# European Union Property Law

## From Fragments to a System

Eveline Ramaekers

# European Union Property Law
## From Fragments to a System

intersentia

METRO

Ius Commune Europaeum

Eveline Ramaekers

European Union Property Law
From Fragments to a System

Intersentia Ltd
Trinity House | Cambridge Business Park | Cowley Road
Cambridge | CB4 0WZ | United Kingdom
Tel.: +44 1223 393 753 | Email: mail@intersentia.co.uk

ISBN 978-1-78068-171-9
D/2013/7849/61
NUR 828


Cambridge – Antwerp – Portland
www.intersentia.com | www.intersentia.co.uk

Cover photo: © rzdeb - iStockphoto

PhD-thesis defended on April 4, 2013 at Maastricht University

## PREFACE AND ACKNOWLEDGEMENTS

'What is the topic of your doctoral dissertation?'

'European Union property law.'

'... Does that exist?'

'That's what I'm trying to find out.'

'And you are dealing with the whole of property law? Isn't that a bit too broad?'

During the four years I spent researching this thesis I was regularly asked these questions. Yes, it was a broad topic. And yes, it was possible to tackle it in four years. I undertook this research project, the aim of which was to establish the status quo of the EU's *acquis* in the area of property law and to propose a framework for its further development, convinced that approaching the topic in its broadest sense was the best (and the only) way to get a complete picture of how much EU property law currently exists, where it is to be found, and whether or not it is developing in a consistent and coherent manner. I was fortunate to be able to build on substantial existing comparative research into the national property laws of the EU Member States, and on research into specific sub-areas of EU property law such as cross-border security rights on movable objects. Have I, by including all aspects of property law, been able to propose a complete system of property law to be developed at EU level? Far from it. There are so many decisions still to be made, so many gaps to fill in, so many bridges to be built. It would be impossible for one person to achieve all that in four years. But I do believe I have been able to provide a detailed overview of the existing EU property law and the fundamentals for its future development.

European Union property law does exist. It is still in its early stages but it is rapidly developing. It has been immensely exciting and fulfilling to be able to work on such a young area of law, where there is still so much to explore and develop. If, with this dissertation, I have been able to make even the most modest contribution to the development of this field I would be tremendously pleased.

During these four years I have had the pleasure to work with and be supported by some extraordinary people. At the ever-existing risk of overlooking someone, I would like to thank a number of friends, family and colleagues. Let me start with my *Doktorvater*, Sjef van Erp. I thank him wholeheartedly for creating an academic environment in which cooperation, loyalty and warmth were key, and in which there was always room for even the most unusual ideas, and for Monday morning cake. I hope to remain a member of his *Doktorfamilie* for many years to come. I also want to thank Bram Akkermans who, with his lively and generous personality and his unrelenting questioning of my research has made me a better academic, and I have come to think of him as one of my dearest friends.

I am grateful for the friends and colleagues from Maastricht, Stellenbosch, Edinburgh, Leuven and many other places, who have made the past four years so memorable. I would like to name in particular my two paranymphs, Gary and Pim, and furthermore Anna, Willem, Tanja, Mariken, Nicole, Katharina, Jennifer, Dalindyebo, Nishara, Maartje, Ronia, Tristan, Wian, Ernst, Jill, Koen and many others.

I would like to thank the members of the reading committee for their academic, and often also personal, support. Jan Smits, who, with the founding of M-EPLI, created an excellent forum to test new research ideas. Andre van der Walt, who has welcomed me many times at the South African Research Chair in Property Law, where I have felt inspired to come up with some of the most fundamental ideas for my dissertation. Hildegard Schneider, who scrutinised my chapter on free movement and property law in its early stages. Reiner Schulze, who gave me the opportunity to spend some time at his *Centrum für Europäisches Privatrecht* in Münster. And Vincent Sagaert, who, through various events of the Ius Commune research school, has regularly provided me with feedback on my research. Thanks are also owed to Arthur Salomons, Kenneth Reid and Eva-Maria Kieninger for evaluating earlier drafts of chapters of my dissertation.

Special thanks to my brother, Pascal, for providing me with the software and the skills necessary to create the cubical images in my thesis, and to my parents for their unconditional support over the years, especially during my move to Oxford when my dissertation was in its final stages.

Last but not least, I want to express my deep-felt appreciation for the love and support of my wonderful fiancé, Rogier, who is always encouraging me to do and be better. Thank you for all the cups of tea, flowers, home-cooked dinners and many, many..... many hot chocolates.

Research for this study was concluded at the end of June 2012. Only minor alterations were made afterwards.

## TABLE OF CONTENTS

# Chapter 1

## PURPOSE AND METHOD OF THE STUDY

> *'Les précautions méthodologiques sont certes utiles mais elles n'offrent qu'une garantie relative: une recherche originale oblige celui qui la parte à construire les outils qui lui sont nécessaires et à pratiquer un certain bricolage méthodologique.'*[1]

### Introduction

Property law was traditionally seen as a nationally-oriented area of law and too politically sensitive to be part of the harmonization debate that was ongoing at the level of the European Union.[2] The differences between English property law, which for the largest part deals with land law,[3] and the continental systems of property law, which deal with immovables and movables equally, were considered to be so large that convergence between the national systems was hardly conceivable.[4] It is sometimes difficult to discern whether such differences are historical 'accidents' or whether they were conscious choices reflecting national preferences and policy decisions.[5] It is not just the supposedly unbridgeable differences between the national systems of property law which have placed property law largely outside the development of European private law. The close link between property law and a country's tax policies and bankruptcy policies contributes to Member States' reluctance to accept regulation by the European Union in the field of property law,

1 Thunis 2003, p. 11. (Methodological precautions are certainly useful, but they only offer a relative guarantee: original research obliges he who commences it to construct the tools which are necessary for him and to engage in a certain methodological do-it-yourself.) [translation ER]

2 See e.g. Van Erp & Akkermans 2010, p. 173; Smits 2010, p. 430; Watson 2000 at para. VIII; Drobnig 1997, p. 492.

3 Van Erp 2006a, p. 1057 *et seq.*

4 See e.g. Goode 1998, p. 456.

5 Keirse & Veder 2010, p. 43-44.

since such regulation might also encroach upon tax law and insolvency law.[6] More generally speaking, the recent credit crisis seems to have renewed feelings of 'economic nationalism'.[7] Something is certainly also to be said for Israël and Saarloos's statement, that discrepancies between national private laws only become noticeable once an internal market has been created, for private law's primary function is not to ensure access to a country's national market but rather to regulate the relations between market participants.[8]

Over the last fifteen years, however, the scene has been changing. The European Union has started to concern itself with areas of property law. Several measures have been enacted that have a direct property law relevance, such as the Financial Collateral Directive,[9] the Late Payments Directive[10] and the Directive on the return of cultural objects unlawfully removed from the territory of a Member State.[11] The recently published Draft Common Frame of Reference (DCFR) should also be mentioned, although it must be noted that this was an academic study rather than EU legislation.[12] The DCFR contains three books on property law: Book VIII on Acquisition and loss of ownership of goods, Book IX on Proprietary security rights in movable assets and Book X on Trusts.[13] It can be seen that, although the EU promulgates legislation in certain specific areas which relate to property law, the picture is very fragmented.

Member States have their reasons to oppose involvement by the EU in property law, but it is not entirely clear what the stance of the EU itself is with regard to property law. As will be seen in Chapter 3, Article 345 of the Treaty on the Functioning of the European Union (TFEU) – which states that nothing in the Treaties shall prejudice the Member States' system of property ownership – is interpreted by the EU institutions as not removing property law from the scope of application of EU law. On the other hand, EU legislation that contains or affects property law does not seem to be created in a consistent and coherent manner.

The central research question of this study consists of three parts: To what extent has the European Union already created property law? Can and should the

6 Goode 1998, p. 455. See also Akkermans 2008, p. 398. The Commission's 2005 Green Paper on Mortgage Credit in the EU provides an example of the close link between property law and tax law, and how action by the EU in one area might affect the other area; COM(2005) 327 final, p. 12 at 43.

7 Mission letter from the President of the European Commission, J.M. Barrosso, 20 October 2009, Pres(2009)D/2250: 'The recent crisis has shown that there remains a strong temptation, particularly when times are hard, to roll back the Single Market and seek refuge in forms of economic nationalism.' To be found at: http://ec.europa.eu/bepa/pdf/ monti_report_final_10_05_2010_en.pdf>.

8 Israël & Saarloos 2007, p. 650.

9 Dir. 2002/47/EC, [2002] *OJ* L 168/43.

10 Dir. 2011/7/EU, [2011] *OJ* L 48/1.

11 Dir. 93/7/EEC, [1993] *OJ* L 74/74.

12 For an overview of the DCFR see Van Erp, Akkermans & Ramaekers 2012.

13 See Van Erp 2008b, p. 20.

European Union harmonize (certain areas of) property law? If so, what would be the best way to do this?

The first aim of this project is therefore to map out the landscape of EU property law. This will include primary and secondary EU law, case law of the European Court of Justice and policy documents.[14] The second step will be to investigate the possibilities for harmonizing property law within the European Union in a more structured manner than is currently the case. In doing so, attention will be paid both to the most suitable form in which to shape EU property law and to its content. The ultimate aim of this project is to propose a framework for further conceptualization and integration of EU property law.

The starting point for this project will not be comparative research of the national systems of the Member States, but the *acquis communautaire*, which will be analysed to see what existing EU law there is that touches upon property law. This is also why the term 'EU property law' is used, as opposed to 'European property law'. The latter may be interpreted as meaning the property law of various European countries and their differences and similarities, while the former means property law as created by or emanating from the EU. In this study, the term 'property law' is used in the private law sense, not in the constitutional sense, meaning that, for instance, Article 1 of the First Protocol to the European Convention on Human Rights - protecting the right to property - will not be dealt with. The analysis of the *acquis communautaire* in the field of property law aims to clarify what problems, (conflicting) solutions and/or gaps there are in EU property law. The final goal of the project is to create a framework that can be used for the future development of EU property law with an aim to increase coherence and consistency in this field of law. National systems of law are set up as internally coherent systems. Whenever EU law is created, the Member States, when implementing that law, somehow have to weave it into the national system. Property law in particular is very systematic and said to be a delicately balanced system. It is therefore important, in the development of EU property law, to strive for coherence and consistency. That way, disruption of the national legal systems is bound to be less, and there will be less need for national law to fill gaps in the European system, which should prevent discrepancies in implementation from Member State to Member State and guarantee the *effet utile* of the European rules. This in turn should promote predictability and legal certainty for parties who are subject to the European rules on property law.[15] One must keep in mind, however, that coherence in a European context may not necessarily mean the same as coherence in a national context, given that European law is of a different nature than national law.

14 *Cf* Van Erp & Akkermans 2010, p. 174.

15 *Cf* Strese 2006, p. 193, where she refers to the *Vorhersehbarkeitsinteresse* (interest in predictability) of market participants: 'Privatrechtsunterschiede [führen] zu einer mangelnden Forhersehbarkeit der Abläufe ausländischen Rechts.'

Possible methods for the implementation of such a framework for the development of EU property law will be looked into as well. Implementation may, for instance, be possible in the form of an optional or mandatory instrument. In that regard, the question will be raised what the competences, if any, of the European Union are to legislate in the area of property law. It is already clear from the European Court of Justice's famous *Tobacco* judgment that Article 114 TFEU, which is the legislative basis for measures concerning the internal market, cannot be used as a general harmonization tool. It can only form a legal basis for harmonization if an actual obstacle to free movement within the internal market can be shown, that is a direct result of a lack of harmonizing measures.[16] Harmonization in the area of property law at the level of the European Union can therefore only take place if a link to the internal market can be established.

The emphasis of this research project lies on the question whether the European Union *can* harmonize property law and, if so, what the best way would be to do that. However, an adjacent question is whether harmonization is at all needed and desirable.[17] It has, for instance, been argued by several authors that harmonization, from an economic perspective, might have more negative than positive results.[18] That literature provides a law and economics perspective to the question of desirability of harmonization. Other starting points to answer the question of desirability can be the cultural perspective - harmonization suppresses local legal diversity - or the perspective of multi-level governance (on which level is a particular area of law best regulated).[19] This thesis only touches upon the desirability question from the point of view of the internal market. It will be argued below and in more detail in Chapter 2, that a degree of harmonization in the field of property law is necessary to improve the functioning of the internal market, given that the differences between the property law systems can and do obstruct free movement.

The current chapter provides the background to the reasons for harmonization and the necessity of this research project and contains an outline of the methodology that will be applied in the following chapters.

## 1. Reasons for the Development of Property Law by the European Union

The submission that there is a need to evaluate the possibilities for harmonizing property law in Europe rests on two pillars. The first pillar concerns the interface between European free movement law and property law; the second pillar concerns

16 Case C-491/01, para. 61. See also Zimmermann 2006, p. 544.

17 *Cf* Dijck & Heuvel 2004, who discuss the role of the 'can you do it-question' (*kan het-vraag*) and the 'should you do it-question' (*moet het-vraag*) in any discussion about the future of property law.

18 See e.g. Van Gerven 2002, p. 163; Wagner 2002, particularly the concluding paragraph at p. 1011 *et seq.*

19 *Cf* Weatherill 2004a, p. 13-15.

the overlap between property law and other areas of private law, especially contract law which has been the object of quite extensive harmonization already.

The differences between the national systems of property law and their mandatory nature, combined with the application of the private international law rule of *lex rei sitae* - pointing to the law of the place where an object is situated as the applicable property law, making it impossible for parties to choose the applicable law to their proprietary relationship - lead to obstacles to the free movement of goods, capital and - to a lesser extent - services and persons. This is the main reason and justification for legislative action in the area of property law by the EU. There is however another important reason. The academic Draft Common Frame of Reference was presented to the Commission in 2009. It contains three books on property law: Book VIII on Acquisition and loss of ownership of goods; Book IX on Proprietary security in movable assets; and Book X on Trusts. These books have been criticized for being incomplete - they do not deal with immovable property[20] - and their quality is arguably affected by the time constraints placed on the project by the Commission.[21] It seems unlikely that the Commission will implement these parts of the DCFR in legislation in the near future. The Commission's Proposal for a Common European Sales Law (CESL), which is based on the work conducted for the DCFR, only implements some of the parts of the DCFR dealing with contract law, but property law is explicitly excluded.[22] However, contract law and property law are - in some legal systems more than in others - inextricably linked with one another, as will be shown below in section 1.2 (*Harmonization of other areas of private law*). The EU has been active in the field of contract law for several decades, but property law (or indeed other areas of private law) are left behind in these developments. The interrelationship between different areas of private law, however, makes it an illusion to believe that development of European contract law can continue completely separately from any development in adjacent areas of private law. But before it can be discussed whether and to what extent the EU should develop property law, it is necessary to gain an overview of the status quo of EU property law. How much EU property law is already there and what does it consist of? Specific parts of property law in an EU context have been the object of study,[23] but as of yet there is no general overview of the whole with a proposal how to move forward in harmonizing European property law in a coherent manner. This study purports to provide such an overview and make a proposal for the future development of EU property law.

20 Van Erp, Akkermans & Ramaekers 2012, p. 5 at footnote 13.
21 Van Erp, Akkermans & Ramaekers 2012, p. 7.
22 COM(2011) 635 final; Preamble at Recital 27.
23 E.g. security rights on movables: Van Erp & Akkermans 2012, Chapter 10; Kieninger 2008a; Kieninger 2006; Kreuzer 1990.

## 1.1. *The Relationship between Free Movement Law and Property Law*

The existing discrepancies between the national property law systems sometimes cause, or may potentially cause, obstacles to the four freedoms within the internal market. The following examples illustrate the type of problems that feature in relation to each of the four freedoms.[24] The interface between free movement law and property law will be further analysed in Chapter 2.[25]

### 1.1.1. Free Movement of Goods

In Germany it is possible to include an extended reservation of ownership clause in a contract, which is called a *Verarbeitungsklausel*. Such a clause allows a seller to reserve ownership, not just of the original goods delivered to the buyer but also of the new product manufactured with those goods. In this manner, the seller is protected against non-payment by or insolvency of the buyer. Consider the case in which a German seller sells goods to a Dutch buyer under such a reservation of ownership clause, and the Dutch buyer uses these goods to manufacture a new product. Subsequently, the Dutch buyer goes insolvent and the German seller attempts to retrieve the newly manufactured product from the insolvent estate of the buyer. According to the private international law rule of *lex rei sitae*, an object is governed by the law of the country where it is located. Therefore, a Dutch judge having to decide on the question who is owner of the new product will apply Dutch property law including the Dutch *numerus clausus*, or closed list, of property rights. Dutch law stipulates that the manufacturer of a new product becomes the owner of that new product.[26] It does not know an extended reservation of ownership clause like German law does, and therefore a Dutch judge will not enforce the *Verarbeitungsklausel* in the contract of sale between the German seller and the Dutch buyer. Through the combination of a rule of private international law - the *lex rei sitae* rule[27] - and a rule of national property law, the German seller loses his ownership of the new product and is unprotected against the insolvency of the buyer.

The reverse situation is also possible. A Dutch seller can include a *Verarbeitungsklausel* in a contract of sale with a German buyer, which becomes valid the moment the goods cross the border into Germany. This is a result of Article 128(2) of Book 10 of the Dutch Civil Code, which allows parties, in deviation from the *lex rei sitae*, to choose the law of the country of destination as the applicable law to a reservation of ownership clause. Such a choice of law is only effective if the object is

24 See also Milo 2003, p. 121.

25 See Van Erp & Akkermans 2010, p. 185: 'The rules on property law of the Member States, it can be concluded, are potentially also subject to negative harmonization. A view on European property law would, therefore, be incomplete without such a perspective.'

26 Art. 16 of Book 5 of the Dutch civil code.

27 The *lex rei sitae* rule and its place in the EU's internal market are discussed more in depth in Chapter 5.

actually imported into the country of destination. In case of insolvency of the German buyer, a German judge, having to decide who the owner of the goods is, will apply German law in accordance with the *lex rei sitae* rule and will acknowledge the *Verarbeitungsklausel* in the contract. The Dutch seller remains the owner of the goods and is protected against insolvency of the German buyer. The result is that it is less attractive for a German seller to export goods to the Netherlands than it is for a Dutch seller to export goods to Germany. The German manufacturer may demand an alternative and probably more costly, security right, or choose not to demand security but raise the price of the product to compensate for the higher risk.[28] This situation constitutes an obstacle to the free movement of goods as prohibited under Article 34 TFEU,[29] given that the Court of Justice of the European Union (CJEU) has decided that any measure that is liable to hinder or make less attractive the free movement of goods is prohibited.[30]

It might be argued that these kinds of situations are so remote that one cannot conclude that there is in fact an obstacle to the free movement of goods. The CJEU judgment in *Krantz*,[31] which will be discussed in Chapter 2, certainly went in that direction. These arguments can be contested. There is a long line of case law from the CJEU that clearly indicates that there is no so-called *de minimis* requirement when it comes to deciding whether a measure forms an obstacle to the free movement of goods.[32] This is also in line with the CJEU's original interpretation of Article 34. In the case of *Procureur du Roi* v *Dassonville*, the CJEU interpreted what was then Article 28 EC as follows: 'All trading rules enacted by Member States which are capable of hindering, directly or indirectly, actually or potentially, intra-community trade are to be considered as measures having an effect equivalent to quantitative restrictions'.[33] In the years following this judgment, the CJEU has mitigated the term 'trading rules' in the sense that *trading* is no longer emphasized and *rules* can be any kind of measure, even non-binding ones.[34]

The conclusion to be drawn from the example given above is that the combination of the *lex rei sitae* rule and the closed and mandatory nature of the different national property laws makes it less attractive for a national from one Member State - in this case Germany - to trade with a national from another Member State - in this case the Netherlands - than it is the other way around. Whether one calls this infringement direct or indirect, actual or potential, is irrelevant given the *Dassonville* judgment.

28 Von Bar & Drobnig 2002, Doc. No. SANCO B5-1000/02/000574, at no. 733.

29 Art. 28 EC reads: 'Quantitative restrictions on imports and all measures having equivalent effect shall be prohibited between Member States.'

30 Unless certain justification requirements are fulfilled; Case C-55/94, *Gebhard* v *Consiglio dell'Ordine degli Avvocati e Procuratori di Milano* [1995] ECR I-4165, para. 37.

31 Case C-69/88, [1990] ECR I-583.

32 Barnard 2007, p. 96. See further case C-448/98, *Guimont* [2000] ECR I-10663, paras. 17-24.

33 Case 8/74, *Dassonville* [1974] ECR 837, at 5.

34 Barnard 2007, p. 92-93.

### 1.1.2. Free Movement of Capital

The purchase of immovable property by a national of one Member State in the territory of another Member State is considered to be a capital movement.[35] National property law rules concerning the acquisition of immovable property have been the subject of CJEU rulings.[36] Areas of Member States that are attractive for winter and summer tourism are targeted by persons wanting to buy holiday homes. These Member States sometimes issue regulations requiring an official statement from the person wishing to buy immovable property in those areas that the property will be used as the primary residence. Through these regulations Member States attempt to avoid the formation of 'tourist colonies'. The CJEU has held such regulations to be in conflict with the free movement of capital. This means that the rules on free movement of capital have a direct impact on the national law concerning acquisition of immovable property.

### 1.1.3. Free Movement of Services

In the context of services, one should primarily think of the creation of security rights. The CJEU recognizes that the grant of a mortgage loan constitutes the provision of a financial service, which is connected to a capital movement.[37] The differences between national mortgage laws can form an obstacle for persons acquiring immovable property in a host Member State, particularly due to the additional costs for the bank granting the loan in acquiring information about mortgage law in the host Member State.[38] These costs are passed on to the person applying for the loan. Proposals such as the Euromortgage - about which more in Chapter 6 - attempt to remove such obstacles. Directive 2006/48/EC relating to the taking up and pursuit of the business of credit institutions (recast) regulates certain aspects of cross-border mortgage loans.[39] The Directive removes those aspects from the scope of application of the free movement of services. All aspects of cross-border mortgage loans not regulated by the Directive continue to be governed by the free movement of services, though.[40]

Free movement of services also comes into play when someone acquires a second residence in another Member State (which, as was seen above, is a capital movement). If that person attracts maintenance or construction services or provides

35 Case C-515/99, *Reisch* [2002] ECR I-2157, para. 29. See also the Nomenclature of capital movements, attached as Annex I to Dir. 88/361/EEC for the implementation of Art. 67 EEC Treaty (free movement of capital), at II – Investments in Real Estate.

36 See cases such as *Trummer* v *Mayer*, *Konle* and *Albore*, which are discussed in Chapter 2, section 4.3. *Obstacles to the free movement of capital.*

37 Case C-222/95, *SCI Parodi* v *Banque Albert de Bary et Cie* [1997] ECR I-3899, para. 8.

38 Von Bar & Drobnig 2002, at no. 527.

39 [2006] *OJ* L 177/1. The Directive is discussed in more detail in Chapter 2, section 5.1.

40 Akkermans 2012a, p. 225.

tourism services or rents out the property to others, then those activities are considered to fall within the scope of the free movement of services.[41] National rules governing the acquisition of immovable property will therefore have to comply with the free movement of services, as well as with the free movement of capital.

### 1.1.4. Free Movement of Persons

Citizens of the European Union enjoy the right to move and reside freely within the territory of the Member States under Article 21 TFEU.[42] The rules on the free movement of persons will be at stake in case of a private individual acquiring a primary or secondary residence in another Member State.[43] Again, national rules governing the acquisition of immovable property may not only come into contact with the rules on free movement of capital and services but also with those on the free movement of persons.

## 1.2. *Harmonization of other Areas of Private Law*

For several decades, work has been ongoing in the harmonization of contract law, mostly in the context of the consumer *acquis*. Certain areas of contract law directly interlink with property law, like cogwheels. Contract law cannot be strictly separated from property law and making changes in contract law will often also affect property law, as was established, *inter alia*, in detail in Von Bar and Drobnig's Study on Property Law and Non-contractual Liability Law as they relate to Contract Law.[44] Harmonization projects in the area of contract law recently culminated in the Common Frame of Reference (CFR). The Draft CFR was published by the Study Group on a European Civil Code and the Research Group on EC Private Law in 2009 and again in 2010 with a complete commentary. The Draft (or Academic) Common Frame of Reference moved from academic to political with the European Commission's Proposal for a Regulation on a Common European Sales Law[45] (CESL) in 2011. Among other things, the CESL contains articles on the requirements for the conclusion of a contract.[46] The conclusion of a contract and the question at what moment ownership passes from seller to buyer are inextricably linked. For instance: in France, ownership passes at the same moment the contract is validly concluded; mere consensus suffices. This is a result of the fact that France has a

41 A-G Geelhoed's Opinion in Joined Cases C-515/99 and C-527/99 to C-540/99, *Reisch*, at paras. 31-33.
42 Art. 21 TFEU: 'Every citizen of the Union shall have the right to move and reside freely within the territory of the Member States, subject to the limitations and conditions laid down in the Treaties and by the measures adopted to give them effect.'
43 A-G Geelhoed's Opinion in *Reisch*, at para. 31.
44 Von Bar & Drobnig 2002. *Cf* also Goode 1998, p. 453 at footnote 1.
45 COM(2011) 635 final.
46 Artt. 30 *et seq.*

consensual transfer system. In Germany on the other hand, a contract alone is insufficient to transfer ownership. The German rules on transfer of ownership require a so-called 'real agreement' (or *dinglicher Vertrag*) to be concluded next to the contract. With the real agreement, the transferor and transferee respectively declare to transfer and accept ownership. This could entail the delivery, i.e. handing over of possession, of an object, or registration. This means that under German law ownership may pass at a different moment than under French law, namely at a later point in time than the time of the conclusion of the contract.[47]

It can therefore be argued that an instrument meant to harmonize contract law needs to be accompanied by an instrument to harmonize property law, in order to create a complete picture and avoid loose ends in the harmonization process. If an instrument that is meant to harmonize contract law only contains provisions on the conclusion of a contract but none on the moment at which ownership passes, it depends on the national legal system whether the conclusion of a contract has property effects. If such a result is not taken into account by the harmonizing instrument, it can lead to disruptions in the national system of property law. The CESL explicitly excludes the transfer of ownership from its scope of application,[48] but mentions the transfer of ownership on several occasions. See, for instance, Article 91:

> 'Article 91
>
> Main obligations of the seller
>
> The seller of goods or the supplier of digital content (in this part referred to as 'the seller') must:
>
> (a) deliver the goods or supply the digital content;
>
> (b) transfer the ownership of the goods, including the tangible medium on which the
>
> digital content is supplied; [...]'

This provision seems to distinguish between delivery and transfer of ownership but, as illustrated above, not all legal systems make this distinction.

The Preamble to the CESL also states, in Recital 16, that 'The Common European Sales Law should be available in particular for the sale of movable goods, including the manufacture or production of such goods, as this is the economically single most important contract type which could present a particular potential for growth in cross-border trade, especially in e-commerce.' This does not necessarily exclude the applicability of the draft CESL to the sale of immovable property, as it should be available *in particular* for the sale of movable goods. What would the consequences be if the draft also became applicable to the sale of immovable prop-

47 For an overview of different transfer systems see Van Erp & Akkermans 2012, Chapter 8. *Transfer*.

48 Preamble to the proposed Regulation, Recital 27.

erty? Could a contract concluded under the CESL for instance, be pre-registered in a land registry and have third party effect?

Parallel to the Common European Sales Law work has been conducted in reviewing the consumer *acquis*. This has led to the adoption of Directive 2011/83/EU on consumer rights,[49] amending Directive 93/13/EEC (unfair terms in consumer contracts) and Directive 1999/44/EC (sale of consumer goods) and repealing Council Directive 85/577/EEC (doorstep selling) and Directive 97/7/EC (distance selling). The adoption of the new consumer rights Directive shows that the threat of incoherence is real where harmonization in the area of contract law is moving forward, but harmonization in the area of property law is staying behind. The Commission's 2006 Green Paper on the Review of the Consumer *Acquis*[50] preceded the adoption of the Directive. In Annex I to the Green Paper a list of questions put to consultation is included. Question 12 reads: 'How should the passing of the risk in consumer sales be regulated?' One of the comments by the Commission to this question was:

> 'At the moment, the issue is regulated differently in the Member States. In some Member States the risk passes to the buyer at the time of the conclusion of the contract while in others property does not pass with the conclusion of the sales contract but with the delivery.
>
> The passing of the risk could be linked to the moment of delivery. Depending on the definition of delivery, this could be at the time when the consumer acquires physical possession of the good or at an earlier stage.'[51]

One of the options provided by the Commission as an answer to Question 12 was that the passing of the risk would be regulated at Union level and be linked to the moment of delivery. Article 20 of the consumer rights Directive now stipulates the following:

> 'Article 20
>
> Passing of risk
>
> In contracts where the trader dispatches the goods to the consumer, the risk of loss of or damage to the goods shall pass to the consumer when he or a third party indicated by the consumer and other than the carrier has acquired the physical possession of the goods. However, the risk shall pass to the consumer upon delivery to the carrier if the carrier was commissioned by the consumer to carry the goods and that choice was not offered by the trader, without prejudice to the rights of the consumer against the carrier.'

49 [2011] *OJ* L 304/64.
50 COM(2006) 744 final.
51 Commission's Green paper of 08/02/2007, COM(2006) 744 final, Annex I, para. 5.4.

The Commission has chosen that the passing of risk occurs upon delivery and not upon the time of conclusion of the contract. This decision could be of direct relevance to the national systems of property law and seems to be most in line with a tradition system of transfer, as is known by German law. It is noteworthy that Recital 51 of the Preamble to the Directive indicates that

> 't]he place and modalities of delivery and the rules concerning the determination of the conditions for the transfer of the ownership of the goods and the moment at which such transfer takes place, should remain subject to national law and therefore should not be affected by this Directive.'

In the DCFR the overlap area between contract law and property law, at least where it concerns transfer of ownership, has been covered: not only does it provide for the conclusion of the contract and the moment of the passing of the risk but also for the moment of the passing of ownership.[52] The new Consumer Rights Directive and the draft CESL only deal with the contractual aspects of a transfer, not with the proprietary aspects. The Directive is of course binding law. Whether and how the draft CESL will be implemented is not yet known at the time of writing. In any event, both these major developments in European private law fail to deal with a crucial area of overlap between contract law and property law.

## 1.3. *Summary*

The fact that a (potential) infringement to the rules on free movement of goods, capital, services and persons can be shown is grounds for researching the possibilities for removing these infringements that hinder free movement within the internal market. Whether these obstacles should be removed through negative or positive harmonization, through mandatory or optional EU law, and what the content of such European rules should be, will be investigated further in Chapters 5 and 6. It is however safe to say already at this point that relying on the CJEU judgments in free movement cases alone will be insufficient to decrease the hindrance to free movement. The main avenue for the CJEU to express itself on rules of European property law is through the preliminary ruling procedure of Article 267 TFEU. Whether it gets a chance to actually do so depends entirely on the decisions of national courts to refer a preliminary question and on the way in which these questions are asked. As a result, case law will only provide a very piecemeal picture and gives rise to a need for harmonization via other means.

The second reason for conducting this study, next to the hindrances to intra-Union trade caused by the diverging national systems of property law, is the fact that the development of EU property law is out of step with the development of EU contract law. The fact that the EU is moving forward in the field of contract law, with the new Consumer Rights Directive and the draft CESL, without equally mov-

52 Artt. II.-4:101 *et seq.*; Art. IV.A.-5:102(1) and Art. VIII.2:101(1)(e).

ing forward in adjacent areas of private law such as property law, has the potential to disrupt the national systems of private law when they have to implement the European contract law rules. This study will therefore lead to a proposal for the development of EU property law.

## 2. The *Acquis* Method: Defining EU Property Law

The ultimate aim of this project is to propose a framework for further conceptualization and integration of EU property law. In order to achieve this goal, the field of EU property law first needs to be delimited to determine what is within its scope. Secondly, attention needs to be paid to main concepts of property law such as ownership, title and possession, which will need to be developed. Currently, these concepts are sometimes used by the European legislature, yet they are not given a clear definition or at least a definition that is workable for both civil and common law systems. For instance, in Directive 93/7 on the Return of Cultural Objects Unlawfully Removed from the Territory of a Member State,[53] the terms 'ownership' and 'owner' are used in Articles 12 and 15 respectively, but a definition is not provided. In Chapter 4 of this study, extensive research will be presented into the use of property law terminology in European legislation. If property law terminology is used in European legislation without being given a European-autonomous interpretation, every Member State will have to interpret such concepts in accordance with its own national system, which in turn leads to discrepancies in the implementation of these European measures.

The first question that needs to be answered is what actually constitutes property law at the level of the European Union. Property law is a very systematic field of law and can be described as being made up of building blocks.[54] It is characterized by mandatory rules. The range of possible answers to questions of property law is generally very narrow: one can, for instance, not deviate from the rules on transfer, so unless these rules are strictly adhered to, the answer to the question whether or not a right has been transferred is no. Whether parties have created a limited property right depends entirely on the *numerus clausus*; intention is irrelevant: if the right is not in the *numerus clausus* then it is not a property right. The main methodological problem of this study is how to define property law at the level of the EU, when EU law is competence-driven and not categorized along the same lines as national law. Below, I will introduce a model I created to solve this particular methodological problem.

EU legislation is competence-driven, meaning that the Commission initiates legislation on the basis of the competences provided for in the Treaties. These competences relate to specific subject matters such as competition, agriculture or

53 [1993] *OJ* L 74/74.

54 Property law has been described in terms of building blocks before: see for instance Heß 1998, p. 514; Stürner 1994, p. 275.

consumer protection. Whether a particular piece of legislation constitutes property law, contract law or even public law or criminal law is usually not indicated, because European law is not divided into areas of law along the same lines as national law is. European legislation is categorized as, for instance, property law by the Member States only, because it influences, on the national level, what they consider to be property law. These national categories of law are irrelevant for EU law: as long as the national implementing measures ensure the effectiveness, or *effet utile*, of the European law, it does not matter what kind of law they constitute at national level. Therefore, to look for something that the European legislature would place under the heading 'EU property law', is a search in vain. Rather, 'EU property law' is a concept that can be placed as an overarching term over that part of the *acquis* that has an effect on what, at the national level, is called property law. This includes not only Treaty law and secondary legislation but also CJEU case law.

A parallel can be drawn with the consumer *acquis*. After the entry into force of the EEC Treaty, the Community started drafting legislation on the basis of the competences provided for in the Treaty. At the beginning of the 21st century the term 'consumer *acquis*' had started to be used to cover a collection of legislative instruments that had not been brought under one heading before. From that moment on, one could say that an area of European law was outlined - just as there are areas of national law like private and public law - which is used to decide which legislation does and which does not fall within the consumer *acquis* 'box'. This 'box' provides a framework for more consistency and coherence with regard to consumer law drafted by the EU. As a result, the concept of consumer (contract) law is given a European content. The Commission's 2006 Green Paper on the Review of the Consumer Acquis, leading to the new Consumer Rights Directive, provides an overview of the questions concerning the consumer *acquis*, which the Commission had to answer in order to decide whether and how to move forward with the harmonization of this area of law. The questions that were dealt with bare a remarkable resemblance to the questions which this research project attempts to answer. The Commission was faced with similar problems as far as the consumer *acquis* is concerned, in comparison to the problems that researchers of European property law face. Issues such as: the scope of the consumer *acquis*, the most appropriate form of a new harmonization instrument, what concepts to define and how to define them, were all part of the Green Paper.[55] The following quotation illustrates how the purpose of the review of the consumer *acquis* resembles the purpose of this research project:

> 'The Review of the Consumer Acquis can provide a unique opportunity to modernise the existing consumer directives, in order to simplify and improve the regulatory environment for both professionals and consumers and improve or extend if necessary

55 *Cf* Commission's Green Paper of 08/02/2007, COM(2006) 744 final, para. 4.6: 'As to the first group, the Commission feels that a consistent definition of the notions of consumer and professional is important since it permits to delimit the scope of the acquis more accurately.'

> the protection offered to consumers. This is fully in line with the modernisation of the Internal Market. To this end, the directives are being reviewed as a whole and individually to identify regulatory gaps and shortcomings affecting all of them as well as problems specific to individual directives.'[56]

The Commission had ascertained that there was inconsistency between directives and that some issues were not dealt with at all. The solution it proposed was a horizontal instrument.[57] The Commission preferred a horizontal approach to a vertical approach, so that issues and terminology common to several directives could be re-regulated in a more systematic manner. This should promote coherence and consistency and prevent further fragmentation.[58] The reasoning put forth by the Commission is relevant for this research project, as it may form a source of inspiration when I discuss the best possible way forward for developing EU property law in Chapter 6 of this study. However, there is one methodological flaw in the outline of the consumer *acquis*. It is a framework that is used for the further coherent development of consumer contract law, and yet the directives selected to be part of the review seem to have been selected relatively randomly, instead of on the basis of clearly outlined criteria. The Consumer Law Compendium indicates that some directives, which are part of the consumer *acquis* under review, seem a bit out of place, whereas others, which one would expect to be included, have not been.[59] The authors note that the selection was not questioned given that it was part of the tender for the Compendium project,[60] but that there were clearly political motives for the choices made.[61] This manner of reviewing the consumer *acquis* feeds the criticism that European private law is a patchwork of measures. They concern several very specific areas but are not based on a well-structured system.[62]

56 2007 Green Paper, para. 2.1.

57 Proposal for a Directive on Consumer Rights at: <http://ec.europa.eu/consumers/rights/docs/COMM_PDF_COM_2008_0614_F_EN_PROPOSITION_DE_DIRECTIVE.pdf>.

58 2007 Green Paper, paras. 3.2 and 4.1-4.2.

59 Consumer Law Compendium, para. 2 'Scope of the Study'. See also 2007 Green Paper, footnote 3: 'It is important to note that what is commonly referred to as the "Consumer Acquis" does not cover all consumer protection legislation in the EU. The recently adopted Directive on Unfair Commercial Practices falls outside the Consumer Acquis for instance. In addition, many provisions aiming at protecting consumers can be found in sector-specific EU legislation, such as legislation in the field of e-commerce, financial services.'

60 Tender B-Brussels: compendium, including a comparative analysis of the Community consumer acquis, 2004/S 80-068070; to be found at: <http://ted.europa.eu/Exec?DataFlow=N_one_doc_access.dfl&Template=TED/N_one_result_detail_curr.htm&docnumber=68070-2004&docId=68070-2004&StatLang=EN#>.

61 Twigg-Flessner 2009, p. 5.

62 Klauer 1998, p. 21: 'Eine häufig geäusserte und nicht ganz unberechtigte Kritik am harmonisierten Gemeinschaftsprivatrecht geht dahin, dass es sich um eine mehr oder weniger zufällig zusammengewürfelte Ansammlung punktueller Regelungen handle, denen keine durchgehende Systematik und kein erkennbares Programm zugrundeliege.'

As said before, the developments in the area of the consumer *acquis* are used as a source of inspiration for this project, which will outline the field of EU property law. To avoid an arbitrary selection of measures, a clear set of criteria will be developed on which to base the selection of *acquis* measures for analysis.

As far as the consumer *acquis* is concerned, one can - on the basis of the foregoing - differentiate between three stages: during the first stage, legislation was 'randomly' issued on the basis of the competences provided for in the E(E)C Treaty and was not necessarily consciously brought under one overarching heading; during the second stage, the concept 'consumer *acquis*' was placed as such an overarching heading on a selection of the *acquis* from the outside; and during the third stage, the consumer *acquis* is used as a framework and filled in more systematically by the EU, as follows, *inter alia,* from the 2007 Green Paper and the subsequently adopted Consumer Rights Directive.

EU property law is currently at stage one: there are a certain number of measures and judgments that are called 'European property law' by national lawyers, because they originate from the European Union and have a bearing on national property law. It is not yet a concept that has a European-autonomous definition, like the consumer *acquis*. The term 'property *acquis*' has not yet been coined. Once this 'box' is created it can be used as a framework and be given a European content and not merely a national content, as has happened with the consumer *acquis*. This would lead to more consistency and coherence. Since EU property law is at stage one, the criterion for calling something EU property law will be that it is European legislation or case law that has a bearing on what is defined as property law at the national level. For this collection of legislation and case law I would create the box 'property *acquis*'. What remains is to define what constitutes property law at the national level. It is here that comparative research has its place in this project.

### 2.1. *Delimiting the Field of Law and Defining its Concepts: the Role of Comparative Research in the Acquis Method*

Although at this first stage EU property law is defined by what is considered to be property law at the national level, this does not mean that concepts found within instruments which form part of the property *acquis* may not already have a European-autonomous definition. For instance, Directive 2000/35/EC on late payments contains a definition of a retention of title clause. This Directive would be part of the property *acquis* because retention of title clauses are considered to be part of property law under the national systems. Nevertheless, this concept now also has a European content. In other words, one has to differentiate between two things: on the one hand, the delimitation of the field of law, namely EU property law and, on the other hand, the definition of concepts that are found within this area of law (such as retention of title, ownership, transfer etc.). Both will be given a European-autonomous content within this study but in a different manner. The part played by comparative legal research in this project is therefore twofold: first, it serves to determine the borders of the field of property law within EU law; second, it is used where lacunae in the *acquis* are discovered that need to be filled. Primary sources underlying the comparative research will be comparative studies such as the Ius Commune Casebook in Property Law,[63] Von Bar's *Sachenrecht in Europa*,[64] the National Reports on the Transfer of Movables in Europe,[65] the *Principles of European Law* published by the Study Group on a European Civil Code,[66] and Akkermans's study of the *numerus clausus* in European property law.[67] As far as concepts of EU property law are concerned, the research will primarily focus on primary and secondary EU law and CJEU case law to see whether definitions of those concepts can already be deduced therefrom. It is only when such definitions do not yet exist that a proposal for such a European-autonomous definition is formed on the basis of comparative research to fill that gap.

The second function of comparative research - to fill conceptual gaps in the property *acquis* - raises the question whether comparative research can at all be used to fill gaps in the *acquis*? In other words, is it methodologically acceptable to use solutions that are found at the national level to supplement a European system of property law? An answer to that question is - at least partially - provided by the CJEU and the Lisbon Treaties themselves. The second function served by comparative research in this study therefore builds on the comparative method as developed by the CJEU.

### 2.1.1. The Comparative Method as Developed by the CJEU

Generally, when the CJEU is faced with a lacuna in European law, it will conduct a comparative study into the solutions provided at national level - in which it is often preceded by the Advocate General - and deliver a judgment with reference to the 'general principles common to the legal systems of the Member States'.[68] The difference between the CJEU and the Advocates-General is that the latter are usually far more explicit than the former in outlining the comparative research conducted.[69] The CJEU may also, on the basis of Article 45 of its Rules of procedure,

63 Van Erp & Akkermans 2012.
64 Von Bar 2000.
65 Faber & Lurger 2008.
66 Study Group on a European Civil Code 2006.
67 Akkermans 2008.
68 Joined cases C-46/93 and C-48/93, para. 27.
69 *Cf* Kakouris 1994, p. 275 and 279. There are exceptions to this however. See, for instance, joined cases 7/56, 3-7/57, *Algera* v *Common Assembly of the ECSC* [1957] ECR, p. 81: 'The possibility of withdrawing such measures is a problem of administrative law, which is familiar in the case-law and learned writing of all the countries of the Community, but for the solution of which the Treaty does not contain any rules. Unless the Court is to deny justice it is therefore obliged to solve the problem by reference to the rules acknowledged by the legislation, the learned writing and the case-law of the member countries .
It emerges from a comparative study of this problem of law that[...]'.

request the Commission to provide it with a comparative study. The comparative approach followed by the Court is justified on the basis of two Treaty provisions: Article 19(1) TEU, which states that the European Union's Courts shall ensure that in the interpretation and application of the Treaty the law is observed, the law here including the general principles common to the Member States;[70] and Article 6(3) TEU which refers to the 'constitutional traditions common to the Member States'. A prime example is the *Brasserie du Pêcheur* case:

> 'Since the Treaty contains no provision expressly and specifically governing the consequences of breaches of Community law by Member States, it is for the Court, in pursuance of the task conferred on it by Article 164 [now 19 TEU] of the Treaty of ensuring that in the interpretation and application of the Treaty the law is observed, to rule on such a question in accordance with *generally accepted methods of interpretation*, in particular by reference to the fundamental principles of the Community legal system and, where necessary, *general principles common to the legal systems of the Member States.*'[71] [emphasis added]

If it follows from the comparative study that a particular solution features in all or the vast majority of Member States, the CJEU can adopt that solution without a problem. If however the solutions existing at the national level are divergent and/or conflicting, the CJEU chooses one of two options: either it chooses not to 'impose a solution which would not meet sufficient support in some Member States to ensure a uniform and effective application of Community law'[72] – which is an understandable step to take but not one that eliminates the lacuna in the *acquis* – or it views this outcome as a justification 'for establishing an autonomous interpretation of the concept in Community law'.[73]

In conclusion, apart from filling lacunae with the use of comparative legal research, the CJEU also develops European-autonomous definitions or 'Community concepts'.[74] In doing so, the Court takes a functional approach in that it develops concepts which serve the purposes of the EU.[75] Sometimes it draws inspiration from national systems,[76] but in the end the definition it decides on is not necessarily equal to the definition of the same concept in the systems of the Member States.[77] In fact, it

70 Kakouris 1994, p. 270 and 273.

71 Joined cases 46 and 48/93, *Brasserie du Pêcheur* [1996] ECR I-1029, para. 27.

72 Lenaerts 2003, p. 893.

73 Lenaerts 2003, p. 896.

74 See case *CILFIT*, *infra* at 3.1. See also Weatherill 2004b, p. 637.

75 *Cf* Kakouris 1994, p. 273: 'The comparative method is in the service of teleological interpretation.'

76 See, for instance, CJEU case C-158/94, *Commission* v *Italy*, at 17: '... the Court noted that it is accepted in Community law, *and indeed in the national laws of the Member States...*' [emphasis added].

77 *Cf* Goode 1998, p. 461: 'It is obvious that if a single set of rules is to be extracted from the divergent rules of national legal systems, changes in at least some national laws are inevitable, and changes in all of them highly probable. [T]he process of harmonisation [does →

could not be, simply because of the large number of States that are currently Member States of the European Union. The definitions of a certain concept at a national level will inevitably be different and may moreover serve a different purpose in the national law than the purpose that needs to be served at Union level.[78] The EU Institutions are all obliged to serve the goals of the Union as laid down in the Treaties.[79] Economic integration is at the heart of these goals.[80]

Advocate-General Fennelly gives a description in the *Jägerskiöld* case[81] of the functional approach adopted by the CJEU. The Advocate-General discusses a line of case law in which the Court was repeatedly asked to define the concept of 'goods' in the context of free movement of goods. The case at hand concerned the question whether electricity could be seen as a good. In paragraph 20 of his opinion, the Advocate-General states the following:

> 'In those cases where the Court has had to resolve the issue, it has followed a functional approach and has avoided an exhaustive definition. [...] In so doing, the Court had regard to [electricity's] treatment as goods in Community law and in the laws of the Member States as well as in the Community's tariff nomenclature.'

The Advocate-General interestingly notes that the CJEU 'has followed a functional approach and has avoided an exhaustive definition'. This approach would also be suitable in the development of European-autonomous concepts of property law, given that 27 Member States would have to be able to accommodate them in what are sometimes still widely differing national systems of property law.[82] Moreover,

not] involve simply the identification of factors common to the legal systems under review. If it did, then the wording of uniform rules governing proprietary rights in commercial assets would indeed be a daunting task, for of all legal constructs the concept of property is the most specific to a given legal system.' See also Smits 2008a, abstract: '[W]hat is best at the national level may not be optimal at the European one.'

78 *Cf* Kakouris 1994, p. 270: 'The rule which constitutes the highest common denominator is usually, but not necessarily, followed. The Court may choose the most appropriate rule, and according to certain authors, it may do so even where the appropriate rule is followed by only one Member State'; Gambaro 1997, p. 503: 'If one accepts the idea that the focus of any possible European law of property must consist in common rules which appertain to the circulation and protection of property in the nature of goods, then it immediately comes to mind that the guidelines must be based on considerations of economic efficiency, and not on the desire to respect the largest possible number of national legal traditions.'

79 Art. 13(1) TEU.

80 *Cf* Klauer 1998, p. 25: 'Gemeinschaftsprivatrecht ist nicht einfach Privatrecht, sondern Teil des Gemeinschaftsrechts und denselben Integrationszielen verpflichtet wie dieses.' (Community private law is not just private law, rather it is part of Community law and it therefore ought to serve the same integration goals.) [translation ER] See also Israël & Saarloos 2007, p. 631.

81 Opinion of A.G. Fennelly in case C-97/98, *Jägerskiöld* [1999] ECR I-8789.

82 See to this extent also Lenaerts 2003, p. 879: '[T]he comparative law method, when applied by the Community judge, is driven by a single *Leitmotiv*, and that is to find through the examination of other legal orders the solution which best suits the objectives of the →

functional concepts of property law are likely to serve the internal market well without being entwined with a doctrinal and historical background as national concepts of property law are.

## 2.2. *The Selection of EU Legislation and Case Law for the Acquis Analysis*

In order to decide what is part of the property *acquis*, the *acquis communautaire* must be analysed. This analysis is intended to provide an overview of the existing and proposed measures that have an influence on property law, the decisions and policy choices that have already been made and the gaps that still remain. For this analysis, a selection of European legislative measures must be made. This, however, raises the preliminary question of how to make such a selection and on the basis of what criteria. When making an analysis of the *acquis*, one runs the risk of randomly going through European legislative measures without a clear goal, which would be very time-consuming and not necessarily lead to results that can be used. Therefore, a tool to make a selection of the *acquis* in an efficient way is required. This selection tool is found in the criterion outlined in section 2: every Treaty Article, secondary legislative measure, and the judgments and policy documents underlying them, that deals with property law or has an impact on national property law, will be part of the selection. As explained in section 2.1 comparative research of the national systems will provide the borders of what falls within the definition of property law at the national level. For instance: property law in some national systems, such as France, includes claims but, in others such as Germany, it does not.[83] By mapping out such differences in definition of property law, a general description of property law can be abstracted.

### 2.2.1. Defining Property Law: Introducing the System-Cube

Every national legal system has its own definition of property law.[84] If it were possible to lay all the definitions of property law that can be found in the national systems of the Member States next to each other, then one of them would inevitably be the narrowest definition and another would be the widest definition, with the other definitions of property law somewhere in between. The selection of the *acquis* will consist of all measures containing property law rules or affecting national property law. Because of the equality principle, the selection of the *acquis* cannot stop at only those measures that concern property law according to the narrowest national definition but has to include all those measures that concern property law

Community [...] and which is acceptable for the different national legal orders responsible for implementing Community law.'

83 §90 German BGB; Art. 516 French CC.

84 Van Erp & Akkermans 2012, Chapter 1 at I.A. *What is 'property' law?*

according to the entire range of national definitions of property law: that means that immovable, movable, and intangible property are all included.[85] The result is the property *acquis*. Once the borders of the property *acquis* have been established, European-autonomous property law rules and definitions - such as owner, immovable, retention of title - can be developed. One major problem in outlining these borders is the fact that the line between property law and contract law is sometimes difficult to draw. Security interests provide one example. The creation of a security interest contains both a proprietary and contractual element: the interest is created by security agreement, which is of course governed by contract law. The secured creditor then receives a property right: he can seize the property which is burdened with the security interest and sell it and repay the debt with the proceeds of the sale. The fact that the secured creditor can do this, and does not have to compete with unsecured creditors, shows that he has a right *in rem* to the property whereas the other creditors merely have a right *in personam* to the debtor. Another example is trusts, which are deeply embedded in common law systems but unfamiliar to civil law systems, although some have adopted 'civil law trusts', such as the French *fiducie* or the German *Treuhand*. The trust involves a 'transfer of the package of in rem rights associated with ownership from the settlor to the trustee'.[86] However, the trustee does not acquire 'full ownership' in the sense that he cannot use the trust property for his own benefit.[87] The trustee is under an obligation to manage the trust for the benefit of the beneficiaries (*cf* a third-party beneficiary contract). The transfer of rights in rem from settlor to trustee is therefore subject to a set of *in personam* duties owed by the trustee to the beneficiaries.[88]

So how then to decide when something is property law and when not? And if something is property law, what does it look like? The first question pertains to the distinguishing features between property rights and personal rights. Whether or not a right is a property right is determined by the principle of *numerus clausus*.[89] According to this principle the list of property rights available to parties is closed. Parties cannot create property rights that do not feature in the *numerus clausus* and they can only give their property rights the content permitted by law. Rights featuring in the *numerus clausus*, and which are therefore property rights, all share two primary characteristics: they are rights against an object, which is reflected by

85 Sparkes 2007, p. 97 *et seq*.

86 Merrill & Smith 2001, p. 844.

87 Lawson & Rudden 2002, p. 86.

88 Merrill & Smith 2001, p. 844. *Cf* also Von Bar & Drobnig 2002, nos. 467-471. In contrast, Gardner describes the duties of a trustee as *in rem* obligations: Gardner 2011, p. 14.

89 The EU Member States generally adhere to the *numerus clausus*, although some more strictly than others. It is in that regard interesting to note a judgment of the French *Cour de cassation* of 31 October 2012 in which the court held that an owner may confer on another person a real right of enjoyment in relation to his object, provided that this does not contravene rules of *ordre public*: 'Vu les articles 544 et 1134 du code civil; Attendu qu'il résulte de ces textes que le propriétaire peut consentir, sous réserve des règles d'ordre public, un droit réel conférant le bénéfice d'une jouissance spéciale de son bien'. Cass. civ. 3ième, No. 11-16304.

the fact that property rights have a *droit de suite*, meaning that they follow the object on which they rest;[90] and they can be invoked *erga omnes* or against the world and not just against one or a number of specific persons.[91] Rights that do not pass through the filter of the *numerus clausus* - i.e. that do not have these characteristics - are not property rights.[92] Once it is established that a right is a property right, the second question - what do they look like and what does the system of property law within which they function look like - can be answered.

To answer this second question, a general model is needed that fits the characteristics of any property law system. Such a model should be able to incorporate the elements all property law systems share in general, without having to study the specifics of the property law of each of the 27 Member States of the European Union.[93] The model must be of a trans-systemic nature.[94] The next section provides such a model, with which all the different elements that make up the system of property law can be construed. It must be noted, that this model shows a standardized system of property law and is not dependent upon a specific national definition of property law.[95] The model is not meant to explain where property rights come from or what their function is but only what they look like. The model shows that the system of property law can be broken down into smaller parts. Once this is done, the building blocks of the system are revealed.[96] All these building blocks together form the system of property law, but each separate property right that one encounters within the system is made up of a particular assembly of some of those building blocks. The model visualizes this internal structure of property law. It consists of a core and a regulatory framework surrounding that core. The core represents the system of property *rights*. The regulatory framework around it -

90 Van Erp 2008b, p. 19.

91 See e.g. Van Erp & Akkermans 2012, p. 51-53; Clarke & Kohler 2005, p. 18.

92 Akkermans 2008, p. 402; Van Erp 2006b, p. 13-14.

93 *Cf* Van Erp 2008b, p. 19.

94 Van Erp 2011b, p. 4: 'Trans-systemic analysis uses the functional method to discover how legal traditions solve particular problems, discovering the underlying values, policy choices, leading principles, concepts, ground rules and more specific technical rules. Through trans-systemic analysis the groundwork (perhaps one could say: the matrix) of legal systems can be found.' See also Van Praagh 2005.

95 *Cf* the distinction made by Hage between doctrinal concepts and internal juridical concepts (*doctrinair en intern juridisch begrip*); he uses the concept of *rechtshandeling* (legal act) to clarify this distinction: 'De karakterisering van rechtshandelingen als handelingen waarmee de handelende personen beogen rechtsgevolgen tot stand te brengen en waaraan het recht de beoogde rechtsgevolgen verbindt omdat ze werden beoogd, is niet gebonden aan een concreet rechtssysteem. Sterker nog, hij abstraheert juist van rechtssystemen door de mogelijkheid te bieden om te beoordelen of een bepaald concreet rechtssysteem het verschijnsel rechtshandelingen kent. De notie "rechtshandeling" waar het hier om gaat is een doctrinaire notie, een begrip ontwikkeld in de rechtsgeleerdheid om bepaalde verschijnselen die relevante kenmerken gemeenschappelijk hebben te kunnen aanduiden. 11. Daar staat tegenover het begrip "rechtshandeling" zoals dat voorkomt in rechtsregels.' Hage 2010, p. 246.

96 Sparkes 2007, p. 128-129.

which I have called the *operating system* – consists of the rules governing these property rights. The operating system contains rules on creation, transfer, registration and destruction. These rules are part of the operating system because they each regulate a different stage in the life of a property right. They inform a person wanting to create a property law relationship how particular property rights can be acquired or passed on to someone else and what these rights can and cannot be used for. They also tell us how a property right may be lost. The operating system also contains rules relating to the third party effect of property rights. One of the distinguishing features of property rights is that they can be invoked *erga omnes*, whereas personal rights can only be invoked against one or several specific persons.[97] Operating rules concerning the third party effect of property rights are therefore, for instance, rules that determine if and when a property right can be invoked against a third party or whether a third party transferee is protected against the invalidity of a previous transfer.

Rules in the operating system are a reflection of underlying principles, such as the principle of transparency.[98] The value that a given system of property law attaches to such principles is reflected in its operating rules. For instance, legal systems in which registration is a constitutive element for the transfer of ownership of an immovable attach a different value to the principle of specificity than legal systems in which registration is not a constitutive element. In Chapter 6, where the creation of a European operating system of property law is discussed, attention will, *inter alia*, be paid to these underlying principles. Choices for particular operating rules at EU level will often be based on the principle of *effet utile*, one of the leading principles of EU law, which purports to guarantee its effectiveness.

The core of the model plus the operating system together form the system of property *law*. In the remainder of this chapter emphasis will lie on the core of the model because it is the most complex part. The following figure visualizes what the entire system of property law looks like. The figures in the next sections further clarify how this model functions.

97 Van Erp 2006a, p. 1051-1052; Akkermans 2008, p. 2.

98 The principle of transparency can be further subdivided into the principle of specificity and the principle of publicity. See Van Erp 2009b.

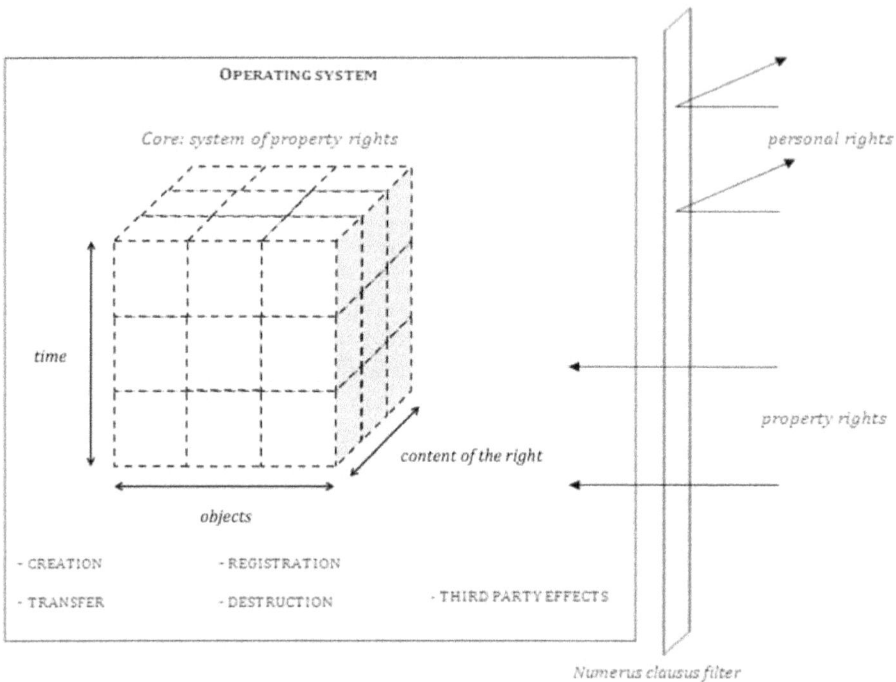


*Figure 1. System of property law*

### 2.2.2. The System of Property Rights: a Three-Dimensional Model

Every property right has three dimensions. The first dimension - the width in my model - consists of the objects, the things that can be the object of property rights. Depending on the legal system, these can either be only corporeal objects or they can include incorporeal objects as well. The second dimension - the depth in my model - consists of the content of the various property rights, i.e. ownership or freehold title and other, limited, property rights, which one can have in relation to the objects. The third dimension of property rights - the height in my model - is the dimension of time. Property rights, as well as the objects on which they rest, can be unlimited or limited in time. For instance, ownership is unlimited in time, but a security right is usually limited to the time during which the underlying claim, which it secures, is being repaid.

There is a constant interplay between the three dimensions of a system of property rights. For instance, in Germany one can only have a right of ownership over corporeal objects, not over incorporeals, yet rights can be transferred and be burdened with limited property rights, such as a usufruct.[99] Emission rights can,

[99] Art. 1068(1) German BGB.

under Dutch law, not be pledged, even though other incorporeal objects usually can.[100]

This three-dimensional model that represents property rights shows the building blocks out of which property rights are made. When visualized, it can be likened to a Rubik's Cube,[101] of which the individual cubes can be detached and re-attached to give different shapes to its width, depth and height. The model, representing the system of property rights, is then visualised in the following manner:

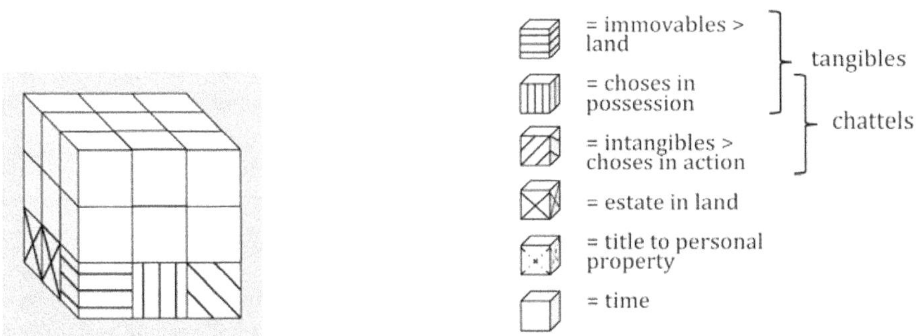


*Figure 2. 'System-Cube' representing the three dimensions of a system of property rights*

The visualization of the three-dimensional model is inspired by the composition of a Rubik's Cube, but the end result is autonomous and differs from the Rubik's Cube in two ways: first, the disks of this cube – the 'System-Cube', see figure 2 – do not rotate, unlike the disks of a Rubik's Cube. Second, the individual cubes of the System-Cube can be detached and re-attached to account for the variables of specific property rights and their objects.[102] Rubik's Cubes cannot be deconstructed (or

100 Art. 16.42(3) of the Dutch Wet Milieubeheer (Law on Environmental Management) reads: 'In afwijking van artikel 228 van Boek 3 van het Burgerlijk Wetboek kan op een gasemissierecht geen recht van pand worden gevestigd.' (In derogation from Article 228 of book 3 of the Civil Code a right of pledge cannot be created on an emission right.) [translation by Akkermans 2011, p. 9].

101 <http://www.rubiks.com/>.

102 The individual cubes of the System-Cube can be detached, because the model that the System-Cube visualizes is based on the French notion of *démembrement*, or subtraction, for the creation of limited property rights. The method of *démembrement* takes as a starting point that the right of ownership contains a number of powers, which can be divided into specific parts. Those parts can be transferred to another person. In the hands of that person, they form a limited property right. In other words, the limited property right consists of fragment of the right of ownership, out of which it was created. The other possibility is to see limited property rights not so much as derived from the powers of the owner, but as a limitation of those powers. Such a limitation entails that those powers that accumulate in the limited →

taken apart) in that way. In other words, it is not so much the way in which the Rubik's Cube functions - i.e. having the capacity to rotate in all directions - that inspired this visualization, but the way in which it is constructed: it is compiled of smaller cubes with different colours,[103] all somehow connected to each other. It is this interconnection between the cubes that forms the essence of the model: the building blocks of the system of property rights are also interconnected. If one is affected, the others are also affected.

### 2.2.3. Practical Application of the System-Cube

With the System-Cube, any given property right can be visualized. I will give a few examples to illustrate. The whole cube will hereafter be called the System-Cube, whereas the individual smaller cubes of which it is made up will be called the minor cubes. The minor cubes each have their own designation, as shown in *Figure 1* above. The three minor cubes in the bottom front row represent, from left to right, immovables and movables (together: corporeals) and incorporeals. The two cubes behind each of these three (forming the dimension of depth) represent the most extensive property right available in a legal system. This would be ownership in civil law systems or freehold title to land or title to personal property in English common law.[104] On top of each minor cube at the bottom of the System-Cube, are stacked two more minor cubes, representing the dimension of time. Two minor cubes on top of the rights-cubes indicate that the right is in principle unlimited in time. Take one away from the top and the right is limited in time. The same goes for the time-cubes placed on top of the objects-cubes: take one away from the top and the object is limited in time.

The full depth of the System-Cube symbolizes the right of ownership or freehold title/title to personal property, since it is the most extensive property right a person can have. By taking minor cubes away from the depth of the System-Cube it is possible to visualize limited property rights. Limited property rights are less extensive than the right of ownership, which is shown by a reduction of the dimension of depth of the System-Cube. If a particular property right only relates to corporeals

property right are not taken away from the person with the more extensive property right, but that this person can, temporarily, simply not make use of those powers. This is the so-called limitation model. See Akkermans 2008, p. 116 and 415.

103 Because this book is printed in black and white the colours have been replaced by patterns, i.e. horizontal stripes, diagonal stripes, etc.

104 In some countries, such as Germany and the Netherlands, it is technically not possible to be an owner of incorporeals. In these systems, the person 'owning' an incorporeal is called the right-holder (*rechthebbende* in Dutch). In the model of the System-Cube, the fact that this 'ownership' is different from ownership of corporeals can be indicated by marking the two minor cubes in the row behind the incorporeal-cube with a dotted X instead of a normal X. However, given that the powers of a right-holder over his incorporeal object are functionally equivalent to the powers that he or she has as owner of a corporeal object, the shape of the cube, as such, need not be changed.

or incorporeals, this can be visualized by taking away minor cubes from the width of the System-Cube. The minor cubes representing the corporeals can be subdivided into movables and immovables, if wanted.[105] The third dimension, of time, is represented by the height of the System-Cube. If a property right is limited in time, or if an object is limited in time (e.g. emission rights), the height of the System-Cube is reduced by taking away minor cubes.

The number of minor cubes, making up the System-Cube, with which one starts, is irrelevant; the principle idea always remains the same. I chose to work with a System-Cube of 3x3x3 minor cubes, because in my opinion this provides a clear visualization of the building blocks that make up property rights. Taking the cube as shown above in *Figure 2* as a starting point, specific property rights in specific countries would have the following composition of minor cubes.

### 2.2.3.1. *A Right of Usufruct*

A right of usufruct can, in Germany and the Netherlands be created both in relation to corporeal and in relation to incorporeal objects. It therefore does not limit the width of the System-Cube. It does, however, limit the depth of the System-Cube, since it is a less extensive right than the right of ownership. It also limits the height of the cube, because both under German and under Dutch law, the usufruct is limited in time in the sense that it ends upon the death of the usufructuary.[106] However, the object as such is in principle not limited in time, so no time-cubes are taken away there. As a result the System-Cube would have the following composition:

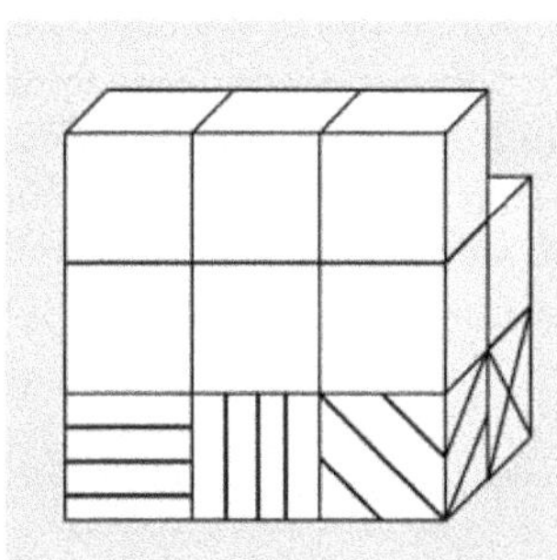

*Figure 3. A right of usufruct in Germany and the Netherlands*

105 I have chosen to do so myself, for the purpose of clarity, but the movables and immovables could just as well be merged into one cube entitled 'corporeals', thereby reducing the width of the System-Cube by one minor cube.

106 Artt. 1030, 1063 and 1068 German civil code; Art. 203 Book 3 Dutch civil code.

*2.2.3.2. A Non-Possessory Right of Pledge on an Incorporeal Object*

A non-possessory pledge created in relation to a claim, as is possible under Dutch law, would affect all three dimensions of the System-Cube. The width is reduced because the object is incorporeal and not corporeal (movable or immovable); the depth is reduced because a right of pledge is less extensive than the right of ownership; and the height is reduced because the right of pledge only exists during the time in which the loan, that the right of pledge is meant to secure, is not yet repaid and the claim still exists. As a result the System-Cube would be composed like this:

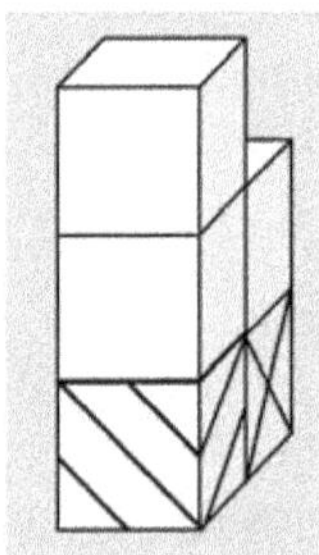

*Figure 4. A non-possessory right of pledge in relation to a claim*

*2.2.3.3. Security Rights in Relation to Corporeal Objects*

A security right created in relation to a corporeal object reduces the width of the System-Cube, because incorporeals are left out; it reduces the depth of the cube because a security right is less extensive than the right of ownership; and the height above the rights-cubes is reduced, because security rights only exist for the duration of the claim that they are meant to secure. A security right in relation to a corporeal object is therefore visualized by the System-Cube in the following way:

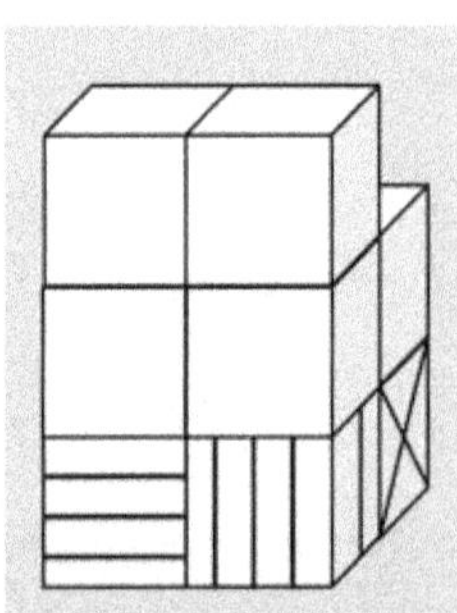

*Figure 5. A security right in relation to a corporeal object*

### 2.2.3.4. *Right of Ownership of Emission Rights*

The right of ownership of emission rights gives yet another shape to the System-Cube. The width is reduced, because emission rights constitute an incorporeal object. The depth is *not* reduced, because it is the right of ownership, the most extensive property right, which is being visualized. The height *is* reduced, but not above the rights-cubes as in the previous examples, because the right of ownership is unlimited in time. The height is reduced above the object-cube, since emission rights are inherently limited in time. They are depleted, used up. This provides the following image:

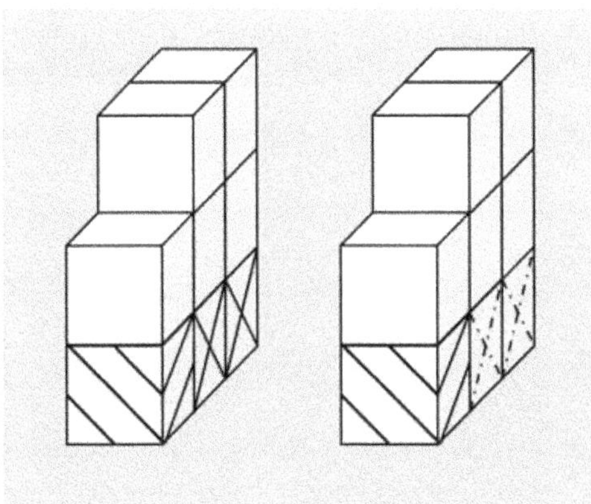

*Figure 6. Right of ownership of emission rights, in France and Germany respectively*

Since it is not technically possible in systems such as Germany to be owner of an incorporeal object, the objects-cubes in the example of *Figure 6* are marked with a dotted ✕instead of a normal ✕. However, since a right-holder in Germany has powers functionally equivalent to those of an owner, the shape of the rights-cubes as such does not have to be altered.[107]

### 2.2.3.5. *Timeshare of Immovable Property*

A person holding a timeshare in, for instance, a holiday home is entitled to that property but only for a limited and specified period of time per year. In other words, timeshares fragment the right of ownership in time.[108] Timeshares were already known in English law, where fragmentation of ownership is possible, but

107 See *supra*, note 104.

108 Timeshares can be set up in different ways under different legal systems, with some regarding them more as proprietary rights and others more as personal rights. More about this in Chapter 4. For the purposes of this section, timeshare is treated as a property right.

civil law systems were not familiar with them until they were introduced by the European Timeshare Directive.[109] Given that civil law systems generally adhere to a uniform concept of ownership, meaning that ownership cannot be fragmented, the introduction of a right that does lead to fragmentation of ownership has caused some difficulties. The Timeshare Directive is dealt with in more detail in Chapter 4.[110] There, the question whether a timeshare is actually a property right or a personal right is also addressed.

If it is assumed that a timeshare is indeed a property right, then the question becomes how the characteristics of this right can be visualized through the System-Cube. The right of ownership is not so much restricted in its content, meaning that the depth of the System-Cube does not need to be reduced, but it is restricted in time, meaning that the height of the minor cubes on top of the rights cubes representing ownership would have to be reduced. Timeshares are therefore represented through the System-Cube in the following way:

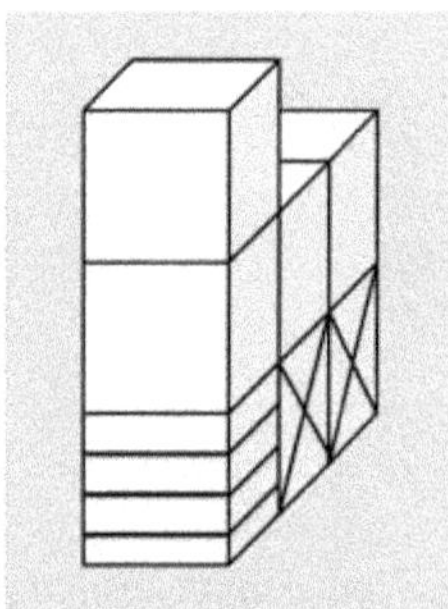

*Figure 7. Timeshare in relation to an immovable object*

### 2.2.4. The System-Cube applied to English Law

The English system of property law is somewhat different from the European continental systems. England is a common law jurisdiction, whereas the European continental countries are predominantly civil law jurisdictions.[111] The separate development in English law of land law and personal property law, and of common law and equity, has led to a fragmented system of property law.[112] Furthermore, while the feudal system of landholding was abolished on the continent after the

109 Dir. 2008/122/EC on the protection of consumers in respect of certain aspects of timeshare, long-term holiday product, resale and exchange contracts [2009] *OJ* L 33/10. This Directive repeals Dir. 94/47/EC.

110 Chapter 4 at 5.7. *Movable/immovable*.

111 'Common law' is hereafter used in the meaning 'as opposed to civil law', not 'as opposed to equity', with the exception of section 2.2.4.1.

112 Akkermans 2008, p. 11.

French Revolution, English land law is still based on feudal concepts of landholding such as fees and estates.[113] Nevertheless, as I argued before, the System-Cube can be applied to any property law system, as long as the building blocks of the System-Cube are properly allocated. It therefore also fits the English system of property rights.

English property law does not know an absolute, unitary right of ownership like the European continental systems do. It takes as a starting point the concept of possession: a person holding a stronger right of possession in relation to a certain object will prevail over a person with a weaker right of possession in relation to that same object.[114] This concept is referred to as 'relativity of title'.[115] It is however a procedural aspect which does not alter the content of a person's right. The search for the strongest right of possession eventually leads to two property rights: a fee simple estate or freehold title, to land, and title to a chattel in personal property law.[116] Just as in civil law systems, where the right of ownership can be regarded as the most extensive property right one can have under a legal system, these two property rights can be seen as the 'most extensive' property rights one can have in English law, in relation to land and personal property respectively. Both the holder in fee simple as well as the holder of title to a chattel are entitled to exclusive possession of the object forever.[117] Other rights to possession exist both in land law and in personal property law, but these property rights are less strong. One exception might be the *demesne* title to land held by the Crown, under which the Crown owns all land.[118] What is essential for the System-Cube is that English property law, just like other systems of property law in Europe, distinguishes between a most extensive property right and less extensive property rights.

Apart from the division between land law and personal property law, English property law also classifies the objects of property rights differently from civil law systems.[119] Tangibles can be subdivided into immovables - which would be subject to land law - and choses in possession - which would be subject to personal property law. Choses in possession and choses in action, the latter being intangibles, can together be classified as chattels, both being subject to personal property law. Taking all of the above into account, the system of property rights in England could then be visualized with the System-Cube in the following manner:

113 Akkermans 2008, p. 11. Also Lawson & Rudden 2002, p. 12-16.
114 Clarke & Kohler 2005, p. 260; Akkermans 2008, p. 417.
115 Clarke & Kohler 2005, p. 386-387; Lawson & Rudden 2002, p. 50-52.
116 Akkermans 2008, p. 417.
117 Akkermans 2008, p. 418; Lawson & Rudden 2002, p. 65 and 80.
118 Lawson & Rudden 2002, p. 78 and 101.
119 For more information on the classification of objects of property rights in English law, see Akkermans 2008, p. 332-334; Clarke & Kohler 2005, p. 18; Lawson & Rudden 2002, p. 19 *et seq.*

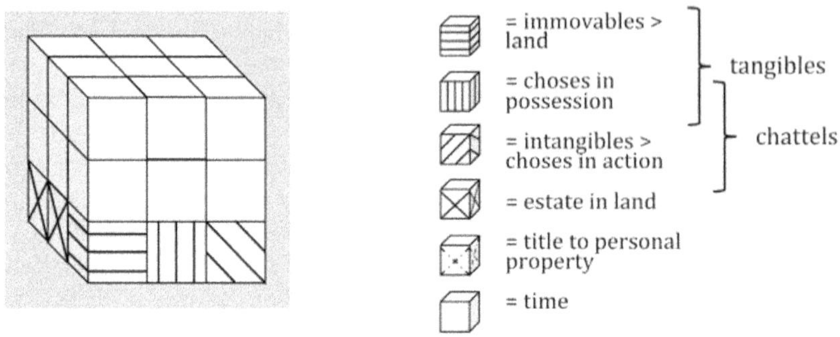


*Figure 8. The system of property rights in English law*

Taking Figure 8, representing the system of property rights in English law, as a starting point, the following figure shows what a fee simple estate in land looks like and what title to a chattel looks like:

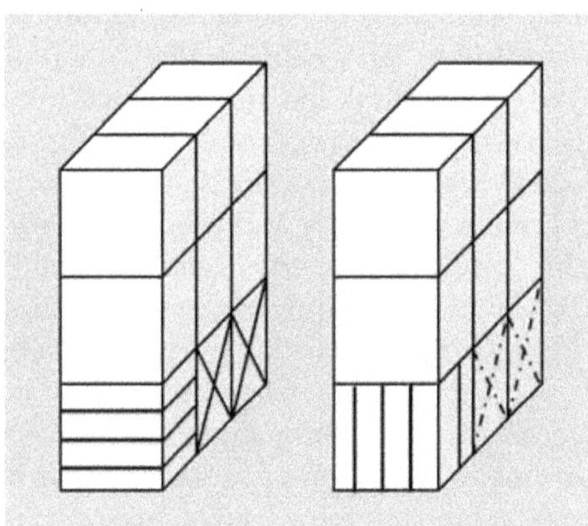

*Figure 9. Fee simple estate in land and title to a chose in possession respectively*

### 2.2.4.1. *Common Law and Equity*

As a result of historical developments, English law consists of two sub-systems: common law and equity.[120] A consequence of this division is the existence of legal as

120 Lawson & Rudden 2002, p. 10-11.

well as of equitable property rights.[121] This division into sub-systems does not prevent the application of the System-Cube. The depth of the Cube represents the range of property rights. The content of the right determines just how deep that dimension is. There is no reason why this range of property rights cannot contain both the legal and the equitable rights. Whether a person holds a property right at law or in equity does not change the content of the right as such, although it may mean that different operating rules apply to the property right. For instance: one kind of operating rules are rules concerning the third party effect of property rights.[122] These rules on third party effect may apply differently depending on whether a person holds a property right at law or in equity. Equitable property rights, for instance, cannot be invoked against a bona fide purchaser for value without notice, whereas legal property rights can.[123] However, a change in the operating rules does not change the parameters of the System-Cube. English property rights, regardless of whether they are legal or equitable property rights, can therefore be visualized through the System-Cube like any other property right.

There is one exception, however, and that is restrictive covenants. Restrictive covenants are English property rights that only exist in equity. A restrictive covenant was first created by the Lord Chancellor's Court in *Tulk* v *Moxhay* in 1848,[124] and was subsequently refined in *Haywood* v *Brunswick Permanent Building Society*[125] and *London County Council* v *Allen*.[126] A restrictive covenant is an agreement between parties that restricts the holder of an estate in land in his use of the land.[127] It requires the existence of a servient and a dominant tenement and the dominant tenement must benefit from the covenant.[128] It must be the intention of the parties that the covenant runs with the land which it burdens.[129] Finally, and this is perhaps the most important aspect and a distinguishing feature from (positive) easements,[130] restrictive covenants must be negative in the sense that they can only entail an obligation for the holder of the servient tenement not to use his property in

121 Akkermans 2008, p. 336; Clarke & Kohler 2005, p. 403 *et seq*. See, for instance, restrictive covenants, which can only exist in equity.

122 *Supra*, section 2.2.1. *Defining property law: introducing the System-Cube*.

123 Akkermans 2008, p. 336-337.

124 *Tulk* v *Moxhay* (1848) 2 Ph 774; Akkermans 2008, p. 363 *et seq*.

125 (1881) 8 QBD 403.

126 [1914] 3 KB 642.

127 *Tulk* v *Moxhay*.

128 *London County Council* v *Allen*.

129 S 79 Law of Property Act 1925.

130 Negative easements are similar to restrictive covenants in that they only entail an obligation for the owner of the servient tenement to refrain from using his land in a certain way, but they seem to be limited to four categories: the right to light, the right to a free flow of air, the right to support of buildings, and the right to a continued flow of water. Lawson & Rudden 2002, p. 154. See also Sara 2011, p. 205, who would however consider the rights to a free flow of air and water to have positive elements in case of a vent or artificial stream, because there is then a defined channel which could be blocked by the servient owner (p. 220).

a certain way.[131] It cannot contain a positive obligation for the holder of the servient tenement to do something with or on the property,[132] nor can it contain a right for the holder of the dominant tenement to do something with or on the servient tenement.

This makes it somewhat difficult to visualize a restrictive covenant through the System-Cube, because it has no content for the 'active side', i.e. the rightholder of the dominant tenement, in the sense that the latter can do something with or on the servient tenement as a result of the restrictive covenant. A restrictive covenant does not give the party benefiting from it any right to do something with the property on which the covenant rests, as would be the case with other limited property rights, most notably positive easements and profits a prèndre. Positive easements grant the party benefiting from them a right to use the servient tenement in a particular way, for instance, to walk over it or run drains underneath it.[133] Profits grant the party benefiting from them a right to take something from the servient land, such as fish (piscary), turf (turbary), or timber (estovers).[134] Restrictive covenants (and negative easements for that matter)[135] do not grant such a right to the owner of the dominant tenement to use or take something from the servient tenement and therefore have a 'negative' content for the owner of the dominant tenement. What it does do, however, is make an addition to the right of ownership of the dominant tenement.[136] For instance, if a restrictive covenant is created to prevent the owner of the servient tenement from developing the land, then that essentially adds the development value of the servient tenement to the dominant tenement.[137] Therefore, while the System-Cube cannot visualize the content of a restrictive covenant as such – since it has only a negative content – it can visualize the fact that a restrictive covenant forms an addition to the right of ownership of the dominant tenement. The result would be this:

131 *Rhone* v *Stephens* [1994] 2 AC 310, HL. See also McFarlane, Hopkins & Nield 2009, p. 928-932.
132 Unless it is made as part of a lease: Akkermans 2008, p. 364.
133 Van Erp & Akkermans 2012, Chapter 3 at II.A.6.; Lawson & Rudden 2002, p. 154.
134 Van Erp & Akkermans 2012, Chapter 3 at II.A.7.
135 Sara 2011, p. 205.
136 *Cf* McFarlane, Hopkins & Nield 2009, p. 923 and 926.
137 Lawson & Rudden 2002, p. 156-157.

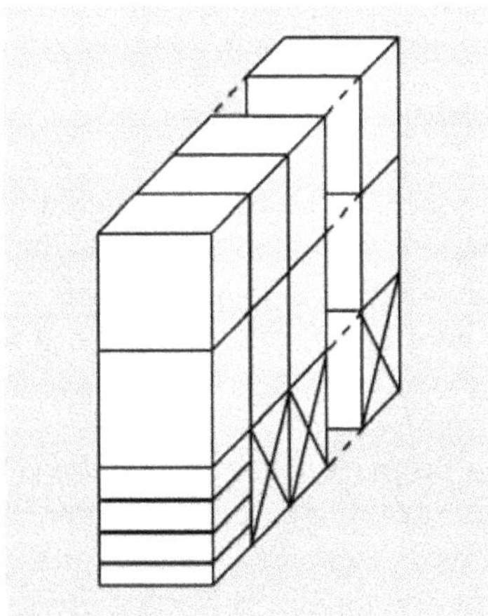

*Figure 10. A restrictive covenant on land*

The minor cube in the front, marked with horizontal stripes, represents the dominant tenement, which is an immovable object. The two minor cubes behind it marked with an X represent the right of ownership in relation to the dominant tenement. Neither the object nor the right of ownership are limited in time, which is why no time-cubes have been removed. The column of minor cubes in the back represents the restrictive covenant which is attached to the right of ownership of the dominant tenement. It is also unlimited in time.

### 2.2.4.2. *Trusts*

The trust is an institution unique to English law and to certain systems based on the English system.[138] Legal scholars have tried to classify it as several different things, among others as a limited property right or as a legal person.[139] The creation of a trust in any event entails a fragmentation of ownership:[140] the powers contained in the ownership right originally held by the settlor are divided amongst the trustees and beneficiaries upon the creation of the trust. The trustees will have the power to manage and dispose of the property, whereas the beneficiaries will have the right to benefit from the property. Gardner defines the trust as:

138 The author assumes that the reader is familiar with the concept of a trust. For a basic explanation of what this concept entails, see, however, Lawson & Rudden 2002, p. 86-88.

139 *Cf* Lawson & Rudden 2002, p. 171.

140 Clarke & Kohler 2005, p. 333.

> '[A] situation in which property is vested in someone (a trustee), who is under legally recognized obligations, at least some of which are of a proprietary kind, to handle it in a certain way, and to the exclusion of any personal interest. These obligations may arise either by conscious creation by the previous owner of the property (the settlor), or because some other legally significant circumstances are present.'[141]

The difficulty for this chapter lies not so much in the question, what a trustee's or beneficiary's interest looks like - if there is a beneficiary; not all trusts have beneficiaries[142] - but rather in the question whether or not the trustee's interest and whether or not the beneficiary's interest is of a proprietary nature. If it is the case that these interests are seen as proprietary, then they can be visualized through the System-Cube just like any other property right.

The trustee has the legal title to the property and can thus be said to be the owner.[143] Of course, being a trustee means being a fiduciary owner, meaning the ownership does not benefit the trustee himself. In that sense, the content of fiduciary ownership clearly differs from outright ownership.[144] Nevertheless, the interest held by the trustee over the trust property is a property right. Whether the right held by the beneficiary (i.e. equitable interest) is a property right is less straightforward. As was seen above in section 2.2.1., the defining characteristics of a property right are that it is a right as against a thing, which can be invoked *erga omnes*. Much depends on the nature of a specific trust, and since there exists a myriad of trusts, it is difficult to give straightforward statements on the nature of a beneficiary's interest. Nevertheless, some general observations can be made. A beneficiary can be said to have an interest against the trust property, if he can dissolve the trust and demand that possession of the trust property is transferred to him under the rule in *Saunders* v *Vautier*.[145] This will be the case where the trust is fixed, held for a sole adult beneficiary of unimpaired capacity, upon whose entitlement there are no conditions.[146] This will also be the case in an exhaustive discretionary trust if all beneficiaries act together as a single beneficiary.[147]

It is clear that a beneficiary can invoke his interest, under certain circumstances, against the trustee. But can a beneficiary invoke his interest *erga omnes*? If not, then it may be doubtful whether a beneficiary's interest is a property right after all. This is a discussion that is far from crystallized. McFarlane and Stevens describe the beneficiary's interest as a right against the trustee's right of ownership.[148] This means that the beneficiary can only invoke his interest under the trust against those third parties who have acquired a right 'that derives from the right which [the

141 Gardner 2011, p. 2.
142 Gardner 2011, p. 6.
143 Clarke & Kohler 2005, p. 334.
144 Gardner 2011, p. 224; Lawson & Rudden 2002, p. 171-173.
145 (1841) 4 Beav 115, Cr & Ph 240. Gardner 2011, p. 223.
146 Gardner 2011, p. 218-219.
147 See e.g. *Re Smith* [1928] Ch 915; *Sainsbury* v *IRC* [1970] Ch 712.
148 McFarlane & Stevens 2010.

trustee] holds on trust for [the beneficiary]'.[149] As a result, the beneficiary can invoke his interest against C if C is given the trust property by the trustee, but the beneficiary cannot invoke his interest against D if D carelessly damages the trust property, for D in that case does not acquire a right in the trust property from the trustee. In accordance with this interpretation, a beneficiary's interest is almost like a semi-property right, in that it can be relied upon against some third parties but not against all third parties. Maitland provided an overview of the different classes of third parties against whom a beneficiary can and cannot invoke his interest.[150] He argued that equitable interests - such as that of a beneficiary under a trust - are not to be seen as property rights, that they are rights *in personam* having only a 'misleading resemblance' to rights *in rem* because a trust will be enforced against persons acquiring legal rights through the trustee, if they knew of or ought to have known of the existence of the trust.[151] On the other hand, a recent Court of Appeal's judgment in *Shell* v *Total*[152] would suggest that a beneficiary's interest is a property right after all, since in that case the applicant was allowed to rely on his beneficial interest directly against the defendant, who negligently damaged the trust property. This judgment has been criticized, however, because it is not clear-cut and may rest on fallacious reasoning.[153]

If it is accepted that a beneficiary's interest under a trust is a property right, then it can be visualized through the System-Cube. The beneficiary's interest is not as extensive as a full right of ownership: the beneficiary may have the right to use and benefit from the object held on trust, but he does not have the right to manage the property and dispose of it. Take as an example a car - i.e. a chattel - held on trust for a sole beneficiary for the duration of his life, that beneficiary's interest in the car could be visualized in the following manner:

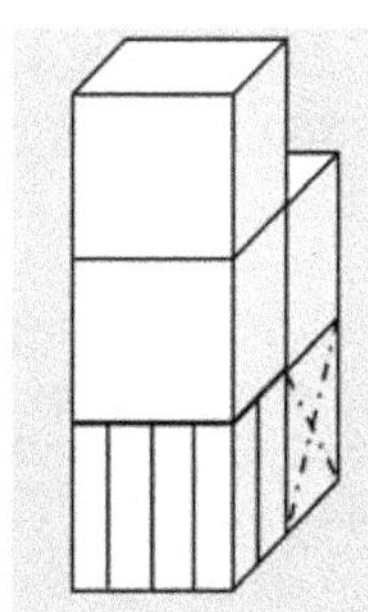

*Figure 11. A beneficiary's interest in a car held on trust*

149 McFarlane & Stevens 2010 at C *Equitable property rights and rights against a right.*

150 Maitland 1936, Lecture IX 'The nature of equitable estates and interests(I)', p. 112 *et seq.*

151 Maitland 1936, Lecture IX 'The nature of equitable estates and interests(I)', p. 115, and Lecture X 'The nature of equitable estates and interests (II), p. 117.

152 [2010] EWCA Civ 180.

153 Rushworth & Scott 2010.

The minor cubes representing time have been reduced by one above the rights-cube (marked with a dotted X), to indicate that the beneficiary's interest is limited to his lifetime.

### 2.2.5. Summary

The model presented above indicates the general characteristics of any property law system, but it can also account for the variables of specific property rights in specific national property law systems. One could debate whether the System-Cube is the preferred way of visualizing the building blocks of property rights; that remains a matter of preference. The underlying model, however, remains the same: a system of property law consists of a core representing the property rights and an operating system around it regulating those rights. The core in turn has three dimensions (width - objects; depth - content of the right; height - time) and in each system the shape of these dimensions shifts depending on the idiosyncrasies of a particular property right.

The model is primarily created to solve the particular methodological problems of this research project. It is not intended for universal application, even though others may be able to use it for different purposes. With this model, I can answer the question how to make a selection of the *acquis communautaire* and on the basis of what criteria. As I said before, every Treaty Article, secondary legislative measure, judgment and policy document that has an impact on property law will be part of the selection. This criterion can now be refined to: every Treaty Article, secondary legislative measure, judgment and policy document that deals with or affects either one of the three dimensions of property rights *or* any of the operating rules will be part of the selection.

## 3. Linguistic Problems: the Method of the Court of Justice of the European Union

The first major methodological issue of this project has been outlined above: to find out what constitutes property law, before the *acquis communautaire* can be analysed and described in order to establish what constitutes EU property law. Once this hurdle is cleared and the analysis of the *acquis* can start, a second problem will undoubtedly be encountered. This is the problem of the multilingual nature of the European Union. There are currently 27 Member States with a total of 23 official languages in the EU. The method developed by the CJEU when dealing with multilingual texts prescribes that all the different language versions must be taken into account on the basis of the principle of equality of languages. However, this method was tailored to an EU with maximum 15 Member States. The official languages spoken in those Member States were relatively understandable for judges who would normally be able to understand a combination of French, English and German. It is uncertain whether this method still fits an EU with 27 Member States and 23 official languages, some of which have much less in common with each other and with the languages of the EU-15. Not all of these languages will be easily understood by all of the judges, nor by academics for that matter. This section is dedicated to explaining the method developed by the CJEU to deal with the multilingual nature of EU law. In the next chapters, especially Chapter 3 dealing with Article 345, this method will be applied and, on occasion, adapted for the idiosyncrasies of this project.

### 3.1. *The Semantic Approach and the Contextual Approach*

The judgments rendered by the Court in cases dealing with interpretation problems show that a hierarchy of interpretative rules exists. The role that languages play in the EU legal order is described in the CILFIT case:[154]

> '18 To begin with, it must be borne in mind that Community legislation is drafted in several languages and that the different language versions are all equally authentic. An interpretation of a provision of Community law thus involves a comparison of the different language versions.
>
> 19 It must also be borne in mind, even where the different language versions are entirely in accord with one another, that Community law uses terminology which is peculiar to it. Furthermore, it must be emphasized that legal concepts do not necessarily have the same meaning in Community law and in the law of the various Member States.
>
> 20 Finally, every provision of Community law must be placed in its context and interpreted in the light of the provisions of Community law as a whole, regard being had to the objectives thereof and to its state of evolution at the date on which the provision in question is to be applied.'

As can be seen from this section of the judgment, the Court takes two steps when interpreting the text of a provision: it starts with a purely textual – or 'semantic' – approach, according to which it compares the different language versions. The Court will thereafter examine the provision in its context, both the immediately surrounding provisions and the other parts of the Treaty, as well as secondary legislation if that legislation touches upon the same subject.[155] If the language versions are unequivocal, the contextual interpretation is intended to confirm this conclusion. If the semantic approach is inconclusive, the contextual interpretation is

154 Case 283/81 [1982] ECR 3415.

155 See also case 30/77, *Bouchereau* [1977] ECR 1999, para. 14: 'The different language versions of a Community text must be given a uniform interpretation and hence in the case of divergence between the versions the provision in question must be interpreted by reference to the purpose and general scheme of the rules of which it forms a part.' The two-step method of interpretation here described applies both to Treaty provisions and to secondary legislation; *Cf* Van Calster 1997, p. 375.

intended to remedy this divergence between the different language versions.[156] The Court's case law provides a number of examples where the semantic method is applied. See, for instance, *Isabelle Lancray* where the Court in paragraph 16 says: 'The wording of the different language versions of the provision in question suggests…'.[157] The Court starts with the use of the semantic approach because of the need for uniformity in interpretation. The result of the fact that all language versions of the Treaty are equally authentic is that the content of the Treaty is not laid down in any of those versions separately but that the content is contained in all those versions together.

The Court is thorough in its analysis. A decision will not be made based on a majority of texts only. First of all, this would go against the rule that all language versions are equally authentic. Secondly, if a decision is based on a common denominator found in a majority of texts but not in all of them, an interesting solution featuring in the minority of texts might be overlooked. This is especially important as it is not always the common denominator that the Court is looking for.[158] Thirdly, basing a decision on the maximum common content could set a poor example for the Member States. A Member State that is unhappy with the way in which legislation develops in a particular area of European law could start looking for differences in wording in the different language versions of the legislative instrument concerned and stick only to the minimum common content. This would be an undesirable hindrance to the unification of that particular area of law.[159] It would equally go against the principle of equality to discount diverging language versions simply because they represent only a small percentage of the Union's population. The CJEU has discarded this suggested approach in case *EMU Tabac*.[160]

It is only when the semantic approach fails to provide a clear answer that the Court turns to the second step: contextual interpretation. An important part of this step in the interpretation process is the intention of the drafters of the - primary or secondary - legislation. However, it was not until 1994 that the documents drawn up during the Intergovernmental Conference of 1957, where the text of the E(E)C

156 See, for instance, case 6/60, *Humblet* [1960] ECR 559, 575, 6th paragraph; case 90/83, *Paterson* v *Weddel* [1984] ECR 1567, para. 12; see also Vismara 2006, p. 67.

157 Case C-305/88 [1990] ECR I-2725. For an overview of cases in which the CJEU applies the semantic approach see Van Calster 1997, p. 370.

158 *Cf* Lenaerts 2003, p. 879.

159 Van Calster 1997, p. 378.

160 Case C-296/95, *The Queen* v *Commissioners of Customs and Excise, ex parte EMU Tabac and others* [1998] ECR I-1605, para. 36: 'Furthermore, to discount two language versions, as the applicants in the main proceedings suggest, would run counter to the Court's settled case-law to the effect that the need for a uniform interpretation of Community regulations makes it impossible for the text of a provisions to be considered in isolation but requires, on the contrary, that it should be interpreted and applied in the light of the versions existing in the other official languages […]. Lastly, all the language versions must, in principle, be recognized as having the same weight and this cannot vary according to the size of the population of the Member States using the language in question.' See also Ioriatti Ferrari 2008, p. 108.

Treaty was decided, were released.[161] Before that time, those documents were unavailable to the Court, let alone to the general public and ascertaining the intention of the drafters of the Treaty was therefore usually impossible.[162] The Court therefore examines a provision in its context. It takes into account the 'general scheme and the purpose of the regulatory system of which the provisions in question form part'.[163] This purposive approach goes hand in hand with the doctrine of *effet utile*: once the purpose of a provision has been established, it will be interpreted further in a way that will 'ensure that the provision retains its effectiveness'.[164]

## Conclusion

This chapter has outlined the two goals of this study: to map out the landscape of EU property law and to propose a framework for further conceptualization of this field of law. The reasons for investigating whether and how the EU should get involved in property law are twofold. First of all, the divergences between the national systems of property law and their closed and mandatory nature, which cannot be avoided through a choice of law, may cause - and do cause - hindrances to free movement within the internal market. The discovery of potential hindrances to free movement functions as a signal that harmonization may be needed. Whether that is indeed the case deserves further research which will be conducted in this study. Secondly, the European Union has been involved in the development of European contract law for several decades, but other areas of private law adjacent to contract law - most notably property law - are left behind in these developments. However, there are too many areas where property law and contract law intertwine, so that moving forward in contract law without also moving forward, at least to a certain extent, in property law could lead to disruptions within the national legal orders that have to implement the European rules on contract law. Having said this, before a discussion about whether and how property law should be developed by the EU can take place, it is important to have an overview of the extent to which the EU has already created property law. This study purports to provide such an overview, focussing on European legislation and case law in the field of property law.

161 Decision No. 359/83 of the ECSC, 5 February 1983 and Regulation No. 354/83 of the EEC and Euratom, concerning the opening to the public of the historical archives of the European Coal and Steel Community, the European Economic Community and Euratom.

162 These documents are now available in the Historical Archives of the European Union at the European University Institute, Firenze, Italy. They can also be consulted in Neri & Sperl 1960, p. 410.

163 Joined cases C-267/95 and C-268/95 [1996] ECR I-6285, paras. 21-22. The wording of this formula has changed somewhat over the years, but the essence has stayed the same; see Fennelly 1996-1997, p. 664-665.

164 Case 187/87 [1988] ECR 5013, para. 19: 'It is to an interpretation to that effect, which is such as to ensure that the provision retains its effectiveness [*effet utile*], that preference must be given, in accordance with a line of decided cases [reference omitted].'

In this chapter, the method has been developed with which the *acquis communautaire* will be analysed for existing property law. To analyse the *acquis* in the field of property law, a selection of measures from the *acquis* will have to be made that deal with property law. Therefore, before it can be established what constitutes EU property law, it has to be established what constitutes property law and where the line is to be drawn between property law and contract law. The distinguishing features of property rights are that they are rights against a thing, which can be relied upon *erga omnes*, as opposed to contractual rights which are rights against a specific person or group of persons only. The principle of *numerus clausus* determines that the list of property rights available within a given system is closed and mandatory. Only rights that are in the *numerus clausus* are property rights and only rights that have the two characteristics just mentioned will be in the *numerus clausus*. The *numerus clausus* thus acts as a filter to draw the line between property rights and contractual rights. Once it has been established that a right is a property right, rules of property law determine how such a right can be created or transferred, whether it must be registered, etc. I have developed a model that shows what a system of property law looks like. It consists of a core, representing the property rights, which is surrounded by an operating system, i.e. the system of rules that governs property rights. The core illustrates the three dimensions of property rights: the first dimension consists of the content of the property right, the second dimension consists of the objects in relation to which a property right can be held and the third dimension represents time, since both a property right and the object on which it rests can be limited or unlimited in time. I have named this core the System-Cube: it illustrates the dimensions of property rights through cubes that represent the building blocks of a property right. The System-Cube was applied to several examples of national property rights to show how its building blocks can visualize any property right from any legal system. At the end of this study, the System-Cube will be revisited and filled in with the data gathered on the status quo of EU property law. The model of property law, including the System-Cube, was developed specifically for the kind of research that I am conducting, where the field of law is largely unexplored and where one therefore has to work with an abstract concept containing the general characteristics of that field of law. The model does not presume to be universally applicable, even though others may be able to use it for different purposes.

While the primary focus of this study is therefore on the *acquis communautaire*, comparative research also plays a role. It is first of all used as a basis to outline the field of property law. Information drawn from comparative research has been used to feed the model that I have developed in this chapter, including the System-Cube. Comparative research will moreover be used at a later point in this study, when the status quo of EU property law is described and when the framework for the future conceptualization of this field of law is developed. Any gaps in EU property law will be able to be filled using examples gathered through comparative research.

Once the status quo of EU property law is clear, this study will provide a framework for the future development of EU property law in a consistent and coherent way. It will deal with both form and content. There are different options for the form which EU property law could take. These possible forms will be explored in depth in Chapter 5, but I will already introduce them briefly here. One possibility would be to lay down a coherent set of property law rules in one regulation or directive, which would be mandatory for the Member States. Drafting a set of regulations or directives, each dealing with a specific issue area of property law might also be possible; they would again be mandatory measures. Whether the EU is allowed to promulgate such measures depends of course on whether the necessary legal basis is available. This is an issue that will be discussed both in Chapter 3 and in Chapter 5. Another option would be for the European Institutions to adopt an inter-institutional agreement. It remains to be seen, however, what could be achieved with this option, as an inter-institutional agreement is only binding on the EU institutions and not on the Member States. A final possibility would be for the EU to adopt an optional instrument on property law that would provide an alternative for parties next to the national systems of property law. Such an optional system is often referred to as the '28$^{th}$ system' to indicate that it exists next to the 27 national systems. However, a 28$^{th}$ system implies that one could choose between one's own system, the 26 other systems of the Member States, and the European system, but in property law there is no such choice of law because the applicable property law will always be the *lex rei sitae*, i.e. the law of the place where an object is situated. If a European alternative was offered, it would therefore not constitute a 28$^{th}$ system but simply a 2$^{nd}$ system.

As far as the content of future EU property law is concerned, there are several examples that can provide inspiration. In this regard one could think of Article 9 of the Uniform Commercial Code or the Cape Town Convention on International Interests in Mobile Equipment, both of which provide for a property security right that can be used in cross-border situations. The developments around a Euro-mortgage and the DCFR are also relevant for this study. All these examples will be explored in the final chapter of this study, which will contain a proposal for the future development of EU property law.

Chapter 2

# PROPERTY LAW AND THE INTERNAL MARKET

## Introduction

The first chapter of this study identified one of the main reasons for researching the development of EU property law as being that the divergences between national systems of property law may cause obstacles to the freedom of movement within the internal market.[1] The effect that the rules of the internal market have on national law is called negative integration. Through negative integration, European law creates the internal market by imposing obligations upon Member States *not* to do something, not to apply certain national legislation. If national law is found to hinder free movement within the internal market, it can no longer be applied, unless the Member State can justify the continuing existence of its law and can show that its law is proportional to the aim it pursues. Negative integration is the opposite of positive integration, by which the EU develops the internal market through European legislation in the form of regulations and directives. These legislative measures impose obligations upon the Member States to *do* something, to change and interpret their national legislation in line with the European rules.

1 There may, of course, be other reasons why businesses or consumers are deterred from entering into cross-border trade than merely a difference in laws. An interesting study in this regard is LOW's *European Contract Law between the Single Market and the Law Market – A Behavioural Perspective*. Some of these deterrents may be practical (e.g. IKEA Belgium will not deliver furniture to people living in the Netherlands for insurance reasons; foreign plugs will not fit into the sockets in your home country; you do not speak the language). Others may be behavioural (*Status quo bias* indicates that as long as there is a default position, people will tend to follow that default position.) Such considerations may lead businesses or consumers to decide not to engage in cross-border proprietary transactions, even if they could be fully informed about foreign law and would therefore not need to worry about, for instance, the costs of acquiring the information. See in particular Low 2011, p. 89-91, 146-150, 256-262, and 268 *et seq*. These considerations, while extremely insightful, fall outside the scope of this study, which focuses only on the effects that differences in national property laws have on people's and companies' decisions to enter into cross-border proprietary transactions.

Positive integration will be dealt with in Chapter 4. The topic of this chapter is negative integration which, in the European Union, is achieved through the rules on the free movement of goods, persons, services and capital.[2] In Chapter 1, a brief introduction was given concerning the possible influence of the four freedoms on national property law. The current chapter investigates whether the rules of national property law indeed fall within the scope of application of the four freedoms and, if so, what the effects of such an application would be. It is meant to explore where the boundaries of the four freedoms lie when it comes to their application to property law.

The possibility that the four freedoms also apply to property law is not often considered. Even though the idea that the four freedoms might also be applicable to private law is not a completely new one,[3] not much is written about the possible influence of the rules on free movement on national property law.[4] National lawyers and courts do not seem to consider that there could be an influence, which is for a large part due to Article 345 TFEU stating that nothing in the Treaties shall affect the Member States' system of property ownership. This will be addressed further Chapter 3. Much more focus is placed on active measures, positive harmonization, undertaken by the EU, which affects property law. This is understandable because these measures are more visible and their effect is perhaps more easily quantifiable. The effect of the rules on free movement is less visible and possibly more indirect, hence the risk of unawareness. But rules of private law are just as capable of creating obstacles to the internal market as rules of public law are.[5] And the effect of the four freedoms on private law could be much more extensive than the effect of the more visible, positive harmonization measures. Precisely for that reason it is important to figure out just how extensive this effect could be.

Apart from unawareness, discomfort also seems to play a part in the limited amount of research done in this area[6] and in the hesitance of the CJEU to test the compatibility of national property law with the internal market rules, as will be shown below in the discussion of the *Krantz* judgment.[7] People seem to be convinced that the application of the four freedoms to private law automatically has drastic consequences, that it will open the flood-gates and that it will disrupt the national system. This is certainly not necessarily the case, however.[8] The application of the internal market rules always occurs in several steps: step 1 – is there an

2 Apart from the four freedoms, negative integration also includes the rules on competition law. They will however not be dealt with here, as that would go beyond the scope of this project.

3 Klauer 1998, p. 17 with further references in footnote 4.

4 Klauer 1998, p. 22.

5 Klauer 1998, p. 62.

6 The application of the four freedoms to private law has even been called a 'horror-image': Steindorff 1994, p. 98.

7 C-69/88, *Krantz* v *Ontvanger der Directe Belastingen* [1990] ECR I-583.

8 Klauer 1998, p. 71.

obstacle to the internal market? If the answer is yes, step 2 follows: is there a possible ground for justification of the national measure? If the answer to that is no, the national measure infringes the internal market rules and will have to be changed or removed; but if the answer to that is yes, step 3 follows: is the national measure proportionate to the aim pursued? If the answer to that is also yes, then the national measure, even though it forms an obstacle to the internal market, is justified and can remain in existence. It will be shown in section 7 that there are quite a large number of possible grounds for justification that have been or may be accepted by the Court. That means that, even though a national measure of private law may initially be caught under one of the free movement articles, in the end nothing much may need to be changed at all, because the measure is justified.

The case law of the CJEU, which interprets the four freedoms in general and which deals with the application of these freedoms to cases relating to property law specifically, will be closely looked at in this chapter. Given the interface between internal market law - especially the free movement of goods and capital - and national property law, which forms one of the two pillars of this research,[9] an important element of this chapter will be an analysis of how the CJEU defines the concept of 'goods' and how it develops this definition. Such an analysis can give an indication as to whether the term 'goods' is given a definition only for the purposes of the internal market or whether it is interpreted in such a way that it can also be used in the context of EU property law.

Another thread running through this chapter is the trend of the CJEU to shift to a market access test, as opposed to a discrimination test, when determining whether a national measure forms an obstacle to the internal market. A discrimination test is applied to catch measures that are of a directly or indirectly discriminatory nature against foreign persons or goods. However, non-discriminatory measures cannot be caught with such a test. Given that even such measures can nevertheless hinder cross-border trade, a test was developed by the CJEU to determine whether they prevent or limit access to the market of a host Member State.[10] It is important to find out for each of the four freedoms which test the CJEU applies because property law is generally applied to anyone and anything within a particular Member State, regardless of whether or not that person or object 'originated' from that Member State. Cases of property law (in)directly discriminating between foreign and domestic persons or between foreign and domestic goods are therefore unlikely.[11] Rules of property law may nevertheless restrict access to the market of a Member

9 Chapter 1, at 1.1. *The relationship between free movement law and property law.*

10 'Host' Member State means the receiving Member State or Member State of destination in a cross-border situation.

11 Klauer 1998, p.64. The agreements that have been made with new Member States upon their accession to the EU, on the acquisition of land in their territories by nationals of the other Member States, are an exception to this. See e.g. Treaty of Accession of Croatia, Annex V *Transitional measures*, [2012] *OJ* L 112/70; *Documents concerning the accession of [...] the Republic of Malta [...]*, Protocol No 6 on the acquisition of secondary residences in Malta, [2003] *OJ* 947.

State. A market access test is therefore needed to determine whether a rule of national property law constitutes a hindrance to free movement. According to the case law of the Court, a market access test (or 'hindrance-test') is by now applied to the free movement of services and persons. For the free movement of capital the Court's case law is less clear-cut. In the free movement of goods, the Court seemed to be going in the direction of a market access test, but the *Keck and Mithouard* judgment caused a lot of uncertainty on this point. That uncertainty has to some extent been relieved by the *Trailers* judgment. Both these cases will be discussed in detail in this chapter. Which test is applied is also relevant to determine what kind of justifications a Member State could rely on to maintain its national measure. In the case of direct or indirect discrimination, only the justifications enumerated in the Treaty are available. This is always a closed list containing justification grounds such as public policy, public security and public health. In the case of non-discriminatory measures which nevertheless pose an obstacle to the internal market, the 'rule of reason' originating from the *Cassis de Dijon* case applies, which provides an open-ended list of possible justifications which are necessary to protect mandatory requirements in the public interest.[12]

A third central theme of this chapter is whether a *de minimis* test is applied when determining if there is an obstacle to the internal market. A *de minimis* test means that there has to be a minimum impact on the internal market before the application of the free movement rules is triggered. A *de minimis* test was unexpectedly applied in one of the cases that will be discussed in depth in this chapter, namely the *Krantz* case.[13] While such a test was generally discarded,[14] it has possibly resurfaced in the development of the market access test.

Finally, it will be shown for each of the four freedoms how they might affect national property law and which part of national property law they could or do affect.

## 1. Cross-border or Purely Internal Situation?

Cases concerning 'purely internal situations' are important for the question whether or not national property law provisions fall within the scope of application of the free movement rules. It could be argued that property relationships are not of a cross-border nature and therefore do not fall under the free movement rules, either due to the nature of the goods (i.e. immovable objects are not transported cross-

12 *Cf* for free movement of services case C-384/93, *Alpine Investments* [1995] ECR I-1141, para. 45, and for free movement of persons case C-55/94, *Gebhard* [1995] ECR I-4165, para. 37. See also Klauer 1998, p. 68. 'Mandatory requirements' is the original wording from the *Cassis* judgment (para. 8 of that judgment). An alternative that is often seen is 'imperative reasons' or 'imperative requirements' (e.g. case C-76/90, *Säger*, para. 15).

13 Case C-69/88, *H. Krantz GmbH & Co.* v *Ontvanger der Directe Belastingen and Netherlands State* [1990] ECR I-583; see *infra*, section 3.4.

14 *Cf* Barnard 2010, p. 78.

border) or because of the fact that the *lex rei sitae* rule always designates one (national) system of property law as the applicable law to a proprietary relationship.[15] However, CJEU cases such as *Pistre, Guimont, Reisch* and *Salzmann* indicate that the chance of a situation being purely internal is becoming more and more remote. *Reisch*[16] and *Salzmann*[17] both concerned the free movement of capital, which is contained in Article 63 TFEU.[18] They have a close connection to property law because they concern the acquisition of immovable property. *Guimont*[19] and *Pistre*[20] do not have this connection to property law; they were cases regarding a national rule for the production of cheese and a national rule regulating labelling respectively, 'standard' free movement of goods cases therefore.[21] Nevertheless, the Court's interpretation of when there is a purely internal situation is of general application to any free movement of goods case, regardless of the type of national rule. Therefore, the Court's ruling in *Guimont* and *Pistre* would also apply to a free movement of goods case concerning property law.

In *Pistre*, the Court starts with the famous *Dassonville*-formula.[22] According to the *Dassonville*-formula, '[a]ll trading rules enacted by Member States which are capable of hindering, directly or indirectly, actually or potentially, intra-Community trade are to be considered as measures having an effect equivalent to quantitative restrictions'.[23] Those measures violate Article 34 TFEU on the free movement of goods. Building on that formula, the Court in *Pistre* then went on to state the following:

> '44 Accordingly, whilst the application of a national measure having no actual link to the importation of goods does not fall within the ambit of Article [34] of the Treaty [reference omitted], Article [34] cannot be considered inapplicable simply because all the facts of the specific case before the national court are confined to a single Member State.
>
> 45 In such a situation, the application of the national measure may also have effects on the free movement of goods between Member States, in particular when the measure in question facilitates the marketing of goods of domestic origin to the detriment of imported goods. In such circumstances, the application of the measure, even if restricted to domestic producers, in itself creates and maintains a difference of

15 *Cf* Akkermans 2012a, p. 206.

16 Joined cases C-519/99 to C-524/99 and C-526/99 to C-540/99, *Reisch and others* v *Bürgermeister der Landeshauptstadt Salzburg and Grundverkehrsbeauftragter des Landes Salzburg* [2002] ECR I-2157.

17 Case 300/01, *Doris Salzmann* [2003] ECR I-04899.

18 Ex Art. 56 EC.

19 Case C-448/98, Criminal proceedings against Jean-Pierre Guimont [2000] ECR I-10663.

20 Joined cases C-321/94, C-322/94, C-323/94 and C-324/94, *Criminal proceedings against Pistre and others* [1997] ECR I-2343.

21 The right to free movement of goods is contained in Art. 34 TFEU (ex Art. 28 EC).

22 Case 8/74, *Procureur du Roi* v *Benoît and Gustave Dassonville* [1974] ECR 837.

23 Para. 5.

treatment between those two categories of goods, hindering, at least potentially, intra-Community trade.'

The Court continues this reasoning in *Guimont*:

> '17 ... The mere fact that a rule is not applied to imported products in practice does not exclude the possibility of it having effects which indirectly or potentially hinder intra-Community trade [...]
>
> 19 Article [34] cannot be considered inapplicable simply because all the facts of the specific case before the national court are confined to a single Member State.'

So far, these two cases only concerned the free movement of goods. Advocate-General Geelhoed discusses the matter of purely internal situations at length in his Opinion in the *Reisch* case, about which more below. In his opinion, the Court had been applying a different line of reasoning depending on which of the four freedoms was at stake. He refers to *Pistre* and *Guimont* and proposes to extend the ruling in those cases to the other three freedoms.

In the context of the free movement of goods, the Court has indicated that it will not refuse to give an answer to a preliminary question in cases where all the elements are confined to a single Member State. Article 34 could still apply to such cases - for example in the event of a national measure prohibiting reverse discrimination - even though strictly speaking there is no cross-border element. An interpretation by the Court is therefore needed and the Court will provide it.[24] As Advocate-General Geelhoed puts it: '[I]t is the nature and substance of the national measure that determine whether the Court answers questions referred to it for a preliminary ruling, not the facts in the main proceedings.'[25] In other words, if the nature and substance of a national measure are such that they potentially hinder the free movement of goods, the Court will examine it under Article 34, regardless of whether the facts of this specific case are all connected to one Member State only.

In the context of the free movement of workers, the freedom of establishment and the freedom to provide services, the Court's interpretation of purely internal situations has been different than in the context of the free movement of goods. Even though it is quick to recognize that there is a cross-border element, it will ultimately refuse to answer the preliminary question if all the facts of the case are linked to a single Member State. With regard to these freedoms, it therefore focuses more on the facts of the case and not on the nature and substance of the national measure.[26]

Advocate-General Geelhoed proposes in *Reisch* that the Court no longer follow this separate line of reasoning for the free movement of persons and services but

24 A.-G. Geelhoed in *Reisch*, paras. 83-88.
25 A.-G. Geelhoed, para. 88.
26 A.-G. Geelhoed, paras. 89-95.

rather that it should also apply *Guimont* to these freedoms.[27] He offers several grounds for this proposition, the most striking of which is the following:

> '100. It is my view [...] that the internal nature of cases such as the present is not very significant. It is *mere coincidence* that all of the parties in the cases referred to the Court are resident in the Member State of Austria.' [emphasis added]

In his view, the nature and substance of a national measure such as the Salzburger Land Transfer Law - which was the national measure in dispute in *Reisch* - may have an external effect, thereby actually or potentially obstructing free movement. In the case of *Reisch* the parties happened to all be Austrian but, argued the Advocate-General, next time they could be German or Italian nationals. It is therefore insufficient to deny the existence of a cross-border element solely based on the fact that all parties involved happen to have the nationality of the Member State imposing the measure.

In the context of the free movement of capital, the Court had not needed to consider purely internal situations any time before the *Reisch* case. According to Advocate-General Geelhoed there is always a cross-border situation as far as the free movement of capital is concerned, since the introduction of the Economic and Monetary Union. Both the investment in immovable property and the financing of that investment are considered to be capital movements.[28] Geelhoed suggests that, since it is not the duty of the Court to investigate whether parties have taken out a mortgage loan and how the institutions lending those mortgage loans operate on the national or European capital market, the Court should leave it up to the national court to raise preliminary questions or not, thereby following the *Guimont* line of reasoning.[29]

The CJEU followed the Advocate-General to a certain extent. It did not explicitly deal with Geelhoed's proposal to extend the *Guimont* judgment to also include the free movement of persons and services. It did, however, take over Geelhoed's suggestion to apply *Guimont* to the free movement of capital. It agreed with the submission by one of the parties that all the facts of the case were restricted to one Member State but held that that was insufficient to conclude that there was no need to answer the preliminary questions referred by the national court. Only if such questions clearly have no connection to the actual case will the Court refuse to reply to them.[30] The Court concluded with a reference to *Guimont*:

27 The facts in *Reisch* will be discussed later in this Chapter because it is an essential case explaining how national property law rules can infringe the free movement of capital: section 4.3. *Obstacles to the free movement of capital.*

28 *Infra*, at section 4.1.

29 A.-G. Geelhoed, paras. 102-111.

30 Joined cases C-515/99, C-519/99 to C-524/99 and C-526/99 to C-540/99, *Reisch and others* [2002] ECR I-2157, paras. 24-26.

> '26. In this case, it is not obvious that the interpretation of Community law requested is not necessary for the referring court. Such a reply might be useful to it if its national law were to require that an Austrian national must be allowed to enjoy the same rights as those which a national of another Member State would derive from Community law in the same situation [reference to *Guimont*].'

This line of case law was confirmed in *Salzmann*. Both Advocate-General Léger and the Court stated - relying on *Pistre, Guimont* and *Reisch* - that the mere fact that all elements of a case are confined to a single Member State does not exclude a possible effect on free movement:

> '26. Ms Salzmann observes [that the national measure] grants Community nationals equal treatment with regard to the acquisition of real property. The lack of prior authorization [...] could, therefore, also be used to refuse to give effect to the acquisition by nationals of other Member States of building plots [...] Consequently, the fact that the material circumstances in the main proceedings are confined to a single Member State is *purely accidental*.'[31] [emphasis added]

The conclusion to be drawn from this line of cases is that - at least for the free movement of goods and capital - the CJEU looks at the nature of the national measure and not to the facts of the case. If the national measure is applied equally to a Member State's own nationals and to the nationals of the other Member States, then the possibility exists that that measure will create a hindrance to free movement. The fact that in a particular case all elements are linked to a single Member State is therefore not decisive.

## 2. Horizontal or Vertical Relationships

It could be argued that the national rules, which are at stake in some of the CJEU cases as discussed in the following sections, are not property law or even private law at all but public law. As a result, those CJEU judgments would not constitute 'European property law'. However, because rules of property law are nearly always mandatory law, it is difficult to draw a strict line between what is private law and what is public law. Property law concerns the vertical relationship between the State and private persons, whereby the State determines, through mandatory legislation, what rights a person can have with regard to an object and how these rights can be created, used and transferred.[32] Of course, property law also governs the relationships between individuals, but they cannot deviate from the mandatory property law provisions, as is allowed in contract law. In that sense, it could be argued that property law is always of a public law nature, in that it is always generated by the State and not by individuals themselves.

31 Case C-300/01, *Doris Salzmann* [2003] ECR I-4899. See also Advocate-General Léger's Opinion of 30 January 2003, paras. 19-32.

32 See e.g. Goode 1998, p. 455.

In a preliminary procedure before the CJEU concerning a proprietary relationship, a private person - relying on free movement rules - will argue that a national rule of property law infringes his free movement rights; he will not contest the individual actions of another private party with whom he has a proprietary relationship.[33] The internal market rules are applied in such a way that national (property) law that infringes them can no longer remain in existence. Because this is *negative* harmonization, the application of the rules of free movement will never actually create new law governing the (proprietary) relationship between individuals. Rather, the free movement rules influence rules of national law, which have an effect within property law. As a result, the free movement rules themselves indirectly have an effect within national property law. That does not necessarily mean that the national rule has to be a property law rule under the national classification.[34] It is the proprietary *effect* that is important; from an EU perspective it is irrelevant whether a national rule is classified as belonging to one or the other area of law.[35] In other words, it does not matter, from the perspective of EU law, whether national law classifies a legal rule or relationship as proprietary, contractual, or anything else. Therefore, CJEU case law on the four freedoms that deals with a national rule, which has an effect in national property law, is included in this chapter as part of EU property law, regardless of whether that rule is - at the national level - classified as public or private law.

## 3. Free Movement of Goods[36]

Goods are meant to circulate freely within the internal market. This follows from Articles 28 *et seq.* TFEU.[37] However, when these goods cross a border into another Member State, the property rights that exist in relation to those goods may be altered or denied access completely due to the application of the private international law rule *lex rei sitae*. The *lex rei sitae* rule entails that the law applicable to a property relationship is the law of the country where the object is situated.[38] If the law of the country where the good is transported to does not recognize a property right created in relation to that good, then that property right may be lost. This may amount to an obstacle to the free movement of goods as contained in Article 34

33 *Cf* Klauer 1998, p. 102-103: 'Da jeder Privatrechtsstreit, der vor den Gerichtshof gelangt, zuvor vor einem nationalen Gericht ausgetragen wird, besteht so gut wie immer ein Ansatzpunkt für ein staatsgerichtetes Verständnis der Warenverkehrsfreiheit. Formaljuristisch ist es nicht das Verhalten der Privatrechtssubjekte, das überprüft wird, sondern die Ausgestaltung des staatlichen (Privat-) Rechts und seine Anwendung durch ein staatliches Gericht.'

34 *Cf* Verhagen 2007a, p. 28.

35 Case 82/71, *SAIL* [1972] ECR 119, para. 5; Case C-20/92, *Hubbard* [1993] ECR I-3777, para. 19.

36 Some of the research conducted for the section on Free movement of goods has been published, together with Bram Akkermans, in the *European Law Journal*: Akkermans & Ramaekers 2013.

37 Ex Artt. 23 *et seq.* EC.

38 Akkermans & Ramaekers 2012.

TFEU. The purpose of this section is to analyse whether and to what extent the free movement of goods applies to property law. There are two possible instances in which property relationships could fall under the scope of application of Article 34: either the concept of goods as used in this Article can be interpreted so as to include property rights; or the doctrine of mutual recognition as developed by the CJEU can be applied to property rights. These two possibilities will be explored below. To determine whether national property law comes within the scope of application of the free movement of goods, it must be classified in accordance with the criteria developed by the CJEU in a long line of case law, most notably the *Keck* case[39] and the *Trailers* case.[40] It will then be established how rules of property law, in combination with the *lex rei sitae* rule, could cause obstacles to the free movement of goods and what those obstacles would consist of. Here, particular attention will be paid to the CJEU's judgment in the case of *Krantz*. Section 3.5. will conclude with an explanation of why the effect of the free movement of goods on national property law is relevant with regard to the System-Cube model of property law as developed in Chapter 1.

### 3.1. *Definition of 'Goods'*

Property rights are by nature intangible. The question to be answered in this section is essentially whether or not the definition of 'goods' in the sense of free movement of goods could also cover intangibles. If it could, then property rights could 'move' freely within the internal market like any other 'good' would be able to. One of the earliest interpretations given by the CJEU of the term 'goods', in the sense of free movement of goods, was in the case of *Commission* v *Italy*: 'By goods [...] there must be understood products which can be valued in money and which are capable, as such, of forming the subject of commercial transactions.'[41]

Later cases provide ample examples of what falls within this definition, such as electricity,[42] natural gas,[43] and even waste.[44] At first view, these examples seem to indicate that the CJEU considers not only tangible objects to be goods but also intangible objects. Advocate-General Fennelly's Opinion in the *Jägerskiöld* case seems to deviate from that interpretation. He expresses his views on the definition of goods in paragraph 20 of his Opinion:

39 Joined cases C-267/91 and C-268/91, Criminal proceedings against Bernard Keck and Daniel Mithouard [1993] ECR I-6097.

40 Case C-110/05, *Commission* v *Italy* (*Trailers*) [2009] ECR I-519.

41 Case 7/68, *Commission* v *Italy*, at 428.

42 Case C-158/94, *Commission* v *Italy*, at 17: '[E]lectricity constitutes a good within the meaning of Article [28] of the Treaty.'

43 Case C-159/94, *Commission* v *France*.

44 Case C-2/90, *Commission* v *Belgium*.

> 'Goods, in the common connotation of the term, possess *tangible physical characteristics*. [...] It might, therefore, appear surprising that the Court has treated electricity, despite its intangible character, as goods. In so doing, the Court had regard to its treatment as goods in Community law and in the laws of the Member States as well as in the Community's tariff nomenclature. To my mind, electricity must be regarded as a specific case, perhaps justifiable by virtue of its function as an energy source and, therefore, its competition with gas and oil.' [references omitted; emphasis added]

According to the Advocate-General, goods can only be tangible objects and the fact that the CJEU included electricity - an intangible object - in the definition of goods was an exception. This exception can be explained, if one takes into account that electricity is treated as a good in several Member States, as the Advocate-General points out.[45]

In this context it is noteworthy that the Commission states in its 'Guide to the Application of Treaty provisions governing the free movement of goods' that goods in the sense of Article 34 'mean all types of imports and exports of goods and products. The range of goods covered is as wide as the range of goods in existence, so long as the goods in question have economic value'.[46] The Commission seems to focus primarily on the economic value, thereby staying close to the CJEU's original interpretation in *Commission* v *Italy* and does not deal with the question whether goods are tangible or intangible. Matters are complicated further by the CJEU's judgment in *Jägerskiöld*, where it states in paragraph 33:

> 'It must also be observed that anything which can be valued in money and which is capable, as such, of forming the subject of commercial transactions does not necessarily fall within the scope of application of [the Treaty provisions relating to the free movement of goods].'

The Court gives a few examples of such things which are covered by the free movement of capital or services, rather than by the free movement of goods.[47] Economic value is thus one element that determines whether something is a good or not, but it is not the only one. Advocate-General Fennelly provides a second element, namely the tangibility of an object. Electricity is 'counted in' with the tangibles by some Member States in their national law, not only because it represents an economic value but also because it is ascertainable: it can be separated and divided into particular quantities and be contained. That also makes it possible

45 See also Barnard 2010, p. 34.

46 Commission's Guide to the Application of Treaty provisions governing the free movement of goods, DG Enterprise and Industry, 2010, section 3.1.2. *Meaning of 'Goods'*; to be found at: <http://ec.europa.eu/enterprise/policies/single-market-goods/files/goods/docs/art34-36/new_guide_en.pdf>.

47 For instance: the organization of a lottery is not an activity relating to 'goods'; it is a provision of a service, even though the lottery distributes lottery tickets. Similarly, granting fishing rights is also a service provision, even though the licence may be laid down in a document. See the Commission's Guide on the free movement of goods, section 3.1.2. *Meaning of 'Goods'*.

to trade in electricity. It is therefore seen as a *product*, a term included in the definition of goods as given by the Court in *Commission* v *Italy*. The Advocate-General followed the practice of the Member States when concluding that electricity was also a good for free movement purposes.

Can this line of reasoning concerning electricity also be applied to property rights, even though they are intangible? To start with, property rights are capable of representing economic value. A right of pledge is worth as much as the underlying debt that it secures. A right of usufruct on a house can be sold, thereby also representing a certain economic value. However, as the Court said, being capable of representing an economic value does not automatically make something a good.[48] The intangible character of property rights continues to prevent them from falling under the definition of goods. It is difficult to associate them with tangible objects, because they are not seen as products. Therein lies the difference between property rights and electricity. As a result, there is no free movement of property rights.[49] For instance: if a Frenchman buys a set of books from a company in England, both the books and the right of ownership to those books move from England to France. This can occur simultaneously or separately, if the right of ownership is transferred sooner than the books themselves are delivered. Given that only the books, as products, and not the right of ownership, are considered goods, the free movement of goods only covers the movement of the books and not the movement of the property right.

However, the conclusion that property rights cannot be viewed as goods by themselves and are therefore not freely tradable, does not mean that property rights cannot cross borders at all. This is explored in the next section.

### 3.2. *Mutual Recognition of Property Rights?*

Property rights may not be able to move freely within the internal market as goods as such, but the doctrine of mutual recognition might be able to provide them with some - limited - movement after all. The CJEU first developed the concept of mutual recognition in the famous *Cassis de Dijon* case.[50] It stated that goods lawfully produced and marketed in one Member State should be recognized as such and allowed access to the markets of the other Member States, without having to comply with additional requirements imposed by the importing Member State. This would otherwise create a double burden on traders trading cross-border who would have to comply both with the law of their own home Member State as well as with the

48 Note that, in line with the Court's case law - *Jägerskiöld* para. 33 - , the fact that property rights are not covered by the free movement of goods does not exclude the application of any of the other freedoms.

49 *Cf*, however, Smits 1998 on free movement of legal rules.

50 Case 120/78, *Rewe* v *Bundesmonopolverwaltung für Branntwein* (*Cassis de Dijon*) [1979] ECR p. 649.

law of the host Member State and therefore hinder intra-Union trade.[51] It follows from *Cassis de Dijon* that Member States are expected to recognize each other's regulatory frameworks within which goods are produced.[52] These regulations all serve similar purposes: to protect consumers, to ensure public health etc. If a good has already met those standards within its own Member State, then that should suffice when it is marketed in other Member States.

The Commission took up this concept of mutual recognition in its White Paper on Completing the Internal Market and used it to develop a new strategy.[53] The concept of mutual recognition could, in the view of the Commission, work to reduce the regulatory burden on traders:

> 77. … 'In cases where harmonisation of regulations and standards is not considered essential from either a health/safety or an industrial point of view, immediate and full recognition of differing quality standards, food composition rules, etc. must be the rule. In particular, sales bans cannot be based on the sole argument that an imported product has been manufactured according to specifications which differ from those used in the importing country.' …
>
> 79. … 'The net long term effect of adopting and implementing this new strategy will be to reduce the regulatory burden on enterprises wishing to operate on a Community wide basis.' […] Similarly the application of the new approach to standardisation and the *move towards the principle of mutual recognition in an increasing number of other areas* will speed up the decision-making process and avoid the need for a further layer of Community rules to be super-imposed on national rules.' [emphasis added]

It seems that the Commission here intends to use the concept of mutual recognition as a kind of back-up or default rule to ensure the functioning of the internal market, in case harmonization measures have not yet been taken or are not deemed to be essential.[54] The Court made a similar statement in the *Cassis de Dijon* case, where it said that

> '[i]n the absence of common rules relating to the production and marketing of alcohol – [pending a legislative proposal] – it is for the Member States to regulate all matters relating to the production and marketing of alcohol and alcoholic beverages on their own territory'.

Nevertheless, such Member State regulations could not cause obstacles to the free movement of goods, unless they were justifiable under any of the mandatory requirements listed by the Court.[55]

51 Case 120/78, *Cassis de Dijon*, para. 14.
52 Similar interpretation given by Kieninger 2002, p. 354.
53 White Paper from the Commission to the European Council: Completing the Internal Market, 14 June 1985, COM(85) 310 final, p. 22.
54 See also Verhagen 2007a, p. 32; Klauer 1998, p. 24.
55 *Cassis de Dijon*, para. 8.

This is an example of how negative and positive integration complement each other.[56] Negative integration, i.e. the free movement rules, prohibit the Member States from applying certain national measures that hinder free movement, thereby opening up the internal market. The doctrine of mutual recognition - as part of the rules on free movement - prohibits a Member State from applying national measures that would hinder access to the market of a product that has already lawfully been marketed in another Member State. However, the rules on free movement have their boundaries. These lie in the justifications such as consumer protection, public policy, or environmental protection that Member States can rely on to keep in force a national measure that otherwise obstructs the free movement. It is here that positive integration through secondary legislative measures such as regulations and directives steps in: if there is a directive that ensures, for instance, the protection of consumers in particular situations, then Member States are no longer allowed to keep their own rules in place for that same purpose.[57] This is because the level of protection is then deemed to be sufficient in all the Member States, given that they all have had to implement that directive.

Could mutual recognition be applied to cross-border property situations? The Commission itself indicates that it is in favour of a certain spill-over of mutual recognition to other areas than free movement of goods. Examples of such spill-over follow *inter alia* from the Commission's White Paper (mutual recognition of tests and certification procedures) but can also be seen in areas such as the CJEU's case law concerning mutual recognition of companies legally established in another Member State.[58] It has also been extended to the free movement of services.[59] If mutual recognition were extended in a similar fashion to property rights, traders would no longer lose their property rights once their goods crossed a border. A country's system of property law could be seen as the regulatory framework under which a property right on an object is validly created. Rules of property law fulfil certain functions: the *numerus clausus* stipulates which property rights are allowed to be created and what their content can and cannot be, to guarantee legal certainty. Rules on transfer and registration of property rights ensure publicity and specificity, so that third parties can be aware of which property rights exist and in relation to what objects they have been established. All these rules fulfil similar functions within the different national property law systems of the Member States.[60]

56 Klauer 1998, p. 23-24.

57 Unless the directive in question aims at a minimum level of harmonization, leaving room for Member States to maintain more stringent consumer protection rules.

58 See cases C-212/97, *Centros*; C-208/00, *Überseering*; and C-167/01, *Inspire Art*. See also Craig & De Búrca 2011, pp. 781-784.

59 Case C-76/90, *Säger* v *Dennemeyer* [1991] ECR I-4221, para. 12. Mutual recognition is also applied to diplomas; see Art. 53 TFEU, and Schneider 1995 and Claessens 2008. See for the mutual recognition of legal parentage and of names Saarloos 2010, p. 302 *et seq*.

60 Van Erp 2009b, pp. 18-21; to be found at: <http://papers.ssrn.com/sol3/papers.cfm?abstract_id=1372166>.

Therefore, if a producer, when marketing a product and creating or transferring certain property rights to that product, has already complied with the property law rules in his country and fulfilled these functions, there should be no need for him to fulfil the same requirements again in the country of import. The property regime under which rights have been created in relation to the product should be recognized by the receiving Member State under the doctrine of mutual recognition.

This provides property rights with a certain ability to move across borders without being destroyed or altered due to the application of the *lex rei sitae* rule. This leaves one other problem, though. If nationals of one Member State have to respect property rights created on products that they buy from sellers from other Member States but are not allowed by their home Member State to create those same property rights, then this causes reverse discrimination.[61] This means that a Member State's own nationals do not have certain rights which nationals from other Member States do have because they receive those rights under EU law in a cross-border setting. These problems could be resolved if full free movement of property rights - in the sense of rights being included in the definition of goods - were allowed. This would effectively lead to the existence of a Europe-wide *numerus clausus,* however, because all the property rights from all the *numerus clausus* of the Member States would be available to all Member States' nationals. Exactly what the consequences would be of applying mutual recognition to property rights and whether mutual recognition could form an alternative to the *lex rei sitae* rule, is explored in more detail in Chapter 5. For now it is important to conclude that the concept of mutual recognition could also be applied to property rights. This in effect creates what could be called a 'shadow-*numerus clausus*'. The national list of property rights is added to by property rights from other Member States. It is a 'shadow' list because these rights must only be recognized; as we have seen, the rules on free movement of goods and mutual recognition are not developed to the extent that nationals of a Member State can themselves make use of those foreign property rights. As will be seen below, the fact that property rights are usually not recognized by a host Member State can and does lead to obstacles to the free movement of goods in the sense of Article 34 TFEU.

### 3.3. *Classifying the Measure: from Keck to Trailers*

Article 34 TFEU differentiates between quantitative restrictions (QRs) and measures equivalent to quantitative restrictions (MEQRs).[62] A national rule of property law in combination with the *lex rei sitae* rule is not likely to constitute a quantitative

61 *Cf* Kieninger 2002, p. 352. 'Reverse discrimination arises when a national of a Member State is disadvantaged because he or she may not rely on a protective provision of Community law when a national of another Member State in otherwise identical circumstances may rely on that same provision': For a general explanation see also Barnard 2010, p. 88, 89 and 228-229.

62 For further information on QR and MEQR and the difference between the two, see Barnard 2010, p. 71 and 73; Craig & De Búrca 2011, p. 638-639.

restriction. It is important to keep in mind that it is not the object which is being refused entry into a Member State but the right resting on that object. If the object were refused, that refusal might amount to a quantity of naught, in which case the refusal would constitute a QR.[63] However, given that we are dealing with a refusal of a foreign property right, not an object, classifying the national measure leading to that refusal as a QR is not in order here.

MEQRs are defined by the Court in the *Dassonville* judgment as '[a]ll trading rules enacted by Member States which are capable of hindering, *directly or indirectly, actually or potentially,* intra-[Union] trade'[64] [emphasis added]. National property law, together with the *lex rei sitae,* could hinder intra-Union trade and therefore constitute a MEQR. Therefore, in order to establish whether Article 34 applies, the national measure must be further classified under two cases of the CJEU clarifying what MEQRs are, namely the *Keck* case and the *Trailers* case.

When the CJEU delivered its *Cassis de Dijon* judgment, it opened up the possibility for many traders to challenge the conformity of provisions of other Member States' law affecting their products. As a result a series of cases was brought before the Court,[65] often referred to as the 'Sunday-trading cases'. In these cases, companies contested national legislation that prohibited the sale of goods on Sundays. This prohibition also applied to products from other Member States. Therefore, the undertakings argued that Article 34 was applicable in these cases.[66] The Court sought to restrict this flow of cases in its decision in *Criminal Proceedings against Keck and Mithouard*:

> 'In view of the increasing tendency of traders to invoke Article 30 of the Treaty as a means of challenging any rules whose effect is to limit their commercial freedom even where such rules are not aimed at products from other Member States, the Court considers it necessary to re-examine and clarify its case-law on this matter.'[67]

In *Keck* the Court restricted its *Cassis de Dijon* case law to rules relating to product characteristics. Examples of product characteristics are labelling, packaging, and ingredients, but the list is not exhaustive. Other measures of national law affecting what has become known as selling arrangements, i.e. measures dealing with how a product is marketed and sold on the territory of another Member State, fall outside the scope of the free movement of goods in so far as their effect is not discriminatory.[68] This means that they must apply to all relevant traders operating within the territory of a Member State and must affect equally, in law and in fact, the

63 Akkermans & Ramaekers 2013 at II.A. *Identifying the measure.*

64 Case 8/74, *Dassonville* [1974] ECR 837, para. 5.

65 Barnard 2010, p. 91-95; Weatherill 2010a, p. 367-371.

66 The first and most well-known of these cases is case C-145/88, *Torfaen Borough Council* v *B&Q plc* [1989] ECR 3851.

67 Case C-267/91, *Criminal Proceedings against Keck and Mithouard* [1993] ECR I-6097, para. 14.

68 Barnard 2010, p. 123-144; Craig & De Búrca 2011, p. 654-661.

marketing of domestic as well as foreign products.[69] As a result the Court has created a complex distinction between rules relating to product characteristics and rules relating to certain selling arrangements. The case, as well as the distinction that follows from it, have been heavily criticized. A number of cases following *Keck* show that there are several types of measures which can hardly be classified as either product characteristics or selling arrangements. Barnard discerns four different types:

> '(1) discriminatory rules regulating sales; (2) rules preventing or (severely) restricting the use of goods; (3) rules preventing or (severely) restricting an activity; and (4) non-discriminatory selling arrangements preventing or restricting access to the market'.[70]

There would appear to be three options for dealing with such measures: (a) under *Keck* but without the reference to certain selling arrangements; (b) under pre-*Keck* cases where the measure is considered to be too remote to affect inter-State trade (thereby effectively applying a *de minimis* test);[71] or (c) as MEQRs which can be justified.[72]

The actual difference between the two categories - product characteristic or selling arrangement - seemed to be whether the national rule imposes a double burden or an equal burden. *Cassis de Dijon* is concerned with double burden rules. These are national rules that impose a double burden on the importer *because* they have to be complied with twice, namely in the home Member State and in the host Member State. They may serve the same purpose in each Member State but their practical application differs in the sense that a trader conducting cross-border business has to perform different acts in both Member States to comply with both sets of rules. Equal burden rules do not impose a double burden, either because they only have to be complied with once, namely only in the host Member State or because they are the same in both the home and the host Member State. In the latter instance it is irrelevant in which Member State the trader wishes to market his products because the circumstances under which they may be marketed - at least with regard to this particular rule - are identical in both Member States. Selling arrangements which do *not* apply in the same way in law and in fact to all producers operating within a Member State create a double burden, which explains why they come within the scope of Article 34 after all. Selling arrangements, which *do* apply in the same way in law and in fact, create an equal burden. They initially fell outside the scope of Article 34 under *Keck*.[73]

Explaining selling arrangements in this manner comes very close to applying a so-called market access test, which is exactly what the Court seems to have been

69 *Keck*, para. 16.
70 Barnard 2010, p. 130.
71 This was the case in the *Krantz* decision, which will be discussed below.
72 Barnard 2010, p. 128-129.
73 *Cf* Craig & De Búrca 2011, p. 655.

doing in cases succeeding *Keck*. In those cases, the Court seems to have moved beyond the product characteristics/certain selling arrangements distinction made in *Keck* towards an approach of market access.[74] In this approach, a measure of national law that hinders a trader in his access to the market of another Member State will fall within the scope of application of internal market law,[75] even if it is indistinctly applicable to both domestic and foreign traders. A pivotal judgment nuancing *Keck* in this respect is *Commission* v *Italy* (*Trailers*).[76] The case concerned Italian legislation prohibiting motorcycles and similar vehicles from towing trailers. A dispute arose as to the question:

> 'of the extent to which and the conditions under which national provisions which govern not the characteristics of goods but their *use*, and which apply without distinction to domestic and imported goods, are to be regarded as measures having equivalent effect to quantitative restrictions on imports within the meaning of Article [34 TFEU].'[77] [emphasis added]

The Court made a number of preliminary observations[78] in which it seemed to recast the classification of measures that existed up until that point under the *Keck* line of case law. First of all, measures of which the object or effect is to treat foreign products less favourably - and are therefore distinctly applicable - must be regarded as MEQRs.[79] Secondly, rules relating to certain product characteristics - even if they are indistinctly applicable - constitute MEQRs and therefore fall under the *Cassis de Dijon* line of case law.[80] Finally, '[a]ny other measure which hinders access of products originating in other Member States to the market of a Member State' must also be considered to be a MEQR within the meaning of Article 34.[81] Apparently there are now three different kinds of MEQR. As a separate category, rules relating to certain selling arrangements that are distinctly applicable - in other words, do not meet the requirements laid down in paragraph 16 of *Keck* that such rules should affect in the same manner, in law and in fact, the marketing of domestic products and of those from other Member States - prevent or hinder access to the market and therefore fall under the *Dassonville* line of case law.[82] As a

74 See, e.g. Case C-319/05, *Commission* v *Germany* (*Garlic Capsule*) [2007] ECR I-9811, Case C-297/05, *Commission* v *The Netherlands* [2007] ECR I-7467. See also Spaventa 2009, p. 917.

75 Craig & De Búrca 2011, p. 662-668; Barnard 2010, pp. 143-144.

76 Case C-110/05, *Commission* v *Italy*, [2009] ECR I-519. In the subsequent case of *Mickelsson and Roos*, the ECJ reiterates the *Trailers* judgment and reaffirms a market access test: case C-142/05, [2009] ECR I-4273, paras. 24-26. See also Barnard 2012, p. 203-209; Weatherill 2010a, p. 380-381; Barnard 2010, p. 106; Spaventa 2009, p. 918.

77 Para. 15 of the judgment.

78 Paras. 33-37 of the judgment.

79 Para. 37 of the judgment.

80 Para. 35 of the judgment.

81 Para. 37 of the judgment.

82 Para. 36 of the judgment. *Cf* Spaventa 2009, p. 919.

result of the *Trailers* case, there are now five different categories of measures that fall under Article 34:

(1) quantitative restrictions (QRs);

(2) distinctly applicable MEQRs (MEQR a);

(3) indistinctly applicable product characteristics (MEQR b);

(4) any other measure hindering market access (MEQR c); and

(5) certain selling arrangements (CSAs).[83]

As regards the CSAs, a two-stage test is applied. If they do not meet the requirements from paragraph 16 of the *Keck* judgment, i.e. if they fail a discrimination test,[84] then they must be classified as a MEQR hindering market access (i.e. category 4).[85] If they do meet the requirements from paragraph 16 of *Keck* - meaning that they are non-discriminatory - then the second test is whether they prevent or hinder market access. If that is the case, they again fall under category 4; if that is not the case, they are exempted from the scope of application of Article 34. This second test possibly includes a *de minimis* requirement,[86] so that only those CSAs that prevent or *substantially* hinder market access are caught under Article 34. The existence of a *de minimis* test in the free movement of goods is discussed in the next section.

The question now is: where do national rules of property law, in combination with the *lex rei sitae* rule, fall under the five categories resulting from *Keck* and *Trailers*?

To start with, it is not likely that a rule of property law would be classified as a QR, unless you perceive an outright refusal of an object as a quantity of naught.[87] A rule of property law can also not be classified as a distinctly applicable MEQR (MEQR a), because such rules apply equally to domestic and foreign traders. This is also true for the *lex rei sitae* rule. The question then becomes whether such rules are product characteristics (MEQR b), or selling arrangements (category 5), or fall under the 'catch-all' category 4 of MEQRs hindering market access (MEQR c).

83 Barnard 2010, p. 142.

84 Klauer 1998, p. 77.

85 *Cf* the Court's judgment in *Gourmet International Products*: 'It should be pointed out that, according to paragraph 17 of [the Court's] judgment in *Keck and Mithouard*, if national provisions restricting or prohibiting certain selling arrangements are to avoid being caught by Art. 30 [now 34] of the Treaty, they must not be of such a kind as to *prevent access to the market* by products from another Member State or to *impede access* any more than they impede the access of domestic products.' [emphasis added] Case C-405/98, *Gourmet International Products* [2001] ECR I-1795, para. 18. Other examples are case C-254/98, *Schutzverband gegen unlauteren Wettbewerb and TK-Heimdienst Sass GmbH* [2000] ECR I-151, para. 29, and case C-384/93, *Alpine Investments* [1995] ECR I-1141, para. 37.

86 Barnard 2010, p. 106-107 and 122.

87 *Supra*, note 61.

The question of classification of property law under the *Keck and Mithouard*-doctrine has been dealt with before but this was prior to the *Trailers* case. Therefore, one was forced to use the *Keck* categories of product characteristics and selling arrangements. A similar problem as described above was encountered, namely that it felt somewhat artificial to classify rules of property law as either product characteristics or selling arrangements, because they really are neither.[88] Kieninger deals extensively with this issue in her PhD thesis.[89] She analyses the effect a property security right has on a product. In her view the availability of a security right directly relates to the product itself, in particular its price. A more expensive property security right - or personal security right - will raise the price to be paid for such a product to compensate for the increase in costs.[90] Hence, there are good arguments to be put forth that property law concerns the characteristics of products themselves. However, the influence of property law on products is not such as to automatically assume that property law always concerns rules relating to product characteristics. Category 3 is therefore also not a likely candidate. This leaves categories 4 and 5.

Classification of rules of property law as measures relating to certain selling arrangements makes more sense. The law of property concerns the way in which a product is 'marketed', it concerns the way in which an object is brought on the market of another Member State. A classification as a certain selling arrangement requires assessing whether the selling arrangement applies in the same way in law and in fact.[91]

The *lex rei sitae* rule, combined with the application of national property law in the host Member State, leads to a different application in law than in fact. Although the *lex rei sitae* rule is almost uniformly applied,[92] the effect of the application of *lex*

88 *Cf* Strese 2006, p. 153-154.

89 Kieninger 1996.

90 Kieninger 1996, p. 152-153: 'Der Preis der Bankdiensleistung wird maβgeblich durch die Qualität der gebotenen Sicherungen bestimmt. Es liegt also wesentlich näher, die genannten Vorschriften als Bestimmungen zu betrachten, die das Produkt "Bankkredit" selbst definieren als als Teil des "environnement juridique" [references omitted]'.

91 See Joined Cases 267 and 258/91, *Keck and Mithouard*:
'16 By contrast, contrary to what has previously been decided, the application to products from other Member States of national provisions restricting or prohibiting certain selling arrangements is not such as to hinder directly or indirectly, actually or potentially, trade between Member States within the meaning of the *Dassonville* judgment (Case 8/74 [1974] ECR 837), so long as those provisions apply to all relevant traders operating within the national territory and so long as they affect in the same manner, in law and in fact, the marketing of domestic products and of those from other Member States.
17 Provided that those conditions are fulfilled, the application of such rules to the sale of products from another Member State meeting the requirements laid down by that State is not by nature such as to prevent their access to the market or to impede access any more than it impedes the access of domestic products. Such rules therefore fall outside the scope of Article 30 of the Treaty.'

92 Kieninger 2002, p. 82 and footnote 380; Sparkes 2007, p. 155.

*rei sitae* is the application of the domestic law of the host Member State. A property right validly created on an object under the law of another Member State is therefore transformed into a receiving-State equivalent or is lost when the receiving property law does not recognize a certain property right or a close equivalent to it. The effect of the application of property law therefore leads to a treatment that is different in fact than it is in law and therefore does not fall under the *Keck and Mithouard* exception.

Consequently, it can be argued that rules of property law must be classified under category four, as MEQRs that hinder access to the market (MEQR c). There are two ways to reach this conclusion. It is possible to view such rules as CSAs but because they do not satisfy the requirements of paragraph 16 of *Keck* they end up being classified as MEQRs c after all. The arguably more correct path would be to state that the classification as CSA is an artificial one and originally born out of necessity because it was the only alternative to product characteristics,[93] which rules of property law are not and that therefore such rules must be placed outright under category four, as MEQRs that hinder market access.

It could be said that rules of private international law are by nature neutral, i.e. non-discriminatory because they do not decide on the substantive matter of a specific case but only indicate which substantive law must be applied. If that is also true for the *lex rei sitae*, then - contrary to what has just been argued - the requirements of paragraph 16 of *Keck* would be fulfilled. Because the measure must then be considered to be indistinctly applicable, the next step is to investigate whether it nevertheless prevents or (substantially) hinders market access. Whether there is an outright refusal (prevention) or merely a hindrance to market access depends on how the foreign property right is received in the host Member State. If there is no equivalent in the national *numerus clausus* to the foreign property right, then the foreign property right will not be accepted and is therefore prevented from accessing the market of the host Member State. If, however, there is a national equivalent then the foreign property right may be recognized and transposed into the national equivalent. That means that there is access to the market for the foreign property right but, because the transposition may have caused a change in the content of the property right, it may still be less attractive for the foreign trader to enter the market of the host Member State. Therefore, even if the *lex rei sitae*, in combination with the national *numerus clausus*, is considered to be non-discriminatory, there is nevertheless a prevention of or hindrance to market access.

### 3.3.1. A *de Minimis* Requirement in Free Movement of Goods?

The starting point is that there is no *de minimis* requirement in the free movement of goods. This follows first of all from the *Dassonville* judgment, according to which all national measures that 'are capable of hindering, directly or indirectly, actually or

93 *Cf* Spaventa 2009, p. 920.

potentially, intra-[Union] trade' form an obstacle to the free movement of goods.[94] The words 'indirectly' and 'potentially' indicate that there does not necessarily have to be an actual or noticeable effect on intra-Union trade for the free movement of goods to apply.[95] This has been repeated in numerous other judgments.[96] One explicit example is Van de Haar, where the Court held:

> '13 It must be emphasized in that connection that Article 30 [now 34] of the Treaty does not distinguish between measures having an effect equivalent to quantitative restrictions according to the degree to which trade between Member States is affected. If a national measure is capable of hindering imports it must be regarded as a measure having an effect equivalent to a quantitative restriction, even though the hindrance is slight and even though it is possible for imported products to be marketed in other ways.'[97]

The conclusion that there is no *de minimis* requirement in the free movement of goods is important for the question whether free movement law applies to property law, given that rules of property law, as they are not necessarily meant to regulate market access, will often cause a potential or indirect hindrance to the internal market, rather than an actual or direct one.

The scene changes, however, with the introduction of the market access test. A market access test, which can also catch non-discriminatory or indistinctly applicable rules, without a *de minimis* requirement would leave very few – if any at all – national measures that would fall outside the scope of application of Article 34 TFEU and would therefore not need to be justified. As Spaventa indicates,

> 'those who advocated the market access test in the past have always attempted to qualify it so as to identify a threshold (through *de minimis* or notions such as a substantial hindrance to market access) below which national rules would not need to be justified'.[98]

This might explain why cases such as *Krantz*, which were adjudicated in the years leading up to the *Keck* judgment, placed certain national measures outside the scope of application of the free movement of goods because their effect on the internal market was 'too indirect and uncertain'. Such rules might have been characterized as certain selling arrangements after *Keck* and be subjected to a market access test, in which case the introduction of a *de minimis* requirement would have made more sense.

94 Case 8/74, *Procureur du Roi* v *Benoît and Gustave Dassonville* [1974] ECR 837, para. 5.
95 Kieninger 1996, p. 137-138.
96 See Barnard 2010, p. 78 and the references in footnote 59.
97 Joined Cases 177 and 178/82, Criminal proceedings against *Jan van de Haar and Kaveka de Meern BV* [1984] ECR 1797.
98 Spaventa 2009, p. 923.

Now that we have seen that rules of property law in combination with the *lex rei sitae* can be classified as a MEQR under Article 34 TFEU, and that those rules can lead to obstacles to the free movement of goods, the next question is what those obstacles actually consist of. This will be illustrated in the following sections, using the CJEU case of *Krantz* as an example.

## 3.4. *Obstacles to the Free Movement of Goods: the Case of Krantz*

There have been numerous cases before national courts, where the fact that goods crossed a border resulted in a complete or partial loss of the seller's property right in relation to those goods (usually a property security right).[99] It is therefore quite peculiar that so far only one such case has made it all the way to the CJEU. This was the Dutch case of *Krantz* v *Ontvanger der Directe Belastingen*.[100] The *Krantz* case provides an interesting practical example of what the obstacles to the free movement of goods, caused by rules of property law, can consist of, which will be explained below. This section will not deal with the question why there has only been one such case in front of the CJEU, as this has been dealt with elsewhere.[101]

### 3.4.1. Facts of the Case

In the case of *Krantz* the CJEU was confronted with a reservation of ownership clause in a contract of sale of a machine concluded between a German company, Krantz GmbH and a Dutch company, J. Krantz & Zoon N.V.[102] The Dutch company placed the machine in its subsidiary company, Vaalser Textielbedrijf B.V. When both of the Dutch companies were declared insolvent, the Dutch collector of taxes seized all movable objects available on the premises of the insolvent companies due to an unpaid amount of taxes by both companies. The machine had not yet been paid for and the German company invoked its reservation of ownership, claiming it was still the owner of the machine and could revindicate it, i.e. claim it back. Based on a provision of Dutch law, the Dutch collector of taxes did not allow this until the German company paid the outstanding amounts in taxes.[103] After payment, the German company went to court claiming that the seizure made by the tax collector

99 To give a few examples: BGH 20. 3. 1963, BGHZ 39, 173 as quoted by Basedow in Basedow 1995, p. 41 and footnote 156; *Corte d'appello Milano* 4. 6. 1956, Foro it. 1957 I 1856; *Hof van Beroep Gent* 29. 10. 1979, *Jurisprudence commerciale de Belgique* (J.C.B.) 1980, 465; *Audiencia Provincial de Barcelona* 13. 9. 1989, Rev. Esp. Der. Int. 42 (1990) 644, as quoted by Basedow, p. 42 and footnotes 158, 159 and 160. See also Kieninger 2008a, p. 188 and 202.

100 Case C-69/88, *H. Krantz GmbH & Co.* v *Ontvanger der Directe Belastingen and Netherlands State* [1990] ECR I-583. *Ontvanger der Directe Belastingen* is translated into the English version of the case as 'collector of direct taxes'.

101 Akkermans & Ramaekers 2013 at III.C. *Why are there no other property law cases?*

102 Akkermans & Ramaekers 2013 at III.B. *The Approach of the European Court of Justice to Movable Property Law.*

103 Art. 16 *Invorderingswet* (Law on the collection of the State's direct taxes).

was contrary to the free movement of goods, in particular Article 34 TFEU, because the application of Dutch law restricted trade between Germany and the Netherlands.[104] The Dutch court asked a preliminary question to the CJEU on this point:

> '(1) Is Article 16 of the Wet op de Invordering van 's Rijks Directe Belastingen ( Law on the collection of the State' s direct taxes ) of 22 May 1845 (Staatsblad 22) to be regarded as a measure having equivalent effect to a quantitative restriction on imports within the meaning of Article 30 of the EEC Treaty [now 34 TFEU] where the Netherlands tax authorities seize goods on the premises of a taxpayer even if those goods are from and are the property of a supplier in another Member State?
>
> (2) If so, is the application of the aforesaid Article 16 none the less justified under Article 36 of the EEC Treaty [now 36 TFEU] on the basis of one of the grounds referred to in Article 36?'

### 3.4.2. Arguments of the parties

Krantz GmbH argued that the right of seizure of the Dutch Tax Authorities infringed Article 30 EEC Treaty (now Art. 34 TFEU). They based this argument on the CJEU's *Dassonville* judgment in which it held that any national measure 'capable of hindering, directly or indirectly, actually or potentially, intra-Community trade' was to be considered as a measure having an effect equivalent to quantitative restrictions and therefore contrary to Article 30 EEC. In the opinion of Krantz GmbH, if it were known in other Member States that the Dutch Tax Authorities had this power, trade with Dutch undertakings on the basis of financing would be drastically reduced. This in turn would hinder intra-Union trade.[105]

The Dutch government put forth several different arguments. First, it stated that the Tax Authorities' right of seizure is not a trading rule as meant in the *Dassonville* judgment.[106] Secondly, the right of seizure is not meant to regulate trade and is equally applicable to all goods present on the land subjected to the right of seizure, regardless of the origin of the goods. Thirdly, the right of seizure would not limit the sales volume, for it does not apply to stocks. Lastly, if the Court should find the right of seizure to be a measure equivalent to a quantitative restriction, the

104 Although the case dealt with Article 30 EEC, later Art. 28 EC, the current Art. 34 in the Treaty on the Functioning of the European Union (TFEU) is identical to the old version. On this case see *inter alia* Kieninger 1996, p. 156-157; Rutgers 1999, p. 197; Barnard 2010, p. 120.

105 Report for the Hearing of case C-69/88, document No. 9003C031, 688J0069, para. 5.

106 Already before *Krantz*, the Court had ceased to emphasize that the rule should be *a trading* rule. Rather, any 'measure', binding or non-binding, legislative or other, could be a measure having an effect equivalent to a quantitative restriction, as long as it fulfilled the *Dassonville* criteria. For a more detailed explanation of this development, see Barnard 2010, p. 74-75 and the cases referred to there, such as the famous *Buy Irish* case.

Dutch government put forth that it was justified to safeguard mandatory requirements in the public interest and was proportionate to the aim pursued.[107]

The Commission argued that the right of seizure could not be seen as a direct or indirect restriction of intra-Union trade, since it did not relate to this trade. Furthermore, there could be no actual hindrance, since seizure is an uncertain event that occurs after goods have been imported into the Netherlands. Finally, there could also not be a potential hindrance, since the import, trade volume and use of the goods that could be seized were not restricted and the importer remained free to decide on his commercial transactions.[108]

### 3.4.3. Opinion of Advocate-General Darmon

Advocate-General Darmon seemed to distinguish three steps that need to be taken in order to establish whether a national measure has infringed the free movement of goods: Is the measure intended to regulate trade? Is there a perceptible effect on imports? And, can the measure be justified under the test developed by the CJEU in *Torfaen Borough Council*, which is meant to discern a legitimate objective of the national measure and the proportionality of its effect?[109]

The Advocate-General's Opinion is to a large extent based on the first step. In his view, '[t]he provisions of the Invorderingswet on the tax authorities' right of seizure is not designed to regulate trade with other Member States'. He seems to conclude that these provisions fall outside the scope of Article 34 TFEU, as they do not relate 'directly and exclusively to the conditions for the production or marketing of certain products or types of products'.[110] With this, he seems to agree with the arguments put forth by both the Commission and the Dutch government.

His second reason for placing the provisions of the *Wet op de Invordering van 's Rijks Directe Belastingen* (Law on the collection of the State's direct taxes; hereinafter *Invorderingswet*) outside the scope of Article 34 TFEU was that they have no bearing on imports (i.e. the second step). He was not convinced by the argument put forth by Krantz GmbH that non-Dutch sellers are reluctant to trade with Dutch buyers because of the possibly negative effects of the application of the *Invorderingswet* on their trade relationship. It can be argued that with that he applied a *de minimis* test which, in his view, results from previous judgments of the CJEU.[111] He draws a parallel with the *Blesgen* and *Forest* cases.[112] In these cases the Court held that the

107 Report for the Hearing of case C-69/88, para. 13.

108 Report for the Hearing of case C-69/88, para. 16.

109 Case C-145/88, *Torfaen Borough Council*, was one of the first so-called Sunday trading cases that led up to the famous *Keck and Mithouard* judgment.

110 A.-G. Darmon's Opinion of 12 December 1989 to case C-69/88, *Krantz*, para. 7.

111 A.-G. Darmon's Opinion, paras. 11, 12 and 16. *Cf* Klauer 1998, p. 90-91.

112 Case 75/81, *Joseph Henri Thomas Blesgen* v *Belgian State* [1982] ECR 1211 and Case 148/85, *Direction générale des impôts and procureur de la République* v *Marie-Louise Forest, née Sangoy, and Minoterie Forest SA* [1986] ECR 3449.

measures that were disputed did not have a bearing on imports, even though it was not unimaginable that removing those measures might increase imports. According to Advocate-General Darmon, if such measures are already considered not to affect trade then that conclusion must *a fortiori* be true for a measure 'whose restrictive effect, whether actual or potential, is simply undetectable'. In his opinion, the Tax Authorities' right of seizure could not possibly be caught by Article 34 TFEU (then Art. 30 EEC).[113]

### 3.4.4. Judgment of the Court

The CJEU was also not convinced by the arguments put forth by Krantz GmbH and held that:

> 'It must, however, be observed that the national provision referred to by the national court applies without distinction to both domestic and imported goods, and does not seek to control trade with other Member States.
>
> [...] Furthermore, the possibility that nationals of other Member States would hesitate to sell goods on instalment terms to purchasers in the Member State concerned because such goods would be liable to seizure by the collector of taxes if the purchasers failed to discharge their Netherlands tax debts is too uncertain and indirect to warrant the conclusion that a national provision authorizing such seizure is liable to hinder trade between Member States.'[114]

The Court seems to rely on the same reasons put forth by the Advocate-General, namely that the national measure does not have as its purpose to regulate trade with other Member States and that its effects on intra-Union trade are too uncertain and indirect. The Court reiterates the *Dassonville* formula but then goes on to state that the circumstances of the case are 'too uncertain and indirect' to warrant the conclusion that there is a hindrance to cross-border trade. It could be said that the Court thereby effectively applied a *de minimis* test.[115]

### 3.4.5. The Obstacles to Free Movement of Goods: Loss of Property Right and Increase in Costs

Whenever goods are moved across Member States' borders, the *lex rei sitae* rule combined with the application of national property law in the receiving Member State leads to a different application in law than in fact to foreign goods and traders, as opposed to national goods and traders. Although rules of private international law are applied in the same manner to both foreign and domestic goods and

113 A.-G. Darmon's Opinion, paras. 14-17.

114 Case C-69/88, *H. Krantz GmbH & Co* v *Ontvanger der Directe Belastingen en de Staat der Nederlanden* [1990] ECR I-583, paras. 10-11.

115 Barnard 2010, p. 122 and 144; Klauer 1998, p. 90-91.

traders, the effect of the application of *lex rei sitae* is the application of the domestic law of the receiving Member State. This entails the application of the *numerus clausus* of the receiving Member State, which means that a Member State's national property law contains a closed list of property rights that cannot be deviated from or added to by private parties.[116] A property right validly created on an object under the law of another Member State will be foreign to the *numerus clausus* of the host Member State. It will therefore either be transformed into a receiving-State equivalent or will be lost when the receiving system of property law does not have a close equivalent to the foreign property right. It is in particular this combination between the *lex rei sitae* rule and the national mandatory character[117] of property law that causes cross-border problems,[118] rather than national property law or the *lex rei sitae* rule on their own.[119] That it is the combination with national law and not just the *lex rei sitae* rule that is the problem will also be illustrated in Chapter 5: it will be shown that replacing the *lex rei sitae* rule with a different rule of private international law will not automatically take away all the obstacles to the internal market as discussed in this chapter.[120] That suggests that the national rules of property law are part of the problem.

The application of property law and the *lex rei sitae* therefore leads to a treatment of foreign property rights - and the holders of those rights and the objects on which they rest - which is different in fact than it is in law. The *Keck and Mithouard* exception therefore does not apply. A certain selling arrangement of this kind will therefore fall under the ambit of Article 34 TFEU. The market access test must determine whether there is an obstacle to the free movement of goods. If the answer is yes then the measure is prohibited, unless it can be justified and the measure deemed proportional. The burden of proof will be on the receiving Member State and no longer on a party claiming incompatibility with Article 34 TFEU.[121]

116 Akkermans 2008, p. 6-7.

117 *Cf* Hesselink, Rutgers & Booys 2007, p. 53.

118 *Cf* Verhagen 2007a, p. 29: 'Wanneer [...] de toepasselijkheid van [...] materieelrechtelijke normen het gevolg is van een objectieve verwijzingsregel, waarvan geen afwijking door middel van rechtskeuze mogelijk is, dan is de uit deze normen voortvloeiende belemmering in ieder geval mede het gevolg van de betreffende verwijzingsregel'; Polak 2006, p. 127: 'As long as divergences exist, problems of private international law will arise as a consequence of the movement of persons, goods, services and capital within the internal market'; Sagaert 2007, p. 301.

119 *Cf* Koch 1995, p. 330: 'Private international law only provides the 'switch' activating the applicable national laws'. See also Kieninger 1996, p. 122. It may be the case that the *lex rei sitae* rule as such hinders free movement within the internal market. This will require further study. The first steps in that direction were made in Akkermans & Ramaekers 2012.

120 Chapter 5, section 3. *EU – Private International Law.*

121 Barnard 2010, p. 136. Justifications and the proportionality test will be dealt with in section 7 of this chapter.

Going back to the *Krantz* judgment, it is not entirely clear why the Court did not investigate the effects of the restrictions to property security further, particularly because cross-border trade on the basis of credit is commonplace.[122] When closely examined, it could very well be that trade between Member States is affected. If a seller is worried that his security right will be lost at the border, he may demand a different, more complex and more expensive, but safer security right, such as a letter of credit.[123] Any additional expenses incurred by the seller in this respect will undoubtedly be reflected in the price of the goods, potentially placing the seller at a disadvantageous position in the market of the host Member State and increasing the cost of the product for the buyer. Alternatively, if the seller is aware that his security right may not be recognized in the Member State of import, he might demand immediate payment from the buyer, before he delivers the goods. Ultimately, he may even decide not to conduct any cross-border business anymore. These situations not only restrict access to the market for the seller but also for the buyer, who is not able to buy a good in another country under the same circumstances as the residents in that country or who will not benefit from a foreign product being brought onto the market in his own Member State.[124]

The reasoning of Advocate-General Darmon in *Krantz* could be relevant in relation to these more expensive security rights. The Advocate-General argued that because of the specific nature of the right of seizure of the Dutch tax authorities, which is restricted to movables available on the premises, but not stocks of the company, the restriction to trade was minimal.[125] If, in his view, there is no discernible restriction to trade, Article 34 TFEU does not apply. However, this leads to the following question: if the seller indeed demands a more costly security right, because his reservation of ownership clause cannot sufficiently protect him due to the application of Dutch rather than German law, does this then not lead to a discernible restriction to trade? After all, establishing such a safer security right increases the cost of the transaction and therefore probably also the price of the product sold. This may eliminate a competitive advantage, which the seller may otherwise have had. The CJEU's judgment in *Oosthoek* is of interest here. In this judgment, the Court held that if a producer has to comply with two legal systems (e.g. that of the home and of the host Member State), this in itself can cause an

122 See e.g. Kreuzer 1990, p. 616-7.

123 *Cf* Bouckaert 2006, p. 183-184.

124 *Cf* Kieninger 1996, p. 156: A Belgian who wants to buy a car in France may run into difficulties when the seller wishes to create a *gage auto* to secure payment of the price. A *gage auto* is a security right not recognized in Belgium. If the French seller is aware of this, he may not want to take the risk and only sell the car upon immediate and full payment. The Belgian is therefore worse off than French citizens, who could acquire the car under the creation of a *gage auto*.

125 Case C-69/88 *H. Krantz GmbH & Co* v *Ontvanger der Directe Belastingen en de Staat der Nederlanden* [1990] ECR I-583, Opinion of A.-G. Darmon, paras. 12, 16.

obstacle.[126] The decision to sell a product under a retention of title clause or under a security right such as a pledge can be seen as a marketing strategy.[127] The CJEU ruled in *Oosthoek*:

> '15. [...] The possibility cannot be ruled out that to compel a producer either to adopt advertising or sales promotion schemes which differ from one Member State to another or to discontinue a scheme which he considers to be particularly effective may constitute an obstacle to imports even if the legislation in question applies to domestic products and imported products without distinction.'[128]

Such a situation is similar to a trader who is forced to establish separate security rights in each country where the goods that he sold might end up if he wants to cover the risk of losing the security right which he established in his own country.[129] The *lex rei sitae*, in combination with a country's national property law under which his security right is not recognized, forces him to do so.

The 'flood-gate' argument could be made against this seemingly very broad application of Article 34 TFEU. It will very often be the case that the law of the host country is simply different from the law of the home country. However, the *Oosthoek* doctrine only applies if the requirements of at least two different legal systems apply simultaneously to one case. The likelihood of this happening is sufficiently limited to exclude a number of cases that would previously also have been brought within the scope of Article 34 by the *Dassonville* formula.[130]

In conclusion, if the *Krantz* case had been of a more general nature than a specific aspect of Dutch procedural law, the result could have been that foreign traders would demand more expensive security rights when trading with Dutch companies. Von Bar and Drobnig's Study on the interaction between contract and property law shows the real concerns that traders have regarding a possible loss of security rights and how much more expensive personal security rights would be.[131] Domestic traders in a purely domestic situation can rely on the national system and will not require the creation of more demanding or more expensive security rights. Moreover, a trader that can effectively make use of a security right will likely lower his interest rate on secured loans.[132] Domestic traders can thus keep their prices lower, thereby gaining a competitive advantage. The negative impact of the *lex rei sitae* rule and the non-recognition by national law of foreign property rights even

126 See e.g. Case C-126/91, *Schutzverband gegen Unwesen in der Wirtschaft e.V* v *Yves Rocher GmbH* [1993] ECR I-2361, para. 10; Case 382/87, *R. Buet and Educational Business Services (EBS)* v *Ministère public* [1989] ECR 1235, paras. 7 and 8. See also Strese 2006, p. 191 who refers to this situation as *Diversifikationszwang*.

127 Kieninger 1996, p. 153-155.

128 Case 286/81, *Oosthoek* [1982] ECR 4575.

129 Kieninger 2008a, p. 225; Verhagen 2007a, p. 30.

130 Klauer 1998, p. 97.

131 Von Bar & Drobnig 2002, nos. 527-529, 733.

132 Kieninger 2004b, p. 7.

causes some smaller businesses to decide not to continue to participate in the internal market at all. Access to the market is thereby clearly hindered. Therefore, the application of the *lex rei sitae* rule in combination with domestic law could result in an actual and substantial hindrance to intra-Union trade under Article 34 TFEU.[133] Whether such a rule can be justified under Article 36 TFEU or one of the mandatory requirements provided by *Cassis de Dijon* will depend on the ground for justification offered by the Member State and the specific circumstances of an individual case.[134]

### 3.5. *The Effect of the Free Movement of Goods on National Property Law*

The free movement of goods may affect national property law through the concept of mutual recognition. If the concept of mutual recognition – as was first developed in the free movement of goods case *Cassis de Dijon* – is also applied to property law, the result would be that Member States must recognize property rights validly established in another Member State, even if these property rights are not present in their own *numerus clausus*. As was seen before,[135] this in effect creates what could be called a 'shadow-*numerus clausus*'. The national list of property rights is in that case supplemented with the property rights of the other Member States' *numerus clausus*. It is a 'shadow' list, because these rights must only be recognized but do not need to be offered within a Member State's own system of property law. As was shown, the rules on free movement of goods and mutual recognition are not developed to the extent that nationals of a Member State can themselves make use of those foreign property rights. If that were the case, the rules on free movement of goods would actually lead to a new, real *numerus clausus* for the Member States, consisting of all the property rights available within the Member States' systems of property law.

## 4. Free Movement of Capital

Under the European Economic Community (EEC) Treaty, the free movement of capital was the least important of the four freedoms.[136] This followed *inter alia* from the wording of Article 67(1) EEC:

> 'During the transitional period and to the extent necessary to ensure the proper functioning of the common market, Member States shall progressively abolish between themselves all restrictions on the movement of capital belonging to persons resident in Member States and any discrimination based on the nationality or on the place of residence of the parties or on the place where such capital is invested.'

133 *Cf* Kieninger 2004b, p. 20-21.
134 *Infra*, section 7.
135 *Supra*, section 3.2.
136 Craig & De Búrca 2011, p. 694.

The free movement of capital touched upon very sensitive areas, such as taxation, exchange rates and currency valuation. Therefore, the capital market was only gradually opened up and liberalized through secondary legislative measures. Under the EEC Treaty, the Articles on the free movement of capital did not have direct effect.[137] The status of the free movement of capital as the 'lesser' of the four freedoms changed dramatically with the entry into force of the Maastricht Treaty in 1993. Article 63 TFEU now reads:

> '1. Within the framework of the provisions set out in this Chapter, all restrictions on the movement of capital between Member States and between Member States and third countries shall be prohibited.
>
> 2. Within the framework of the provisions set out in this Chapter, all restrictions on payments between Member States and between Member States and third countries shall be prohibited.'

Free movement of capital became a fully-fledged freedom and Article 63 (ex Art. 56 EC) now has direct effect, meaning that it can be invoked by private persons before national courts.[138] This development also brought an increase in the case law of the CJEU on free movement of capital. Unlike in the area of free movement of goods, where there is really only one case - *Krantz* - on the influence of that freedom on national property law, there are several cases in the area of free movement of capital that are relevant for national property law. Before studying those cases it is important to establish first what actually constitutes a capital movement in the sense of Article 63 TFEU.

### 4.1. *What Constitutes a Capital Movement?*

The Treaty itself does not specify what a capital movement is. Therefore, Directive 88/361/EEC for the implementation of Article 67 of the (EEC) Treaty[139] is indicative for defining what a capital movement is.[140] A number of capital movements are specified in the Nomenclature in Annex I of the Directive. The list is not exhaustive.[141] Noteworthy in relation to property law are the following capital movements: II - Investments in Real Estate; III - Operations in Securities normally dealt in on the Capital Market; IV - Operations in Units of Collective Investment Undertakings; V -

137 Case 203/80, *Criminal proceedings against Guerrino Casati* [1981] ECR 2595, para. 19. See also Steiner & Woods 2009, p. 385.

138 Joined cases C-163/94, C-165/94 and C-250/94, *Sanz de Lera and others* [1995] ECR I-4821, para. 48. See also Steiner & Woods 2009, p. 387.

139 [1988] *OJ* L 178/5.

140 Case C-222/97, *Trummer and Mayer* [1991] ECR I-1661, para. 21.

141 'This Nomenclature is not an exhaustive list for the notion of capital movements - whence a heading XIII - F. "Other capital movements - Miscellaneous". It should not therefore be interpreted as restricting the scope of the principle of full liberalization of capital movements as referred to in Article 1 of the Directive.'

Operations in Securities and other Instruments normally dealt in on the Money Market; VII - Credits related to Commercial Transactions or to the Provision of Services in which a Resident is participating; VIII - Financial Loans and Credits; IX - Sureties, other Guarantees and Rights of Pledge; XII - Physical Import and Export of Financial Assets; and of course XIII - Other Capital Movements, F - Miscellaneous. So far, a lot of the case law of the Court on the free movement of capital concerned the acquisition of immovable property (i.e. investments in real estate) and 'golden shares' cases.[142] National rules on the acquisition of land have sometimes been held to pose an obstacle to the free movement of capital. In general, it can be observed that the free movement of capital relates more to immovables, whereas the free movement of goods relates more to movables.

## 4.2. *Discrimination or Market Access Test: a de Minimis Requirement in Free Movement of Capital?*

The Court shows a tendency to move towards a market access test, in line with its case law regarding the other freedoms. An important case in that respect is *Commission v Portugal*,[143] in which the Court held the following:

> '44. [...] Article 73b of the Treaty lays down a general prohibition on restrictions on the movement of capital between Member States. That prohibition goes beyond the mere elimination of unequal treatment, on grounds of nationality, as between operators on the financial markets.
>
> 45. Even though the rules in issue may not give rise to unequal treatment, they are liable to impede the acquisition of shares in the undertakings concerned and to dissuade investors in other Member States from investing in the capital of those undertakings. They are therefore liable, as a result, to render the free movement of capital illusory (see, in that regard, Joined Cases C-163/94, C-165/94 and C-250/94 *Sanz de Lera and Others* [1995] ECR I-4821, paragraph 25, and Case C-302/97 *Konle* [1999] ECR I-3099, paragraph 44).'

Consequently, not only discriminatory but also non-discriminatory measures can be caught under Article 63 TFEU.[144] It seems that the *Keck* distinction between product characteristics and selling arrangements is not applied by analogy to the free movement of capital. The market access test is thus applied to any kind of national measure liable to hinder the free movement of capital. The Court only does not do so in cases where it considers the effect on the market too remote and indirect. This seems to be the only - slight - limitation to the market access test.[145]

142 See e.g. case C-367/98, *Commission* v *Portugal* [2002] ECR I-4731.

143 Case C-367/98, *Commission* v *Portugal* [2002] ECR I-4731. See also case C-174/04, *Commission* v *Italy* [2005] ECR I-4933, para. 12: 'Article 56 EC draws no distinction between discriminatory and non-discriminatory measures'. See further Barnard 2010, p. 569-571.

144 Craig & De Búrca 2011, p. 695.

145 Barnard 2010, p. 572.

It is not entirely clear whether the Court applies a *de minimis* test in free movement of capital cases. It seems to do so only in cases where the national measure is non-discriminatory.[146] It is interesting to note, however, that in the cases discussed here in section 4,[147] the argument that the effect of the measure on the internal market was too uncertain and indirect to be caught under the free movement of capital was never made.[148]

### 4.3. *Obstacles to the Free Movement of Capital*

With regard to the free movement of capital, there are quite a number of cases that provide examples of how European law has an effect within national property law.

The case of *Trummer* v *Mayer* was adjudicated before the Euro was introduced. Mr. Mayer, residing in Germany, sold a share in the ownership of a property situated in Austria to Mr. Trummer, residing in Austria. The purchase price was denominated in German Marks. The parties applied to an Austrian District Court for registration of the transaction in the land registry. The registration of the mortgage that the parties had created to secure payment of the purchase price was however refused because Austrian law stipulated that a mortgage could only be created in Austrian Schillings. According to Trummer and Mayer, this law was incompatible with the free movement of capital.

The CJEU first established that the creation of a mortgage indeed constituted a capital movement.[149] It then held that the national law indeed hindered the free movement of capital:

> '26 The effect of national rules such as those at issue in the main proceedings is to weaken the link between the debt to be secured, payable in the currency of another Member State, and the mortgage, whose value may, as a result of subsequent currency exchange fluctuations, come to be lower than that of the debt to be secured. This can only reduce the effectiveness of such a security, and thus its attractiveness. Consequently, those rules are liable to dissuade the parties concerned from denominating a debt in the currency of another Member State, and may thus deprive them of a right which constitutes a component element of the free movement of capital and payments [...].
>
> 27 Furthermore, the rules at issue may well cause the contracting parties to incur additional costs, by requiring them, purely for the purposes of registering the

146 See, for instance, case C-412/97, *ED Srl* v *Italo Fenocchio* [1999] ECR I-3845, para. 11. *Contra* Steiner & Woods 2009, p. 389. Something similar can be seen in the context of the free movement of services and persons: *infra*, sections 5.2 and 6.1.

147 I.e. *Trummer* v *Mayer*, *Reisch* etc.

148 See also Landsmeer 2001, p. 60.

149 *Trummer and Mayer*, para. 23: 'Moreover, mortgages represent the classic method of securing a loan linked to a sale of real property, which is a transaction covered by the nomenclature. In those circumstances, a mortgage must be regarded as constituting an "other guarantee" within the meaning of point IX of the nomenclature, headed "Sureties, other guarantees and rights of pledge".'

> mortgage, to value the debt in the national currency and, as the case may be, formally to record that currency conversion.
>
> 28 In those circumstances, an obligation to have recourse to the national currency for the purposes of creating a mortgage must be regarded, in principle, as a restriction on the movement of capital within the meaning of Article 73b of the Treaty.'

It is interesting to note that the Court refers to the additional costs that the parties may incur to comply with the national law. As was seen before in the context of free movement of goods,[150] a national rule that results in additional costs for parties that enter into cross-border trade is for that reason often considered by the Court as an obstacle to the internal market.

The CJEU also developed a line of case law on the acquisition of immovable property and authorization and declaration procedures that needed to be fulfilled before such an acquisition. In the *Konle* case,[151] Mr. Konle, a German national, wanted to buy a plot of land in Austria but was confronted with the Tyrol Law on the Transfer of Land. This Law stipulated that the acquisition of land in that area was subject to authorization by the authority responsible for land transactions. Authorization would be refused if the acquirer failed to show that the land would not be used for a secondary residence. Such legislation is meant to prevent the creation of 'holiday colonies', areas where foreigners only come during the winter or summer season but which are deserted during the rest of the year. According to the CJEU, such legislation constitutes, by its very purpose, a restriction on the free movement of capital.[152] It accepted that the legislation could be justified by objectives of town and country planning. However, the legislation failed the proportionality test that every justification ground must pass. The Court held that the same objectives could be achieved by less far-reaching measures, namely by virtue of a prior declaration system, instead of a prior authorization system. A Member State would be allowed to ensure adherence to such a system in several ways, such as imposing a fine, ordering the compulsory sale of the land or declaring the sale void, if the requisite prior declaration was not obtained by the person seeking to acquire immovable property within that Member State.[153]

The *Albore* case also concerned a prior authorization procedure.[154] This time, two German nationals wanted to buy immovable property in an area of Italy that was designated as being of military importance. Italian law stipulated that, for such a transfer, prior authorization needed to be acquired from the Prefect of the

150 *Supra*, section 3.4.5.

151 Case C-320/97, *Konle* [1999] ECR I-3099.

152 Para. 39.

153 Paras. 40-48.

154 Case C-423/98, *Alfredo Albore* [2002] ECR I-5965. Other examples of cases concerning a prior authorization procedure are case C-452/01, *Margarethe Ospelt and Schlössle Weissenberg Familienstiftung* [2003] ECR I-9743 on the acquisition of agricultural plots, and cases C-358/93, *Criminal proceedings against Bordessa and others* [1995] ECR I-361 and C-163/94, *Criminal proceedings against Sanz de Lera and others* [1995] ECR I-4821 on the transfer of bank notes.

province in question. However, Italian nationals were not required to get this authorization. The Court first of all held that the fact that the buyers of the property had German nationality was sufficient to constitute a cross-border element, making European law applicable: the purchase of immovable property in a Member State by a non-resident constitutes a capital movement in the sense of Article 63 TFEU. The Italian law was directly discriminatory on the basis of nationality, causing an obstacle to the free movement of capital that could only be justified by any of the limited number of grounds laid down in Article 65 of the Treaty. Although the law might pursue a justified aim, - i.e. public security - it failed to fulfil the proportionality test. The Italian government was unable to show that non-discriminatory treatment of the nationals of all Member States would create a real and serious military risk that could not be avoided by less far-reaching means.

The *Reisch* case was concerned with both a prior authorization procedure and a prior notification procedure.[155] Austrian law stipulated that persons wanting to buy building plots in certain areas needed to submit a declaration to the relevant authorities first, stating that they had Austrian nationality or the nationality of one of the EU or EEA Member States and did not intend to use the building plot for a secondary residence.[156] Several Austrian nationals who had bought or tried to buy such building plots started proceedings before the national court, either because they had been fined for not notifying the acquisition of building plots in time or because they had not been granted the authorization needed to buy such plots.[157] As the Court had already held in *Konle*, a prior authorization procedure was not compatible with EU law and could not be justified, since the aim that it pursues can be achieved by less far-reaching means, namely a prior declaration procedure. The Court therefore deemed the declaration procedure to be compatible with the free movement of capital, especially because, as an a priori measure, it provides more legal certainty and prevents the difficulties that come with having to reverse a transfer of land.

The *Burtscher* case also concerned a prior declaration procedure, which was in principle held to be in violation of the free movement of capital, with reference to *Reisch*.[158] A particular problem in this case was the penalty that was imposed on the person acquiring the land, when he or she failed to submit the declaration in time. The penalty entailed the retroactive invalidity of the property transaction. Because

155 Joined Cases C-515/99, C-519/99 to C-524/99 and C-526/99 to C-540/99, *Reisch and others* v *Bürgermeister der Landeshauptstadt Salzburg and others* [2002] ECR I-2157.

156 In some cases, prior authorization was required if the land transfer agent (*Grundverkehrsbeauftragter*) doubted that the building plots would be used in accordance with the declaration.

157 This case concerned Austrian law, applied to Austrian nationals buying land in Austria. This seems to be a so-called purely internal situation, to which EU law would not be applicable. The Court held that this was not the case, though. See *supra*, section 1. *Cross-border or purely internal situation?*

158 Case C-213/04, *Ewald Burtscher* v *Josef Stauderer* [2005] ECR I-10309, para. 43.

the penalty would be imposed automatically once the time limit for submitting the declaration had passed, the Court deemed it to be disproportionate to the aim pursued.[159] The Court held:

> '[F]or no reason deriving from infringement of the applicable substantive rules, such a penalty radically calls into question an agreement expressing the intentions of the parties and cannot therefore reflect the requirements of legal certainty, which are particularly important in relation to property acquisitions. [...] such a measure is excessive in so far as it has automatic consequences for late submission of the declaration, prohibiting [the competent] authority from examining whether, on the merits, the proposed acquisition complies with the applicable planning rules.'[160]

What all these cases have in common, is that they make it less attractive for foreigners to acquire immovable property in the host Member State than it is for nationals of that Member State. Nationals of a Member State are more likely than foreigners to acquire immovable property in that State for their primary residence or (for countries not in the Euro-zone) are more likely to acquire a mortgage loan to buy immovable property denominated in the currency of their own Member State. Because the national measures disputed in these cases were held to violate the free movement of capital, they had to be changed or could no longer be applied. This means that, by applying the rules on free movement of capital to these national measures, a person would be free to use the immovable property they acquired in accordance with their own wishes, e.g. as a secondary residence rather than a primary residence. In this way, the free movement of capital affects a person's right of ownership over the immovable property.[161]

A recent development potentially affecting the free movement of capital is the stream of petitions received by the European Parliament from home owners on the Spanish Costas, concerning the Spanish *Ley de Costas* or Coastal Law. This Law was originally passed in 1988 but only started to be applied as of 2008.[162] During that time, the development of private homes as well as holiday complexes on the Spanish Costas grew exponentially. Under the Coastal Law a strip of land six metres from the edge of the sea inland is declared public property, effectively reducing the private properties bordering on the coast, the owners of which are losing their mooring, patio and often part of their front rooms.[163] The petitioners mostly complain that the application of the Coastal Law amounts to a (partial)

159 Town and country planning and the maintenance of a permanent population and economic activity independent of the tourist sector; *Burtscher*, para. 46.

160 *Burtscher*, paras. 56-59.

161 *Cf* Akkermans 2012a, p. 232; Van Erp 2006b, p. 8.

162 Wallis & Allanson 2011, p. 21.

163 Wallis & Allanson 2011, p. 21. See also Parliamentary Question for written answer to the Commission by Angelika Niebler, No E-002649/2011, 'Expropriation of property under the Spanish law on coastal protection'.

expropriation of their property.[164] However, given that many of the home owners in the affected regions are nationals from other Member States,[165] the free movement of capital could also be jeopardized, if it is taken into consideration that the acquisition of immovable property in another Member State constitutes a capital movement in the sense of Article 63 TFEU.[166] Furthermore, as one of the petitioners pointed out, the Coastal Law might also infringe Article 50(2)(e) TFEU, which states that a national of one Member State should be enabled to acquire and use land and buildings situated in the territory of another Member State.[167]

If it transpires that the Spanish Coastal Law indeed violates these Treaty provisions, then it will be up to the Spanish authorities to present a ground for justification of the Coastal Law and to show that this Law is proportionate to the aim it pursues, which is to provide a protected strip of public access to the coast and prevent further loss of coastline to rampant development.[168] If such a justification ground is found to be unacceptable, or if the measure is deemed to be disproportionate, by the CJEU, then the Coastal Law may not be enforced. If that is the case, then the Treaty provisions on free movement of capital and freedom of establishment will have protected the property rights of the owners of the coastal properties.

### 4.4. *The Effect of the Free Movement of Capital on National Property Law*

The case law of the CJEU as described in this section on free movement of capital affects national property law in a number of ways. First of all, cases such as *Reisch*, *Konle* and *Burtscher* influence, at the national level, the formalities that need to be fulfilled for acquiring ownership of a plot of land. They therefore affect national rules on the transfer of a property right. Secondly, they affect the content of a property right, namely the right of ownership. The aforementioned cases affect the way in which individuals are allowed to use their right of ownership. Under the national rules that were at stake in these cases, an owner would only have been able to use the immovable property he or she acquired as a primary residence. But under the application of the rules on free movement of capital, Member States are expected to also allow an owner to use the immovable property as a secondary

164 See for a list of petitions European Parliament Doc No. CM\785693EN.doc, to be found at: <http://www.europarl.europa.eu/meetdocs/2009_2014/documents/peti/cm/785/785693/785693en.pdf>.

165 See another list of petitions, European Parliament Minutes Meeting of 23 May 2011, from 15.00 to 18.30, and 24 May 2011, from 9.00 to 12.30, Brussels, to be found at: <http://www.europarl.europa.eu/meetdocs/2009_2014/documents/peti/pv/868/868535/868535en.pdf>.

166 See *supra*, section 4.1. *What constitutes a capital movement?*

167 Petition 0174/2008 by Mr. Jose Ortega (Spanish), on the alleged abusive application of the Spanish law of the coasts in relation to property rights.

168 Wallis & Allanson 2011, p. 21.

residence. The content of his right of ownership is thereby broadened. Finally, the free movement of capital might also come to protect national property rights in immovable property by shielding them from the devastating effects of the Spanish Coastal Law as described in the previous section.

## 5. Free Movement of Services

The free movement of services is laid down in Article 56 TFEU.[169] The free movement of services and the free movement of capital are closely connected to each other. Whenever a person or company acquires immovable property, the acquisition as such is governed by the free movement of capital, but the financing of the acquisition is governed by the free movement of services. The CJEU held in the *Parodi* case that the grant of a mortgage loan by a bank or other credit institution established in one Member State to a borrower established in another Member State - a so-called home loan - constitutes the provision of a service.[170] Therefore, if national rules make it impossible or more difficult to grant or acquire such a loan, both the lender and the borrower would be able to contest those rules, relying on the free movement of services. According to the Court in *Luisi and Carbone*, the free movement of services entails not just the freedom to provide a service, but also the freedom to receive a service, which is why both lender and borrower could contest national law that they perceive to infringe the free movement of services.[171]

Directive 2006/48/EC relating to the taking up and pursuit of the business of credit institutions (recast)[172] regulates certain elements of the service provision by financial institutions. The area where the Directive applies is outside the scope of application of the general rules on the internal market. Situations not covered by the Directive are still governed by the free movement of services and the Court's judgment in *Parodi*.[173] The Directive is dealt with in more detail below, in section 5.1.

It follows from the *Parodi* judgment that there is a close relationship between free movement of capital and services with regard to financing the acquisition of immovable property. The case concerned the grant of a mortgage loan by a Dutch bank to a French company, expressed in German DM. Such a loan is classified as a 'provision of services connected with movement of capital'.[174] The general question

169 Ex Art. 49 EC. Art. 56 TFEU reads: 'Within the framework of the provisions set out below, restrictions on freedom to provide services within the Union shall be prohibited in respect of nationals of Member States who are established in a Member State other than that of the person for whom the services are intended.
The European Parliament and the Council, acting in accordance with the ordinary legislative procedure, may extend the provisions of the Chapter to nationals of a third country who provide services and who are established within the Union.'

170 Case C-222/95, *SCI Parodi v Banque Albert de Bary et Cie* [1997] ECR I-3899, para. 8.

171 Cases 286/82 and 26/83, *Luisi and Carbone* v *Ministero del Tesoro* [1984] ECR 377, para. 16.

172 [2006] *OJ* L 177/1.

173 Akkermans 2012a, p. 235.

174 Case C-222/95, *Parodi* [1997] ECR I-3899, para. 8; A.G. Elmer's Opinion, para. 13.

is: do banking services connected with a movement of capital fall under the provisions on free movement of services? According to the Court's case law, this is indeed the case, provided that the form of movement of capital in question has been liberalized.[175] The freedom to provide services and the free movement of capital are thus interconnected. This follows from Article 58(2) TFEU (ex Art. 51(2) EC): 'The liberalization of banking and insurance services connected with movements of capital shall be effected in step with the liberalization of movement of capital.' The Community's internal market was only gradually opened up to the free movement of capital.[176] Only capital movements that have been liberalized through secondary EU measures, i.e. to which the internal market has been opened up, can be subject to the free movement of capital and services. Grants by financial institutions of medium- and long-term loans, including mortgage loans, are a liberalized capital movement under Article 3 of the First Capital Directive,[177] in connection with Annex I List C and Annex II, VIII.A to that Directive. The free movement of services thus applies to the grant of such loans.[178]

Advocate-General Elmer felt, in his Opinion in the *Parodi* case, that, with a view to Article 58(2) TFEU, both the free movement of capital and the free movement of services rules should be applied in cases concerning a service by a financial institution connected to a capital movement. There moreover seems to be a hierarchy between the two freedoms, according to the Court:

> '10. It follows that the only case in which the Treaty provisions on services do not apply to banking services is where there is a restriction on the free movement of capital relating to such transactions which is compatible with Community law.'[179]

In conclusion: it must first be established whether a particular capital movement is liberalized. Once this has been established, the free movement of capital rules are applied first, where after the free movement of services rules are applied. If it is established that there is an obstacle to the free movement of capital, which is nevertheless compatible with EU law, then the free movement of services rules will not be applied.

## 5.1. *Directive 2006/48/EC*

Directive 2006/48 relating to the taking up and pursuit of the business of credit institutions (recast)[180] indicates in its preamble that it 'constitutes the essential

175 Case C-484/93, *Svensson and Gustavsson*, para. 11.

176 *Parodi*, para. 11.

177 EEC Council: First Directive for the implementation of Article 67 of the Treaty, *OJ* 43 English special edition 1959-1962, p. 49.

178 *Parodi*, paras. 14 and 17.

179 CJEU in *Parodi*.

180 [2006] *OJ* L 177/1.

instrument for the achievement of the internal market from the point of view of both the freedom of establishment and the freedom to provide financial services, in the field of credit institutions'.[181] It operates on the basis of mutual recognition of financial institutions.[182] Once a financial institution has been authorized in its home Member State, it should be able to establish branches and provide its services in the other Member States.[183] The Directive provides for a number of situations in which a financial institution should *not* be authorized by its home Member State and all authorizations must be notified to the Commission.[184] Articles 29 to 37 of the Directive allow the host Member State to demand information or withdraw authorization from a foreign financial institution offering its services in the host Member State.[185] Furthermore, the financial institution will have to comply with the national laws of the host Member State, which would *inter alia* mean that, in accordance with the *lex rei sitae*, a financial institution providing a loan to a client can only secure that loan with a security right valid under the law of the host Member State. Any additional costs incurred by the financial institution from having to obtain authorization from, and complying with the laws of, the host Member State, will undoubtedly be passed on to the recipient of the financial service. This may result in an obstacle to the free movement of services. Matters covered by the Directive, which are primarily the supervision of credit institutions, their financial solvability and overview of their activities,[186] fall outside the scope of application of the free movement of services. Other aspects of cross-border financing for home loans that are not covered by the Directive are still governed by the free movement of services and the CJEU's *Parodi* judgment. This is likely to be the case for a country's property law provisions.[187] Therefore, national property law provisions restricting the provision or receipt of a cross-border financial service such as a home loan have to be objectively necessary for the aim they pursue and should not go beyond what is necessary to achieve that aim.

181 Recital 3.

182 Preamble, recitals 7 and 10. The Directive thereby provides another example of mutual recognition being used in another area than the free movement of goods; see *supra*, section 3.2.

183 Preamble, recital 14. See also Akkermans 2012a, p. 243.

184 Artt. 6-22.

185 Akkermans 2012a, p. 234.

186 Akkermans 2012a, p. 235.

187 Akkermans 2012a, p. 235.

## 5.2. *Discrimination or Market Access Test: a de Minimis Requirement in Free Movement of Services?*

The CJEU applies a market access test and not merely a discrimination test with regard to the free movement of services.[188] Therefore, even non-discriminatory measures that nevertheless hinder access to the market in some way can be caught under the provisions on free movement of services.[189] Furthermore, the difference made in *Keck* between product characteristics and selling arrangements is not extended to the free movement of services.[190] Therefore, something that might be considered a selling arrangement under the free movement of goods, and which might for that reason escape scrutiny under Article 34, will not fall outside the scope of application of Article 56.[191] Whether a *de minimis* rule is applied in relation to free movement of services is a little less certain. It seems that a *de minimis* rule is only applied in cases concerning a non-discriminatory measure, as a way to mitigate the potentially very wide scope of application of the market access test.[192]

## 5.3. *Obstacles to the Free Movement of Services*

Both the provider as well as the receiver of a financial service may experience difficulties in a cross-border situation. As said before, the financial service provider must comply with the national law of the host Member State. Therefore, if he wishes to create a security right, to secure an underlying loan, on an immovable object located in the host Member State, the *lex rei sitae* rule obliges him to create a security right in conformity with the national law of the host Member State.[193] The need to comply with the national law of the host Member State as a result of the *lex rei sitae* rule is not covered by Directive 2006/48. The question whether this situation hinders the cross-border provision of financial services therefore remains to be decided on the general rules on free movement of services and the Court's *Parodi* case law.[194] Having to create a 'foreign' security right requires extra effort, for instance, information gathering,[195] extra costs, and the risk assessment made by the provider of the loan may differ depending on whether the security right it receives is national and familiar or foreign and unfamiliar. This will either be a disadvantage to the service provider, or to the person acquiring the loan, to whom the additional

188 See *inter alia* case C-76/90, *Säger* v *Dennemeyer* [1991] ECR I-4221, para. 12; case C-3/95, *Reisebüro Broede* v *Sandker* [1996] ECR I-6511, para. 25.

189 Craig & De Búrca 2011, p. 806.

190 Case C-384/93, *Alpine Investments* [1995] ECR I-1141, paras. 32-36.

191 Craig & De Búrca 2011, p. 807.

192 See e.g. Cases C-51/96 and 191/97, *Deliège* [2000] ECR I-2549; Case C-190/98, *Graf* [200 ECR I-493. See also Craig & De Búrca 2011, p. 808.

193 Akkermans 2012a, p. 235.

194 Akkermans 2012a, p. 235.

195 *Cf* Strese 2006, p. 191.

costs may be passed on in the form of a higher interest rate. The fact that it is (potentially) more costly, either for the service provider or for the service recipient, to conclude a cross-border mortgage loan than it is to conclude a mortgage loan within their own Member State, may make cross-border mortgage loans less attractive than domestic mortgage loans. This could be seen as a hindrance to the free movement of services, resulting from the application of the *lex rei sitae* rule which does not allow for the creation of a foreign mortgage right on immovable property within the host Member State.

It is not just financial services that are relevant here. Advocate-General *Geelhoed* explained in his opinion in the *Reisch* case that national law prohibiting a person to use immovable property as a secondary residence not only contradicts the free movement of capital but also of services. A secondary residence might be used by the owner to rent out to others during the time that he himself does not occupy it. This is a service that the owner could not provide if the owner were obliged to use the building as primary residence. Furthermore, by acquiring an immovable object, the owner not only becomes a potential service provider but also a potential receiver of services. This could be services connected with the building itself, such as maintenance or construction work or services relating to tourist activities.[196] In this way, the free movement of services facilitates the acquisition of immovable property in a similar way as the free movement of capital does.[197] It therefore has an indirect effect on national property law in the sense that the acquirer of the immovable has more freedom to make use of his right of ownership of the immovable due to the application of the free movement rules than he would have had under the national law.

## 5.4. *The Effect of the Free Movement of Services on National Property Law*

If the free movement of services rules indeed facilitate the acquisition of immovable property like the rules on free movement of capital do and extend what an owner of that property can do with it beyond what would have been allowed under national law – like using the property as a holiday home as opposed to a primary residence – then the freedom of services rules and the *Parodi* judgment of the CJEU affect the content of a national property right. Furthermore, if it is indeed the case that the *lex rei sitae* rule in combination with the national *numerus clausus* makes it impossible for financial service providers and recipients to conclude a cross-border mortgage loan on the basis of the law of the home Member State, rather than the host Member State, then those rules may be affected by the application of the free movement of services.

196 A.-G. Geelhoed's Opinion to *Reisch*, paras. 31-33.

197 See the series of cases on free movement of capital and the acquisition of immovable property discussed in section 4.3.

## 6. Free Movement of Persons

The right to free movement of persons is contained in Article 20(2)(a) TFEU, which states that '[c]itizens of the Union shall enjoy the rights and be subject to the duties provided for in the Treaties. They shall have, inter alia: (a) the right to move and reside freely within the territory of the Member States'. Free movement for workers specifically has been laid down in Article 45 TFEU (ex Art. 39 EC). The free movement of persons is worked out in detail in Directive 2004/38/EC.[198]

### 6.1. *Discrimination or Market Access Test: a de Minimis Requirement in Free Movement of Persons?*

The Court applies a market access test in the area of free movement of persons as well as to the other freedoms.[199] Furthermore, as with the other freedoms, a *de minimis* requirement only seems to be applied to non-discriminatory national measures, which may nevertheless hinder access to the market of the host Member State. Both Advocate-General Fennelly and the CJEU itself explicitly dealt with this in the *Graf* case.[200] Just as with the free movement of services, the *Keck* distinction between product characteristics and selling arrangements is not applied to the free movement of persons. However, the reasoning of the Court behind the *Keck* distinction, namely the removal of non-discriminatory measures that do not substantially hinder access to the market from the scope of application of the rules on free movement, may also underlie the application of a *de minimis* requirement for non-discriminatory measures in the other freedoms, including the free movement of persons.[201]

Interestingly, the case *Corsica Ferries France* provides a very explicit statement by the CJEU that there is actually no *de minimis* requirement in any of the four freedoms:

> 'As the Court has decided on various occasions, the articles of the EEC Treaty concerning the free movement of goods, persons, services and capital are fundamental Community provisions and any restriction, even minor, of that freedom is prohibited.'[202]

198 [2004] *OJ* L 158/77.

199 Case C-415/93, *Bosman* [1995] ECR I-4921, para. 96; case C-19/92, *Dieter Kraus* v *Land Baden-Württemberg* [1993] ECR I-1663, para. 32; case C-464/02, *Commission* v *Denmark* [2005] ECR I-7929, paras. 34-36. See also Craig & De Búrca 2011, p. 730-732.

200 Case C-190/98, *Volker Graf* v *Filzmoser Mashinenbau GmbH* [2000] ECR I-493. A.-G. Fennelly at para. 32 of his Opinion; the CJEU at paras. 24-5 of its judgment.

201 Barnard 2010, p. 242 *et seq.*, with further references there.

202 Case C-49/89, *Corsica Ferries France* v *Direction générale des douanes françaises* [1989] ECR I-4441, para. 8. See, for instance, also case 167/73, *French Merchant Seamen* [1974] ECR 359, para. 46: 'It thus follows from the general character of the prohibition on discrimination in Article →

However, this case was decided before the development from a discrimination test to a market access test really took place. It is safe to say that those developments nuanced the Court's statement in *Corsica Ferries*.

## 6.2. *Obstacles to the Free Movement of Persons*

Citizens of the European Union have the right to move and reside freely within the territory of the Member States. This right is granted to them by Articles 20(2)(a) and 21(1) TFEU and by Directive 2004/38/EC on the right of citizens of the Union and their family members to move and reside freely within the territory of the Member States.[203]

The differences between the national systems of property law could lead to obstacles for persons making use of their freedom to move. A corollary to the right to move and reside freely in other Member States would have to be the right to freely acquire immovable property.[204] With regard to the free movement of establishment, this corollary right to acquire immovable property has been recognized by the CJEU.[205] It is currently laid down in Article 50 TFEU:[206]

> '1. In order to attain freedom of establishment as regards a particular activity, the European Parliament and the Council, acting in accordance with the ordinary legislative procedure and after consulting the Economic and Social Committee, shall act by means of directives.
>
> 2. The European Parliament, the Council and the Commission shall carry out the duties devolving upon them under the preceding provisions, in particular:
>
> [...] (e) by enabling a national of one Member State to acquire and use land and buildings situated in the territory of another Member State, in so far as this does not conflict with the principles laid down in Article 39(2)'. [emphasis added]

48 [EEC] and the objective pursued by the abolition of discrimination that discrimination is prohibited even if it constitutes only an obstacle of secondary importance'.

203 [2004] *OJ* L 158/77.

204 *Cf* Bright & Bright 1998, p. 365.

205 Case 305/87, *Commission* v *Greece* [1989] ECR 1461, para. 22: 'In particular, as is apparent from Article 54(3)(e ) of the [EEC] Treaty and the General programme for the abolition of restrictions on freedom of establishment of 18 December 1961 (*Official Journal*, English Special Edition, Second Series IX, p. 7), the right to acquire, use or dispose of immovable property on the territory of a Member State is the corollary of freedom of establishment.' See also case C-302/97, *Konle*, para. 22.

206 Ex Art. 44 EC. See also Bright & Bright 1998, p. 365.

Advocate-General Geelhoed stated in his Opinion in the *Reisch* case[207] that it should not matter, whether a building is acquired to be used as a secondary residence or a primary residence:

> 'A private individual acquiring a secondary residence may do so, firstly, with the aim of occupying it himself for part of the year. Activities relating to the free movement of persons will then be in issue: (the right of) residence in another Member State. Although secondary residences are usually occupied for only a limited period of the year, such occupancy none the less has something permanent about it.'[208]

Therefore, national rules such as the ones discussed under the free movement of capital, which restrict an acquirer of immovable property in the use of that property,[209] can also be seen as a hindrance to the free movement of persons.

Other problems arise when a person acquires a property right in relation to an object by way of succession. Consider the following example: a French person domiciled in Paris at the time of his death leaves a right of usufruct over his car to his daughter, who lives in London. The car is situated in London at the time of death of the testator. According to English private international law movable assets devolve in accordance with the *lex domicilii* of the deceased.[210] The *lex domicilii* in this example is French law. This means that French law governs the right of usufruct created in relation to the car which is situated in England.

If this situation had not been one of succession but one of transfer *inter vivos*, it would not have been possible to create a right of usufruct in relation to the car: English law would have applied as the *lex rei sitae* and the English *numerus clausus* does not know a right of usufruct. If the usufruct had been created while the car was still in France and the car had only afterwards been driven to England, the French right of usufruct would either be transformed into an equivalent right under the English *numerus clausus* or would not be accepted in England and therefore would have been lost at the border. It is not quite clear whether or not this is also what happens to a foreign usufruct that enters England under a will. The adherence to the *lex domicilii* as opposed to the *lex rei sitae* suggests that the usufruct would in any event be recognized as validly created by the testator and acquired by his daughter under French law. Whether the French usufruct could also be enforced by the testator's daughter in England remains to be seen. It would appear that this would not be possible if the object was not a car but land situated in England, because succession to immovable property is governed by the *lex rei sitae*.[211] The

207 Joined Cases C-515/99, C-519/99 to C-524/99 and C-526/99 to C-540/99, *Reisch and others* [2002] ECR I-2157.

208 A.-G. Geelhoed's Opinion to *Reisch*, para. 31.

209 *Supra*, at section 4.3.

210 Garb & Wood 2010, p. 243 at 15.99 and 15.102.

211 Garb & Wood 2010, p. 243 at 15.99 and 15.102.

Regulation on international succession[212] would bring a change in that respect, as it would abolish the *lex rei sitae* rule for succession to immovable property. This would mean that 'English courts [might be required] to recognize and enforce a French *usufruit* over land in England'.[213] One might deduce from the fact that the *lex domicilii*, and not the *lex rei sitae*, is applied to successions to movable property that the attitude to recognition and enforcement of foreign property rights over movable objects is different and that - to return to our example - the testator's daughter might be able to enforce her French right of usufruct over the car in England. It has however proven difficult to find legislation or case law which confirms this.

The Commission considers the fact that persons have difficulties asserting rights acquired under a will in the context of an international succession to constitute a hindrance to the free movement of persons. This follows from its 2009 Proposal for a Regulation on international successions.[214] These difficulties arise because rules of Member States governing international successions differ and the Regulation - which has in the meantime become law[215] - therefore purports to eliminate the obstacles to the free movement of persons that arise out of those differing national laws, thereby enabling 'people living in the European Union to organize their succession in advance and effectively to guarantee the rights of heirs and/or legatees and of other persons linked to the deceased, as well as creditors of the succession.'[216] The Impact Assessment attached to the Proposal shows that an estimated 450,000 successions in the EU have an international dimension.[217] An international dimension can arise if the deceased's property is located in more than one Member State, if the deceased had a different nationality from the Member State of his last habitual residence or if the potential heir lives in a different Member State than the testator. Given that approximately eight million EU citizens have made use of their right to free movement, the likelihood that a succession has an international dimension increases.[218] Heirs in international successions are faced with legal uncertainty, increased costs and time delays. The Impact Assessment refers to

212 Regulation 650/2012/EU on jurisdiction, applicable law, recognition and enforcement of decisions and acceptance and enforcement of authentic instruments in matters of succession and on the creation of a European Certificate of Succession, [2012] OJ L 201/107. More about this Regulation in Chapter 4.

213 Garb & Wood 2010, p. xxxvi.

214 Proposal for a Regulation on jurisdiction, applicable law, recognition and enforcement of decisions and authentic instruments in matters of succession and the creation of a European Certificate of Succession, COM(2009) 154 final. See Preamble at Recital 6, and the Explanatory Memorandum to the Proposal at 1.2.

215 Reg. 650/2012/EU, [2012] *OJ* L 201/107.

216 Explanatory Memorandum to the Proposal, at 3.1. *Legal basis*.

217 Impact Assessment at 3.3. *Scope of the problem*. See also Gaillard & Trautman 1987, p. 313 and fn. 11: '[R]eports of the practice before notaries contain numerous examples of trusts used for purposes of succession to immovables in civil-law countries. [...] In France, for example, public notaries report about 100 cases a year involving trusts having to do with immovable assets located in France.'

218 Ramaekers 2012, p. 1.

examples of heirs having to renounce their rights to a succession because their enforcement in another Member State would have been too expensive.[219] The Impact Assessment calculates an estimated cost of international successions of four billion Euro per annum to EU citizens.[220] If the status quo is maintained, those costs are estimated to double within a period of ten years,[221] resulting in a potentially significant hindrance to the free movement of persons. The Regulation on international successions might be able to reduce that hindrance.

### 6.3. *The Effect of the Free Movement of Persons on National Property Law*

The Regulation on international successions could have an impact not only on the national private international rules governing successions (such as the *lex rei sitae* and the *lex domicilii*) but also on the national *numerus clausus* of the Member States, which would be faced with foreign property rights acquired in a succession. According to Salla Saastamoinen, Head of the civil justice unit, DG Justice, Freedom and Security, of the European Commission at the time the Proposal for the Regulation came out, succession is considered to be property law, not family law.[222]

Furthermore, the free movement of persons could affect national property law in a similar way as the free movement of capital and the free movement of services could, given that a corollary to the right to move and reside freely within the EU, enjoyed by all EU citizens, is the right to acquire immovable property in another Member State. Any national restrictions concerning the acquisition of immovable property may fall foul of the rules on free movement of persons.

## 7. Justification Grounds

Once it has been established that the four freedoms apply to rules of property law, and that those rules directly or indirectly, actually or potentially hinder free movement within the internal market, a Member State can attempt to maintain its national legislation by invoking a ground for justification. It is important to deal with a particular case in this order: it must first be determined whether the free movement rules apply; then it must be determined whether they are infringed by the national measure (e.g. a rule of property law); finally, it must be determined whether or not that national measure can be justified. If the application of the free movement rules is denied at the outset because of a 'too indirect and uncertain' effect on the internal market,[223] something which, as we have seen in this chapter,

219 Impact Assessment at 3.3.
220 Impact Assessment at 3.3.
221 Impact Assessment at 4.1. How would the problem evolve, all things being equal?
222 Ramaekers 2012, p. 2. See also the Explanatory Memorandum to the Regulation, at 3.1. *Legal basis*.
223 The Court took this route in *Krantz*: *supra*, section 3.4.4.

should only be taken into account in the case of a non-discriminatory measure which restricts access to the market or because the national law is highly likely to be justified anyway, one foregoes what Klauer calls the 'signal function' of the application of the free movement rules:

> 'A review, whereby an obstacle to the internal market is determined, but which nevertheless declares this obstacle to be justified on the basis of mandatory requirements in the public interest, is not at all a useless exercise. It is exactly these cases that possess an important *signal function*, in that they point out where private law does not comply adequately with the internal market and at what point potential harmonisation efforts should be initiated.'[224] [translation ER]

In other words, it is important to establish first whether a national rule falls within the scope of application of the free movement provisions, and whether the free movement is hindered by the national measure, before discussing the justifiability of the national measure. Only by following these steps can obstacles to the internal market be discovered, even if they are justifiable for the moment and can the Commission decide whether or not to take legislative action to remedy these obstacles.

If a Member State invokes a justification ground, the CJEU evaluates it on the basis of two criteria: whether the national rule pursues an aim which constitutes a mandatory requirement in the public interest; and whether the rule is proportionate to the aim pursued. The proportionality test will be dealt with separately in section 7.1. It is moreover important to keep in mind that grounds for justification must be analysed on a case-by-case basis. It can therefore not be said that if a particular justification ground has been accepted by the CJEU once that it can always be relied on in the future.

Several justification grounds could be, and have been, invoked. For directly and indirectly discriminatory measures, only the limited list of justifications as provided in the Treaty applies. Article 36 TFEU offers a set of justifications that may be used by a Member State to justify a measure infringing the free movement of goods.[225] Articles 45, 52 and 65 contain similar provisions for the other freedoms.

224 Klauer 1998, p. 73-74: '[E]ine Überprüfung, die ein Hindernis für eine Grundfreiheit konstatiert, dieses Hindernis jedoch aus zwingenden Allgemeinwohlinteressen für gerechtfertigt erklärt [ist] keineswegs vergebene Mühe. Gerade solche Fälle besitzen eine wichtige Signalfunktion, indem sie darauf hinweisen, wo es an der Funktionsadäquanz des Privatrechts für den Binnenmarkt fehlt und an welcher Stelle eventuelle Harmonisierungsbemühungen ansetzen sollten.'

225 Art. 36 (ex Art. 30 EC) reads: 'The provisions of Articles 34 and 35 shall not preclude prohibitions or restrictions on imports, exports or goods in transit justified on grounds of public morality, public policy or public security; the protection of health and life of humans, animals or plants; the protection of national treasures possessing artistic, historic or archaeological value; or the protection of industrial and commercial property. Such prohibitions or restrictions shall not, however, constitute a means of arbitrary discrimination or a disguised restriction on trade between Member States.'

One possible justification ground is public policy. Public policy is of special relevance for property law because of the mandatory character of many property law rules, the *numerus clausus*, the closed list of property rights, in particular. The *numerus clausus* limits parties in the creation of property rights: it determines what property rights they can create, how to create them and what the content can or cannot be. In many legal systems the mandatory character of property law is achieved by determining that the rules are of public policy. As a result, parties may not deviate from them by contract.[226] Rules of private international law are often also rules of public policy. The private international law rule *lex rei sitae* is almost always of public policy, so private parties cannot deviate from it. It can therefore be assumed that Member States would offer public policy as a justification ground for maintaining their rules of property law.[227] It must be noted, that this concerns public policy as interpreted under national private law, but there is no reason to assume that it would not be covered by the public policy exception of Article 36 TFEU.[228]

For non-discriminatory measures, a Member State can also rely on the open-ended list of mandatory requirements in the public interest, as originally developed under the *Cassis the Dijon* case law of the CJEU.[229] These justification grounds must be of a non-economic nature.[230] An argument often made by property lawyers is that the application of European law to national property law could force a Member State to make changes that could disrupt the coherence of the national system of property law.[231] For instance, if foreign property rights would have to be accepted under the doctrine of mutual recognition, as developed in the area of free

226 Perhaps the best example of this is offered by French law in Art. 6 *Code civil*, which states: 'On ne peut déroger, par des conventions particulières, aux lois qui intéressent l'ordre public et les bonnes moeurs' (One may not deviate, by private agreement, from the laws that concern public policy and good morals [translation ER]). See also Art. 3 *Code civil*: 'Les immeubles, même ceux possédés par des étrangers, sont régis par la loi française.' (Immovables, even those possessed by foreigners, are governed by French law. [translation ER]).

227 One should keep the following in mind, however: 'That something has long been practised by Europeans is not enough for it to merit respect.' Weatherill 2004b, p. 652. Moreover Flessner 2010, p. 134: 'Gegen die Berufung auf den Typenzwang lässt sich zunächst dasselbe einwenden wie gegen das Argument mit den Verkehrsinteressen generell. Sie blockiert die Bewegungsfreiheit der Beteiligten viel zu pauschal, zur Wahrung eines dogmatischen Prinzips und ohne Rücksicht darauf, ob im konkreten Fall der Rechtsverkehr durch die Rechtswahl überhaupt nachteilig betroffen wäre.'

228 Hartkamp 2007, p. 13; Barnard 2010, p. 151.

229 Case 120/78, *Rewe-Zentral AG* v *Bundesmonopolverwaltung für Branntwein* (*Cassis de Dijon*) [1979] ECR 649, para. 8: 'Obstacles to movement within the Community resulting from disparities between the national laws relating to the marketing of the products in question must be accepted in so far as those provisions may be recognized as being necessary in order to satisfy mandatory requirements relating in particular to the effectiveness of fiscal supervision, the protection of public health, the fairness of commercial transactions and the defence of the consumer.'

230 Barnard 2010, p. 165-171.

231 *Cf* Kieninger 2008a, p. 190.

movement of goods, the balance that is achieved at a national level through the national system of property rights could be jeopardized. It is likely that the CJEU would accept the argument regarding the coherence of the system as a legitimate aim to be pursued. It has already accepted this argument in tax law cases and insurance cases.[232]

Another ground for justification could be the protection of creditors. The existence of property rights outside the property rights recognized by the national systems of property law may lead to difficulties in insolvency situations. Property security rights offer the holder priority in insolvency. Partly because of this effect their creation and existence is strictly regulated. The forced recognition of a foreign property security right can lead to the forced recognition of priority. Creditors can be expected to take the existence of security rights under their own national law into account, and may even be expected to find out if their debtor has created property security rights, but they can perhaps not be expected to know about the existence and scope of foreign rights that also give priority. It would moreover be very difficult to establish ranking in the first place between property security rights created in several Member States. This line of argumentation has also been used in company law cases, where it was accepted as a ground for justification.[233]

These three grounds - public policy, coherence of the system and protection of creditors - seem to offer the most likely grounds for justification of a national rule of property law that hinders free movement within the internal market.[234] However, even if such a ground for justification is accepted, the measure, i.e. the *lex rei sitae* rule in combination with the applicability of national property law that leads to the transformation or even complete loss of the foreign property right, must still pass the proportionality test.

### 7.1. *Proportionality*

The proportionality test generally consists of two elements: suitability and necessity. Is the measure suitable for the aim to be achieved and is the measure necessary in the sense that there are no less restrictive means that could achieve the same aim?[235]

Member States may argue that their system of property law is of public policy and that they are allowed to organize their own system of property law,[236]

232 See, for instance, case C-204/90, *Bachmann* [1992] ECR I-249, paras. 17-28; case C-279/93, *Schumacker* [1995] ECR I-225, para. 40; case C-35/98, *Verkooijen* [2000] ECR I-4071, para. 56. See also Steiner & Woods 2009, p. 390 and Craig & De Búrca 2011, p. 696 with further references in footnote 24.

233 Case C-167/01, *Kamer van Koophandel en Fabrieken voor Amsterdam* v *Inspire Art Ltd.* [2003] ECR I-10155, para 135.

234 See also Akkermans & Ramaekers 2013 at II.C. *Are there grounds for justification?*

235 Craig & De Búrca 2011, p. 94.

236 Wilmowsky 1996, p. 136.

especially because there is no coherent European system of property law yet.[237] This argument may be used by Member States as a basis for their reasoning that their internal system is balanced - e.g. to protect unsecured creditors - on national property rights alone. However, an outright refusal to recognize foreign property rights may go further than necessary to achieve the aim of protecting unsecured creditors.[238] Additional registration requirements might be able to serve the same purpose without the secured creditor losing his rights, thereby preventing unsecured creditors from receiving unreasonably extensive protection at the disadvantage of secured creditors.[239] Such requirements could be comparable to labelling requirements often imposed by the Court in free movement of goods cases. Labelling requirements are regarded as less far-reaching than an outright refusal of access of a product to a Member State's market.[240]

Swiss law provides an interesting example in this regard. Article 102(2) of the Swiss Private International Law Statute (or *Bundesgesetz über das Internationale Privatrecht*) provides that when an object, in relation to which a reservation of ownership has been validly established in another country, comes into Switzerland, the foreign reservation of ownership is allowed to remain in existence for three months.[241] During that period, the reservation of ownership must be registered in accordance with Swiss law to comply with the Swiss requirements for a valid reservation of ownership.[242] In this way, Swiss law essentially provides a '*terme de grace*' for foreign reservation of ownership clauses.[243] This example shows that there already exists in practice a less far-reaching measure than an outright and immediate refusal of a foreign property right at the border.

The argument that the internal coherence of the system of property rights needs to be protected from too much European influence can also be questioned. The argument is used in social security and tax cases but will only be accepted by the CJEU if the national system is indeed applied coherently.[244] When this is not the case, such a ground for justification will not be proportional to the aim pursued. Studies have shown that national systems of property law, although Member States

237 Kieninger 2008a, p. 190.

238 See also Akkermans & Ramaekers 2013 at II.D. *Proportionality*.

239 Wilmowsky 1996, p. 148-149; Case 178/84, *Commission* v *Germany* [1987] ECR 1227, para 28.

240 Barnard 2010, p. 175 *et seq*.

241 Art. 102(2) Swiss IPRG reads: 'Gelangt eine bewegliche Sache in die Schweiz und ist an ihr im Ausland ein Eigentumsvorbehalt gültig begründet worden, der den Anforderungen des schweizerischen Rechts nicht genügt, so bleibt der Eigentumsvorbehalt in der Schweiz noch während drei Monaten gültig.' See also Van der Weide 2006, p. 38-39.

242 Art. 715(1) Swiss Civil Code (ZGB): 'Der Vorbehalt des Eigentums an einer dem Erwerber übertragenen beweglichen Sache ist nur dann wirksam, wenn er an dessen jeweiligem Wohnort in einem vom Betreibungsbeamten zu führenden öffentlichen Register eingetragen ist.'

243 Snijders 2006, p. 156; Von Bar & Drobnig 2002, No. 735; Kreuzer 1990, p. 625-626.

244 Kieninger 1996, p. 191.

may want to defend this, are not completely internally coherent.[245] A justification on this ground is therefore not likely to be accepted.

Finally, it is also doubtful whether the argument that foreign property rights are not recognized, because creditors must be protected against unknowable rights, will hold under the proportionality test. Many Member States know, within their own system, non-possessory security rights which are not visible to the outside world because possession is not transferred. Examples are the Dutch non-possessory pledge or the German transfer of ownership for security purposes and reservation of title clauses in general.[246] Sometimes, publicity is ensured through registration, but this is not always the case. As a result, creditors already have to take into account the possibility that security rights exist without their knowledge.[247] An interesting example in this regard is provided by a German judgment of the *Landesgericht* (LG) Bremen of 2 April 1959. The court recognized outright an American non-possessory 'maritime lien'. It held that such recognition did not violate the German principles underlying the possessory right of pledge, given that these principles had been breached already anyway with the introduction into German law of the *Sicherungseigentum*.[248] It is difficult to argue that having to take into account non-possessory, invisible, security rights is acceptable for domestic but not for foreign security rights, especially because publicity through registration could also be achieved for foreign security rights, albeit that a more complex system may be needed. As Flessner states, it is illogical to elevate the protection of third parties to the status of 'Ideal' in private international law, whereas internally the protection of third parties seems less important.[249]

All in all it can be concluded that, while there may be several grounds to justify that national rules of property law and the *lex rei sitae* (potentially) hinder free movement within the internal market, which will be accepted by the CJEU, it may be difficult for Member States to prove that these national measures are proportional to the aims they pursue. This will have to be evaluated on a case-by-case basis.

## Conclusion

This chapter has explored the application of the rules on the four freedoms to property law. The boundaries of the scope of application of the free movement rules are not exactly known, but it follows from the CJEU's case law that they are interpreted very broadly. In addition, the CJEU's very narrow interpretation of

245 Rutgers 1999, p. 202; Struycken 2007, p. 368 *et seq*; Akkermans 2008, p. 528; Verhagen 2007a, p. 38.
246 Van Erp & Akkermans 2012, p. 476, Note 4 to excerpt 5.50 (E&W).
247 *Cf* Kieninger 1996, p. 167, 181.
248 LG Bremen 2 April 1959, IPRspr. 1960/1961, No. 43 as discussed and referred to by Van der Weide 2006, p. 109-110.
249 Flessner 2010, p. 136.

what constitutes a so-called purely internal situation makes it difficult to argue that property law cases fall outside the scope of application of the free movement rules, because there is no cross-border element to them. Even with regard to property law, purely internal situations remain the exception and not the rule.

The purpose of this chapter was to determine whether the rules on the four freedoms can be applied to property law and if so, whether the differences between the national property law systems, in combination with the *lex rei sitae* rule, infringe the rules on free movement. A final step was then to see whether such infringements could be justified. To answer these questions, two sub-topics have been addressed.

The first sub-topic was the question, whether the Court applies a discrimination test or a market access test to determine whether a national rule infringes the rules on free movement. This is important because rules of national property law will generally apply equally to all goods and persons within a Member State's territory, regardless of the country of origin. They are therefore non-discriminatory measures, which can only be caught with a market access test and not with a discrimination test. With regard to the free movement of capital, services and persons a market access test is indeed applied. The situation under the free movement of goods is less straightforward, due to the distinction that the Court has made in its *Keck* judgment between rules relating to product characteristics and rules relating to selling arrangements. Initially, the Court seemed to go back to a discrimination test for rules relating to selling arrangements - and property law rules must probably be classified as rules relating to selling arrangements. However, the *Trailers* case has re-drawn the lines between product characteristics, selling arrangements and other measures having an effect equivalent to quantitative restrictions and has confirmed the trend towards a market access test in the area of free movement of goods. A market access test can therefore be used across the board to determine whether or not property law and the *lex rei sitae* hinder any of the four freedoms.

The second sub-topic was the question whether there is a *de minimis* requirement when applying the rules on free movement. With regard to the free movement of goods, the starting point was always that there was no *de minimis* requirement. With the introduction of a market access test, however, a *de minimis* requirement seems to be applied by the Court sometimes to mitigate the potentially far-reaching effects of the market access test. With regard to the other freedoms, there also seems to be no *de minimis* requirement, except in cases that concern a national non-discriminatory measure, to which, again, a market access test is applied. One has to keep in mind, though, that, even if there is a *de minimis* requirement, this does not necessarily mean that property law rules cannot be caught under the rules on free movement. It is submitted that the effect on the internal market from the differing national property law systems in combination with the *lex rei sitae* rule is sufficiently substantial to fulfil a *de minimis* requirement. The *Krantz* case was the only case in which this was contested, but national cases show that cross-border trade is indeed substantially hindered by the differences between national systems of property law and the inability for traders to choose the applicable law to their property relationship due to the *lex rei sitae*.[250]

The CJEU held in *Krantz* that the effect of the national measure was indeed too indirect and uncertain to bring the case within the scope of the free movement of goods. It has however been argued that this holding was incorrect.[251] The essence of the *Krantz* case was the recognition of a foreign property security right and thereby automatically the problem of ranking of several security rights - including a foreign security right - in insolvency proceedings. This ranking includes rights held by the tax authorities. Under Dutch law, the rights held by the tax authorities rank higher than a reservation of ownership clause. Because the German reservation of ownership clause held by Krantz GmbH was not recognized outright in the Netherlands but transferred into a Dutch reservation of ownership, Krantz GmbH lost their ownership when the tax authorities executed their rights and seized all the goods present at the debtor's premises. When *Krantz* is considered from this perspective, it is not at all an 'unusual constellation of facts' as the Court referred to it. Rather, such property security rights frequently need to be taken into account in insolvency proceedings. I would agree with Klauer that

> '[i]f the seller assumed that the buyer would stay solvent and willing to pay, then he would not need to create a security right. It is simply naive to assume, that the actions of a supplier would not be affected, if he had to fear that his security right would be lost or that its effectiveness would be diminished when crossing the border.'[252]

It was unfortunate that the CJEU applied a *de minimis* test in *Krantz* because it brought the case outside the scope of application of the free movement of goods, thereby precluding the possibility to discuss possible justification grounds and their proportionality to the aim pursued.[253]

These two sub-topics form the foundation to the argument that the rules on the four freedoms can indeed be applied to national rules of property law. The rules on free movement of goods are more likely to deal with situations involving movable objects; the rules on the other freedoms are more likely to deal with situations involving immovable objects.[254] It was thereafter established that the

250 Kieninger 2004b contains 15 case studies on this exact problem.

251 *Supra*, section 3.4.5. See also Kieninger 1996, p. 157: 'Selbst wenn man also eine de minimis-Regel für richtig halten würde, könnte die Spürbarkeit in den hier interessierenden Fällen nicht verneint werden.'

252 Klauer 1998p. 91: 'Ginge der Verkäufer davon aus, dass der Käufer zahlungsfähig und zahlungswillig bleibt, so bräuchte er kein Sicherungsmittel zu vereinbaren. Es ist geradezu naiv anzunehmen, es habe keinen Einfluss auf die Handlungsweise eines Lieferanten, wenn dieser befürchten muss, dass seine Sicherungsmittel beim Überschreiten der Grenze untergehen oder in ihrer Wirksamkeit beeinträchtigt werden.' [Translation in text by ER]

253 See also *supra*, section 7.1.

254 So far, there has been no case law concerning free movement law and claims; *cf* Kieninger 2004b, p. 18 *et seq*.

differences between the national systems of property law, in combination with the *lex rei sitae* rule, can cause obstacles to the internal market. Because movables cross borders, the seller of those goods is confronted with a possible loss of his property rights in relation to those goods, resulting in an increase in costs for the seller or price for the buyer,[255] because more expensive security rights are needed or because the seller calculates the risk that he loses his rights to the goods into the price of the goods. That can also mean that the seller looses a competitive edge on the market, which he might otherwise have had. He may even decide not to conduct cross-border business anymore. We have also seen that the rules on free movement of capital, persons and services can have an effect within national property law because they prohibit certain national rules that limit the possibilities of acquiring immovable property (e.g. *Reisch*) or because they prohibit certain national rules that limit the possibilities of providing or acquiring financial or other services related to the acquisition of immovable property (e.g. *Parodi*).

However, the fact that national property law rules can fall under the scope of application of the rules on free movement does not necessarily mean that they need to be changed or removed at national level. It is very likely that the Court will accept grounds for justification offered by the Member States to maintain those rules. The most likely grounds for justification are public policy, to maintain the coherence of the national property law system and to protect creditors. Whether these justification grounds can be invoked, and whether the way in which Member States try to achieve these aims is proportionate, is for the Court to decide on a case-by case-basis. In any case, it is important to go through all these steps instead of taking a shortcut, like the Court did in *Krantz,* in order to fulfil the 'signal function' towards the Commission that harmonization might be needed.[256]

Finally, every section on one of the four freedoms was concluded with an explanation of how the rules on that particular freedom (potentially) affect national property law. They may lead to the recognition of foreign property rights by receiving Member States and may broaden the possibilities to acquire and use immovable property in another Member State.

255 *Cf* Strese 2006, p. 194.
256 *Supra,* section 7.

Chapter 3

# THE EU'S COMPETENCE TO REGULATE PROPERTY LAW

## Introduction - The Relationship between European Law and Property Law

The previous chapter, which explored the relationship between the rules on free movement within the European Union's internal market and national rules of property law, showed that the differences between the Member States' national property laws and their mandatory character can and do lead to obstacles to the internal market. This can be seen as an indication that the EU should become involved in property law so as to reduce or remove these obstacles to the internal market. This chapter therefore investigates whether and to what extent the European legislature would have the competence to regulate matters of property law. Article 345 of the Treaty on the Functioning of the European Union (TFEU) is crucial in this respect. The Article reads: 'The Treaties shall in no way prejudice the rules in Member States governing the system of property ownership.'

It is not entirely clear what the meaning of this provision is and whether or not it says anything about the competence of the EU to legislate in the field of property law. It is therefore important, before discussing to what extent the EU should regulate or harmonize property law, to uncover the meaning of Article 345 TFEU. This chapter presents the results of extensive research into the origins of Article 345 and its present-day use by the European Institutions. The chapter ends with an analysis of the potential legal bases which the European legislature could use to enact rules of property law, provided that Article 345 does not prevent it from doing so.

## 1. Article 345 of the Treaty on the Functioning of the European Union[1]

The meaning and scope of Article 345 TFEU are not entirely clear. Not much is known about the origins of the Article, nor about its exact meaning and effect on the rest of the Treaty or on national law. The phrasing of the Article is unfortunate, its wording is so broad that the meaning becomes difficult to determine. Looking purely at the wording of Article 345, it could be argued that property law is exempted from the influence of European law.[2] The Article seems to indicate that property law is exclusively for the Member States to regulate and, therefore, that the European legislature has no competence to legislate in this area. However, reality shows a different picture than a literal reading of the Article would suggest. There is existing European legislation that deals with property law – as will be seen in Chapter 4 –, there is proposed legislation that will deal with property law and there are several decisions of the Court of Justice of the European Union (CJEU) that deal directly and indirectly with matters of property law.[3] In other words, it seems that Article 345 does not prevent the European legislature from acting, nor does it seem to prevent the CJEU from making a ruling that has far-reaching effects in the area of property law.[4]

The uncertainty surrounding the Article's scope and meaning could be the reason that legal scholars, the European Commission and the CJEU all seem uncertain how to handle this Article. Moreover, the cases where Article 345 TFEU comes up are not usually fundamental cases in the development of EU law. Perhaps these reasons also explain why literature and case law on Article 345 is hardly available.[5]

1 Part of the research underlying this chapter was previously published in the European Law Journal, in an article co-authored with Bram Akkermans: Akkermans & Ramaekers 2010.

2 See for a discussion of Art. 345 TFEU *inter alia* Van Erp 2006b, p. 6-7; Akkermans 2008, p. 508-509; Caramelo Gomes 2008, p. 239; Sagaert 2007, p. 301-333.

3 See, for instance, Dir. 2002/47/EC of the European Parliament and the Council of 6 June 2002 on financial collateral arrangements; Green Paper Mortgage Credit in the EU, COM(2005) 237 final; White Paper on Mortgage Credit Markets; COM(2007) 807 final; Reg. 650/2012/EU on international successions, [2012] *OJ* L 201/107; and CJEU Case C-367/98, *Commission* v *Portugal* [2002] ECR I-4731, para. 48; Case C-483/99, *Commission* v *France* [2002] ECR I-4781, para. 44; Case C-503/99, *Commission* v *Belgium* [2002] ECR I-4809, para. 44; Case C-302/97, *Klaus Konle* v *Republik Österreich* [1999] ECJ I-3099; and Joined Cases C-515/99, C-519/99 to C-524/99 and C-526/99 to C-540/99 *Hans Reisch and others* v *Bürgermeister des Landeshauptstadt Salzburg and others* [2002] ECR I-2157.

4 *Cf* Case C-117/06, *Möllendorf and Möllendorf-Niehuus* [2007] ECR I-8361 and its discussion in Van Erp 2009a and Lavranos 2008.

5 Riegel exclaimed in 1979 already: 'Es ist erstaunlich, dass es zu diesen Fragen kaum Literatur gibt, obwohl sie doch von zentraler Bedeutung sind für die bisherige und künftige Rechts- und Integrationsentwicklung der EWG.' (It is astonishing, that there is hardly any literature regarding these questions, even though they are of crucial importance for the current and future legal and integration development.) [translation ER]; Riegel 1979, p. 744-749. See however Caramelo Gomes 2008, p. 239; Devroe 1997; Bartels 1995.

This chapter purports to provide more clarity concerning the meaning of Article 345 as well as to investigate its use and interpretation in both legislation and case law. In order to do so, several steps will be taken in line with the methodology followed by the CJEU as outlined in Chapter 1.[6] In subsequent order, this chapter will deal with the linguistic interpretation of the Article, its historical development, as well as its current application by the European Commission, European Parliament and, finally, the European Court of Justice. The Article will be evaluated both from the point of view of European law and from the point of view of property law.

Taking a look at the existing legislation as well as future legislation is increasingly becoming more relevant with the nationalization of banks by Member States in the current financial crisis. One of the questions in the work of the European Commission is whether such nationalization is to be considered as State aid under Article 106 TFEU. If Article 345 would prevent the application of European law to national property law, the measure nationalizing a financial institution would possibly be exempted from scrutiny under European law and therefore also from the supervision of the European Commission under Article 106.

## 2. Methodology of the CJEU

The Treaty of Rome, also known as the E(uropean)E(conomic)C(ommunity) Treaty, was originally drafted in French. The predecessor of Article 345 in the EEC Treaty was Article 222. As this thesis is written in English, emphasis will lie on a comparison between the French and English language versions of Article 345 TFEU. However, the comparison will not stop there. Given that all language versions of the Treaties are equally authentic, a linguistic comparison based solely on the French and English language versions would constitute an insufficient basis for any conclusion that would be drawn concerning the meaning of Article 345.[7] The Courts of the European Union have to take into account all language versions when interpreting a provision of the Treaties.[8] This causes very particular problems of a linguistic nature. The method of legal interpretation adopted by the CJEU to cope with these problems has been described in Chapter 1 and it will now be applied to Article 345. With the use of the Court's method, the meaning of Article 345 may be uncovered. It is however important to note at this point that it would be very difficult, if not practically impossible, to research all the different language versions of Article 345. Furthermore, it would not be necessary to do so as the wording of the Article has not changed since it was drafted in 1957 and the wording has barely changed since its early predecessor - Article 83 of the Treaty establishing the European Coal and Steel Community (ECSC), which was only authoritative in

6 Chapter 1 at 3. *Linguistic roblems: the method of the Court of Justice of the European Union.*

7 This follows from Article 314 EC, which lists the 23 authentic versions of the Treaty. See also EEC Council Regulation no. 1, 6 October 1958, *OJ* L 17/385.

8 The Treaty on European Union and the Treaty on the Functioning of the European Union [2010] *OJ* C 83/13 and 83/47.

French - was drafted. What is even more, Article 345 'is in the unique position of deriving its authority directly from the Schuman Declaration of 9 May 1950, on which it has been based'.[9] The key terms in Article 345, which will be discussed below, have literally been taken over from the Schuman Declaration, at least as far as the French version is concerned: 'L'institution de la Haute Autorité ne préjuge en rien du régime de propriété des entreprises.'[10]

It is for these reasons that the research into the meaning of Article 345 will be limited to the four original drafting languages - French, German, Dutch and Italian - with special emphasis on French; the English version, being a later translation, will be reviewed against the four original versions.

## 3. Interpretation of Article 345 TFEU

Research that has been conducted over the last decades shows that neither the scope of application nor the exact meaning of Article 345 is clear from its wording.[11] In this paragraph, Article 345 is dissected into three different parts. These parts are evaluated together in an attempt to determine the precise meaning of the Article. For reasons outlined above,[12] I rely mostly on the French version of Article 345, which reads: 'Les traités ne *préjugent* en rien *le régime de la propriété* dans les États membres.' [emphasis added]

The term *préjugent* is evaluated in subsection 3.1; subsection 3.2 is devoted to the evaluation of the expression *régime de la propriété*; and the expression *Les traités* is dealt with in subsection 3.3.

### 3.1. *Linguistics: Prejudice, Prejudge or Preclude?*

Article 345 states that the Treaties shall in no way *prejudice* Member States' rules governing the system of property ownership. The term 'prejudice' is a vague term and it is unclear whether or not it means that the EU legislature will refrain from interfering in the property law systems of the Member States. The examination into this is further complicated by the fact that the different language versions of Article 345 and its surrounding provisions do not always match. For example:

The English version of Article 345 reads: 'The Treaties shall in no way *prejudice* the rules in Member States governing the *system of property ownership*.' [emphasis added]

The French version reads: 'Les Traités ne *préjugent* en rien le *régime de la propriété* dans les États membres.' [emphasis added]

9 A.G. Colomer's Opinion to joined cases C-367/98, C-483/99 and C-503/99 [2002] ECR I-4731, para. 45.

10 The full text of the Declaration can be found at: <http://www.robert-schuman.eu/declaration_9mai.php>.

11 Bartels 1995, p. 244-51; Sagaert 2007, p. 302 *et seq.*

12 Section 2.

The German version reads: 'Die Verträge *lassen* die *Eigentumsordnung* in den verschiedenen Mitgliedstaaten *unberührt.*' [emphasis added]

The Dutch version reads: 'De Verdragen *laten* de regeling van het *eigendomsrecht* in de lidstaten *onverlet.*' [emphasis added]

The Italian version reads: 'I trattati lasciano del tutto *impregiudicato* il *regime di proprietà* esistente negli Stati membri.' [emphasis added]

First of all, it is doubtful that 'to prejudice' is the most correct interpretation of the French *préjugent*. Article 55 TFEU (which used to be Article 294 EC, directly preceding Article 295 EC which is now 345 TFEU) uses the French term *préjudice*, which is also translated into English as prejudice.[13] One would think that the drafters had reasons for using different terms in French, but this difference in terminology between these Articles cannot be seen in the English language version. As a result, the English version uses a term with an uncertain sense, whereas the corresponding term in the four original language versions is clearer.[14] A comparison with the original language versions will have to indicate how the term prejudice is to be understood.

The precursor of Article 345 TFEU is Article 83 ECSC. Unlike the TFEU, the ECSC Treaty is only authoritative in French: Article 100 ECSC states that the treaty is 'rédigé en un seul exemplaire'.[15] Article 83 ECSC reads: 'L'institution de la communauté ne préjuge en rien le régime de propriété des entreprises soumises aux dispositions du présent Traité'. The term *préjuge* is used in the French version of both Article 83 ECSC and Article 345 TFEU.[16] It was already used in the Schuman Declaration. The equivalents of *préjugent* in the German and Dutch versions of Article 295 EC are *lassen unberührt* and *laten onverlet* respectively. These two expressions match; they both mean that something remains unaffected. The same goes for the Italian *lasciano impregiudicato*. Together they all match the original French expression. The French term *préjugent* is even a bit stronger in the sense that not only the systems of property ownership in the Member States remain unaffected after the entry into force of the Treaties, but it also seems to imply that the Treaties did not prejudge[17] the systems of property ownership of the Member States as they existed when the Treaties were first drafted to create the European Communities. The compatibility of the national systems of property ownership with the Treaties at

13 Art. 55 reads: 'Member States shall accord nationals of the other Member States the same treatment as their own nationals as regards participation in the capital of companies or firms within the meaning of Article 54, without prejudice to the application of the other provisions of the Treaties.'

14 Van Calster 1997, p. 374.

15 The English version states 'drawn up in a single original'. See also Van Calster 1997, p. 366.

16 Because of the change from 'This Treaty' to 'The Treaties', Art. 345 now uses the word *préjugent* instead of *préjuge*.

17 'Prejudge' is incidentally the (non-official) translation of *préjuge* in the Schuman Declaration.

that moment was assured, as was the neutral stance of the European Communities towards these systems after entry into force of the Treaties.[18]

A comparison between Article 345 TFEU and Article 346 TFEU (ex Art. 296 EC) reveals more about the use of the term prejudice. Article 346, which is also an Article that deals with exceptions to the Treaties, uses the English term preclude. It seems therefore that there is a difference between the term prejudice and the term preclude in the terminology of the EU Treaties. The French version uses the words *préjugent* in Article 345 and *ne font pas obstacle* in Article 346. This different wording could be the result of a difference in subject of the sentence: *le présent Traité* in 295 EC, *les dispositions du présent Traité* in 296 EC, but the difference in terminology seems to suggest a different meaning. The translation of *ne font pas obstacle* with preclude in the English version is accurate as preclude means preventing something from happening before it even takes place. It is therefore different from prohibiting, banning or disallowing. The term *préjugent,* which translates into the English version as prejudice, is more complicated. Prejudice as a verb generally means to cause harm to. Therefore a negative wording with the verb prejudice should be interpreted as 'without causing harm to something'.[19]

When applied to the Treaties, there is therefore a difference: preclude, preventing the application of the provisions of the Treaties in the first place is stronger than prejudice, just not causing harm to national legal systems. With respect to Article 345, therefore, the Treaties may apply but just as long as they do not cause harm to the rules governing the system of property ownership in the Member States. This seems to match the conclusion drawn above, that *préjuge/lässt unberührt/laat onverlet/lascia impregiudicato* means that nothing in the Treaties will *affect* the systems of property ownership in the Member States. However, to prejudice, understood as will not cause harm to, is less neutral than *préjuge;* it is more negative. Nevertheless, when compared to the original four language versions, it can be understood that the expression 'shall in no way prejudice' refers to the neutral stance that is taken by the European Union with regard to the way in which Member States regulate their system of property ownership.

## 3.2. *History of the Article: Relating to Undertakings or not?*

In the Treaty of Rome that was negotiated during 1955 and 1957 and signed in Rome on 25 March 1957, Article 222 EEC stated in French, as English was not yet an official language:[20] 'Le présent Traité ne préjuge en rien le régime de propriété dans les Etats Membres.'

18 Groeben 1997, 5/386-5/387.

19 The meaning of the terms used in English in this section have all been derived from the Oxford English Dictionary.

20 French was the original drafting language. However, the initial four official languages in which the Rome Treaty was drafted were French, German, Dutch and Italian. Due to the principle of equality of languages, all four versions were – with retroactive effect as it were – →

It is unclear what is exactly meant by the words *régime de propriété* or, in English, system of property ownership. A look at the *Travaux Préparatoires* of the EEC Treaty may provide more insight into the meaning of Article 345 (ex Art. 222 EEC). First of all, the search shows that the wording of the Article has differed in earlier versions of the draft of the Treaty. During the negotiation process, there were several groups dealing with the wording of the Article. The *Groupe de Rédaction* proposed the first wording on 5 December 1956:[21] 'Le présent Traité ne préjuge en rien le régime de propriété des moyens de production existant dans la Communauté.'[22]

On 18 January 1957 a special group of experts (the *Groupe du Marché Commun* (GMC)) created to assist the *Comité des Chefs de Délégation*, the gathering of delegation leaders that made most of the decisions on the content of the draft Treaty, proposed a revised version: 'Le présent Traité ne préjuge en rien le régime de propriété des entreprises soumises aux dispositions du Traité.'[23]

In the text of the GMC the archaic use of the words 'means of production' had been changed to ownership of undertakings, most likely modernizing the text but not substantially altering the content of the Article. On 21 January 1957, the same group of experts deleted the last part of the sentence *soumises aux dispositions du Traité*. This left a version of the text that is almost identical to the version that would make it into the Treaty of Rome. The only difference remained in the reference to undertakings (*des entreprises*) qualifying the system of ownership (*régime de propriété*). During an Intergovernmental Meeting (IGC) in March 1957 and not during an official meeting devoted to the wording of the Treaty provisions, the *Chefs de Délégation* met, on 6 March 1957, and removed the expression *des entreprises* from the text of the Article.[24] The changes made to the text of the Article therefore provided Article 222 EEC with its final wording.

The *Travaux Préparatoires* of Article 222 EEC do not mention more than the chronological order of the changes that have been made to the draft version of the Treaty. They do not explain why these changes were made, nor do they provide insight into whether or not the changes made, in particular by the *Comité des Chefs de Délégation*, were intended to enlarge the scope of application of the Article. As the text of the Article can be directly traced to the Schuman Declaration, it seems that altering the meaning of the Article would have been an important decision. Earlier

equally authentic; *Cf* Van Calster 1997, p. 369. The languages of the acceding Member States became equally authentic to the others upon the moment of their accession, following the Accession Treaties and Art. 55 TEU, ex Art. 314 EC.

21 Conseil des Communautés Europeennes, Archives Historiques, Negociations des Traités Instituant la communauté Economique Europeenne et la communaute europeenne de l'energie atomiche, CM 3, N. 0261, Conférence intergouvernementale: Historique des articles 210 à 225 du traité instituant la CEE.

22 Doc. MAE 641/56 (Art. 9).

23 Doc. MAE 177/57 and Doc. MAE 243/57 (Art. 43 *quater*).

24 Doc. MAE 786/57 (Art. 282).

writings concerning the meaning of Article 345 occasionally mention that this expression is left out of the final version, only to then continue by either sidestepping this point completely or by merely mentioning that further background information is not available and leaving it at that.[25] The fact that the Article was amended by the *Chefs de Délégation,* and not during an intergovernmental conference at a political level by the Ministers themselves, seems to suggest it was a mere change of wording.[26] Moreover, the lack of attention to the change seems to suggest it was considered unimportant.

In line with this reasoning, it has sometimes been concluded that Article 345 therefore deals with the ownership of undertakings only; in other words, that the European Union will not concern itself with whether undertakings are publicly or privately owned.[27] See, for instance, a statement by the CJEU in the case *Commission* v *Portugal*:

> '[Article 345 TFEU] merely signifies that each Member State may organise as it thinks fit the system of ownership of undertakings whilst at the same time respecting the fundamental freedoms enshrined in the Treaty.'[28]

This is an interesting interpretation, but whether it is correct remains unclear, just as it remains unclear why the *Chefs de Délégation* removed the reference to undertakings from the wording of the Article. If this was just an aesthetic change, the focus of the Article on means of production or undertakings subject to the Treaties remains. However, the removal of undertakings from the wording of the Article seemingly broadens its scope beyond ownership of undertakings to systems of ownership in general. Advocate-General Jacobs in his Opinion in *Spain* v *Council* carefully remarks that perhaps the reference to undertakings was removed because the Treaty not only applies to Member States but also to private individuals.[29] This, however, is a conclusion that can only be drawn in hindsight. It was through the judgments of *Van Gend & Loos*[30] and *Costa* v *E.N.E.L.*[31] that the ECJ established that the E(E)C Treaty entailed rights and obligations for individuals as well, and then only those Articles of the Treaty that were sufficiently clear and precise. These judgments were rendered after the entry into force of the Treaty and there is thus no reason to assume that the drafters of the Treaty intended its Articles to be directly applicable to individuals. The wording of the Article alone is insufficiently clear and

25 *Cf* Riegel 1979, p. 746.

26 The *Travaux Préparatoires* of the meeting of 6 March 1957 do not mention any explanation on the change in wording. MAE 786/57, Art. 232, Fiche CM3-NEGO-000268.

27 Devroe 1997.

28 Case C-367/98, *Commission* v *Portugal* [2002] ECR I-4731, para. 28.

29 Opinion delivered on 9 March 1995; para. 29.

30 Case 26/62, *Van Gend & Loos* [1963] ECR 1.

31 Case 6/64, *Costa* v *E.N.E.L.* [1964] ECR 585.

precise to have a bearing on private individuals and cannot provide complete clarity on its scope.[32]

More clarity is provided by looking back into history even further than the time the *Travaux Préparatoires* were drafted. As previously mentioned, it follows from the *Travaux Préparatoires* for Article 345 (then Art. 222) that one of the earlier versions of the Article read 'le régime de propriété des entreprises'.[33] This is not surprising, given the wording of Article 83 of the Treaty on the European Coal and Steel Community (ECSC) which was the precursor of Article 345 TFEU.[34] Unlike the TFEU, the ECSC Treaty was only authoritative in French: Article 100 ECSC states that the treaty is 'rédigé en un seul exemplaire'.[35] The term *préjuge* is used in the French version of both Article 83 ECSC and Article 345 TFEU. As was mentioned before,[36] it was also already used in the Schuman Declaration.

The interpretation given by the Court to Article 345, as can be deduced from the abovementioned judgment of *Commission* v *Portugal*, seems to lie closer to the earlier draft of Article 222 EEC, which in turn seems inspired by the text of Article 83 ECSC and the *Schuman* Declaration. Next to that, the Commission's interpretation of Article 345 as well seems to be in line with the previous versions of what used to be Article 295 EC. Its interpretation is referred to as the 'neutrality principle':

> 'The Treaty of Rome (Article 222) clearly establishes that each Member State is entitled to decide on the most appropriate form of property ownership. The Commission has

32 The Advocate-General himself concludes, regardless of his own statement, that Art. 345 is probably only relevant for nationalisation and privatisation of undertakings; para. 29. See further on the addressees of Art. 345: Burghardt 1969, p. 71. The author would agree with Riegel (Riegel 1979, p. 746), that the decision to leave out the reference to undertakings might seem to broaden the scope of the article and might cast doubt to the submission that it nevertheless still only applies to undertakings. ('Gerade die Tatsache aber, dass man letztlich eine weitere Fassung gewählt hat als ursprünglich, spricht doch eher dafür, dass dies dann auch so gemeint ist, zumal der EWGV im Gegensatz zum EGKSV ja nicht nur für Unternehmen relevant ist. Deshalb sind an der Folgerung, Art. 222 EWGV betreffe dennoch nur die Eigentumsordnung der Unternehmen, erhebliche Zweifel angebracht.') However, since there is no evidence in case law or otherwise that supports this view, we are forced to conclude, as we have, that Article 345 TFEU is still to be interpreted as referring to the ownership of undertakings only.

33 Conseil des Communautés Europeennes, Archives Historiques, Negociations des Traités Instituant la communauté Economique Europeenne et la communaute europeenne de l'energie atomiche, CM 3, N. 0261, Conférence intergouvernementale: Historique des articles 210 à 225 du traité instituant la CEE.

34 *Supra*, at section 3.1.

35 The English version states 'drawn up in a single original'. See also Van Calster 1997, p. 366.

36 *Supra*, section 2. *Methodology of the CJEU.*

therefore never taken any position on the question of public ownership and has always scrupulously ensured neutrality in its dealings with different forms of ownership.'[37]

Finally, the explanatory memoranda of the governments of the initial six Member States clarify why it is specifically the ownership of *undertakings* that is emphasized. The German *Bundesregierung,* for instance, commented that Article 222 EEC was in the Treaty because no other provision in the Treaty and no measure of the Community Institutions should be allowed to have the purpose or effect of nationalizing or privatizing undertakings.[38] Also Italy and France wanted Article 222 in the Treaty out of concern that the Community would interfere with their practice of nationalizing certain industries.[39]

Therefore, even though the reference to undertakings has been removed from Article 345 TFEU, all the above-mentioned sources indicate that the Article should still be interpreted as though that reference was still there.[40] On the basis of a historical interpretation, Article 345 therefore relates to the neutrality of the Treaties in respect to the ownership, private or public, of undertakings only.

### 3.2.1. Article 345 TFEU as seen from the Point of View of Property Law

The rules mentioned in Article 345 are the rules governing the system of property ownership, or in French *le régime de la propriété*. The Article does not state the rules of property ownership but the rules on the *system* of property ownership. It is here that an additional argument may be found in property law, rather than in European law, that might clarify the meaning of the Article.

In property law it is uncommon to speak of the system of ownership, except when defining types of ownership such as fragmented or unitary concepts of

37 EC Bulletin 7/8-1991, point 1.2.75. See further Annex 1 (Definition of terms) to the Commission White Paper on Services of General Interest: 'The term "public undertaking" is normally also used to define the ownership of the service provider. The Treaty provides for strict neutrality. It is irrelevant under Community law whether providers of services of general interest are public or private; they are subject to the same rights and obligations.' COM(2004) 374 final.

38 Rieber 1957, 312: 'Durch den Vertrag soll nicht in die rechtlichen Bestimmungen der Mitgliedstaaten eingegriffen werden, durch die das Eigentum geregelt wird. Das gilt besonders für das Eigentum an Unternehmen. Keine Bestimmung des Vertrags darf daher so ausgelegt werden und keine Maßnahme der Organe der Gemeinschaft darf zum Ziele haben, ein Unternehmen in Gemeinwirtschaft zu überführen oder umgekehrt ein im Gemeineigentum stehendes Unternehmen zu privatisieren.'

39 See, for instance, Schwarze 2000, 2334; Léger 2000, 1879; Sauter 1998, 57. One of the earliest examples is the nationalisation of the Italian electricity sector, which led to the famous *Costa* v *E.N.E.L.* judgment (Case 6/64 [1964] ECR 1141). The Commission answered to a written question from Philipp MEP concerning this intended nationalisation, that in accordance with Article 222 EEC every Member State has the right to change the system of property ownership in a sector of its economy: *OJ* 1962, No. 121, 2715-2716.

40 See, for instance, also VerLoren van Themaat 1982, p. 365.

ownership.[41] The addition of the term 'system' therefore suggests that we are not dealing with the right of ownership itself but rather with the way in which the right of ownership can be held. Burghardt gave a similar explanation only a few years after the entry into force of the EEC Treaty. According to him, the term 'system' refers to the collection of rules that regulate ownership in the broadest sense, including the rights and obligations that are attached to the right of ownership and the way in which the right of ownership can be used but also nationalizations, privatizations and expropriations.[42] He emphasized that 'system of property ownership' - and the equivalents in the original four languages - is not normally used as a legal technical term. More recently, Advocate-General Colomer gave a statement to the same effect in his Opinion of 6 November 2008 in the *Commission* v *Italy* case:[43]

> 'I therefore repeat my view that the expression "system of property ownership" contained in Article 295 EC refers not to the civil rules concerning property relationships, but to the ideal body of rules of every kind, including public law rules, which are capable of granting ownership rights in respect of a business; in other words, rules which allow the person vested with such rights to exercise decisive influence on the definition and implementation of all or some of its objectives; [...].'

In other words, a wording leaving out the word system would immediately provide a different meaning to Article 345 for a property lawyer: rules of the Member States governing *property ownership* would imply a direct effect on the right of ownership itself. It is in this regard important to refer to Article 91 of the Treaty establishing the European Atomic Energy Community (EAEC), which corresponds to Article 83 ECSC and Article 345.[44] This Article states:

> 'Le régime de propriété applicable à tous objets, matières et biens qui ne font pas l'objet d'un droit de propriété de la Communauté en vertu du présent chapitre est déterminé par la législation de chaque État membre.'[45]

A difference is made in this Article between the *régime de propriété* - system of property ownership - and a *droit de propriété* - right of ownership. For a property

41 Van der Walt & Kleyn 1989, p. 213-60.

42 Burghardt 1969, p. 18-19. See also Grabitz 2005, Art. 295 EGV, 1; Lenz 1999, 1978; Bartels 1995, p. 246.

43 Case C-326/07 [2009] ECR I-2291, para. 36. See also his earlier Opinion to joined cases C-367/98, C-483/99 and C-503/99, *Commission* v *Portugal*, at para. 54.

44 And to Art. 125 EEA, which will be discussed in section 5.2.

45 The English version states: 'The system of ownership applicable to all objects, materials and assets which are not vested in the Community under this Chapter shall be determined by the law of each Member State.' Originally the Treaty was only authentic in four languages - Art. 225 EAEC: 'This Treaty, drawn up in a single original in the Dutch, French, German and Italian languages, all four texts being equally authentic, shall be deposited in the archives of the Government of the Italian Republic, which shall transmit a certified copy to each of the governments of the other signatory States.'

lawyer these are two different things. The German version of the Article provides the same results: the German version differentiates between the term *Eigentumsordnung* (system of property ownership) and the term *Eigentumsrecht* (right of ownership). The system of property ownership concerns the entire body of rules that regulates the way in which the right of ownership is held, whereas the term ownership - or *droit de propriété/Eigentumsrecht* - refers to the (content of) the right of ownership itself.[46] Article 345 TFEU is therefore concerned with the subjects of the property relationship, namely undertakings. It excludes the application of the Treaties to the question whether these undertakings are held in private ownership - by shareholders - or in public ownership - by a Member State government. Given the limitation to undertakings, Article 345 is concerned only with legal persons and not natural persons as the subjects of the property relationship, which means that it has no bearing on consumers. Most importantly, the Article does not concern the content of the right of ownership, nor does it concern what types of things (e.g. tangibles or intangibles) can form the objects of a right of ownership. This means that undertakings, and the question whether or not they are owned publicly or privately, *are excluded* from the scope of application of the Treaties, but that national rules governing the right of ownership and the objects of ownership *are not excluded* from the scope of application of the Treaties.

Concluding, on the basis of the foregoing, that 'system of property ownership' refers not to the right of ownership itself but only to the way in which it is held, the continued reference to undertakings and whether they are held in public or private ownership becomes easier to understand.

### 3.2.2. Private or Public Property Law?

Another possibility would be to distinguish, with regard to the interpretation of 'system of property ownership', between private property law and public property law. Private property law would then be the area of law regulating relationships of persons with regard to objects, in civil law countries primarily to be found in the civil code. Public property law would include areas of law such as planning law, environmental law, land taxation and possibly even human rights law: think of the right to property as laid down in Article 1 of Protocol I to the European Convention on Human Rights and in Article 17 of the EU Charter of Fundamental Rights and similarly the right to property as laid down in many constitutions of the EU Member States.[47] Article 345 TFEU could in that case be interpreted as excluding from the scope of the Treaty only one of these two branches of property law, namely

46 See to this effect Groeben 1997, 5/386-5/387. The same is true for the Italian version, which differentiates between *il regime di proprietà and un diritto di proprietà.*

47 See e.g. Art. 14 of the German *Grundgesetz,* Art. 14 of the Dutch *Grondwet,* Art. 17 of the French *Déclaration des Droits de l'Homme et du Citoyen de 1789,* and Art. 42 of the Italian *Costituzione.*

public property law.[48] This interpretation can be deduced from the focus placed on ownership of undertakings in previous versions of Article 345.

Whether the European legislature would actually distinguish between private property law and public property law in this manner remains to be seen. As explained in Chapter 1,[49] the EU generally does not classify legislation in areas of law along the same lines as national legislatures do because EU law is competence-driven. Nevertheless, presuming that the European legislature would distinguish between private and public property law, one has to conclude, on the basis of the other findings described in this chapter, that Article 345 would exclude *public* property law from the scope of application of the Treaties, but not *private* property law. Whether ownership of an undertaking is in the hands of the State or in private hands, i.e. whether an undertaking is nationalized or privatized, would be classified as public property law. This is in line with the previous conclusion that Article 345 only concerns the system of property ownership of undertakings and not the entire private law area of property law.

It may be difficult to draw a strict line separating public from private property law, and this line may of course be drawn differently in different Member States. National rules on expropriation, for instance, are arguably more of a public law nature and would because of Article 345 TFEU not be 'prejudiced' by the Treaties. Until the EU Charter of Fundamental Rights became binding with the entry into force of the Lisbon Treaty it was more likely, however, that the EU would not interfere with national rules on expropriation, not because of Article 345 TFEU, but because that was the domain of Article 1 First Protocol of the European Convention on Human Rights. However, since the right to property is now also protected under Article 17 of the Charter, national rules on expropriation may fall within the scope of application of the Treaties after all, in spite of Article 345. It always remains the case, though, that the Charter only applies to Member States when they are implementing EU law. Therefore, national rules on expropriation that have nothing to do with the implementation of EU law - and they probably do not - will not be affected by the Treaties.[50]

On the other hand, national rules excluding certain objects from private ownership (and which therefore regulate which types of things can be the objects of

48 The author wishes to thank Professor George Gretton, University of Edinburgh, for suggesting this possible interpretation of Article 345 TFEU.

49 Chapter 1 at 2. The acquis method: defining EU property law.

50 *Cf* case 40/11, *Yoshikazu Iida* v *Stadt Ulm* (8 November 2012, n.y.r.), para. 78: 'As to the fundamental rights mentioned by the referring court [...] it must be borne in mind that, in accordance with Article 51(1) of the Charter [of Fundamental Rights], its provisions are addressed to the Member States only when they are implementing European Union law. Under Article 51(2) of the Charter, it does not extend the field of application of European Union law beyond the powers of the Union, and it does not establish any new power or task for the Union, or modify powers and tasks as defined in the Treaties. Accordingly, the Court is called on to interpret, in the light of the Charter, the law of the European Union within the limits of the powers conferred on it (see *Dereci and Others*, paragraph 71).'

the right of ownership)[51] may be considered to be more of a private law nature. Given that Article 345 would not apply to such rules, they would come under the scope of application of the Treaties. This argument is supported by what was seen in Chapter 2 with regard to the Spanish *Ley de Costas*.[52] This Spanish law excludes certain coastal regions from private ownership and is likely to be in violation of the Treaties' rules on free movement of capital.

### 3.3. *'The Treaties' to which Article 345 TFEU Refers*

The words 'the Treaties' in Article 345 refer to the TEU and the TFEU. They seem to refer to the free movement of goods, persons, services and capital, the rules of EU Competition law, as well as the Articles in the Treaties providing rights directly, for instance, Article 9 TEU that creates European citizenship and Articles 20 *et seq.* TFEU attaching rights to European citizenship, and the Articles providing a legal basis for secondary EU legislation.[53] There are other Articles in the TFEU that also exempt the application of the Treaty but which use different words. For example, Article 346 TFEU mentions 'the provisions of the Treaties' rather than 'the Treaties' only. Article 55 TFEU (ex Art. 294 EC) mentions 'the other provisions of the Treaties'.[54] It is unclear whether there is a difference between these two wordings.[55]

The short wording 'the Treaties' leaves open whether secondary EU legislation can be enacted contrary to Article 345 TFEU, in the sense that it affects the Member States' rules on their system of property ownership. It would then technically be the secondary European legislation that would be contrary to Article 345 and no longer the provisions in the Treaties themselves. This question is relevant as Article 345 is occasionally used by Members of the European Parliament or by the European Commission to attempt to prevent secondary legislation from being enacted.[56] As will be shown in Chapter 4, the EU has already enacted a number of regulations and directives that have an effect on the national systems of property law. It would appear that in those instances Article 345 has not prevented the European legislature from legislating.

51 See *supra*, section 3.2.1.

52 Chapter 2, section 4.3. *Obstacles to the free movement of capital.*

53 On rights derived from Art. 21 TFEU (ex Art. 18 EC) see Case C-353/06, *Grunkin-Paul* [2008] ECR I-7639.

54 See also Artt. 25 (to the other provisions of the Treaties), 122 (to the other procedures provided for in the Treaties), 140 (to the other provisions of the Treaties), 212 (to the other provisions of the Treaties), 226 (to the powers conferred by the Treaties), 262 (to the other provisions of the Treaties), and 325 (to the other provisions of the Treaties).

55 It might be that this difference has gone unnoticed thus far.

56 See e.g. Green Paper on Wills and Succession COM(2005) 65 final and the questions of the Members of the European Parliament mentioned *infra* in section 4.

### 3.4. *Combining the Above: a Possible Interpretation of Article 345 TFEU*

Taking all of the above into account, it is possible to formulate a most likely interpretation of Article 345, against which the current use and interpretations by the European legislature and Courts can be tested. The following interpretation will be revisited in the conclusion of this chapter to see whether the interpretation is sufficiently accurate or might need adaptation in light of, for instance, CJEU judgments.

Article 345 TFEU, formerly 295 EC and 222 EEC, is an Article that limits, but does not prevent, the application of the Treaties as a whole to the way in which rules of a Member State deal with the right of ownership of undertakings. The Article does not provide powers to the European Union to legislate in the field of property law, nor does it give powers to the Member States.[57]

The conclusion can be drawn from analysis of the *Travaux Préparatoires* and the predecessors of Article 345 - in particular Article 83 ECSC - that Article 345 only concerns the private or public ownership of undertakings, with which the EU shall not concern itself and which can thus be regulated by the Member States themselves,[58] especially since there is no apparent reason why the reference to undertakings was removed from the final version of the Article.

## 4. Article 345 TFEU in EU Legislative Work

The linguistic, historical and contextual interpretation of Article 345 provides a better overview of the scope and meaning of the Article than a mere literal interpretation does. Additionally, the way the Article is used in practice must also be considered. Such an examination is necessary to see whether the intention of the drafters of the Treaty was followed or whether, over time, the Article has gained a different meaning from the one originally intended by the drafters.

Because Article 345 does not offer a legal basis for secondary European legislation, it is difficult to find instances where Article 345 is used in a systematic way. Nonetheless, there are certain subject areas where Article 345 is dealt with more often than others. Competition Law, in particular State aid, and Enlargement are the two main fields in which the Article has been used. However, the use and interpretation of the Article are not always consistent.

When Article 345 is mentioned in relation to Competition Law, the European Commission usually recalls that this Article relates to the principle of neutrality. By using that term the Commission wishes to show that the Treaty is neutral concerning the question whether a company - or undertaking - is in public or private

57 As may be implied from Joined Cases C-92/92 and C-326/92, *Phil Collins* v *Imtrat Handelsgesellschaft mbH and Patricia Im- und Export Verwaltungsgesellschaft mbH* and *Leif Emanuel Kraul* v *EMI Electrola GmbH* [1993] ECR I-05145, paras. 18, 27.

58 See Craig & De Búrca 2011, p. 1073.

ownership, i.e. whether the shares in such a company are held by the State or by private shareholders. For example, in its Notice on the Application of Article 87 and 88 of the EC Treaty (now Artt. 107 and 108 TFEU) to State aid in the form of guarantees, the Commission states:

> 'This Notice applies without prejudice to Article 295 of the Treaty [now Art. 345 TFEU] and thus does not prejudice the rules in Member States governing the system of property ownership. The Commission is neutral as regards public and private ownership.
>
> In particular, the mere fact that the ownership of an undertaking is largely in public hands is not sufficient in itself to constitute a State guarantee provided there are no explicit or implicit guarantee elements.'[59]

This use of Article 345 is in conformity with the interpretation of the Article as presented above. It is this interpretation that is most often used by the European Commission in its documents.[60] Moreover, this interpretation is used by institutions of the European Union involved in the legislative process. For example, the Committee of the Regions states in a Resolution on Enlargement:

> '15) Deplores the fact that the Commission systematically recommends accelerating the pace of privatisation in its monitoring reports on the acceding countries. It must be recalled that Article 295 EC provides neutrality of EU legislation as regards property. Privatisation is not an aim in itself and should not be confused with opening of market access in the sectors where the EU is competent to regulate. The social impact of opening market access in the applicant countries should be closely monitored;'[61]

The European Council conclusions of the Laeken Council on Services of General Interest of 17 October 2001 mention in recital 18:

> '18. As regards the means to ensure the compensation, Member States have in fact a large margin of discretion. Depending on the specific needs of the undertakings concerned, these can receive annual subsidies, a preferential fiscal treatment, lower social contributions etc. The decisive element for the Commission lies in the fact that the value of these advantages does not exceed the extra-costs of the undertakings concerned for the provision of a service of general economic interest. Similarly, in accordance with Article 295 the Commission's approach is neutral as regards the public or private nature of the undertakings concerned. This choice is entirely up to the Member States.'[62]

Despite this seemingly uniform interpretation of the Article, the European Institutions, especially the European Commission, do not always act in conformity with

59 Commission Notice 2008/C 155/02, *OJ* 20.6.2008, C 155/11.

60 See, *inter alia*, COM(2004) 327 final, 20, COM(2007) 529 final, 6, COM(2007) 530 final, 6, COM(2007) 532 final, 6.

61 Committee of the Regions Resolution on Enlargement, 2004/C 73/16.

62 Council Conclusions of 17 October 2001, COM(2001) 598 final.

the general interpretation of the Article. In the past decades several Members of the European Parliament have asked questions on the use of Article 345 TFEU as a restriction on the competences of the European Union. In answering these questions the Commission is a lot less clear as to its meaning.

On 16 October 1997 MEP Watts asked the European Commission whether 'there are any restrictions placed on the purchase of a property in EU Member States for non-nationals of that State?' The Commissioner for the Internal Market Monti answered:

> 'The Honourable Member's questions concern, without reference to a particular Member State, the purchase of real estate in one Member State by nationals of another Member State. The Commission would recall earlier parliamentary questions concerning property acquisition in particular Member States ((See, for example, written questions No E-1032/96 by Mr Böge, OJ C 297, 8.10.1996; No 2491/95 by Mr Sakellariou, OJ C 66, 4.3.1996. )). (…)
>
> While the EC Treaty in no way prejudices the system of ownership in Member States (Article 222), rules will remain subject to the fundamental rule of non-discrimination at the basis of Articles 6, 48, 52 and 59 and measures to give effect to certain of these Articles, as well as the prohibition of all restrictions, subject to the usual exceptions, on cross border capital movements (which includes the acquisition of real estate) provided in Article 73b.'[63]

On 1 December 1998 MEP Angelilli asked a question to the Commission regarding a campaign to save an authentic Italian farm, which had been State owned, from the hands of a commercial company that might use the building for non-farming purposes. The Commissioner for Agriculture, Rural Development and Fisheries Fischler answered:

> 'Under Article 222, the EC Treaty does not in any way prejudice the rules in Member States governing the system of property ownership. There are no Directives or other acts in Community law containing provisions allowing agricultural cooperatives or workers to exercise a right of pre-emption when the holding on which they work is sold. Any provisions establishing such a right for the above entities, to which the Honourable Member refers, would thus be governed exclusively by national law.'[64]

Moreover, on 8 June 1998 the Commissioner for Competition Van Miert recalled the more generally accepted meaning of Article 345 TFEU by stating:

63 Written Question E-3216/97 by Mark Watts (PSE) to the Commission (16 October 1997).
64 Written Question E-3543/98 by Roberta Angelilli (NI) to the Commission (1 December 1998).

> 'The Commission shares the Honourable Member's view that the Treaty is neutral with respect to the ownership of business, a principle laid down in Article 222 of the EC Treaty.'[65]

This last interpretation was confirmed by Commissioner Bolkenstein:

> '5. Article 295 of the EC Treaty stipulates that This Treaty shall in no way prejudice the rules in Member States governing the system of property ownership. Member States therefore have the right to nationalise or to privatise.'[66]

However, Article 345 TFEU has also been used to deny competence of the European Union. For example, on 11 March 2003, MEP Borghezio asked the Commission a question relating to property caught up in an inheritance that would not be released by the Italian State. Commissioner Vitorino answered:

> 'The Commission does not have a general competence as regards the fundamental rights under the terms of the treaties on European Union and establishing the European Community. It could intervene only in the event of violation of the fundamental rights in the field of application of Community legislation, which does not seem to be the case related to the property of the letters of the late Mrs Petacci. Indeed the regulation of property comes under the responsibility of the Member States. In fact, Article 295 of the EC Treaty provides that: This Treaty shall in no way prejudice the rules in Member States governing the system of property ownership.'[67]

Interestingly, the most deviating interpretation of the Article comes from the Commissioner for Enlargement Verheugen. On several occasions Members of the European Parliament asked him on the involvement of property law in the negotiations with the new Member States. He answered, *inter alia*:

> 'The confiscation to which the Honourable Member refers took place before the entry into force of the Treaty of Rome. Article 295 (former Article 222) of the EC Treaty states that the Treaty should in no way prejudice the system of property ownership in the Member States. The matter therefore falls within the jurisdiction of the candidate countries themselves and not the European institutions. Consequently, the system of ownership is not being discussed in the accession negotiations, nor is the Commission carrying out any investigations.'[68]

And:

65 Written Question E-1564/98 by Marie-Noëlle Lienemann (PSE) to the Commission (20 May 1998).
66 Written Question E-0476/03 by Erik Meijer (GUE/NGL) to the Commission (20 February 2003).
67 Written Question P-0818/03 by Mario Borghezio (NI) to the Commission (11 March 2003).
68 Written Question E-0530/01 by Cristiana Muscardini (UEN) to the Commission (22 February 2001).

> 'Poland is currently not a member of the Union. If the EC Treaty in its Article 295 (ex-Article 222) explicitly states that this treaty shall in no way prejudice the rules in Member States governing the system of property ownership, then, a fortiori, the Community has no competence to intervene in property issues in countries that apply for membership. Therefore, the issue is, and would be even if Poland were already member of the Union, one for national law rather than Community law.'[69]

One of the clearest explanations of Verheugen's point of view comes from an answer to a question raised by Doorn MEP on the restitution of property stolen from Jewish Citizens. The Commissioner stated:

> 'The situation with regard to property rights is, however, due to the war and post-war history of the candidate countries particularly complex. It cannot be overlooked that expropriations took place long before the creation of the Community and the entering into force of the Treaty of Rome and are therefore, in principle, not relevant for the transposition and the implementation of the Union-acquis in the candidate countries.
>
> Problems related to the restitution of confiscated properties are therefore essentially the responsibility of each candidate country, and, as the case may be, of the European Court for Human Rights. Candidate countries have hitherto chosen approaches, which they consider most appropriate to their historical, social and economic context. Even where no specific legislation has been enacted, each individual has the right to take his or her case to the courts under existing legislation. After the accession to the Union, and within the scope of application of the EC-Treaty, any discrimination on the grounds of nationality (of a Member State) or based on racial or ethnic origin, religion or belief, will be prohibited.'[70]

In the view of the Directorate General on Enlargement, property law matters are complicated and especially outside the scope of the Treaties. The fact that property relations originate from before the entry into force of the Treaty is a complicating factor that, according to the Commissioner, cannot be solved.

The different explanation of the Directorate General on Enlargement from the Directorates General on Competition and Internal Market seems difficult to explain. Of course, the sensitivity of negotiations with the new Member States that acceded in 2004 must have played a role. Many of the Eastern European Member States did, and sometimes still do, impose restrictions on the acquisition of ownership of immovables by foreigners. The line of reasoning of Commissioner Verheugen does not seem to make sense. If Article 345 limited the competence of the European Union on national property law matters, the special agreements made with some Member States on the special status of immovable property law in their systems would have become redundant. Protocol no. 6 to the Accession Agreements with the 10 New Member States reads:

69 Written Question P-3012/00 by Ursula Stenzel (PPE-DE) to the Commission (19 September 2000).

70 Joint answer to Written Questions E-0194/02, E-0195/02, E-0196/02 and E-0197/02 given by Mr. Verheugen on behalf of the Commission, *OJ* 12.2.2002, C309E, 15.

> 'Bearing in mind the very limited number of residences in Malta and the very limited land available for construction purposes, which can only cover the basic needs created by the demographic development of the present residents, Malta may on a non-discriminatory basis maintain in force the rules on the acquisition and holding of immovable property for secondary residence purposes by nationals of the Member States who have not legally resided in Malta for at least five years laid down in the Immovable Property (Acquisition by Non-Residents) Act (Chapter 246).'[71]

A similar exception exists for Denmark in the Treaty on European Union concluded in Maastricht in 1992. The protocol on the acquisition of property in Denmark states: 'Notwithstanding the provisions of this Treaty, Denmark may maintain the existing legislation on the acquisition of second homes.'

It seems that, save for a few instances in which the European Commission has given a functional interpretation to Article 345, the Article does not confer any exclusive powers to the European Union or the Member States to deal with property law. Instead, the Institutions only use the Article to confirm the neutrality of the Treaties to questions of private or State ownership of companies.

Article 345 therefore, in both its historical interpretation as well as in its current application by the European Union legislature, confirms a principle of neutrality regarding the ownership of undertakings in the Member States. Interpretations emphasizing that the removal of the words 'of undertakings' in Article 345 enlarged the scope of application of the Article do not find evidence of this in the use of the Article by the Institutions.

## 5. Interpretation of Article 345 TFEU by the Court of Justice of the European Union

In addition to the use of Article 345 by the European Union's Institutions that deal with the drafting of legislation, the Article is also interpreted by the Court of Justice of the European Union (CJEU). The interpretation of the Article by the CJEU offers clarity to its meaning and additional content.

In 1984 the CJEU dealt with an Irish Act that forced landowners to sell their land by forced sale to the Irish authorities for the purposes of increasing the size of holdings of land. The Act was stated to exist in order to ensure economic viability of land use.[72] The Irish Land Commission had proceeded to buy a piece of land owned by Robert Fearon and Company Limited. Before deciding on the case, the Supreme Court of Ireland brought a preliminary question to the European Court of Justice questioning the conformity of the Irish Act with the freedom of establishment. As a central part of these proceedings the question on the meaning of Article 222 EEC

71 *Documents concerning the accession of the Czech Republic, the Republic of Estonia, the Republic of Cyprus, the Republic of Latvia, the Republic of Lithuania, the Republic of Hungary, the Republic of Malta, the Republic of Poland, the Republic of Slovenia and the Slovak Republic to the European Union*, Protocol No. 6 on the acquisition of secondary residences in Malta, *OJ* 23.9.2003, 947.

72 Case 182/83, *Robert Fearon and Company Ltd* v *The Irish Land Commission* [1984] ECR 3677.

(now 345 TFEU) arose. The European Commission argued that 'the system of compulsory acquisition by public bodies is part of the system of property ownership in Ireland' and that therefore the question should be answered negatively.[73] The ECJ felt otherwise and held:

> '6. That conclusion cannot be accepted. By virtue of Article 54 (3)(E) of the Treaty, the restrictions on the acquisition and use by a national of one Member State are among those which are to be abolished with a view to the realization of freedom of establishment. Similarly, the Council's 'programme général pour la suppression des restrictions à la liberté d'établissement' (General Programme for the Abolition of Restrictions on the Freedom of Establishment) of 19 December 1961 (Journal Officiel 1962, p. 36) lists, among the restrictions on freedom of establishment to be abolished, provisions or practices which provide for less favourable rules for nationals of another Member State in regard to compulsory acquisition.
>
> 7. Consequently, although Article 222 of the Treaty does not call in question the Member States' right to establish a system of compulsory acquisition by public bodies, such a system remains subject to the fundamental rule of nondiscrimination which underlies the Chapter of the Treaty relating to the right of establishment.'[74]

The case of *Fearon* shows how the interpretation of the European Court of Justice is very different from the general interpretation of the European Commission. According to the CJEU the meaning of Article 345 is not to exclude the application of the Treaties to questions of State or private ownership at all but is rather to emphasize how, according to the Treaties, these powers might belong to the Member States, but not as far as the exercise of those powers is concerned. When dealing with lawmaking competences at the national level, the Member States must take into account the fundamental freedoms enshrined in the TFEU, in this case the free movement of persons in the form of the freedom of establishment.

A similar interpretation by the Court can be found in cases dealing with the ownership of shares. Companies issue special shares to avoid hostile takeovers, known as golden shares. These shares are 'golden' because of the special voting rights attached to them. The ECJ delivered similar judgments in these cases as it did in *Fearon*. See, for instance, *Commission* v *Portugal*:

> 'However, those concerns cannot entitle Member States to plead their own systems of property ownership, referred to in Article 222 of the Treaty, by way of justification for obstacles, resulting from privileges attaching to their position as shareholder in a privatised undertaking, to the exercise of the freedoms provided for by the Treaty. As is apparent from the Court's case-law (Konle, cited above, paragraph 38), that article

[73] Case 182/83, *Fearon* [1984] ECR 3677, para. 6.

[74] Case 182/83, *Fearon* [1984] ECR 3677, paras. 7 and 8.

> does not have the effect of exempting the Member States' systems of property ownership from the fundamental rules of the Treaty.'[75]

Apart from these cases that deal with more general issues of property law, the CJEU has delivered a line of case law regarding intellectual property law. This case law applies to Article 345 in full and would therefore also apply to the application of the Article to other areas than just intellectual property law. This case law centres on a fundamental distinction made between the existence and exercise of property rights. This distinction was first drawn by the CJEU in the case of *Consten & Grundig*.[76] According to the CJEU Article 345 does not exclude any influence of EU law on the exercise of national 'industrial' property rights. The existence of such rights, in the eyes of the CJEU, remains untouched by the Treaty. This distinction has become a fundamental starting point of the Court's reasoning and was repeated in following cases, such as *Parke Davis* and *Deutsche Grammophon*.[77] All these cases concerned the application of the Treaty articles on the four freedoms and competition law to national legislation.

Following the viewpoint of the CJEU, Member States may be free under the Treaty provisions to legislate in the area of property law. In the exercise of that freedom as well as in respect to the exercise of the property rights so created, the provisions of the TFEU apply. The same would apply in case there is European legislation dealing with aspects of property law. In *Commission* v *Italy* and *Commission* v *UK* the ECJ held that just because there was no positive harmonization, i.e. secondary legislation, in the area of intellectual property law yet, that did not authorize the Member States to adopt legislation that violated the free movement or competition rules.[78] This difference was clarified by the ECJ itself in *Spain* v *Council*: the existence v. exercise dichotomy is only applicable in cases of negative harmoni-

75 Case C-367/98, *Commission* v *Portugal* [2002] ECR I-4731, para 48. See also Case C-483/99, *Commission* v *France* [2002] ECR I-4781, para. 44, and Case C-503/99, *Commission* v *Belgium* [2002] ECR I-4809, para. 44.

76 Joined Cases 56 and 58/64 [1966] ECR 429, 345, para 6. See also Schwarze 2000, p. 2335; EP Fact Sheet 3.4.4. of 10 November 2000 at 2(a); Bartels 1995, p. 247.

77 Case 24/67, *Parke Davis* [1986] ECR 81, 72; Case 78/70, *Deutsche Grammophon* [1971] ECR 487, para. 11: 'Although the Treaty does not affect the existence of rights recognized by the legislation of a Member State with regard to industrial and commercial property, the exercise of such rights may nevertheless fall within the prohibitions laid down by the Treaty'.

78 Case C-235/89, *Commission* v *Italy* [1992] ECR I-777, para. 14: 'However, the provisions of the Treaty, and in particular Article [295] … cannot be interpreted as reserving to the national legislature, in relation to industrial and commercial property, the power to adopt measures which would adversely affect the principle of free movement of goods within the common market as provided for and regulated by the Treaty.' More generally A.-G. Colomer's opinion to joined cases C-367/98, C-483/99 and C-503/99, at para. 67: 'Article 295 EC does not detract from application of the fundamental rules of the Treaty'; Case C-30/90, *Commission* v *UK* [1992] ECR I-829, paras. 16-18.

zation, not in cases that concern the making of European legislation in this area.[79] The ECJ stated:

> 'Thus, far from endorsing the argument that rules concerning the very existence of industrial property rights fall within the sole jurisdiction of the national legislature, the Court was anticipating the unification of patent provisions or harmonization of the relevant national legislation. … [The Union] may use Article [352] as the basis for creating new rights superimposed on national rights'.[80]

Therefore, the scope of the Union's competence to harmonize in this area of law is not influenced by the distinction made by the CJEU between the existence and exercise of intellectual property rights.

It is remarkable that the Court has never provided any argumentation as to why this distinction between positive and negative harmonization should be made. It cannot be deduced from the wording of Article 345 itself.[81] It seems to be a reaction of the Court to an incorrect interpretation of Article 345 by the Member States involved in the aforementioned cases. These Member States based their argumentation in those cases on Article 345 to justify their national legislation concerning intellectual property rights. Given the fact that the current version of Article 345 does not mention that ownership is restricted to undertakings, it may be understood why Member States wrongly rely on that Article in these intellectual property law cases.

It would have been more correct if the ECJ had held that Article 345 is not concerned with intellectual property law and that therefore the Article is not applicable in those cases. Instead, however, the ECJ seems to have attempted to find a response to the arguments put forth by the Member States. The result of this is the existence v. exercise dichotomy. Although the Court never directly states so, this doctrine seems to be inspired by Article 30 EC, now Article 36 TFEU. The possible justification for the protection of industrial and commercial property provided by that Article safeguards the existence of intellectual property rights unless the

79 Case C-350/92, *Kingdom of Spain* v *Council of the European Union* [1995] ECR I-01985, paras. 18-22. Also A.-G. Jacobs' Opinion to this case, para. 20: 'The case-law cited by Spain does indeed distinguish between the existence of intellectual property rights and their exercise. It does so, however, in relation to the application of substantive Treaty rules, such as Articles 30, 36, 85 and 86, and not with a view to determining the scope of the Community's competence to harmonize national legislation, or to introduce new rules. Such is the tenor of *Consten and Grundig* v *Commission, Parke, Davis v. Centrafarm, Deutsche Grammophon* v *Metro, Commission* v *United Kingdom* and *Commission* v *Italy* [references omitted], and numerous other cases which could be cited, most of which are dealt with by the Commission in its observations.' See further Drasch 1998, 128.

80 Case C-350/92, *Kingdom of Spain* v *Council of the European Union* [1995] ECR I-01985, paras. 19 and 23. See also ECJ Opinion 1/94 on the Competence of the Community to conclude international agreements concerning services and the protection of intellectual property [1994] ECR I-5267, para. 59.

81 Riegel 1979, p. 745.

exercise of those rights constitutes a means of arbitrary discrimination or a disguised restriction on trade between Member States.[82] Interpreting Article 345 to only apply to the exercise of intellectual property rights therefore ensures consistency with Article 36 TFEU.

Thus far, the existence v. exercise dichotomy has only been applied in intellectual property law cases; it seems that such reasoning also applies to property law in the more classic meaning of the term. In any case, the very few cases that have come before the Court of Justice, most often dealing with the freedom of establishment and the freedom of capital, do seem to answer to the dichotomy as they all concern the exercise of property rights rather than their existence.[83] However, the dichotomy as such remains unmentioned by the Court.[84]

## 6. Article 345 TFEU in the Debate on Privatizations and Nationalizations

To start from the presumption that Article 345 does indeed concern the public or private ownership of undertakings - a presumption which is for an important part fed by the Schuman Declaration and its historic context - leads to an extensive body of literature and EU documents concerning privatization and nationalization matters. Especially those books and articles providing background information to the Schuman Declaration indicate why the eventual Article 345 TFEU would be specifically about the ownership of *undertakings*. For instance, Marie-Thérèse Bitsch writes in her *Histoire de la construction européenne de 1945 à nos jours* about the role of nationalization procedures and the possible accession of the United Kingdom to the ECSC. She describes how the fact that the UK was about to nationalize both its coal and its steel sector should not have posed an obstacle to its accession to the ECSC,

82 See Barnard 2007, p. 176.

83 A.-G. Stix-Hackl seems to suggest something similar in her Opinion to case C-436/03, *European Parliament* v *Council of the European Union* [2006] ECR I-3733: 'The counter-argument put forward by the Parliament, that the case-law relates to intellectual property law and that this has special status because of Article 295 EC, is not tenable. First, Article 295 EC does not just cover intangible rights such as trade marks. Second, that provisions itself has only limited significance in that area: [reference omitted] thus the corresponding exercise of proprietary rights, for instance, is undeniably governed by the Treaty, that is to say by the other provisions of primary law.' (paras. 69 and 70).

84 See, in particular, Case C-302/97, *Klaus Konle* v *Republik Österreich* [1999] ECJ I-3099, and Joined Cases C-515/99, C-519/99 to C-524/99 and C-526/99 to C-540/99, *Hans Reisch and others* v *Bürgermeister des Landeshauptstadt Salzburg and others* [2002] ECR I-2157. Moreover, see Case C-503/04, *Commission* v *Germany* [2007] ECR I-6153 in which the ECJ holds that the particular features of the system of property ownership in a Member State cannot justify the continuation of a failure to fulfil obligations which consists of an obstacle to, in that case, the freedom to provide services, and Case C-117/06, *Möllendorf and Möllendorf-Niehuus* [2007] ECR I-8361 in which the ECJ holds that a transfer of ownership of land may be blocked on the basis of secondary European legislation in case one of the parties is registered as a potential terrorist.

since those sectors were also nationalized in France and, most importantly, since Schuman's Declaration stated that 'l'institution de la Haute Autorité ne préjuge en rien du régime de propriété des entreprises'.[85]

At the time of creation of the ECSC Treaty, the future Member States' coal and steel industries varied considerably as far as the influence - or lack thereof - of the national governments was concerned. The idea behind Article 83 ECSC and later 222 EEC was to prevent the Community institutions and other Member States from interfering with those industries' structure.[86] It appears that this desire to prevent intervention did not just underlie Article 83 ECSC but has continuously been adhered to throughout the years, up to the present day.[87] In the 1980s, the French government carried out a series of nationalizations. Questions were asked about these intended nationalizations in the European Parliament, in relation to Article 222 EEC. It follows from the answers given by the Commission representative that the Community would not interfere with France's decision to extend its public sector.[88]

Most recently, Article 345 was discussed in a 'golden-shares' case brought by the Commission against Italy.[89] Advocate-General Colomer, in his Opinion of 6 November 2008, reiterated that Article 345 (then Article 295) has solely to do with the ownership of undertakings and expressed his dizappointment that the ECJ in its judgments continuously ignores the matter of the scope and application of Article 345. The CJEU has made clear, however, that the Member States cannot plead their systems of property ownership to escape application of the fundamental (free

85 See *supra*, section 2.

86 See, for instance, Verhoeven 1996, p. 863; Burdeau 1984, p. 56; Marenco 1983, p. 496; Colliard 1965, p. 3 and 5.

87 Perhaps one of the most famous nationalisation cases was that of the Italian electricity sector that led to the *Costa* v *E.N.E.L.* case in the early sixties (case 6/64). The ECJ itself, however, did not specifically refer to Art. 222 EEC in that case. It was, however, touched upon by the Commission: Virole 1965, p. 396.

88 Written Question No. 1091/81 by Mrs Charzat; Written Question No. 1161/81 by Mr Damseaux; see also the Commission representative's answer to Written Question No. 1156/81 by Mr Damseaux concerning aid granted by the Belgian government to firms in difficulties: 'Article 222 of the EEC Treaty states that [ ...; reference omitted]. The Belgian State may therefore acquire a holding in a firm in the same way as any natural or legal person.' All these Questions can be found in *OJ* C 38, 15 February 1982. See also Burdeau 1984, p. 55.

89 Regarding the 'golden-shares' cases, see *supra*, section 5. More recent (i.e. from the past ten years) documents discussing Article 345 in the context of nationalisations and interpreting it according to the principle of neutrality include Commission Decision of 2 April 2008 on State aid C 41/07 (ex NN 49/07) which Romania has implemented for Tractorul, *OJ* L 263/5, para. 34; Commission Notice on the application of Articles 87 and 88 of the EC Treaty (now 107 and 108 TFEU) to State aid in the form of guarantees, *OJ* C 155/10, point 1.5; Opinion of the European Economic and Social Committee on The future of services of general interest, *OJ* C 309/135, point 10.8.

movement) rules of the Treaty.[90] Here again the influence of the existence v. exercise dichotomy can be seen.

It may never be known one hundred percent for sure why the wording of Article 345 was changed to no longer include the reference to undertakings, as there are no available documents clarifying this decision and all the people who took part in drafting the Article are most likely no longer with us to answer that question. Smit and Herzog provide the following possible explanation in their Commentary:

> 'Considerations undoubtedly similar to those leading to the inclusion of Article 83 in the Coal and Steel Treaty seem to have been instrumental in the adoption of Article 222 of the Treaty establishing the European Economic Community. [...] The change in wording may have been due to an inability of the negotiators to reach agreement on a more precise formula [reference omitted], but was undoubtedly also influenced by the European Economic Community's much wider scope of activities.'[91]

Thus, whatever the reasons for altering the text of the Article, practice, at least in nationalization/privatization matters, suggests that the rationale behind it has not changed since the Treaties were first enacted.

## 7. Preliminary Conclusions

The foregoing shows that Article 345 is not always interpreted consistently. The Article originates directly from the famous Schuman Declaration of 9 May 1950. Through the Schuman Declaration the provision made its way into the European Coal and Steel Community Treaty (Article 83), the Euratom Treaty (Article 91), the European Economic Community Treaty (Article 222), the Treaty Establishing the European Community (Article 295), as well as the European Economic Area Agreement (Article 125) and now finally into the Treaty on the Functioning of the European Union (Article 345). Throughout the years, even with the modernization and modification of the Treaties, the phrasing of the provision has not changed.

The preparatory documents (*Travaux Préparatoires*) regarding Article 345 (then Art. 222 EEC) reveal ambiguity as to its scope of application. It remains unclear whether the change from the original wording including the words *des entreprises* (of undertakings) to the final version, that does not mention this limitation, has any significant effects. Taking into consideration the interpretation of the European Institutions, of the European Commission and of the European Court of Justice in

90 A.-G. Colomer's Opinion in case C-326/07, *Commission* v *Italian Republic* [2009] ECR I-2291. See also his joined opinion in cases C-436/00 and 98/01, *Commission* v *Spain and Commission* v *UK* [2003] ECR I-4581, para. 37: 'In any event, the judgments, without stating why, ignore the question of the application and scope of Article 295 EC. That cannot be done with impunity, even in the name of the fundamental freedoms, since in the scheme of the Treaty Article 295 EC is as important as they are.'

91 Smit & Herzog 1976-1996, at 6-216.64.

particular, it seems there is no reason to assume that the removal of the reference to undertakings has changed the scope of application.

However, occasionally Article 345 continues to be used, both by the Member States as well as by the European Institutions, to prevent the application of the Treaties to the law of property in general. The most likely interpretation of the Article, however, does not leave room for such a conclusion. The Article embeds the principle of neutrality, under which the Treaties are neutral as to whether an undertaking is held in public or private ownership; to be more specific, whether the Member State or one of its organs, or private individuals owns the shares in such a company.

It seems, therefore, that the Treaties cannot apply to nationalization of companies in the Member States. However, under the case law of the European Court of Justice, the rules of the internal market remain applicable with regard to the exercise, by the Member States, of their competence to nationalize. The existence v. exercise dichotomy, although originating in cases dealing with intellectual property rights, applies in general: the Treaties are neutral to the existence, i.e. the question of nationalization itself, but do interfere in the way in which the nationalization takes place. A nationalization of a bank by a Member State to save it from insolvency is therefore allowed under the rules of the Treaties. However, the nationalization must be in conformity with the four freedoms and, in particular, competition law. It is all the more strange, therefore, that Article 345 is rarely mentioned in this context.

Article 345 is occasionally used in a way not consistent with this interpretation. This applies to the European Institutions as well as to the Member States. Even though the European Court of Justice seems to be the only European Institution with a consistent and correct interpretation of the Article, because of the incorrect use of it by the Member States in the procedures the Court is forced to go into aspects of the Article it would normally not consider.[92]

Article 345 is occasionally also discussed, usually by academics, in the context of the harmonization of private law. In these discussions the question is raised whether Article 345 obstructs the development of a European property law. However, the interpretation of the Article as developed in this chapter shows that there is no reason to assume Article 345 would form an obstacle to the development of a European property law. The next question is then, of course, whether the EU would have the competence to enact legislation dealing with property law. Is there a legal basis in the TFEU upon which such legislation could be created?

## 8. Legal Basis

This section will first explore the possible legal bases - if any - for the EU to promulgate legislation in the area of private law, in particular property law. Next to

92 See, for example, Joined cases 56 and 58/64, *Consten & Grundig* [1966] ECR 429, 345. See further, *supra*, section 5.

the question whether the TFEU provides a legal basis at all, the principle of subsidiarity needs to be taken into account: even if there is a legal basis for the EU to draft legislation in the area of property law, that does not necessarily mean that the EU *should* make use of this power.[93] And if it decides to do so, the legislation that ensues should be suitable to attain the purpose for which it was drafted and should not go beyond what is necessary to attain that purpose. In other words, the legislation should be able to withstand a proportionality test.

The legal bases contained in the TFEU can be divided into three categories: specific legal bases, such as Article 169 TFEU on consumer protection; general legal bases, in particular Article 115 TFEU (ex Art. 95 EC); and Article 352 (ex Art. 308 EC) as 'residual' legal basis.[94] The focus will be on those articles that may provide the EU with a legal basis to create substantive property law. However, the competence to create private international law rules will also be taken into account. I concluded in Chapter 2 that the private international law rule *lex rei sitae* is no longer appropriate within the internal market and that changing it may improve the situation for persons entering into cross-border property relationships. Whether this is a feasible option will be further explored in Chapter 5.

Article 5(2) TEU (ex Article 5 EC) lays down, in its first section, the principle of attributed competences or the principle of conferral.[95] This principle entails that the EU can only make legislation in those areas for which the competence is explicitly granted by the Treaties.[96] Once it has been established that the EU has the competence to legislate in a certain area, the way in which this competence can be used is governed by the principles of subsidiarity and proportionality as laid down in Article 5(3) and (4) respectively.[97]

The nature of the national law (e.g. public or private law) is irrelevant for the question, whether the EU has the competence to harmonize.[98] The competences laid

93 Weatherill 2004b, p. 658.

94 *Cf* Heiderhoff 2007, p. 5.

95 Art. 5(2) TEU reads: 'Under the principle of conferral, the Union shall act only within the limits of the competences conferred upon it by the Member States in the Treaties to attain the objectives set out therein. Competences not conferred upon the Union in the Treaties remain with the Member States.'

96 Craig & De Búrca 2011, p. 73; Strese 2006, p. 65.

97 Art. 5(1) reads: 'The limits of Union competences are governed by the principle of conferral. The use of Union competences is governed by the principles of subsidiarity and proportionality.'

98 Case 11/70, *Internationale Handelsgesellschaft* [1970] ECR 1125, para. 3: 'Recourse to the legal rules or concepts of national law in order to judge the validity of measures adopted by the institutions of the Community would have an adverse effect on the uniformity and efficacy of Community law. The validity of such measures can only be judged in the light of Community law. In fact, the law stemming from the Treaty, an independent source of law, cannot because of its very nature be overridden by rules of national law, *however framed*, without being deprived of its character as Community law and without the legal basis of the Community itself being called in question.' [emphasis added]

down in the Treaties are functional.[99] Harmonization of private law will therefore not normally be an aim in itself but a means to achieve a different purpose, for instance, the further development of the internal market or the protection of consumers. The way in which harmonization takes place may differ when it concerns private law, due to the specific characteristics of this area of law, but that is a different matter.[100]

The possible legal bases for legislation in the area of property law range from specific to general and would have to be followed by the Commission in that order: only if there is no specific legal basis for the harmonization of property law can any of the general legal bases be used. As such, there is no specific legal basis in the TFEU for legislation in the area of property law or private law in general.[101] In that respect, the Lisbon Treaty has not brought anything new in relation to the EC Treaty.[102] However, the specific legal bases in Article 50(2)(e) TFEU (freedom of establishment through acquisition of land in another Member State; ex Art. 44(2)(e) EC) and/or in Article 169 TFEU (consumer protection; ex Art. 153 EC) might be relied upon by the Commission to legislate in the area of property law.[103] It must be noted, however, that these two legal bases are so far mostly hypothetical, for separate reasons. Article 169 has often been mentioned as a theoretical legal basis for European private law, but because measures concerning consumer law often also facilitate the internal market, Article 114 (ex Art. 95 EC) is usually chosen as the legal basis, instead of Article 169.[104] This is also the case for the Consumer Rights Directive.[105] Article 50(2)(e) may have more potential as a legal basis for European property law than Article 169, but so far it seems to have never been considered as such.[106] In any case, if these specific legal bases prove to be unusable, the Commis-

99 See e.g. Strese 2006, p. 111: 'Es kann insoweit von dem Prinzip funktional definierter Handlungsbefugnisse im Gegensatz zu rechtsgebietlich definierten Zuständigkeiten gesprochen werden.'

100 Strese 2006, p. 51 and 63. Strese even takes it one step further, claiming that, like no other area of law, private law is pre-eminently suited to realise the internal market: 'Die Grundlagenrolle des Privatrechts innerhalb der Gemeinschaft ist unbestritten. [reference omitted] Wie kein anderes Rechtsgebiet ist es dazu geeignet, die Schaffung des Binnenmarktes durch die Realisierung der Grundfreiheiten zu fördern.' (p. 52).

101 Hesselink, Rutgers & Booys 2007, p. 70.

102 Roth 2009, p. 26.

103 Art. 47(2) EC (now Art. 53 TFEU) has on occasion been used as a legal basis for instruments that are relevant within the context of this research, namely a number of banking directives. However, because it is not immediately evident why this provision was chosen as a legal basis, and because the wording of the Article has changed significantly since the Lisbon Treaty entered into force, it will not be dealt with here. See however also Strese 2006, p. 103.

104 Keirse & Veder 2010, p. 48; Strese 2006, p. 106.

105 Dir. 2011/83/EU on consumer rights, amending Dir. 93/13 and Dir. 1999/44 and repealing Dir. 85/577 and Dir. 97/7, [2011] *OJ* L 304/64.

106 Bright & Bright 1998 mentions Art. 50(2)(e) (then Art. 54(3)(e)) in the context of the four freedoms and land (p. 365), but does not go into its potential as a legal basis for the development of European rules of property law.

sion could resort to the general, functional legal bases of Article 114 or 115 TFEU (ex Art. 95 and 94 EC resp.).[107] It must be noted, though, that Article 115 requires unanimity in the Council, that the Parliament merely needs to be consulted and that only directives can be issued on its basis.[108] Furthermore, the explicit requirement that measures adopted on this legal basis must directly affect the establishment or functioning of the internal market also narrows the scope of application of this provision.

On the other hand, with regard to Article 114[109] the CJEU's famous *Tobacco*-judgment(s) must be taken into account.[110] The ECJ held that Article 95 EC (now Art. 114 TFEU) cannot be used as a *carte blanche* to enact legislation for the internal market.[111] This Article can only be used as a legal basis for measures which actually contribute to the elimination of obstacles to the internal market.[112] This includes already existing obstacles as well as obstacles 'which may well arise'.[113] The mere existence, therefore, of divergences or differences between the systems of the Member States is not enough to be able to use Article 114 as a legal basis. This is only possible if the effect of these differences is that they hinder the functioning of the internal market.[114] This was confirmed more recently by the Court in *Vodafone and others* v *Secretary of State*.[115]

107 *Cf* Hesselink, Rutgers & Booys 2007, p. 44; Müller-Graff 2004, p. 78.

108 Keirse & Veder 2010, p. 6-7. Art. 115 TFEU reads: 'Without prejudice to Article 114, the Council shall, acting unanimously in accordance with a special legislative procedure and after consulting the European Parliament and the Economic and Social Committee, issue directives for the approximation of such laws, regulations or administrative provisions of the Member States as directly affect the establishment or functioning of the internal market.'

109 Art. 114(1) TFEU reads: 'Save where otherwise provided in the Treaties, the following provisions shall apply for the achievement of the objectives set out in Article 26. The European Parliament and the Council shall, acting in accordance with the ordinary legislative procedure and after consulting the Economic and Social Committee, adopt the measures for the approximation of the provisions laid down by law, regulation or administrative action in Member States which have as their object the establishment and functioning of the internal market.'

110 For an extensive discussion of the CJEU's line of case law following *Tobacco I*, see Weatherill 2006.

111 Case C-376/98, *Germany* v *Parliament and Council* [2000] ECR I-2247, paras. 83-84.

112 Or to the removal of appreciable distortions of competition: para. 108 of the judgment; Weatherill 2004b, p. 644. Distortions of competition are however not relevant here. See also Basedow *et al.* 2011, p. 20.

113 Case C-376/98, *Germany* v *Parliament and Council*, paras. 95-96. See also Van Gerven 2002, p. 165.

114 *Cf* Akkermans 2008, p. 500: 'In order to harmonise private law, therefore, the Community legislature must not only show divergences between the various national legal systems, but must also show that these divergences lead to an obstacle to the functioning of the Internal Market'; see also Keirse & Veder 2010, p. 7; Strese 2006, p. 210. See subsequently, in case C-380/03, *Tobacco II* [2006] ECR I-11573, para. 37: 'While a mere finding of disparities between national rules is not sufficient to justify having recourse to Article 95 EC, it is otherwise where there are differences between the laws, regulations or administrative provisions of the →

The effect of the differences between the national systems of property law is indeed that they hinder the functioning of the internal market. It is not so much the mere existence of these differences that has this effect, but rather the mandatory and closed character of each Member State's system of property law.[116] The *lex rei sitae* protects this closed character by always allocating a proprietary relationship to the law of the *situs* of the object concerned. The *numerus clausus* of the *situs* does not permit the entry of foreign property rights, which means that those rights will either not be allowed entry into the host Member State or will be transposed into the nearest equivalent right available in the *numerus clausus* of the host Member State. This may make intra-Union trade less attractive for the party whose property right is lost or altered at the border. Property law differs in this regard from contract law. The Max Planck Research Paper on Policy Options for Progress Towards a European Contract Law mentions that '[m]arket participants established in different Member States are said to face the same divergences, as well as the same possibilities to avoid certain national contract laws, by way of choice of law.'[117] Because there is generally no choice of law in property law (the *lex rei sitae* rule cannot be deviated from), market participants cannot get around the differences in national property laws and the obstacles they cause to intra-Union trade.[118]

A separate difficulty with Article 114 is that it is meant for the 'approximation' of national rules. It would depend on the type of legislative action in the field of property law that might be taken in the future whether or not it would amount to approximation: a mandatory instrument would probably fulfil this requirement, but an optional instrument would not so much amount to approximation (harmonization), but rather to the creation of new, autonomous EU law.[119] For this reason, Article 352 TFEU (ex Art. 308 EC) may be a more appropriate legal basis.[120]

Article 50(2)(e) TFEU seems to be less well-known but is potentially of great importance to the development of European property law. Article 50 reads:

Member States which are such as to obstruct the fundamental freedoms and thus have a direct effect on the functioning of the internal market'.

115 Case C-58/08, *Vodafone and others* [2010] ECR I-4999, paras. 32-33. See also Weatherill 2011, p. 831-832 and 841-842.

116 *Cf* Polak 2006, p. 127-128.

117 Basedow *et al.* 2011, p. 21.

118 In this light it is interesting to read the CJEU's statement in *Alsthom Atlantique*, that 'parties to an international contract of sale are generally free to determine the law applicable to their contractual relations and can thus avoid being subject to French law'; Case C-339/89, *Alsthom Atlantique* v *Sulzer* [1991] ECR I-107, para. 15. This was one of the reasons why the French law in question was held not to infringe the free movement of goods and EU competition law. This seems to suggest that, where parties are not able to choose the applicable law to their relationship - as is the case in property law -, the relevant national law might infringe EU law. *Cf* Von Wilmowsky 1998, p. 6.

119 Weatherill 2010b, p. 67.

120 *Infra*, p. 131 *et seq*. See also Basedow *et al.* 2011, p. 19 and 26.

> '1. In order to attain freedom of establishment as regards a particular activity, the European Parliament and the Council, acting in accordance with the ordinary legislative procedure and after consulting the Economic and Social Committee, shall act by means of directives.
>
> 2. The European Parliament, the Council and the Commission shall carry out the duties devolving upon them under the preceding provisions, in particular: [...]
>
> (e) by enabling a national of one Member State to acquire and use land and buildings situated in the territory of another Member State, in so far as this does not conflict with the principles laid down in Article 39(2).'

Similarly, the General Programme for the Abolition of Restrictions on the Freedom of Establishment[121] lists as one of the obstacles to be removed in order to facilitate the free movement of establishment national measures which make it less attractive for nationals of another Member State to acquire, use or dispose of movable or immovable property or rights therein.[122] After extensive research, I have only been able to identify a single source referring to Article 50(2)(e) as a possible legal basis for European property law or private law.[123] If this Article is mentioned at all, focus is more often placed on sub-subsection g.[124]

An example may illustrate how this provision could be used as a legal basis for European property law: ECJ cases such as *Reisch*, which were discussed in Chapter 2, indicate that there are several Member States that have legislation in force, which restricts the owner in his use of the immovable property he acquired in that particular Member State. It follows from these judgments that such legislation is in principle held to form an obstacle to the internal market. In particular instances, the CJEU has accepted grounds for justification of the national measure, but as was also described in Chapter 2, justifications always have to be considered on a case-by-case basis. Keeping in mind the interaction between negative and positive harmonization, and the signal-function fulfilled by the CJEU's judgments towards the Commission,[125] the following steps might be taken: the CJEU's judgments, in terms of negative harmonization, indicate that there is national legislation restricting the acquisition of land, thereby forming an obstacle to the internal market. The Commission could pick up on this and initiate positive harmonization in the form of a directive (Art. 50(2)(e) does not provide for the enactment of regulations).[126] The Commission could propose a Directive on the acquisition of land/immovable property in other Member States on the basis of Article 50(2)(e) TFEU, taking into account the judgments of the CJEU on cross-border acquisition of

121 18 December 1961, *OJ* 1962, p. 36.

122 General Programme for the Abolition of Restrictions on the Freedom of Establishment, Title III. See also case 182/83, *Fearon* v *Irish Land Commission* [1984] ECR 3677, para. 6.

123 Bright & Bright 1998, p. 365.

124 See, for instance, Strese 2006, p. 63; Groeben 1997, p. 1365 *et seq.*

125 Chapter 2, section 7. *Justification grounds.*

126 *Cf* Barnard 2010, p. 567.

immovables and the justification grounds that were accepted in those judgments. Furthermore, Article 50(2)(e) might also be a proper legal basis for the creation of a 'Eurotitle' or 'Euromortgage'. These would be European property rights that could be used to acquire immovable property across the border. The creation of European property rights is discussed in detail in Chapter 6.

Article 169 TFEU (ex Art. 153 EC) lays down that the Union shall promote the interests of consumers and ensure a high level of consumer protection. Those objectives must be attained, however, 'through measures adopted pursuant to Article 114 in the context of the completion of the internal market', according to Article 169(2)(a). Legislation enacted under Article 169(2)(a) must therefore comply with the same requirements as legislation enacted under Article 114. It must also be determined whether or not European rules on property law would be aimed at consumer protection or whether they would be aimed at the protection of business. In the latter case, Article 169 would not be a suitable legal basis. It follows from Chapter 2 of this study that, from a point of view of property law, the free movement of capital concerns primarily situations of cross-border C2C transactions of immovable property. Article 169 is only intended for B2C transactions. As far as the free movement of goods is concerned, Chapter 2 has shown that in the context of property law we are mostly dealing with cross-border B2B transactions on the basis of credit. Article 169 does not cover B2B transactions either.[127]

Measures not aimed at the completion of the internal market, but envisaged to 'support, supplement and monitor the policy of the Member States' can be taken under Article 169(2)(b). A binding instrument containing European rules of property law would replace rather than supplement the Member States' policy and would therefore not fulfil the requirements of Article 169(2)(b).[128] Whether an optional instrument would support and supplement the Member States' policy is also doubtful because it would promote the EU's policy.[129] It is therefore unlikely that Article 169, whether under subsection 2(a) or 2(b), could provide a suitable legal basis for the enactment of secondary legislation dealing with property law.

The legal basis of last resort, so to speak, is Article 352 TFEU (ex Art. 308 EC). It can only be used if the Treaty provides no other legal basis.[130] A noteworthy difference in wording between the old Article 308 EC and the new Article 352 TFEU is the omission of the phrase 'in the course of the operation of the common market'.[131] This entails a significant broadening of the scope of application of Article

127 *Cf* Basedow *et al.* 2011, p. 25.
128 Roth 2009, p. 28.
129 Roth 2009, p. 28.
130 Opinion 2/94, *Accession by the Community to the European Convention for the Protection of Human Rights and Fundamental Freedoms* [1996] ECR I-1759, para. 29.
131 Weatherill 2010b, p. 67. Art. 352(1) reads: 'If action by the Union should prove necessary, within the framework of the policies defined in the Treaties, to attain one of the objectives set out in the Treaties, and the Treaties have not provided the necessary powers, the Council, →

352 TFEU. On the other hand, unanimity is required in the Council, which may be difficult to achieve with 27 Member States. Another important change is the addition of paragraph 3, which states that '[m]easures based on this Article shall not entail harmonization of Member States' laws or regulations in cases where the Treaties exclude such harmonization.' This prohibition was not part of the old Article 308, which meant that it could be (and was) used more often than would now be possible to legislate in certain areas as long as there was political consensus. This provision, however, does not provide an obstacle to the harmonization of property law because the Treaties do not explicitly exclude such harmonization.

The Court clarified what kind of legislative measures Article 114 and Article 352 can be used for in case C-436/03, *Parliament* v *Council*.[132] The Parliament contested the legal basis that was used to adopt Regulation 1435/2003/EC on the Statute for a European Cooperative Society (SCE). The legal basis used was Article 352 (ex Art. 308 EC), but the Parliament was of the opinion that Article 114 (ex Art. 95 EC) should have been used. In its view, the term 'approximation' in Article 114 does not only imply substituting European law for national law, as the Council argued, but that it can also be 'carried out by supplementing national law by creating European legal forms'.[133] It was also of the opinion that the SCE was not a new European-autonomous form of company because the Regulation did not provide for the exhaustive organization of such a company and referred on several occasions to national law. According to the Council, the SCE is a European-autonomous legal form, supplementing the cooperative societies under national law, thereby not 'approximating' national law in the sense of Article 114. The only legal basis left was therefore, in its opinion, Article 352. The ECJ agreed with the Council. It held that European legislation, which harmonizes national law by substituting it with European law, should be adopted on the basis of Article 114. European legislation which leaves national law unchanged, but supplements it with a new, European legal form – such as was the case with the SCE, but also, for instance, with European-autonomous intellectual property rights[134] – should be adopted on the basis of Article 352 because it 'cannot be regarded as aiming to approximate the laws of the Member States'.[135]

What role Article 352 can in the end play for the harmonization of property law depends on the suitability of the other possible legal bases for such harmonization, given that they have priority over Article 352.[136] In any case, the ECJ's judgment in the *Parliament* v *Council* case needs to be taken into account: if European property law is created in such a way that it substitutes national legislation,

acting unanimously on a proposal from the Commission and after obtaining the consent of the European Parliament, shall adopt the appropriate measures. [...]'.

132 [2006] ECR I-3733.

133 Para. 20.

134 Para. 25. See also Roth 2009, p. 30 and Craig & De Búrca 2011, p. 317.

135 Paras. 44-46.

136 *Cf* Strese 2006, p. 120.

with the object of the establishment and functioning of the internal market, then Article 114 is the appropriate legal basis. If on the other hand European property law is created in a way which supplements national law with new, European legal forms, then Article 352 is likely to be the appropriate legal basis, in the absence of any other legal basis.

A final option could be to use Article 81(2)(c) TFEU (ex Art. 65 EC) as a legal basis. It is true that this provision only contains a legal basis for the creation of private international law (PIL) rules, not for substantive (private) law, which is why I discuss it separately from all the other legal bases. However, it is argued in Chapter 2 and Chapter 5 of this study that the *lex rei sitae* rule, which is the general private international law rule as regards property law, is no longer suitable in the context of the internal market. Changing this rule may solve some of the problems that the differing national property law systems cause within the internal market. This is one of the options which will be discussed in Chapter 5. For that reason, I wish to point out already here that Article 81(2)(c) would provide the EU with the competence to adopt PIL rules. It must be noted at the outset, however, that this legal basis can only be used for an instrument that is applicable in cross-border situations, not for one that also applies to internal situations.[137] Furthermore, the territorial application of a measure taken on the basis of Article 81 will be limited, due to the opt-in position of the United Kingdom, Ireland and Denmark.[138] On the other hand, it is also noteworthy that Article 81(2) provides for the adoption of measures '*particularly* when necessary for the proper functioning of the internal market' [emphasis added]. This wording is slightly different from the wording of Article 65 EC, which stated 'in so far as necessary for the proper functioning of the internal market'. The new wording of Article 81(2) seems to imply that it also provides for the adoption of legislation which is not necessarily only needed for the internal market.[139]

## 8.1. *Subsidiarity and Proportionality*

None of the competences mentioned in the previous section are exclusive competences for the EU.[140] They are all shared competences and therefore both the EU and the Member States are in principle allowed to legislate in these areas.[141] However, Member States may only make use of their competence to the extent that the EU has not (yet) done so. This implies that at a certain point, in any of these areas, full

137 Art. 81(1) TFEU speaks of 'civil matters having cross-border implications'; see also Keirse & Veder 2010, p. 52.

138 Protocol (No. 21) on the Position of the United Kingdom and Ireland in respect of the Area of Freedom, Security and Justice, [2010] *OJ* C 83/295, and Protocol (No. 22) on the Position of Denmark with Annex, [2010] OJ C 83/299. See also Basedow *et al.* 2011, p. 18.

139 Saarloos 2010, p. 312.

140 Artt. 3 and 4 TFEU.

141 Art. 2(2) TFEU.

harmonization may be reached, i.e. that the EU has used its competence to regulate a certain area exhaustively and that, as of that point, there is no competence left for the Member States. This is in particular true with regard to the internal market, large parts of which have already been subject to harmonization.[142] In any case, as regards all these areas of competence, the EU legislature must take into account the principles of subsidiarity and proportionality during the legislative process. This follows from Article 5(3) and (4) TEU, and Protocol (No2) to the Lisbon Treaties on the Application of the Principles of Subsidiarity and Proportionality.[143]

The principle of subsidiarity determines whether the EU *should* use its competence: is the EU better suited to regulate a certain area of law than the Member States are?[144] Weatherill points out that, in light of the CJEU's case law, the subsidiarity principle has lost much of its significance as regards European private law. If the purpose of an EU measure is to eliminate barriers to trade between Member States caused by differences between the national laws, then according to the Court this is a purpose that cannot be better achieved by the Member States individually, but must be achieved at EU level.[145] Advocate-General Fennelly expressed the same view in his Opinions in *Germany* v *Parliament and Council*[146] and *Imperial Tobacco*:[147]

> 'Where disparate national rules give rise either to obstacles to trade in goods or the provision of services or to distortions of competition, the Community has an interest in achieving uniformity of trading conditions which is quite distinct from its interest in the substantive content of the uniform rules adopted. The coordination or approximation of national rules which affect economic activity is the very essence of these competences, *provided* it serves the purposes of the internal market, and is not merely an instrument for achieving some separate, materially defined objective. *It is clear that only the Community can adopt measures which satisfy these requirements.*' [emphasis added]

The principle of proportionality determines that if the EU has the competence to legislate, and under the subsidiarity principle the EU should legislate and not the Member States, that legislation should be suitable for the aim it pursues and not go beyond what is necessary to achieve that aim.[148] The CJEU applies a marginal test: only if the measure is 'manifestly inappropriate' with regard to the aim which it pursues will the Court strike it down. The EU legislature is thus given a broad

142 *Cf* Sparkes 2007, p. 119.

143 [2010] *OJ* C 83/206.

144 *Cf* Wagner 2002, p. 1000: 'These differences counsel in favour of a principle of subsidiarity: since people are different and even groups of people hold different sets of preferences, the power to legislate should be fixed at the lowest, rather than the highest, political level.'

145 Weatherill 2010b, p. 64 with reference to case C-491/01, *R* v *Secretary of State, ex parte BAT and Imperial Tobacco*. See also Basedow *et al.* 2011, p. 23.

146 Case C-376/98 [2000] ECR I-2247.

147 Case C-74/99 [2000] ECR I-8599. See also Müller-Graff 2004, p. 79.

148 Craig & De Búrca 2011, p. 94; Strese 2006, p. 69.

discretion.[149] It might further be argued that minimum harmonization is more proportional than maximum harmonization as it is a less far-reaching measure.[150] That argument can be countered with the suggestion that minimum harmonization will not eliminate the divergences between national laws that may have been the initial reason for legislating in the first place, given that Member States would be able to maintain legislation that goes beyond the minimum level ensured by the European legislation.[151]

On a separate note, it used to be the case under the Amsterdam Treaty's protocol on subsidiarity and proportionality that directives were preferred to regulations as less far-reaching measures,[152] but this is no longer so under the Lisbon Treaties' protocol on subsidiarity and proportionality.[153] The Protocol has, however, introduced a so-called yellow card and orange card procedure.[154] Article 6 of the Protocol provides national parliaments with the opportunity to send in a reasoned opinion, within eight weeks from the date of transmission of a draft legislative act, stating why it considers that that draft legislative act does not comply with the principle of subsidiarity.[155] Article 7(2) of the Protocol determines that if the reasoned opinions from the national parliaments represent at least one third of the votes allocated to the national Parliaments, the draft must be reviewed. The Commission may then decide to maintain, amend or withdraw the draft, giving reasons. This is the yellow card procedure. Article 7(3) then determines that if the reasoned opinions represent at least a simple majority of the votes, the proposal must be reviewed. If the Commission then decides to maintain the proposal, it must justify in a reasoned opinion why it feels that the proposal complies with the principle of subsidiarity. This reasoned opinion will be submitted to the union legislator for consideration, upon which the Parliament and Council may terminate the proposal if it is considered to be incompatible with the principle of subsidiarity. This is the orange card procedure.[156] It is important to note that these procedures

149 Case C-380/03, *Germany* v *Parliament and Council* ('*Tobacco-II*') [2006] ECR I-11573, para. 145: 'With regard to judicial review of the conditions referred to in the previous paragraph, the Community legislature must be allowed a broad discretion in an area such as that involved in the present case, which entails political, economic and social choices on its part, and in which it is called upon to undertake complex assessments. The legality of a measure adopted in that sphere can be affected only if the measure is *manifestly inappropriate* having regard to the objective which the competent institutions are seeking to pursue'. [emphasis added].

150 Strese 2006, p. 229.

151 *Cf* Basedow *et al.* 2011, p. 24.

152 Protocol XXI to the Treaty of Amsterdam, [1997] *OJ* C 340/105.

153 Protocol (No. 2) on the Application of the Principles of Subsidiarity and Proportionality, [2010] *OJ* C 83/206.

154 *Cf* Craig & De Búrca 2011, p. 96-97.

155 Art. 6 of the Protocol does not mention the principle of proportionality. Weatherill 2006, p. 857-858.

156 Weatherill 2006, p. 853.

apply to legislative proposals drafted on the basis of Article 352 TFEU,[157] but not to proposals on the basis of Article 114 TFEU. They are therefore potentially only of limited significance in ensuring a proper review of the question, whether or not the Union legislature has complied with the principle of subsidiarity.[158]

## Final conclusions

As was seen in this chapter, Article 345 TFEU, which states that 'The Treaties shall in no way prejudice the rules in Member States governing the system of property ownership', does not remove the whole of property law from the scope of application of EU law. Historical research into Article 345's predecessors and the *Travaux préparatoires,* as well as a linguistic analysis of the Article and a review of the CJEU's interpretation of Article 345 have revealed no plausible explanation why the reference to ownership *of undertakings* was removed from the final version of what is now Article 345. As a result, the prevailing interpretation of Article 345 is still that it only refers to the question of whether an undertaking is publicly or privately owned. A Member State's decision to nationalize or privatize a company remains a matter for that Member State, as long as the nationalization or privatization does not interfere with the provisions of the Treaties on free movement and competition.

The CJEU may soon shine a new light on Article 345. On 24 February 2012 the Dutch supreme court (*Hoge Raad*) asked the CJEU preliminary questions on Article 345 in three separate but connected cases.[159] These cases revolved – as far as Article 345 is concerned – around the so-called *privatiseringsverbod,* or ban on privatization, resulting from the Dutch *Besluit aandelen netbeheerders.*[160] Directives 2003/54/EC[161] and 2003/55/EC[162] form the original background to the Dutch Decree. According to these Directives, distribution system operators of electricity or gas must be independent in terms of their organization and decision making from other activities not related to distribution.[163] The Directives were implemented in the Netherlands through the *Interventie- en Implementatiewet* (Intervention- and Implementation

157 Art. 352(2) reads: 'Using the procedure for monitoring the subsidiarity principle referred to in Article 5(3) of the Treaty on European Union, the Commission shall draw national Parliaments' attention to proposals based on this Article.'

158 Weatherill 2006, p. 857-858.

159 *De Staat der Nederlanden* v *Essent BV and Essent Nederland BV,* LJN: BQ9210, HR, 10/03851; *De Staat der Nederlanden* v *Eneco Holding NV,* LJN: BQ9212, HR, 10/03852; and *De Staat der Nederlanden* v *Delta NV,* LJN: BQ9214, HR, 10/03853.

160 Decree on shares in system operators. [translation as used on <http://curia.europa.eu> in the English version of the Reference for a preliminary ruling, Pending Cases C-105, 106 and 107/12].

161 Dir. 2003/54/EC concerning common rules for the internal market in electricity, [2003] *OJ* L 176/37.

162 Dir. 2003/55/EC concerning common rules for the internal market in natural gas, [2003] *OJ* L 176/57.

163 Art. 15(2) and Art. 13(2) respectively.

Law), which adapted the 1998 *Elektriciteitswet* (Law on electricity) and the *Gaswet* (Law on gas). These were later adapted again by the *Wet onafhankelijk netbeheer* (Law on independent network operation). The latter Law entailed a fragmentation of ownership, leaving the economic ownership of the networks with the distribution system operators (*netbeheerders*). On the basis of this latter Law, the Decree laid down that shares in the distribution system operators could not be held by private parties. This ban on privatization was contested by Essent, Eneco and Delta. The Dutch *Hoge Raad* stayed the proceedings and asked the CJEU the following preliminary question:[164]

> 'Must Article 345 TFEU be interpreted as meaning that the 'rules in Member States governing the system of property ownership' also include the rule in respect of the absolute ban on privatisation which is at issue in the present case, as set out in the Besluit aandelen netbeheerders (Decree on shares in system operators), in conjunction with Article 93 of the Elektriciteitswet 1998 (1998 Law on electricity) and Article 85 of the Gaswet (Law on gas), under which shares in a system operator can be transferred only within the circle of public authorities?'

At the time of writing,[165] no date has yet been scheduled for the Advocate-General's Opinion or for the hearing of these cases. However, since they are potentially of vital importance for the interpretation of Article 345, they will be closely followed.

Since Article 345 does not remove the whole of property law from the influence of EU law, the next question is whether or not the EU might have the competence to legislate in the field of property law. Several possible legal bases for such legislation were discussed in this chapter: Article 50(2)(e) on the freedom of establishment and the acquisition of immovable property in another Member State; Article 169 on consumer protection; Article 114 on the internal market; Article 81 for measures of private international law; and Article 352 as a legal basis of last resort. Article 50(2)(e) is a potential candidate for European measures of property law, but only for those specifically aimed at facilitating the cross-border acquisition of land. Article 169 is not a likely candidate because it can only be used for measures concerning B2C transactions, whereas cross-border transactions involving property law are more likely to be B2B transactions (in the context of free movement of goods) or C2C transactions (in the context of free movement of capital). Moreover, Article 169 refers to Article 114 as far as measures regulating the internal market are concerned. Article 114 may be a suitable legal basis for the enactment of European rules of property law but it requires approximation of national laws, which may be the case if the European property law rules would be mandatory, but not if they would be optional.[166] In line with the Court's *Tobacco* case law, it must also be kept

164 The *Hoge Raad* also asked a second and third question, but those are not relevant here. They can be consulted on the Curia website.

165 May 2012.

166 The form of future European measures on property law (mandatory or optional; regulation or directive, etc.) will be discussed in detail in Chapter 5.

in mind that measures enacted under Article 114 must genuinely have as their objective the removal of (existing or future) obstacles to the internal market or the elimination of appreciable distortions of competition.[167] For property law, this requirement may be fulfilled due to the fact that it is closed and mandatory, meaning that parties cannot get around the obstacles caused by the differences in national property laws through a choice of law.[168] Article 81 is primarily meant as a legal basis for the enactment of measures on private international law.[169] However, given that Chapter 2 of this study identified the private international law rule of *lex rei sitae* as one of the factors causing difficulties in cross-border property relationships (next to the diverging national substantive property laws), Article 81 may serve as a legal basis for a European measures intended to alter or replace the *lex rei sitae*.[170] Furthermore, Article 81 can only be used to enact measures applicable in cross-border situations, not for measures that also apply to purely internal situations. Finally, Article 352 might be used as a legal basis if none of the other legal bases are available. Article 352 has traditionally been used for legislation creating European-autonomous legal concepts or structures, such as the Societas Europaea or the Community trade mark. According to the CJEU, this type of legislation cannot be based on Article 114 TFEU as it does not lead to approximation of national laws. Article 352 might therefore be a suitable legal basis for a future optional instrument on EU property law. It must be noted, though, that Article 352 requires unanimity in the Council, something which may be difficult to achieve with 27 (soon to be 28)[171] Member States.

If it is established that the Treaties do indeed attribute the competence to the EU to regulate matters of property law, then it must still be established whether this regulation should occur at EU level as opposed to at national level and what the least far-reaching measure is that the EU could take to achieve its goals. In other words, the European legislature must adhere to the principles of subsidiarity and proportionality. Whether or not these two principles really curb and streamline the EU's legislative activity remains to be seen. The CJEU's case law seems only to have set a 'drafting guide'[172] for the European legislature, rather than actually clarify and enforce subsidiarity and proportionality. As long as certain key terms are inserted into the proposal for or preamble of a regulation or directive, the measure will pass muster. An effect on the internal market must be shown to be *direct*, or a distortion of competition to be *appreciable*, or the emergence of obstacles *likely*, etc.,[173] but often these key phrases are inserted but not elaborated on. See, for instance, Recital 36 of

167 *Cf* Weatherill 2011, p. 831.
168 See *supra*, section 8.
169 Basedow *et al.* 2011, p. 17-18.
170 This option will be explored in Chapter 5.
171 See the Treaty of Accession of Croatia of 24 April 2012, *OJ* L 112/10. The Treaty enters into force on 1 July 2013 (Art. 3(3)).
172 Weatherill 2011.
173 Weatherill 2011, p. 832-833.

the Late Payments Directive,[174] one of the measures discussed in the next chapter as relating to property law, which states that '[i]n accordance with the principle of proportionality, as set out in [Article 5 TEU], this Directive does not go beyond what is necessary in order to achieve that objective.' This meagre application of the principles of subsidiarity and proportionality is primarily a problem with regard to Article 114 TFEU, though. Legislation based on other, more sector-specific legal bases, such as Article 169(2)(b) or Article 50(2)(e), tends to be drafted with more regard for subsidiarity and proportionality.[175]

Now that the question whether or not the Treaties attribute the competence to the EU to legislate in the field of property has been evaluated, we turn to the already existing legislation to see whether and to what extent it already deals with property law.

174 Dir. 2011/7/EU on combating late payments in commercial transactions, [2011] *OJ* L 48/1.
175 Weatherill 2011, p. 833.

Chapter 4

# SUBSTANTIVE PROPERTY LAW AND PROPERTY LAW TERMINOLOGY IN PRIMARY AND SECONDARY EU LAW

## Introduction

It was seen in the previous chapter that there are several potential legal bases for the EU legislature to enact measures that concern property law. This chapter provides an overview of the extent to which the EU has already enacted legislation in the area of property law. The chapter consists of two parts. Part I provides an overview of the currently existing secondary EU legislation that deals with property law, directly or indirectly. The search for instruments relating to property law is difficult because most of the relevant provisions are 'hidden' within regulations or directives,[1] whose overall subject matter is usually not property law, but which may nevertheless contain property law elements. This is largely the result of the competence-driven nature of EU legislation.[2] Nevertheless, secondary EU legislation that is not at first view aimed at regulating an area of property law often has a bearing on property law because it contains property law terminology or because it contains provisions which either lay down substantive EU rules of property law or which affect the national systems of property law. The legislation discussed in Part I is presented in reverse chronological order to show the most recent developments first.

Part II explores the use of property law terminology in the Lisbon Treaties and in secondary EU legislation. This part of the chapter is intended to uncover what terminology the EU legislature uses, how it is used, and whether the terms used are given a European-autonomous definition in the legislation. Taken together, both parts of this chapter have as their purpose to find out whether or not the contours of

1 As Drobnig put it: 'As is well known, the voluminous 'statute book' of the European Union contains – hidden away among a mass of innumerable regulations and directives dealing with economic regulation and deregulation – a very small number of private law provisions'; Drobnig 1997, p. 491.

2 See Chapter 1, at 2. *The acquis method: defining European property law.*

a system of property law at EU level can already be seen to be emerging. The central question of this chapter is therefore: when can it be said that an EU Treaty or secondary legislative measure contains property law? To elaborate: is it sufficient that a Treaty or secondary measure contains property law terminology? Or can it only be said to concern property law if it contains substantive rules regulating matters of property law? In reality, the one is inextricably linked to the other. Substantive rules of property law are expressed in the language of property law, in words that are specifically used - and sometimes invented - to describe concepts and relationships in property law. For that reason, EU measures which either contain property law terminology or concern substantive property law are all taken into account in this chapter. An overview of the terminology used is essential in trying to build a coherent system of property law for the EU. Of particular interest are terms that have been defined. They may be used as a starting point in the process of building such a system. If there is no consistency or coherence in the use of terms yet, then this is something that will need to be improved upon in future legislation.

Certain types of documents have been excluded from the search. Decisions, although a binding legislative measure under Article 288 TFEU just as regulations and directives, have not been included in the search. The volume of search results, if decisions had been included, would simply have been too large to process. Furthermore, decisions generally have a specific addressee; they are not addressed to all the Member States. They can therefore not be relied on when forming a system of property law for the EU in its entirety. It must also be noted that not a single search entry yielded only decisions as a result, without also bringing up regulations and/or directives. CJEU case law and Advocates-General's opinions have also been excluded, because this chapter focuses on the legislative side of the formation of EU property law, not on the judicial side. Elsewhere in this book, in the context of negative harmonization through the four freedoms, CJEU judgments have been included and discussed in more detail. In this Chapter, which focuses primarily on positive harmonization through legislation, CJEU case law is only mentioned where it clarifies a term contained in legislation that was found with the list of search terms. However, I intend to repeat the search with the same list of terms used for this research in CJEU judgments and AG's opinions in future research.

In order to maintain an overview of the different ways in which EU legislation relates to property law, the legislative measures analysed in this chapter have been categorized in the following way: first, a division is made between those measures that concern substantive property law and those that only contain property law terminology; secondly, a division is made between those measures that concern substantive property law directly and those that only concern it indirectly; and thirdly a division is made between those measures that define certain terms, which are normally part of property law in the national systems and those that only use these terms but do not define them. Direct measures of EU property law are those measures that deal with matters of property law directly. These are, for instance, the

Directive on the Return of Stolen Cultural Objects, which contains rules on third party protection, the Late Payments Directive, which contains rules on retention of title, and the Insolvency Regulation, which contains rules on security rights.[3] Indirect measures of EU property law are those measures, which do not purport to change national rules of property law or add new rules, but which nevertheless affect the national systems of property law, be it intentionally or unintentionally.[4]

The measures discussed in this chapter can thus be grouped in the following way:

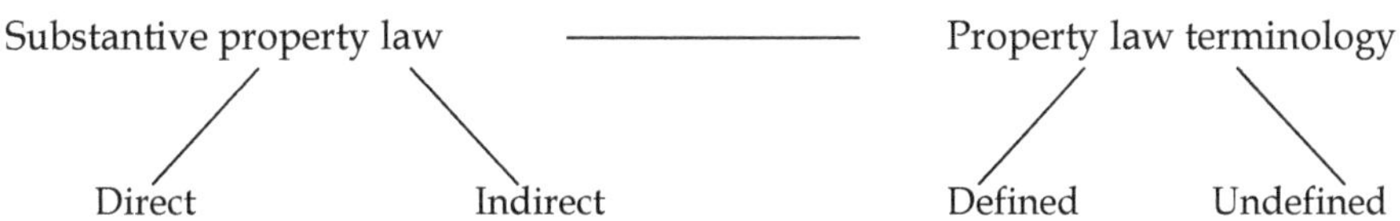


With regard to property law terminology, it must be noted that the Draft Common Frame of Reference and the subsequent Proposal for a Regulation on a Common European Sales Law[5] both contain definitions of terms that are relevant for property law. However, given that they are not (yet) part of the *acquis communautaire* they have not been included in the search conducted for this chapter. They will, however, serve as inspiration for the framework for future EU property law to be constructed in the final chapter of this thesis.

The information and analysis presented in both Part I and Part II will be brought together in a Conclusion at the end of this chapter.

## Part I - Substantive EU Property Law

## 1. Direct EU Property Law

### *1.1. Regulation 650/2012/EU on International Successions*[6]

A European Regulation on international successions has been in the making since 2006 when the Commission published a Green Paper on Succession and Wills.[7] On 23 May 2012 the Parliament and Council adopted the Regulation in its final form

3 *Cf* Akkermans 2011, p. 3.
4 *Cf* Akkermans 2011, p. 7.
5 COM(2011) 635 final.
6 Reg. on jurisdiction, applicable law, recognition and enforcement of decisions and acceptance and enforcement of authentic instruments in matters of succession and on the creation of a European Certificate of Succession, [2012] *OJ* L 201/107.
7 Green Paper of 1 March 2006 on Succession and Wills, COM(2005) 65 final. See also Ramaekers 2012.

but it has not yet entered into force at the time of writing.[8] The Regulation is intended to remove obstacles to the free movement of persons within the internal market 'who currently face difficulties in asserting their rights in the context of a succession having cross-border implications.'[9] The Regulation has been based on Article 81(2)(c) TFEU, meaning that it primarily contains private international law rules. However, its impact on national substantive property law is potentially great.

Article 21 of the Regulation states that the law applicable to a succession shall be the law of the State in which the deceased had his habitual residence at the time of death.[10] The Regulation grants people a limited choice of law so that they may choose, as the applicable law to their succession, the law of the State whose nationality they possess at the time of making the choice or at the time of death.[11] Perhaps the most important provision is Article 23, which states that the law determined pursuant to Article 21 or 22 shall govern the succession *as a whole*. This provision could have a substantial impact on the private international law of Member States where currently different conflict rules apply depending on the nature of the object. This is, for instance, the case under English law - where rights to movables acquired under a succession are governed by the *lex domicilii* and rights to immovables are governed by the *lex rei sitae*[12] - although at this moment the UK has decided to opt out of the Regulation.[13]

The impact on property law results from Article 31 of the Regulation. This Article reads as follows:

> 'Where a person invokes a right *in rem* to which he is entitled under the law applicable to the succession and the law of the Member State in which the right is invoked does not know the right *in rem* in question, that right shall, if necessary and to the extent possible, be adapted to the closest equivalent right *in rem* under the law of that State, taking into account the aims and the interests pursued by the specific right *in rem* and the effects attached to it.'

Recital 15 of the Preamble states that the Regulation should not affect the *numerus clausus* of rights *in rem* of a Member State, in other words that the receiving Member State should not be required to recognize a right *in rem* that is unknown to its own *numerus clausus*. Yet, Recital 16 and Article 31 require adaptation of an unknown right *in rem* to the closest equivalent under the law of the receiving Member State. This requirement of mutual recognition of property rights may affect national property law significantly. For instance, Member States may have difficulty adapting

8 June 2012. The text of the Regulation can be found at: <http://register.consilium.europa.eu/pdf/en/12/pe00/pe00014.en12.pdf#page=2>.

9 Recital 7.

10 Unless the deceased was manifestly more closely connected with another State; Art. 21(2).

11 Art. 22(1).

12 Garb & Wood 2010, p. 243 at 15.99 and 15.102.

13 Recital 82.

unusual[14] property rights such as the German *Reallast*, entitlements acquired under an English trust or the Dutch right of *usufruct* which, unlike, for instance, French or German law, does not entail an obligation to maintain and preserve the object.[15]

As will be seen below in section 3.9 of Part II of this chapter, the EU so far adhered to the *lex rei sitae*. What is not known at this moment is how the EU interprets the *lex rei sitae*. Different Member States interpret the *lex rei sitae* in different ways,[16] but no measure of EU secondary legislation currently provides insight into an interpretation of the *lex rei sitae* by the EU. What is clear is that the Regulation on international successions is a clear deviation from the *lex rei sitae* in favour of the *lex domicilii* and limited choice of law, albeit in succession law and not (yet) in general property law.

## 1.2. *Regulation 207/2009/EC on the Community Trade Mark (codified version)*[17] *and Regulation 6/2002/EC on Community Designs*[18]

Regulation 207/2009/EC on the Community trade mark codifies Regulation 40/94/EC and its several amendments. Regulation 40/94 is thereby repealed.[19] Regulation 207/2009 provides for a Community trade mark, which 'shall have equal effect throughout the Community'.[20] The Preamble indicates that the 'barrier of territoriality', which holders of national trade marks face, cannot be removed through approximation of laws. The Community therefore found it necessary to create a Community trade mark which can be used throughout the Community in a uniform manner.[21] The legal basis for this instrument is Article 308 EC (now Art. 352 TFEU). What this Regulation essentially does, is provide an optional Community trade mark which exists next to the national trade marks.[22] The concept of trade mark is given a European-autonomous interpretation. Registration is required to obtain a Community trade mark.[23]

Several provisions in this Regulation are of particular interest from a property law point of view. First of all, Community trade marks, as objects of property law, are to be dealt with under the law of the Member State where the proprietor has his seat or domicile or where he has an establishment.[24] That would, for instance, mean that a transfer of a Community trade mark – the trade mark is transferable on the

14 Unusual in the sense that they are only known in a very limited number of Member States.
15 Akkermans 2011, p. 10 *et seq.*
16 Akkermans & Ramaekers 2012b.
17 [2009] *OJ* L 78/1.
18 [2002] *OJ* L 3/1.
19 Preamble at (1) and Art. 166.
20 Art. 1(2).
21 Preamble at (4).
22 Preamble at (6).
23 Art. 6.
24 Art. 16(1).

basis of Article 17 of the Regulation - is governed by the rules of the relevant Member State on transfer of ownership of intangible property. Nevertheless, Article 17(6) stipulates that '[a]s long as the transfer has not been entered in the [Community] Register, the successor in title may not invoke the rights arising from the registration of the Community trade mark'. In other words, without entry in the Register,[25] the transfer is valid but cannot be invoked vis-à-vis third parties.[26] Secondly, on the basis of Article 19, Community trade marks may be given as security or be the subject of rights *in rem*. Unfortunately, it is not clarified anywhere in the Regulation what such rights *in rem* might be.[27] Presumably, these are the rights *in rem* available at national level and yet they may be entered in the Register of Community trade marks and published. In any case, this Regulation does view intangible objects, namely trade marks, as possible objects of rights *in rem* or property rights.[28] This may be valuable information when establishing, on the basis of the System-Cube developed in Chapter 1, what EU property law looks like. Finally, the Community trade mark - if properly filed - has priority over any later trade mark and other national right.[29]

Regulation 6/2002/EC on Community designs is similar to the Regulation on the Community trade mark. It, too, was adopted on the basis of Article 352 TFEU. Like the Regulation on the Community trade mark, it provides a European design which can be used throughout the EU. A Community design as an object of property shall be governed by national law.[30] A Community design is transferable, but until the transfer is registered the successor in title may not invoke the rights arising from registration.[31] A Community design may be given as security or be the subject of rights *in rem*.[32] This is another example of an intangible object which is capable of being the object of property rights.

### 1.3. *Regulation 1346/2000/EC on Insolvency Proceedings*[33]

This Regulation governs cross-border insolvency procedures. It focuses in particular on matters of applicable law.[34] However, it also contains several provisions which

25 Art. 87 'Register of Community trade marks'.

26 Art. 23(1): 'Legal acts referred to in Articles 17, 19 and 22 concerning a Community trade mark shall have effects vis-à-vis third parties in all the Member States only after entry in the Register.'

27 The Dutch version of the Regulation speaks of *zakelijke rechten*, the German version of *Dingliche Rechte*, the French version of *droits réels*.

28 *Cf* Bright & Bright 1998, p. 370.

29 Art. 29(2). See also the website of the Office for Harmonization in the Internal Market (Trade Marks and Designs) at: <http://oami.europa.eu/ows/rw/pages/CTM/tenReasons.en.do>, at 9 'Community trade marks as prior rights in all the member states of the European Union'.

30 Art. 27.

31 Art. 28.

32 Art. 29.

33 [2000] *OJ* L 160/1.

are relevant from a property law point of view. Article 5 of the Regulation refers in section 1 to 'rights *in rem*'.[35] What these rights entail is further clarified in section 2:

> '(2) The rights referred to in paragraph 1 shall in particular mean:
>
> (a) the right to dispose of assets or have them disposed of and to obtain satisfaction from the proceeds of or income from those assets, in particular by virtue of a lien or a mortgage;
>
> (b) the exclusive right to have a claim met, in particular a right guaranteed by a lien in respect of the claim or by assignment of the claim by way of guarantee;
>
> (c) the right to demand the asset from, and/or to require restitution by, anyone having possession or use of them contrary to the wishes of the party so entitled;
>
> (d) a right *in rem* to the beneficial use of assets.'

This section does not tell us what constitutes a right *in rem* in a European-autonomous sense; rather it is a functional description of the competences attached to rights *in rem*.[36] The reason for this absence of a definition is that the drafters did not want to risk including in their description rights *in rem* which would not be considered as such under national law or the other way around, risk excluding rights *in rem* which would be considered as such under national law.[37] The line is drawn at 'an unreasonably wide interpretation of the national concept of a right *in rem* to include, for instance, rights simply reinforced by a right to claim preferential payment'.[38] Essentially, the principle of *numerus clausus* is applied, but without being given any content: there is a description of what constitutes a right *in rem*, but there is no list of specific rights *in rem*.

Even though it does not provide a definition as such, the provision nevertheless provides important insights into what national legal relationships are considered by EU law to involve a property right.[39] Categories a and b concern security rights. They include the assignment of a claim by way of guarantee as a security right, in deviation from the way in which some Member States would view

34 Preamble, Recital 8.

35 Art. 5(1) states: 'The opening of insolvency procedures shall not affect the rights *in rem* of creditors or third parties in respect of tangible or intangible, movable or immovable assets - both specific assets and collections of indefinite assets as a whole which change from time to time - belonging to the debtor which are situated within the territory of another State at the time of opening of the proceedings.'

36 *Cf* Sagaert 2007, p. 309. The French version of the Regulation speaks of *droits réels*, the German version speaks of *dingliche Rechte*, and the Dutch version speaks of *zakelijke rechten*.

37 See the *Vírgos/Schmit* report on the Convention of Insolvency Proceedings of 3 May 1996, Council doc. no. 6500/1/96, at 100. The report can be found at: <http://globalinsolvency.com/sites/globalinsolvency.com/files/insolvency_report.pdf>. See also Israël 2005, p. 278.

38 *Vírgos/Schmit* report, at 102.

39 *Cf* Van Erp & Akkermans 2010, p. 174-175; Israël 2005, p. 277-278.

this.[40] Category c concerns remedies relating to rights *in rem* and category d concerns rights to use. Furthermore, section 1 gives an indication as to what the objects of these rights *in rem* could be, namely tangible and intangible assets and movable and immovable assets. It also indicates that these assets do not necessarily need to be specified; they may also be 'collections of indefinite assets as a whole which change from time to time'. This definition seems similar to that of an English floating charge.[41] A floating charge is a charge - security right - hovering over a changing class of assets, only attaching to specific assets at the moment of crystallization.[42] The *Vírgos/Schmit* report indeed states that security rights such as the English floating charge can be characterized as rights *in rem* for the purposes of the Insolvency Convention (now the Insolvency Regulation).[43] Similar provisions can be found in Directive 2009/138/EC (Solvency II),[44] Directive 2001/24/EC on the reorganization and winding up of credit institutions[45] and Directive 2001/17/EC on the reorganization and winding-up of insurance undertakings.[46]

Section 3 of each of these provisions states that '[t]he right, recorded in a public register and enforceable against third parties, under which a right *in rem* within the meaning of paragraph 1 may be obtained, shall be considered a right *in rem*'. This resembles the German concept of *Vormerkung* - or 'priority notice' - to which one can resort in order to protect a claim to the granting of a right in a piece of land or in a right burdening a piece of land.[47] According to the regulation and directives discussed here, the right registered through such a priority notice is considered to be a right *in rem*. This could have some interesting consequences.[48] Member States that know priority notice, but in which priority notice does not turn the registered right into a property right, are overruled by the Insolvency Regulation in cross-border insolvency situations. The Insolvency Regulation does turn such pre-registered rights into property rights, provided that they are enforceable against third parties. This may in effect mean an addition to the national *numerus clausus* with this right *in rem* resulting from the Insolvency Regulation. The *Vírgos/Schmit* report itself states that Article 5(3) of the Insolvency Regulation is a departure from the general statement that the characterization of a right as a right *in rem* must be sought in the applicable national law.[49] Here, the Regulation provides a

40 Sagaert 2007, p. 309.
41 *Cf* Sparkes 2007, p. 414.
42 Lawson & Rudden 2002, p. 144.
43 *Vírgos/Schmit* report, at 104.
44 [2009] *OJ* L 335/1, Art. 286.
45 [2001] *OJ* L 125/15.
46 [2001] *OJ* L 110/28, Art. 20. Note that this Directive's validity will end on 31 October 2012 as it has been repealed by Dir. 2009/138 (Solvency II).
47 § 883(1) German civil code; translation from Kiiver & Kornet 2010, p. 295.
48 *Cf* Sagaert 2007, p. 308.
49 *Vírgos/Schmit* report, at 101.

much more European-autonomous interpretation of what constitutes a right *in rem*.[50]

Article 7 of the Regulation deals with reservation of title. This combination of terms is somewhat confusing, as civil lawyers would generally speak of reservation of ownership, whereas English lawyers would speak of retention of title.[51] A reservation of ownership is in principle just a contractual clause. It therefore depends on its effect in insolvency proceedings whether it retains its proprietary character as well. If a reservation of ownership clause is not recognized in insolvency, it loses its proprietary character. If, on the other hand, it is recognized in insolvency, it retains its proprietary character. The Insolvency Regulation guarantees the recognition of reservation of title clauses both in the case of insolvency of the buyer as well as in the case of insolvency of the seller.[52] In conclusion, the Insolvency Regulation grants property effect to reservation of title clauses.

## 1.4. *Directive 2008/48/EC on Credit Agreements for Consumers*

The Directive on credit agreements for consumers[53] was enacted because of the development of new credit instruments and because of the increasing availability of cross-border credit.[54] The Directive provides protection for consumers entering into cross-border credit agreements. It is a full harmonization Directive: Member States are not allowed to introduce or maintain national provisions other than those laid down in the Directive.[55] One of the issues regulated by the Directive is the assignment (or *cession* in the French version)[56] of rights flowing from a consumer credit agreement. The Directive provides the following in Article 17:

> 'Assignment of rights
>
> 1. In the event of assignment to a third party of the creditor's rights under a credit agreement or the agreement itself, the consumer shall be entitled to plead against the assignee any defence which was available to him against the original creditor, including set-off where the latter is permitted in the Member State concerned.
>
> 2. The consumer shall be informed of the assignment referred to in paragraph 1 except where the original creditor, by agreement with the assignee, continues to service the credit vis-à-vis the consumer.'

50 For a more detailed discussion of the Insolvency Regulation, from the point of view of insolvency law rather than property law, see Israël 2005, Chapter Eight. *Council Regulation 1346/2000 on Insolvency Proceedings.*

51 Akkermans 2011, p. 4; Van Erp & Akkermans 2010, p. 177. For the difference between the two, see Akkermans 2008, p. 418-420.

52 Artt. 7(1) and (2); see also Akkermans 2011, p. 4-5 and Van Erp & Akkermans 2010, p. 178.

53 [2008] *OJ* L 133/66.

54 Preamble at 4 and 5.

55 Preamble at 9.

56 For a discussion of the terms 'assignment' and 'cession' in EU legislation see *infra*, Part II at 2.4. *Transfer/convey/assign/cession.*

Of particular interest is section 2 of this provision, which stipulates that the consumer (i.e. the debtor of the credit agreement) shall be informed of the assignment. This is a rule of property law generally also followed in national systems, but they sometimes permit assignment (or cession) of claims without informing the debtor (*debitor cessus*). This is, for instance, the case in Dutch law. Article 94(3) of Book 3 of the Dutch civil code provides for such a 'silent cession' (*stille cessie*). Banks in particular make use of silent cessions. Their preference for silent cessions as opposed to cessions whereby their debtors are informed stems from a desire to avoid negative publicity or a loss of confidence in the bank by its clients.[57] Banks fear that such negative publicity or loss of confidence might result from informing their debtors that claims have been assigned to obtain financing. Article 17 of the Directive on consumer credit agreements has been implemented by the Dutch legislator in Article 69 of Book 7 of the civil code.[58] It would appear that Article 7:69 now precludes silent cessions in the case of consumer credit agreements, in deviation from general Dutch property law which allows silent cessions.[59] This may pose a barrier for banks wanting to assign their claims as collateral for a loan.[60]

### 1.5. *Directive 2006/112/EC on the Common System of Value Added Tax*

Directive 2006/112 recasts the Sixth Council Directive 77/388/EEC on the harmonization of the laws of the Member States relating to turnover taxes.[61] The legal basis for this Directive was Article 93 EC (now Art. 113 TFEU), although the legal bases for Directive 77/388 were Articles 99 and 100 EEC (now Artt. 121 and 122 TFEU). The Directive will hereafter be referred to as 'the VAT Directive'. Of interest to this study are first of all Articles 14-16 of Directive 2006/112. Even though the order of the different parts of the provision has been changed in relation to its predecessor – Article 5 of Directive 77/388 – the content is still the same.

Article 14(1) defines the supply of goods as 'the transfer of the right to dispose of tangible property as owner'. What is interesting is that the transfer of a *right* is seen as the supply of *goods*. This seems out of line with the definition of goods as developed in the context of free movement of goods, which requires an object to be tangible for it to fall under the free movement definition of goods.[62] As was shown in Chapter 2, the rules on free movement of goods only govern the movement of the good itself, not the movement of any property rights resting on that good.[63] In

57 Scheltema 2011, p. 283-284.

58 Section 2 of that Article reads: 'De consument wordt geïnformeerd over de in lid 1 bedoeld overdracht, behalve indien de oorspronkelijke kredietgever, in overleg met de verkrijger tegenover de consument het krediet verder beheert.'

59 Scheltema 2011, p. 285-286.

60 Scheltema 2011, p. 285-286.

61 Dir. 2006/112/EEC, [2006] *OJ* L 347/1, Preamble, Recital 1.

62 See Chapter 2, section 3.1. *Definition of 'goods'*.

63 Section 3.1. *Definition of 'goods'*.

contrast, the VAT Directive governs the movement - or transfer - of the property right. This makes sense in a tax-related context. Whether a person or company has to pay turnover taxes, and how much, depends on whether a transfer provides them with ownership of (or an equivalent property right in relation to) certain property, not on whether the property is in their possession. According to the CJEU in the *Safe BV* case,[64] the 'supply of goods' must be interpreted in the following manner:

> '7 It is clear from the wording of this provision that "supply of goods" does not refer to the transfer of ownership in accordance with the procedures prescribed by the applicable national law but covers any transfer of tangible property by one party which empowers the other party actually to dispose of it as if he were the owner of the property.
>
> 8 This view is in accordance with the purpose of the directive, which is designed inter alia to base the common system of VAT on a uniform definition of taxable transactions. This objective might be jeopardized if the preconditions for a supply of goods - which is one of the three taxable transactions - varied from one Member State to another, as do the conditions governing the transfer of ownership under civil law.'

The CJEU here takes a functional approach to the transfer of ownership as a supply of goods, regarding it independently from any national requirements for a transfer of ownership.[65]

Article 20 of the Directive concerns the intra-Community acquisition of goods and states that this 'shall mean the acquisition of the right to dispose as owner of movable tangible property dispatched or transported to the person acquiring the goods, by or on behalf of the vendor or the person acquiring the goods, in a Member State other than that in which dispatch or transport of the goods began'. What exactly does the 'right to dispose as owner' mean? Obviously, an owner - in the civil law sense - would have that right. But does that include a Common law freeholder? Could it include someone holding a security right/security ownership who could sell/keep the object if the underlying debt is not repaid? If that is indeed the case, then, for the purposes of the Directive, the intra-Union acquisition of goods would entail the cross-border(!) acquisition of property rights. As we know, though, that would be problematic due to the *lex rei sitae* rule which might alter the property right as soon as it crossed a border, or even cause it to disappear completely.[66]

Article 15(1) indicates what is in any case to be treated as tangible property, namely 'electricity, gas, heat, or cooling energy and the like',[67] things which are not necessarily tangible, but are nevertheless treated as such. Article 15(2) then provides

64 Case C-320/88, *Staatssecretaris van Financiën* v *Shipping and Forwarding Enterprise Safe BV* [1990] ECR I-285.

65 See also Bright & Bright 1995, p. 665.

66 See for a more detailed discussion of the *lex rei sitae* and the problems it causes in intra-Community trade in Chapter 2, at 3.4.5.

67 Provision in its amended form in accordance with Dir. 2009/162/EU.

the Member States with several options of things they may regard as tangible property:

> '(a) certain interests in immovable property;
>
> (b) rights *in rem* giving the holder thereof a right of use over immovable property;
>
> (c) shares or interests equivalent to shares giving the holder thereof de jure or *de facto rights of ownership or possession* over *immovable property* or part thereof.'[68]

Again, it is interesting to see that it is not so much the objects themselves that are part of the description of tangible property (or goods, as was shown before with regard to the supply of goods), but the rights over or interests in these objects. This optional part refers to immovable property only, leaving the impression that the preceding (mandatory) parts refer to movable property.

To get a better overview of how exactly this Directive has influenced property law at a national level, it would be interesting to see how it has been implemented in several Member States.

In the Netherlands, the Directive has been implemented through the *Wet op de omzetbelasting 1968*.[69] The provisions concerning the supply of goods have been implemented in Articles 3 and 3a of the Statute. The Dutch legislature has chosen to include immovable property as well, on the basis of Article 15(2) of the Directive. In accordance with the CJEU's judgment in the case of *W.M. van Tiem* v *Staatssecretaris van Financiën*,[70] this choice has certain consequences. The Court held in paragraph 24 of its judgment that

> 'where a Member State has availed itself of the possibility afforded by Article [15(2) of the] Directive to consider rights in rem giving the holder thereof a right of user over immovable property to be tangible property, the reference to *transfer* in the first paragraph of [Article 14] must be interpreted as including the *creation* of such a right in rem' [emphasis added].

This judgment makes not only the transfer of a right to dispose as owner of an immovable taxable under the Directive, but also the creation of such a right over an immovable.

Attention must further be drawn to Article 3(7) of the *Wet op de omzetbelasting 1968*, which states: '*Goederen zijn alle voor menselijke beheersing vatbare stoffelijke objecten, alsmede elektriciteit, gas, warmte, koude en dergelijke.*'[71]

68 Emphasis has been added to indicate the remarkable use of property law terminology in this provision.

69 Statute on turnover taxation 1968.

70 Case C-186/89, [1990] ECR I-4363.

71 'Things are all corporeal objects susceptible to human control, including electricity, gas, heat, cold and the like.' Translation based on the translation of Artt. 3:1 and 3:2 Dutch civil code (BW) as provided in Kiiver & Kornet 2010.

This definition is peculiar, given the distinction that the Dutch civil code (BW) makes between *zaken* (objects) - which are corporeal objects susceptible to human control - and *goederen* (things) which are all objects and all patrimonial rights (*vermogensrechten*). The definition in Article 3(7) seems to be a result of the fact that the Dutch version of the Directive speaks of *levering van goederen* as the equivalent to the English 'supply of goods'. Apparently, *goederen* has a different meaning in a European law context than it does in the Dutch private law context.

Germany has indicated that implementation measures are in its view unnecessary.[72] The same is true for Belgium,[73] Spain[74] and Portugal.[75] The United Kingdom has implemented the Directive by way of the Value Added Tax Act 1994.[76] The United Kingdom, like the Netherlands, has also chosen to include immovable property in its implementing legislation. This can be derived from Schedule 4 attached to the VAT Act on 'Matters to be treated as supply of goods or services'. Section 1(4) states: 'The grant, assignment or surrender of a major interest in land is a supply of goods.' It is not specified what a major interest in land is, but presumably, on the basis of the Law of Property Act 1925, this would in any event be the two common law estates in land, the fee simple estate and the term of years absolute. The fact that the UK has included immovable property in the VAT Act means that the CJEU's judgment in *Van Tiem* also applies here. The UK legislation would appear to be in conformity with this judgment, given that it considers both the grant as well as the assignment of an interest in land as a supply of goods, meaning both are taxable in accordance with the Directive.

## 1.6. *Directive 2002/47/EC on Financial Collateral Arrangements*[77]

The Financial Collateral Directive regulates aspects of transactions between banks and other large financial institutions.[78] Financial collateral arrangements are defined in Article 2(1)(a) as 'a title transfer financial collateral arrangement or a security financial collateral arrangement'. The first type of financial collateral arrangement would be 'translated' in national property law as a transfer of ownership (or title to goods) for security purposes. The second type of arrangement is one whereby the debtor grants the creditor a security right to secure payment of an underlying

72 See: <http://eur-lex.europa.eu/LexUriServ/LexUriServ.do?uri=CELEX:72006L0112:EN:NOT#FIELD_DE>.

73 See: <http://eur-lex.europa.eu/LexUriServ/LexUriServ.do?uri=CELEX:72006L0112:EN:NOT#FIELD_BE>.

74 See: <http://eur-lex.europa.eu/LexUriServ/LexUriServ.do?uri=CELEX:72006L0112:EN:NOT#FIELD_ES>.

75 See: <http://eur-lex.europa.eu/LexUriServ/LexUriServ.do?uri=CELEX:72006L0112:EN:NOT#FIELD_PT>.

76 For an overview of the Value Added Tax Act in relation to land see Sparkes 2007, p. 137 *et seq.*

77 [2002] *OJ* L 168/43.

78 Van Erp & Akkermans 2010, p. 178.

claim.[79] According to Recital 10 of the Preamble to the Directive, the scope of application is limited to 'those financial collateral arrangements which provide for some form of dispossession'.[80] In other words, non-possessory security rights - like the Dutch silent pledge - are not covered.

One the one hand, the Directive creates substantive rules of EU property law. On the other hand, it has led to some changes in national property law. The substantive EU property law rules consist of the fact that Article 5 of the Directive allows the holder of a security right to keep the collateral for him- or herself in case of default payment by the debtor, something which is generally not allowed in property law.[81] Article 5 also allows the creditor to return like objects to the debtor in the place of the original object, again something which is not normally allowed under property law.[82] At the national level, the Directive has led to changes in French law - Article 2364 *Code civil* now also allows the creditor to keep the objects under security in case of non-performance by the debtor.[83] In the Netherlands, the Directive was implemented through Articles 51-56 of Book 7 of the Dutch civil code. The first type of financial collateral arrangement - the title transfer arrangement - was problematic for Dutch law because Article 3:84(3) of the Dutch civil code stipulates that legal acts purporting to transfer a thing for security purposes cannot form a valid title for transfer.[84] Article 7:55 Dutch civil code has remedied this conflict by stipulating that a transfer for the performance of a title transfer financial collateral arrangement is not a transfer in the sense of Article 3:84(3) Dutch civil code.[85]

79 Van Erp & Akkermans 2010, p. 179.

80 Recital 10: 'This Directive must however provide a balance between market efficiency and the safety of the parties to the arrangement and third parties, thereby avoiding inter alia the risk of fraud. This balance should be achieved through the scope of this Directive covering only those financial collateral arrangements which provide for some form of dispossession, i.e. the provision of the financial collateral, and where the provision of the financial collateral can be evidenced in writing or in a durable medium, ensuring thereby the traceability of that collateral.'

81 Art. 5(1). See also Van Erp & Akkermans 2010, p. 179; Sagaert 2007, p. 325.

82 Art. 5(2).

83 Van Erp & Akkermans 2010, p. 180, note 8. See also Sagaert 2007, p. 324.

84 *Cf* Sagaert 2007, p. 324.

85 Art. 7:55: 'Een overdracht ter nakoming van een financiëlezekerheidsovereenkomst tot overdracht is geen overdracht tot zekerheid of een overdracht die de strekking mist het goed na de overdacht in het vermogen van de verkrijger te doen vallen in de zin van artikel 84 lid 3 van Boek 3.' For a more detailed discussion of the effects of the financial collateral Directive on Dutch law, see Van Vliet 2005.

## 1.7. *Directive 2000/35/EC on Combating Late Payments in Commercial Transactions*[86]

This Directive - which is succeeded by Directive 2011/7/EU,[87] to be implemented by 16 March 2013 - regulates cases of non- or late payment in cross-border commercial transactions.[88] One of the functions of the Directive is to guarantee the effectiveness of retention of title clauses.[89] The Directive defines retention of title clauses as 'the contractual agreement according to which the seller retains title to the goods in question until the price has been paid in full'.[90] This corresponds to the standard retention of title or reservation of ownership clauses known in the Member States. Extended reservation of ownership clauses such as they exist in Germany[91] are however not part of the Directive.[92] Directive 2011/7 will only alter the numbering but not the wording of the relevant provisions.[93]

It is a pity that the original proposal for the Directive was not followed, for it contained a uniform rule on a simple retention of title clause, which would have had to be recognized in all Member States. It also would have included a provision stipulating that retention of ownership clauses should be able to be invoked in insolvency proceedings. The latter provision did not make it to the final version. As regards the former, the Directive in its final form contains a reference to private international law: creditors should be able to exercise a retention of title throughout the Community 'if the retention of title clause is valid under the applicable national provisions designated by private international law'.[94] The national provisions designated by private international law will be the *lex rei sitae*.[95] In theory, this could lead to the non-recognition of a foreign retention of title clause if it does not comply with the formalities for such a clause in the host Member State, although that would go against the *effet utile* of the Directive.[96] Given, however, that all Member States provide for a simple retention of title clause under their national law, problems of non-recognition will be minimal.

86 [2000] *OJ* L 200/35.
87 [2011] *OJ* L 48/1.
88 Preamble to Dir. 2000/35, at 7-12. See also Akkermans 2011, p. 4.
89 Art. 4(1) of the Directive: 'Member States shall provide in conformity with the applicable national provisions designated by private international law that the seller retains title to goods until they are fully paid for if a retention of title clause has been expressly agreed between the buyer and the seller before the delivery of the goods.'
90 Art. 2(3).
91 Van Erp & Akkermans 2012, p. 499 *et seq.*, section IV.A.6. *Manufacturing of the assets under retention of title*; Milo 2003, p. 133-134.
92 *Cf* Sagaert 2007, p. 319.
93 Art. 2(3) becomes Art. 2(9); Art. 4 becomes Art. 9.
94 Preamble, Recital 21; Art. 4(1). See also Kieninger 2004b, p. 23-24.
95 *Cf* Milo 2003, p. 121.
96 Milo 2003, p. 137.

## 1.8. *Directive 93/7/EEC on the Return of Stolen Cultural Objects*[97]

The Directive on the return of stolen cultural objects provides Member States with a procedure to retrieve cultural objects unlawfully removed from their territory from the possessor or holder of such an object in another Member State.[98] Even though the Directive focuses on a specific issue - stolen cultural objects only - its effect on national property law is potentially great. Generally, a good faith acquirer for value of a cultural object will be considered the owner of that object, at least until it is discovered that the object was unlawfully removed from another Member State.[99] However, within the scope of application of the Directive, the object must nevertheless be returned to the Member State from which it was stolen.[100] This obligation under the Directive has led to some changes in the Member States' property law. In the Netherlands, for instance, the civil code contains a rule - Article 86 of Book 3 of the civil code - protecting good faith acquirers who acquire an object for value from a party who did not have the power to dispose over an object, against revindication by the original owner. This rule, however, conflicts with the obligations imposed by the Directive. As a result, a provision was added to the Dutch civil code stating that Article 86 of Book 3 of the civil code cannot be invoked against a Member State reclaiming a stolen cultural object, provided that the conditions of the Directive are fulfilled.[101] In conclusion, a choice has been made in the Directive not to protect third parties who acquired a cultural object for value and in good faith, but to protect the rights of the Member State from whose territory the object was unlawfully removed. This is in contrast to the law of some Member States which does protect the rights of third parties over the rights of the original owner in certain circumstances.

There is a proposal for a codified version of the Directive[102] but this will leave the text of the Directive practically unaltered. The terminological implications of the Directive will be discussed in Part II of this chapter.

97 [1993] *OJ* L 74/74.
98 Art. 5.
99 Akkermans 2011, p. 3.
100 Van Erp 2006b, p. 8.
101 Art. 86a of Book 3 Dutch civil code. See Akkermans 2011, p. 3.
102 COM(2002) 873 final.

## 2. Indirect EU Property Law

### 2.1. *Regulation 881/2002/EC Imposing certain Specific Restrictive Measures Directed against certain Persons and Entities Associated with Usama bin Laden, the Al-Qaida Network and the Taliban*[103]

Regulation 881/2002/EC was adopted under the Common Foreign and Security Policy.[104] It implements several UN Security Council Resolutions and provides for sanctions to be taken against certain persons suspected of terrorist activities. One of the sanctions is to freeze all financial assets of such a person, group of persons or organization.[105] An ECJ judgment, *Möllendorf*,[106] exemplifies how these sanctions can affect a person's property and his or her capacity to dispose freely of it.

The facts of the case were as follows: Gerda Möllendorf and Christiane Möllendorf-Niehuus (the sellers) concluded a contract of sale for land and buildings, which they owned in Berlin, with Salem-Abdul Ghani El-Rafei, Kamal Rafehi and Aqeel A. Al-Aqeel (the buyers). The purchase price had been paid and the transfer of ownership was provisionally registered in the German Land Registry. However, before the transfer could be finally registered, the Registry found out that one of the buyers was blacklisted in Annex I to Regulation 881/2002. The Registry therefore rejected the application for final registration. Proceedings concerning this rejection were started and reached the *Kammergericht* in Berlin. In order to understand the impact of this rejection, it is important to know several things about the transfer of ownership of immovable property under German law. Such a transfer first of all requires a valid title (in this case the sales agreement), but it also requires an agreement for the actual transfer of the right of ownership and for this agreement to be registered in the Land Registry.[107] According to the *Kammergericht*, the freezing of a person's assets affects his capacity to dispose of them and the Land Registry must take this into account when deciding whether or not to finalize the registration of the transfer of ownership.[108]

Because this case required an interpretation by the ECJ of Regulation 881/2002, the *Kammergericht* stayed the proceedings and asked the ECJ for a preliminary ruling. The ECJ held the following:

> '[T]he answer to the questions referred must be that in a situation where both the contract for the sale of immovable property and the agreement on transfer of ownership of that property have been concluded before the date on which the buyer is included in the list in Annex I to Regulation No. 881/2002 and where the sale price has

103 [2002] *OJ* L 139/9.
104 Legal bases: Artt. 60, 301 and 308 EC (now Artt. 75, 215 and 352 TFEU).
105 Art. 2.
106 Case C-117/06, *Möllendorf and Möllendorf-Niehuus*, [2007] ECR I-8361.
107 See Artt. 873 and 925 German Civil Code (BGB).
108 A.-G. Mengozzi's Opinion to case C-117/06, *Möllendorf*, at paras. 41-42; Lavranos 2008, p. 139.

> also been paid before that date, Article 2(3) of that regulation must be interpreted as *prohibiting the final registration*, in performance of that contract, of the transfer of ownership in the Land Register subsequent to that date.'[109] [emphasis added]

It follows from this judgment that the blacklisting and subsequent freezing of assets under Article 2(3) of Regulation 881/2002 has several effects on national property law. Primarily, it affects a person's power to dispose over his assets,[110] which is generally an essential requirement for the transfer or creation of a property right. Furthermore, in the *Möllendorf* case, it affected the *Vormerkung* which had already taken place. *Vormerkung* is a concept of German property law, meaning preliminary registration. Preliminary registration of a contract of sale for an immovable property in the Land Registry can be done immediately after the conclusion of the contract and provides the buyer with an *Anwartschaftsrecht*, which protects him against insolvency of the seller or acts of the seller which purport to transfer ownership of the immovable to a third person.[111] This *Anwartschaftsrecht* - or expectation right as it is often translated - was essentially lost by the buyer the moment he was blacklisted.

## 2.2. *Directive 2003/87/EC Establishing a Scheme for Greenhouse Gas Emission*[112]

The emission rights Directive establishes a Community-wide trading scheme in so-called emission allowances. The scheme is meant to reduce the volume of greenhouse gasses emitted into the atmosphere each year. An 'allowance' is defined in Article 3 as

> 'an allowance to emit one tonne of carbon dioxide equivalent during a specified period, which shall be valid only for the purposes of meeting the requirements of this Directive and shall be transferable in accordance with the provisions of this Directive'.

Companies are expected to reduce their greenhouse gas emissions. Excess emission rights can be traded with other companies.

Article 3 prescribes that emission rights shall be transferable and it is in this respect that the Directive has impacted national property law. Emission rights, as

109 Para. 80 of the judgment. See also Van Erp 2009a, p. 265 *et seq.*

110 A.-G. Mengozzi, para. 70: 'That said, I would observe that Article 2(3) of Regulation 881/2002, by prohibiting in general terms, [...] the making available of economic resources to the persons mentioned in Annex I to that regulation, imposes a relative prohibition of disposal that of course covers every act which, under national law of a Member State, may be prescribed for the transfer of ownership, or even mere possession, of immovable property.' See also ECJ, paras. 60-62 of the judgment.

111 Van Erp & Akkermans 2012, Chapter 8, Note 7 under excerpt 8.55 (DE), and section II.A.2.g. *The priority notice* (*Vormerkung*) on p. 870 *et seq.*

112 [2003] *OJ* L 275/32.

objects of property law,[113] can be transferred making use of the national system of transfer. The Netherlands has a causal tradition system of transfer, meaning that, for a valid transfer, an underlying agreement (or title), which is and remains valid, and delivery (or a deed and registration) are required.[114] However, the nature of emission rights makes it difficult for them to be transferred under this system. Emission rights are used up: once the greenhouse gasses have been emitted, the rights expire. If, by the end of the year, the underlying agreement - and therefore the entire transfer - became invalid for some reason, it would hardly be possible to return the emission rights to the original seller, given that they have been depleted. The Dutch legislature has therefore had to make an exception to the general transfer system for the transfer of emission rights. Article 16.42 of the Dutch law implementing the Directive states the following:

> '1. Voidance, avoidance or rescission of the agreement that led to the transfer, has, after the transfer has been completed, no consequences for the validity of the transfer.
>
> 2. Every condition in relation to the transfer ends at the moment that transfer has been effected.
>
> 3. In derogation from article 228 of book 3 of the Civil Code a right of pledge cannot be created on an emission right.'[115]

This provision implements an abstract system of transfer whereby invalidity of the underlying agreement (title) does not affect the validity of the transfer. The Dutch legislature chose this system of transfer of emission rights, because it felt that it was essential that holders of emission rights should be able to rely on the fact that they can actually use their emission rights.[116] In addition, the Dutch legislature has excluded the possibility to create a right of pledge on an emission right because emission rights, due to their temporary character, are hardly a suitable collateral to secure a claim.[117] It is noteworthy, however, that neither the French, nor the

113 In the Netherlands they are considered to be *vermogensrechten* (patrimonial rights) because they represent a certain value and are transferable; see Akkermans 2011, p. 8; Kortmann 2005, p. 393.

114 Van Vliet 2000, p. 133.

115 1. Nietigheid, vernietiging of ontbinding van de overeenkomst die tot de overdracht heeft geleid, heeft, nadat de overdracht is voltooid, geen gevolgen voor de geldigheid van de overdracht.
2. Elk voorbehoud met betrekking tot de overdracht is uitgewerkt op het moment dat de overdracht tot stand is gekomen.
3. In afwijking van artikel 228 van Boek 3 van het Burgerlijk Wetboek kan op een broeikasgasemissierecht geen recht van pand worden gevestigd. [transl. by Akkermans 2011, p. 9]

116 MvT, *Kamerstukken II*, 2003/04, 29 565, nr. 3, p. 73. See also Kortmann 2005, p. 394.

117 *MvT, Kamerstukken II*, 2003/04, 29 565, nr. 3, p. 74: 'Emissierechten zijn als gevolg van hun tijdelijk karakter nauwelijks een geschikt verhaalsobject.'

German, nor the English legislature have excluded the possibility to pledge emission rights in their implementing legislation.[118]

Through the Emission Rights Directive, the EU legislature has introduced a new object of property law,[119] and an intangible one at that.[120] As the example of Dutch law shows, incorporating this new object into the existing national system of property law is not always without problems. The Emission Rights Directive provides an example indicating that a coherent European system of property law may be desirable in which European-autonomous 'creations' of property law - be they rights, objects etc - can function smoothly.[121]

## 2.3. *Natura 2000*

Natura 2000 forms the core of the EU's nature and biodiversity policy.[122] It establishes a network of nature protection areas through two directives: the Habitats Directive[123] and the Birds Directive.[124] If an area is designated as a Special Area of Conservation or Special Protection Area under either one of these directives, the owner of this land is restricted in what s/he can do with it. This follows, for instance, from Article 6(3) of the Habitats Directive:

> 'Any plan or project not directly connected with or necessary to the management of the site but likely to have a significant effect thereon, either individually or in combination with other plans or projects, shall be subject to appropriate assessment of its implications for the site in view of the site's conservation objectives. In the light of the conclusions of the assessment of the implications for the site and subject to the provisions of paragraph 4, the competent national authorities shall agree to the plan or project only after having ascertained that it will not adversely affect the integrity of the site concerned and, if appropriate, after having obtained the opinion of the general public.'

This means, for instance, that hunting certain species of animals is not allowed and that construction, or any other activity that risks disturbing the habitat of certain species, is not allowed either. The same is true for the disturbance of plant life.[125] Similar provisions concerning the preservation of certain bird species can be found

118 Kortmann 2005, p. 396.
119 *Cf* Akkermans 2008, p. 502.
120 Sagaert 2007, p. 310. Emission trading rights are essentially public law licenses. There has been some discussion in Dutch administrative law as to whether these are transferable; see Teuben 2005 at 2.5.1.3 *Overdraagbaarheid*.
121 *Cf* Van Erp 2006a, p. 1065-1066.
122 <http://ec.europa.eu/environment/nature/natura2000/index_en.htm>.
123 Dir. 92/43/EEC on the conservation of natural habitats and of wild fauna and flora, [1992] *OJ* L 206/7.
124 Dir. 2009/147/EC on the conservation of wild birds, [2010] *OJ* L 20/7.
125 See Artt. 12 and 13 of the Habitats Directive.

in the Birds Directive.[126] In essence, through these directives an owner can be restricted in the exercise of his right of ownership of a particular area of land by a public law measure.

## 2.4. *Directive 93/13/EEC on Unfair Terms in Consumer Contracts*[127]

The Unfair Terms Directive is meant to aid consumers when concluding cross-border contracts for the supply of goods or services, by ensuring that unfair terms are removed from those contracts.[128] Because the Directive applies to goods and services,[129] it will affect movable property law: contracts concluded for the creation, transfer or destruction of property rights in relation to movable objects will fall under the scope of application of the Directive.[130] Whether the scope of the Directive extends to contracts relating to immovable property remains to be seen.[131] The English and German versions - using the terms 'goods' and *Güter* respectively - might indicate that the Directive does not cover contracts relating to immovable property. The French and Dutch versions on the other hand - using the terms *biens*[132] and *goederen* respectively - might indicate that the Directive does cover contracts relating to immovable property, given that these terms cover both movable and immovable property in their respective national systems.[133] The Explanatory Memorandum to the original Commission proposal stated:

> 'It cannot be assumed that consumers who cross frontiers to buy goods or services, or to *invest or acquire property* in other Member States, have understood and agreed the terms of a contract they have made, if they do not speak the local language or are unfamiliar with the local law.'[134] [emphasis added]

On this same issue a question was asked by European Parliamentarian Yves Verwaerde, who wished to know '[w]hat specific measures [...] the Commission plan[s] to adopt to increase legal protection for those acquiring immovable property in the European Community [...]?'.[135] The Commission's representative answered that the proposal for the Unfair Terms Directive 'offers considerable protection in relation to contracts for any kind of consumer purchase'. The final version of the Directive no longer contains the reference to the investment or acquisition of property. Bright ventures to say that the specific exclusion of immovable property

126 Artt. 5-8.
127 [1993] *OJ* L 95/29.
128 Preamble, Recital 10.
129 Art. 4.
130 Akkermans 2010a, p. 14.
131 Bright & Bright 1995, p. 655.
132 *Cf* Schulte-Nölke, Twigg-Flessner & Ebers 2008, p. 367.
133 *Cf* Bright & Bright 1995, p. 664.
134 COM(90) 322 final of 3 September 1990, p. 2.
135 Written Question No. 2325/90 by Yves Verwaerde, [1991] *OJ* C 177/9.

from a number of directives may indicate that, in the absence of any such exclusion, immovable property is normally covered.[136] This is certainly a possibility. Below, under the heading *Movable/immovable*, it is shown that the term immovable is often used to exclude immovable property explicitly from the scope of application of a directive or regulation. The absence of such an exclusion from the Unfair Terms Directive, together with the Explanatory Memorandum and the Parliamentary Question just mentioned,[137] may indicate that the Unfair Terms Directive should be read as including contracts relating to immovable property. This argument is supported by a judgment of the English Court of Appeal in which Laws LJ states the following:

> 'I am unable to perceive any rationale for the exclusion of land transactions from the [Unfair Terms] Directive's scope. Such an exclusion would cut across the grain of the legislation's aim to provide "a high level of protection". I agree [...] that one would expect to find such an exclusion expressly provided for; and it is not to be found.'[138]

Contracts for the supply of services are not restricted by the Directive to movable property only, thus services relating to immovable property may be covered.[139] A mortgage loan, for instance, could be seen as the provision of a (financial) service.[140] Bright draws a parallel with the VAT Directive in which the creation of rights in immovable property is classified as a supply of goods or services.[141] A parallel can also be drawn with the Doorstep Selling Directive.[142] The ECJ held in the *Dietzinger* case, which involved the Doorstep Selling Directive, that '[t]he grant of a credit facility is indeed the provision of a service [in the sense of the Directive]'.[143]

In conclusion, it would seem that the scope of application of the Unfair Terms Directive not only includes contracts for the supply of goods or services in relation to movable property but also such contracts in relation to immovable property.

## 2.5. *Directive 85/577/EEC on Contracts Negotiated away from Business Premises ('doorstep selling directive')*

The starting point in this Directive is that it excludes contracts relating to immovable property from its scope of application. This follows from Article 3(2) of the

136 Bright & Bright 1995, p. 666.
137 See *supra* note 135.
138 *R. (on the application of Khatun)* v *Newham LBC*, [2005] QB 37.
139 Akkermans 2010a, p. 14.
140 Bright & Bright 1995, p. 662.
141 Bright & Bright 1995, p. 669. For a more detailed discussion of the VAT Directive see *supra*, section 1.5.
142 See *supra*, section 1.5.
143 Case C-45/96, *Bayerische Hypotheken- und Wechselbank AG* v *Edgard Dietzinger*, [1998] ECR I-1199, para. 18.

Directive.[144] At first glance, therefore, the Directive appears not to concern matters of property law. However, Article 3(2) has been interpreted by the ECJ in such a way that it can actually have an effect on national rules of property law. The cases *Heininger*,[145] *Schulte*[146] and *Crailsheimer*[147] all involved investment deals - for instance to renovate residential apartment blocks - consisting of an agreement to purchase immovable property and a credit agreement (or loan agreement) to finance the purchase, with the immovable property as collateral.[148] When the deals turned out to be bad investments, it proved impossible to cancel the purchase agreements, even though the deals had been concluded in what the Directive would consider to be 'doorstep' conditions.[149] The parties in these cases then tried to challenge the credit agreements under the Directive, arguing that the purchase agreements formed an economic unit with the credit agreements so that, if the credit agreements could be cancelled under the Directive, the purchase agreements should also be able to be cancelled. The Court however held that a credit agreement falls within the scope of the Directive but that the effects of a cancellation of that agreement on the purchase agreement are to be governed by national law.[150] However, cases such as *Heininger, Schulte* and *Crailsheimer* arise mainly if the consumer has not been told of his doorstep right of cancellation.[151] The consumer cannot avoid exposure to the risks of a bad investment if he is not informed in time of his right of cancellation.[152] If this is the case, Member States are required 'to ensure that their legislation protects consumers who have been unable to avoid exposure to such risks, by adopting suitable measures to allow them to avoid bearing the consequences of the materialization of those risks.'[153] In other words, Member States are to ensure the *effet utile* of the Directive. If linked contracts are involved such as in the abovementioned cases, the *effet utile* of the Directive may not be realized if consumers can only withdraw from the credit agreement but not from the purchase agreement.[154] Therefore, the effects of these judgments may be direct in causal systems (both causal consensual and causal tradition systems), where ownership

144 See Art. 3(2): 'This Directive shall not apply to: (a) contracts for the construction, sale and rental of immovable property or contracts concerning other rights relating to immovable property. Contracts for the supply of goods and for their incorporation in immovable property or contracts for repairing immovable property shall fall within the scope of this Directive.'

145 Case C-481/99, *Heininger*, [2001] ECR I-9945.

146 Case C-350/03, *Mr and Mrs Schulte* v *Deutsche Bausparkasse Badenia AG*, [2005] ECR I-9215.

147 Case C-229/04, *Crailsheimer Volksbank*, [2005] ECR I-9273.

148 Sparkes 2007, p. 205.

149 Sparkes 2007, p. 205.

150 *Schulte*, at 68.

151 Sparkes 2007, p. 244.

152 *Schulte*, at 98-99.

153 *Schulte*, at 101.

154 Akkermans 2010a, p. 7.

passes upon conclusion of the agreement.[155] In abstract tradition systems, where the transfer of ownership depends not only on a valid agreement but also on an act of delivery, property law rules may have to be altered or added to, to conform with the Directive.[156]

## Part II - Terminology

### 3. Searching for Property Law Terms

During the search for property law aspects in EU law it became clear that, while there are only very few measures that actually contain substantive property law, measures containing property law terminology can be found frequently. The research for this part of the chapter was conducted on the basis of a list of search terms. The list was compiled on the basis of knowledge gained through several years of researching comparative and European property law. The literature consulted for this research shows that there is a basic set of terms used within the field of property law to describe the core concepts and relationships.[157] This information was used to decide what terms would be included in the list of search terms. The search was conducted with the use of the EUR-lex database[158] and with the use of the Google search engine. The list of search terms and a description of how the search was conducted are provided below:[159]

- owner/ownership/proprietor
- possessor/possession
- in rem/in re
- real right/personal right
- proprietary
- numerus clausus
- lex rei sitae
- transfer
- convey* *with* land
- assign* *with* claim
- cession
- pledg* (to find pledge, pledgor, pledgee and any variation of the verb to pledge)
- mortgag* (to find mortgage, mortgagor, mortgagee and any variation of the verb to mortgage)

155 *Cf* Hoge Raad 10 August 2012, BW4992, 11/01768.

156 Akkermans 2010a, p. 7.

157 See, for instance, Lawson & Rudden 2002, Sparkes 2007, Baur, Baur & Stürner 2009, Libchaber 2004, Asser & Hartkamp 2011, Von Bar 2000, Faber & Lurger 2008, Van Erp 2009b.

158 <http://eur-lex.europa.eu/en/index.htm> Simple Search.

159 The search was conducted between April 2010 and March 2012. Legislation enacted after that time is not included.

- hypothec* (to find hypothec, hypothecor, hypothecee)
- lien* *except* client
- charge/floating charge/fixed charge
- estate
- tenure
- freehold* (to find freeholder as well)
- free simple
- lease* (to find leasehold and leaseholder as well)
- tenancy/tenancies
- title to *with* interest in/legal title
- retention of title/reservation of ownership
- servitude
- usufruct* (to find usufructuary as well)
- easement
- restrictive covenant
- emphyteusis
- superficies
- trust* (to find trustee as well)
- beneficiary *with* trust
- movable* (to find both movable(s) and immovable(s))
- tangible* except tangible evidence/contribution/criteria (to find both tangible(s) and intangible(s))
- corporeal* (to find both corporeal(s) and incorporeal(s))

Compiling a list of search terms was not the most difficult part of this research. EUR-lex seemed the logical search engine to use for searching property law terminology in EU legislation. A simple search by word in title and text was the first step. The search results were then narrowed down by indicating that the type of document should be a regulation or directive. Other refining tools used were the EXCEPT and WITH fields, providing the possibility to exclude or include a term or terms in combination with the main search term.[160] However, the EUR-lex search engine has a number of shortcomings, which are felt in particular when looking for terms that have a colloquial meaning in addition to their legal meaning, such as assignment or title. It is impossible in EUR-lex to separate a term's legal meaning from its colloquial meaning. One cannot tell a search engine to look for title 'in the property law sense'; it takes a human brain to understand such a contextual qualification.

Secondly, it is not possible to manipulate what comes in front of your search term. To clarify: an asterisk (*) can be used as a so-called wild card to tell the search

160 For instance: convey WITH land will only yield documents that contain both these words. Lien EXCEPT client will only yield documents that contain the word lien, but not the word client.

engine to fill in the blanks. For instance, EUR-lex makes a search for own* possible, which yields documents containing terms such as owned, owner and ownership. Unfortunately, it also yields documents with words such as known or down. Due to these limitations in the search engine, some search terms yield (tens of) thousands of results, a quantity of data impossible to manage in the context of a PhD research project. This problem is exacerbated by the fact that, unlike many other search engines, EUR-lex does not display the context - i.e. sentence or paragraph - in which the searched term appears, so that one could immediately infer from the context whether the document is relevant or not. One can, for instance, quickly deduce from context whether 'assignment' is used in the meaning of task or in the meaning of transfer of a claim.

Thirdly, EUR-lex also renders search results of measures which are no longer in force. That means having to check for each individual measure whether or not it has expired or been replaced by a new measure. I did this for every measure enacted before the year 2000. Furthermore, it renders amendments separately from the original document - usually, there is no consolidated version. That means that the amendments must be compared to the original to find out whether anything relevant from a property law point of view has been added or removed by the amendment. One final problem is that the search results cannot be downloaded into, for example, an excel file where they could be archived for later use.

EUR-lex's advanced search engine does not solve these problems. It is not user friendly, does not yield certain results of which you know are 'out there' and, while it does allow you to be somewhat more detailed with the search terms, for some search terms this still does not reduce the number of results to a manageable level, due to some of the other difficulties described above. Unfortunately, the EUR-lex helpdesk was unable to help me to solve these problems, primarily because the solution lies in a reprogramming of EUR-lex itself (for instance, so that it provides the context of the search term, like Google and others do).

In conclusion: the EUR-lex search engine is not suitable to do a search for certain terms. The term ownership, for instance, is found in approximately[161] 451 regulations and 126 directives; the term transfer is found in approximately 1896 regulations and 427 directives. Processing these results would either require an enormous amount of time, or a group of researchers. Different ways to do the search were therefore necessary. I decided to use EUR-lex only for terms that yield no more than 20 pages of results, containing a maximum total of 200 search results. Where the number of results exceeded 20 pages, I used Google as an alternative search engine. Google has a few important advantages over EUR-lex. Most importantly, Google displays the context in which the search term appears, making the selection process of relevant documents much quicker. Furthermore, Google provides a number of tools to conduct a very detailed search. It is possible to

161 Given that the search conducted for this chapter took place within a certain time frame - April 2010 until March 2012 - these numbers may have slightly changed since then.

instruct Google to only search for results in EUR-lex, by including in the search 'site:eur-lex.europa.eu'. By adding 'intitle:"EN"' the search results are restricted to documents whose webpage has EN in the title, meaning that you only get the English version of an EUR-lex document. Moreover, I added the phrase 'having regard to', because the preamble of a regulation or directive always starts with this phrase. Conversely, Google allows you to exclude certain terms – I chose to exclude 'judgment of the court' and 'opinion of the advocate general', given that I was only looking for regulations and directives. Finally, Google allows one to search for terms that appear close to each other in the text – the AROUND function. This function helped with searches for terms which otherwise, even in Google, simply rendered far too many results. 'Possession' rendered 1210 results in Google, i.e. 51 pages of search results. Taking into account that the vast majority of search results will either be using possession in a sense not relevant for property law, or will use the term in a property law sense but not define it, they are a lot less relevant for the research than the handful of measures hidden in that jungle of search results that possibly do contain a definition of the term possession that is meaningful in the property law sense. When it proved impossible to go through all the search results – which was the case with possession and also with transfer – the next best thing was to try and find measures in which the term possession is defined. Looking at how regulations and directives are generally drafted, such a definition will either be found under the heading 'definitions' or in a sentence containing the words 'shall mean' or 'shall in particular mean'. Google's AROUND function makes it possible to search for possession not more than, say, 50 words removed from the word definitions. The search then includes 'possession AROUND(50) shall mean'. The end result is a search term that, for example, looks like this: '["in rem" AND "having regard to" site:eur-lex.europa.eu intitle: "en" – "judgment of the court" – "opinion of the advocate-general"].'[162]

Only one problem remained: copying several of the searches already conducted with EUR-lex in Google showed that not all search results that should come up, did come up. This appeared to be an indexing problem: anything not indexed by Google cannot be found. Having run this problem by a Google employee revealed that – for reasons unknown – some EUR-lex documents have been indexed by Google in their .pdf format only, not in their .html format. They sometimes do not show up in the search, because they do not always have EN in their title. The Google contact person suggested changing intitle:"EN" to inurl:"EN", because the .pdf documents did have EN in their URL. This created more problems than it solved, however. The number of additional, irrelevant search results that show up because they contain the letters 'en' in their URL referring to something other than the English language version was entirely disproportional to

162 For possession, the search term would look like this: ["possession" AROUND(50) "shall mean" AND "having regard to" site:eur-lex.europa.eu intitle:"en" –"judgment of the court" – "opinion of the advocate-general"].

the number of relevant search results missing because of this indexing problem. I therefore decided to leave the search query as before and accept the minute risk that the one regulation or directive containing a term which could not be searched with EUR-lex and which has actually been defined in a European-autonomous way did not show up in the search results.

While EUR-lex contains a very valuable, extensive database, often with documents going far back in time to the early years of the EU, difficulties with its search engine are not something that I alone have experienced in my research. Ronny Patz's blog and the comments it has received[163] is a testimony to the despair felt by many a researcher when trying to make sense of the EUR-lex search engine. In the end, most people - including myself - find themselves resorting to Google, which tends to deliver the sought after document much more easily. A Council document of 15 December 2010 entitled "New EUR-lex" indicates that EUR-lex is currently under revision.[164] I wrote to the Council and suggested that they consider a Google-like function for EUR-lex, which displays with each search result the sentence or paragraph in which the search term features. This function would enable a speedier selection of relevant search results than EUR-lex currently does because in EUR-lex one has to open and search in each individual search result for the sought-after term.

### 3.1. *Language of the Search*

The search was conducted in English, since that is currently the most commonly used working language of the EU.[165] Sometimes, however, the wording of a provision was ambiguous. In such instances a comparison was made with, first of all, the French version, French being one of the original languages and still one of the primary working languages of the EU Institutions; and secondly, with the Dutch and German versions, both also being original languages. The results of the search will show that a wide variety of property law terminology is already being used in secondary EU legislation, albeit in different contexts. This chapter provides an overview of what terminology is used, how it is used and in what context and whether any definitions are given. From this overview conclusions will be drawn regarding the extent to which the EU legislature uses property law terminology and whether or not its use is consistent and coherent. These conclusions will form the starting point for Chapter 6, in which a framework for the future development of EU property law will be developed.

163 <http://polscieu.ideasoneurope.eu/2011/01/13/the-quest-for-eu-documents-an-exemplary-journey/>.

164 Doc No. 17427/10, to be found at: <http://register.consilium.europa.eu/pdf/en/10/st17/st17427.en10.pdf>.

165 English has gradually taken over from French, which used to be the main working language. The CJEU forms an exception by still using French as the primary working language.

Each of the following sections analyses a property law term or group of terms as used in the Treaties and in secondary legislation. The searched terms have been printed in bold in the text, as well as in the quotations of legislation.

## 3.2. *TEU and TFEU*

The TEU does not contain any of the search terms in the list. The TFEU, on the other hand, does. Several provisions mention the term *own* or *ownership*, the most prominent of course being Article 345.[166] Furthermore, Article 75 TFEU reads:

> 'Where necessary to achieve the objectives set out in Article 67, as regards preventing and combating terrorism and related activities, the European Parliament and the Council, [...], shall define a framework for administrative measures with regard to capital movements and payments, such as the freezing of funds, financial **assets** or economic gains belonging to, or *owned* or held by, natural or legal persons, groups or non-State entities.'

It thus contains several of the search terms.

*Property* is the search term most often found. Apart from Article 345, it also features *inter alia* in Article 335:[167]

> 'In each of the Member States, the Union shall enjoy the most extensive legal capacity accorded to legal persons under their laws; it may, in particular, acquire or dispose of *movable* and *immovable property*.'

Other examples include Article 50(2)(e) which mentions 'to acquire [...] *land*';[168] Article 64 which mentions *real estate*; Article 192(2)(b) again mentioning *land*;[169] and Articles 318 and 321 both again mentioning *assets*. Neither Treaty contains any definitions of property law terms, however.

166 'The Treaties shall in no way prejudice the rules in Member States governing the system of property *ownership*' [emphasis added]; see Chapter 2. See also Art. 123(2).

167 The other articles are 36, 118, 207 and 262 TFEU, although in these articles the term is used in the sense of intellectual property (rights).

168 Art. 50(2)(e) was also mentioned in Chapter 2 as a possible legal basis for rules of European property law.

169 Art. 192 also forms the Legal basis for Dir. 2003/87/EC on greenhouse gas emissions and for Dir. 2004/35/EC on environmental liability.

## 4. Defined Property Law Terms

### 4.1. *Right in Re(m)/Real Right/Personal Right*

The search for rights *in re(m)* led to a number of results, amongst others Regulation 593/2008/EC ('Rome I'), Regulation 44/2001/EC ('Brussels I') and Regulation 207/2009/EC on the Community trade mark (codified version).[170]

The Rome I Regulation[171] excludes from its scope of application contracts relating to rights *in rem* in immovable property; their validity is determined by the law of the country where the property is situated.[172] The Regulation is silent on rights *in rem* in movable property. The Brussels I Regulation[173] stipulates what is the competent court in matters relating to rights *in rem* in immovable property.[174] It does not give a definition of rights *in rem* - neither does the Rome I Regulation - and is silent on rights *in rem* in movable property. The Commission's proposal for the recasting of Brussels I,[175] however, provides for a new provision concerning rights *in rem* and possession in movable property.[176] Again, there will not be a definition of rights *in rem*.[177] In addition, several authors have expressed the opinion, in response to the Green Paper and subsequent Proposal for the review of Brussels I, that the scope of the provision should only include rights *in rem* in relation to tangible movable property and that rights *in rem* in intangible movable property should be excluded.[178] The main argument put forth in this respect is that the connecting factor to determine which court shall have jurisdiction is the *situs* of the object and that the *situs* of intangible assets is difficult to establish.

While the Brussels I Regulation does not provide a definition of rights *in rem*, there is an ECJ judgment concerning the Brussels Convention - the predecessor to Brussels I - that makes the fundamental distinction between rights *in rem* and rights *in personam*. This case, *Lieber v Göbel*,[179] revolved around the question, whether compensation for use of a dwelling after a failed property transfer was covered by

170 The term rights *in re* was found only once, in Dir. 2001/24/EC.

171 Reg. 593/2008/EC on the law applicable to contractual obligations, [2008] *OJ* L 177/6.

172 Preamble, at 27; Artt. 4(1)(c), 6(4)(c) and 11(5).

173 Reg. 44/2001/EC on jurisdiction and the recognition and enforcement of judgments in civil and commercial matters [2001] *OJ* L 12/1.

174 Artt. 6(4) and 22(1).

175 COM(2010) 748 final.

176 Art. 5(3) of the Proposal: 'The following courts shall have jurisdiction: [...] 3. as regards *rights in rem* or possession in moveable property, the courts for the place where the property is situated.' For a detailed discussion of this proposed provision, see Franzina 2011.

177 *Cf* Franzina 2011, p. 5.

178 Franzina 2011, p. 8-10; Dickinson 2009, at 50; Review of the Brussels I Regulation (EC 44/2001) - Comments from the United Kingdom, at 44.

179 Case C-292/93, *Norbert Lieber* v *Willi S. Göbel and Siegrid Göbel*, [1994] ECR I-2535.

the term right *in rem* under Article 16(1) of the Brussels Convention.[180] The Court stated, in paragraph 14:

> 'The difference between a right in rem and a right in personam is that the former, existing in an item of property, has effect against the whole world, whereas the latter can only be claimed against the debtor.'

This statement is based on the Schlosser Report, which first - in an EU context - described the difference between rights *in personam* and rights *in rem*.[181] This characterization of rights *in rem* is repeated in the *Virgos/Schmit* report.[182] According to this report rights *in rem* have two characteristics, namely a direct and immediate relationship with the asset they cover independent of any relationship between the holder of the right *in rem* and another person; and an absolute nature meaning that they are enforceable *erga omnes*.[183] The same characteristics of rights *in rem* are applied by the Court, not only in *Lieber* v *Göbel* but also in *Webb* v *Webb*[184] and in *Reichert*.[185] The latter two cases both concerned the Brussels Convention. According to these cases, the Brussels Convention - now the Brussels I Regulation - only applies to actions *in rem* that are based on a right *in rem*,[186] i.e. actions

> 'which seek to determine the extent, content, ownership or possession of immovable property or the existence of other rights *in rem* therein and to provide the holders of those rights with the protection of the powers which attach to their interest'.[187]

Rights *in rem* are then described as 'rights directly relating to the property which are enforceable against the whole world'.[188]

The distinction between rights *in rem* and rights *in personam* presupposes the existence of a *numerus clausus* - or closed list - of property rights. Rights *in rem*, being defined as having effect against the whole world, will be limited in number and content precisely because of this effect.[189] It can further be assumed that this interpretation given by the Court of rights *in rem* is a European-autonomous interpretation. The Court stated in *Reichert* that 'an independent definition must be given in Community law to the phrase "in proceedings which have as their object rights in rem in immovable property"'.[190]

180 Para. 8 of the judgment.
181 Schlosser Report, [1979] *OJ* C 59/71, para. 166.
182 See *supra*, Part I, section 1.3.
183 *Vírgos/Schmit* report, at 103.
184 Case C-294/92, *Webb* v *Webb*, [1994] ECR I-1733.
185 Case C-115/88, *Mario P.A. Reichert and others* v *Dresdner Bank*, [1990] ECR I-27.
186 *Webb* v *Webb*, para. 14.
187 *Reichert*, para. 11.
188 *Webb* v *Webb*, para. 15.
189 Akkermans 2008, p. 6-7.
190 *Reichert*, para. 8. With regard to the same provision - Art. 16(1) of the Brussels Convention - that was at stake in *Reichert*, the Court gave such an independent definition to the term →

Regulation 207/2009 on the Community trade mark stipulates that 'A Community trade mark may [...] be given as security or be the subject of rights in rem'.[191] This provision gives some indication as to the types of objects in relation to which a person can have a right *in rem*. Given that a trade mark is an intangible object, the fact that one can have a right *in rem* in relation to it stands in stark contrast to what has been said earlier about objects of rights *in rem* under the Brussels I Regulation. A broader definition of rights *in rem* can be found in the Insolvency Regulation (1346/2002/EC) and similar regulations. See for a discussion of these regulations and the Regulations on the Community trade mark and design further above, Part I on Substantive EU Property Law.

The search for *personal right* did not yield any results and the search for *real right* only yielded one result in Regulation 1722/2005/EC[192] where it is observed that a time-share constitutes a real right in at least one Member State.[193]

## 4.2. *Property/Assets/Things/Objects*

These terms yielded by far the most results - tens of thousands. There are several reasons why this happened. First of all, these words can be used in a property law context but they also have a colloquial meaning. Secondly, and this is particularly true for 'things' and 'objects', they are 'empty' terms: they do not really have an independent meaning but derive their meaning from context. A thing can be anything; so can an object. 'Assets' can be understood in the economic sense, meaning things(!) that have an economic value. But a character trait or physical appearance can also be someone's 'greatest asset'. Property, depending on the context, can mean land, ownership, or characteristic. The search results were not significantly diminished by trying to link these terms to another search term or to the term 'definition' or 'shall mean', as was, for instance, possible with the term 'possession'. The search for these terms could therefore not be conducted directly. This was not a problem, however. Any definitions of property or assets to be found in the *acquis* are found automatically because other terms that are part of such a definition have been sought for. For instance, a definition of assets was found in Regulation 881/2002/EC imposing certain specific restrictive measures directed against certain

'tenancies of immovable property' in case 241/83, *Rösler* v *Rottwinkel*, [1985] ECR 99, paras. 24-25.

191 Reg. 207/2009/EC (codified version) on the Community trade mark, Art. 19(1); see further *supra*, Part I at 1.2. The same is stipulated for the Community design in Reg. 6/2002/EC.

192 [2005] *OJ* L 276/5.

193 Annex to the Regulation, under Principal 9, 1.4.3. *Time-sharing accommodation.*

persons and entities associated with Usama bin Laden, the Al-Qaida network and the Taliban[194] as a result of the search for 'tangible' and 'movable':

> 'Article 1
>
> For the purpose of this Regulation, the following definitions shall apply: [...]
>
> (2) "economic resources" means *assets* of every kind, whether tangible or intangible, movable or immovable, which are not funds but can be used to obtain funds, goods or services.'[195]

A definition of property can be found in Directive 2005/60/EC on the prevention of terrorist financing:[196]

> 'Article 3
>
> For the purposes of this Directive the following definitions shall apply: [...]
>
> (3) "property" means assets of every kind, whether corporeal or incorporeal, movable or immovable, tangible or intangible, and legal documents or instruments in any form including electronic or digital, evidencing title to or an interest in such assets [...].'[197]

It was possible to search for the term proprietary. The most interesting result from that search was Regulation 385/96/EC on protection against injurious pricing of vessels.[198] Article 1 of this Regulation contains principles and definitions and states in section 3(e):

> 'For the purpose of this Regulation: [...]
>
> (e) the term 'ownership interest' shall include any contractual or *proprietary* interest which allows the beneficiary or beneficiaries of such interest to take advantage of the operation of the vessel in a manner substantially comparable to the way in which an owner may benefit from the operation of the vessel.'

194 [2002] *OJ* L 139/9. The phrase found in Art. 1(2) of this Regulation can be found in all regulations 'imposing restrictive measures'. *Cf* also Dir. 98/26/EC on settlement finality in payment and securities settlement systems, [1998] *OJ* L 166/45:
'Article 2:
For the purpose of this Directive: [...]
(m) 'collateral security' shall mean all realisable *assets* provided under a pledge (including money provided under a pledge), a repurchase or similar agreement, or otherwise, for the purpose of securing rights and obligations potentially arising in connection with a system, or provided to central banks of the Member States or to the future European central bank.'

195 See also Art. 286 of Dir. 2009/138/EC (Solvency II), [2009] *OJ* L 335/1.

196 [2005] *OJ* L 309/15.

197 See also Art. 1(1)(D) of Dir. 2001/97/EC on prevention of the use of the financial system for the purpose of money laundering, [2001] *OJ* L 344/76.

198 [1996] *OJ* L 56/21.

This provision shows a differentiation between contractual and proprietary rights and equates all rights that are substantially comparable to ownership with ownership.

## 4.3. *Possessor/Possession*

Apart from the terms owner or ownership, which will be discussed below under *Undefined property law terms*, the terms possessor and possession are also used. *Possessor* is found in only one directive, namely the Directive on the return of cultural objects, which provides a definition not only of possessor but also of holder:[199]

> 'Article 1
>
> For the purposes of this Directive; [...]
>
> 6. "*Possessor*" shall mean the person physically holding the cultural object on his own account.
>
> 7. "Holder" shall mean the person physically holding the cultural object for third parties.

Two things can be said about this provision: first of all, even though the definitions are only 'for the purposes of this Directive', they may nevertheless be of more general use for other legislation. As long as there is no other legislative measure that gives a different definition to the same term, this definition is the current one within the *acquis*. Secondly, these definitions seem to be quite well in line with the way in which these concepts are defined in most national systems.[200] This might make it easier for them to be adopted as general European property law terms than it is for other terms because problems with implementation may be fewer. The term holder,

199 Council Directive 93/7/EC of 15 March 1993 on the return of cultural objects unlawfully removed from the territory of a Member State, [1993 *OJ* L 74/74.

200 *Cf* some of the other language versions:
- in German:
'6. "Eigentümer": die Person, die die tatsächliche Sachherrschaft über das Kulturgut für sich selbst ausübt;
7. "Besitzer": die Person, die die tatsächliche Sachherrschaft über das Kulturgut für andere ausübt.'
- in Dutch:
'6. "bezitter": degene die een cultuurgoed feitelijk houdt voor zichzelf;
7. "houder": degene die een cultuurgoed feitelijk houdt voor een ander.'
- in French:
'6) "possesseur": la personne qui a la détention matérielle du bien culturel pour son propre compte;
7) "détenteur": la personne qui a la détention matérielle du bien culturel pour compte d'autrui.'
The terminology in German national property law is more complicated: it distinguishes between mittelbares and unmittelbares Fremdbesitz and Eigenbesitz.

although not searched for specifically, came up in another regulation as a result of the search for *possession*. 'Holder' is defined in Regulation 1221/2008/EC[201] as 'any natural or legal person physically in possession of the products concerned'. This Regulation does not specify whether that means in possession for himself or in possession for someone else.

By limiting the search for possession to definitions only, the number of search results was greatly reduced. Possession is, for instance, used in Regulation 108/2006/EC:[202]

> '38. When an entity obtains financial or non-financial assets [...] by taking *possession* of collateral it holds as security or calling on other credit enhancements (e.g. guarantees), and such assets meet the recognition criteria in other Standards, an entity shall disclose:'

Possession is also used in Directive 72/159/EC on the modernization of farms:[203]

> 'Article 6 [...]
>
> 2. If the development plan contains a proposal for extending the area of the farm, the enlarged area shall consist of: - the land already in the **possession** of the farmer;
>
> - land in respect of which he has been given a legally enforceable promise entitling him to *possession*.'

In the first example the term possession is clearly used in a property law sense: in the execution of security rights taking possession of the collateral that is held as security is usually the first step. In the second example it is less clear whether or not the term possession is used in a property law sense because it is not specified what a 'legally enforceable promise' entitling someone to possession would be.

## 4.4. *Transfer/Convey/Assign/Cession*

The search for the term transfer was made difficult by the vast amount of search result it generated: around 18,000 results in EUR-lex. A Google search still rendered 3,300 results. The search was therefore focused on finding a definition of the term transfer. A selection of the most interesting results is presented here. One example is Regulation 73/2009/EC[204] in which the term transfer is defined in Article 23(1):

201 Regulation amending Reg. 1580/2007 laying down implementing rules in the fruit and vegetable sector as regards marketing standards, [2008] *OJ* L 336/1. It was this amendment that added the definition of holder.

202 Amending Reg. 1725/2003/EC adopting certain international accounting standards, [2006] *OJ* L 24/1.

203 [1972] *OJ* L 96/1.

204 [2009] *OJ* L 30/16.

> 'For the purpose of this paragraph, "*transfer*" shall mean any type of transaction whereby the agricultural land ceases to be at the disposal of the transferor.'

Another example is Regulation 385/96/EC, where the term transfer is present in the definition of 'sale':

> 'Article 1
>
> Principles and definitions [...]
>
> (d) the term "sale" shall cover the creation *or transfer* of an ownership interest in the vessel, except for an ownership interest created or acquired solely for the purpose of providing security for a normal commercial loan.'

This provision differentiates between an outright transfer of ownership and a transfer of ownership for security purposes. There are many more examples to be found.[205] I will not mention all of them here; more information can be found in the Annex attached to this chapter.

The term *convey*[206] was coupled with the term land because it otherwise returned too many search results and because convey is the term normally used in English law for the transfer of land. This search rendered three results but only one of them actually had to do with the transfer of land.[207]

In searching for the use of the term *assign(ment)*, a combination was made with the term 'claim', for it was otherwise impossible to separate the term assignment in the property law sense from the term assignment in the sense of 'task'. Article 14(3) Rome I gives a definition of assignment:[208] 'The concept of assignment in this Article includes outright transfers of claims, transfers of claims by way of security and pledges or other security rights over claims.'

This is a clear definition, with the exception perhaps of the use of the word 'included', which would suggest that the definition is not exhaustive. The definition is however so broad that one wonders what else it could cover.

The term 'assign' is used in many more regulations and directives, although the Rome I Regulation is the only measure defining the term. See, for instance, Directive 2009/44/EC amending Directive 98/26/EC on settlement finality in payment and securities settlement systems and Directive 2002/47/EC on financial collateral arrangements as regards linked systems and credit claims:

205 One of the more prominent is Dir. 86/635/EEC on the annual accounts and consolidated accounts of banks and other financial institutions which, in Art. 12, sets out in detail what sale and repurchase transactions are.

206 Searched as convey* so as to also find conveyance or conveyancing.

207 See Art. 5(1) of Dir. 72/160/EC on farming and agricultural areas. The other two search results were Reg. 1126/2008/EC and Reg. 1910/2005/EC, both adopting certain international accounting standards.

208 Verhagen & Dongen 2010, p. 5.

> 'Article 2
>
> Amendments to Directive 2002/47/EC [...]
>
> '3. [...] Member States shall ensure that debtors of the credit claims may validly waive, in writing or in a legally equivalent manner:
>
> (i) their rights of set-off vis-à-vis the creditors of the credit claim and vis-à-vis persons to whom the creditor *assigned*, pledged or otherwise mobilised the credit claim as collateral;'

In Directive 2006/112/EC on the common system of value added tax, not only the term assignment is used but also the term *cession*:[209]

> 'Article 199
>
> 1. Member States may provide that the person liable for payment of VAT is the taxable person to whom any of the following supplies are made: [...]
>
> (f) the supply of goods following the *cession* of a reservation of ownership to an **assignee** and the exercising of this right by the *assignee*;'[210]

On the one hand it might seem surprising that a fairly complex construction such as a cession of a reservation of ownership is taken into account in European legislation. On the other hand, this makes more sense if one takes into consideration that both directives using the term cession - Directive 2006/112 and Directive 2006/69[211] - are tax directives. In the context of taxes it is not unusual that complex proprietary relationships are constructed in an attempt to reduce the amount of taxes that have to be paid. What is perhaps more important is that these two directives use the term cession, whereas otherwise the term assignment is used. Assignment is the proper term in English law for the transfer of a claim, but cession just seems to be a direct translation of the civil law concepts of *Zession* or *cession*, which are used in the German and French versions of the directives and it does not combine well with the use of the word assignee in the same sentence.

209 The term assignment can be found in quite a number of other directives and regulations, amongst others in Dir. 2008/48/EC on credit agreements for consumers, [2008] *OJ* L 133/66:
'Article 17
Assignment of rights
1. In the event of *assignment* to a third party of the creditor's rights under a credit agreement or the agreement itself, the consumer shall be entitled to plead against the assignee any defence which was available to him against the original creditor, including set-off where the latter is permitted in the Member State concerned.
2. The consumer shall be informed of the *assignment* referred to in paragraph 1 except where the original creditor, by agreement with the assignee, continues to service the credit vis-à-vis the consumer.' [emphasis added]

210 *Cession* of a reservation of ownership is also mentioned in Dir. 2006/69/EC, [2006] *OJ* L 221/9.

211 See *infra*, section 5.1.1. *Retention of title/reservation of ownership*.

## 5. Undefined Property Law Terms

### 5.1. *Owner/Ownership/Proprietor*

Searching for the terms owner and ownership was not possible with the EUR-lex search engine. Ownership rendered around 5,000 results, owner and owners together rendered around 9,000 results. With Google it was possible to narrow the number of search results down to around 700 results each. There are nevertheless still many examples to choose from. A selection is presented here. One example is Article 56 of Regulation 2009/207/EC on the Community trade mark:[212]

> 'Article 56
>
> Application for revocation or for a declaration of invalidity
>
> 1. An application for revocation of the rights of the *proprietor* of a Community trade mark or for a declaration that the trade mark is invalid may be submitted to the Office: [...]
>
> (c) where Article 53(2) applies, by the *owners* of the earlier rights referred to in that provision or by the persons who are entitled under the law of the Member State concerned to exercise the rights in question.' [emphasis added]

The only definition of owner found was a rather circular one, in the sense that the owner is the one having ownership. This definition is contained in Directive 2002/60/EC,[213] Article 2:

> 'For the purposes of this Directive: [...]
>
> "*owner*" shall mean any person or persons, either natural or legal, having ownership of the pigs, or charged with keeping the said animals, whether or not for financial reward.'

Variations on the term ownership, such as 'full ownership' or 'ownership rights', also exist. See, for instance, Directive 2002/47:

> 'Article 2
>
> Definitions
>
> 1. For the purpose of this Directive: [...]
>
> (b) "title transfer financial collateral arrangement" means an arrangement, including repurchase agreements, under which a collateral provider transfers *full ownership* of financial collateral to a collateral taker for the purpose of securing or otherwise covering the performance of relevant financial obligations;' [emphasis added]

212 [1994] *OJ* L 11/1.

213 Directive laying down specific provisions for the control of African swine fever, [2002] *OJ* L 192/27.

'Ownership rights' are mentioned in Directive 2004/39/EC on markets in financial instruments:[214]

> Article 4(1)(1): [...]
>
> (a) the *ownership rights* of third parties in instruments and funds must be safeguarded, especially in the event of the insolvency of the firm or of its proprietors, seizure, set-off or any other action by creditors of the firm or of its proprietors; [emphasis added]

Regulation 113/2010/EU[215] uses the concept 'economic ownership' and defines it in Article 19(1)(c) as:

> '"[E]conomic *ownership*" means the right of a natural or legal person to claim the benefits associated with the use of a vessel or aircraft in the course of an economic activity by virtue of accepting the associated risks.'

One wonders what the difference would be between ownership, full ownership and ownership rights. The term proprietor is also used relatively frequently.[216] Whether this should be seen as an alternative to owner or whether it has a separate meaning does not become clear. In Article 56(1) of Regulation 2009/207,[217] the terms proprietor and owner are even used next to each other; the same is true for Article 4(1)(1)(a) of Directive 2004/39.[218]

214 [2004] *OJ* L 145/1. 'Ownership interests' are mentioned in Reg. 904/2010/EU on administrative cooperation and combating fraud in the field of value added tax, [2010] *OJ* L 268/1, Art. 54.

215 [2010] *OJ* L 37/1.

216 Reg. 1346/2000/EC on insolvency proceedings speaks of '[t]he proprietor of the right in rem': Preamble, Recital 25. Reg. 696/93/EEC, [1993] *OJ* L 76/1, on the statistical units for the observation and analysis of the production system in the Community, uses both the term ownership as well as the term proprietorship.

217 *Supra*, Part II, section 3.1.

218 Other examples can be found, such as Art. 1 of Regulation 881/2002/EC imposing certain specific restrictive measures directed against certain persons and entities associated with Usama bin Laden, the Al-Qaida network and the Taliban, [2002] *OJ* L 139/9:
'For the purpose of this Regulation, the following definitions shall apply: [...]
3. "freezing of funds" means preventing any move, transfer, alteration, use of or dealing with funds in any way that would result in any change in their volume, amount, location, *ownership*, possession, character, destination or other change that would enable the use of the funds, including portfolio management.' Art. 3 of Directive 2006/114/EC on misleading and comparative advertising (codified version), [2006] *OJ* L 376/21:
'In determining whether advertising is misleading, account shall be taken of all its features, and in particular of any information it contains concerning: [...]
(c) the nature, attributes and rights of the advertiser, such as his identity and assets, his qualifications and *ownership* of industrial, commercial or intellectual property rights or his awards and distinctions.'

### 5.1.1. Retention of Title/Reservation of Ownership

Even though the correct phrase is either retention of title or reservation of ownership,[219] I decided also to conduct a search for reservation of title and retention of ownership in case these combinations are used in EU legislation. *Retention of title* was only found in Directive 2011/7/EU on late payments. The late payments Directive has been discussed in more detail in Part I of this chapter. *Reservation of ownership* can be found in the Directive 2006/112/EC on VAT and in Directive 2006/69/EC, both of which mention the possibility of a cession of a reservation of ownership. *Retention of ownership* yielded no results; *reservation of title* yielded four results, the most prominent of which is the Solvency II Directive:[220]

> 'Article 282
>
> Right to lodge claims
>
> 1. Any creditor, including public authorities of Member States, whose habitual residence, domicile or head office is situated in a Member State other than the home Member State shall have the right to lodge claims or to submit written observations relating to claims. [...]
>
> 3. Except in cases where the law of the home Member State otherwise allows, a creditor shall send to the competent authority copies of any supporting documents and shall indicate the following: [...]
>
> (c) whether he alleges preference, security in rem or *reservation of title* in respect of the claim;'

Apart from the Late Payments Directive, none of the other measures found - even though interesting - provide a definition of reservation of ownership or retention of title.

## 5.2. *Interest in/Title to*

Searching for the terms *interest* or *title* on their own proved impossible because of their many meanings outside property law and because of the fact that most regulations and directives are subdivided into Titles. All of those regulations and directives that are subdivided into Titles will come up in a search for the word *title*. I therefore decided to search for the terms *title to* together with *interest in* as this is usually the way in which they are used in a property law context. This led to some interesting results. Regulation 1126/2008/EC, adopting certain international accounting standards,[221] alternates between the use of 'title to' and 'interest in' (for instance: title to land at one point and interest in land at another point). All the

219 Akkermans 2008, p. 419.

220 Dir. 2009/138/EC, [2009] *OJ* L 335/1.

221 [2008] *OJ* L 320/1.

regulations concerning certain restrictive measures in respect of a particular country contain the phrase 'title to, or interest in, [...] assets'.[222] It is of course impossible to say which language version was drafted first, and therefore which version was a translation of which, but in the German, French and Dutch versions 'title to' is translated respectively with *Eigentum*, *droit de propriété* and *eigendom*, whereas 'interest in' is translated respectively with *Beteiligung an*, *intérêt sur* and *belang in*. In other words, 'title to' in these language versions refers to ownership, whereas 'interest in' is not translated in the other versions with a property right.

A search for *legal title* also rendered a few results.[223] One of those was Directive 91/674/EC on the annual accounts and consolidated accounts of insurance undertakings.[224] It uses the term legal title in Article 2:

> '2. Funds [...] which an insurance undertaking administers in its own name but on behalf of third parties must be shown in the balance sheet if the undertaking acquires *legal title* to the assets concerned.'

'Acquires legal title' is translated in other language versions as *wird Rechtsinhaber* (DE), *est titulaire* (FR), and *is rechthebbende* (NL).

## 5.3. *Tenure/Tenancy*

The term *tenure* can be found in quite a number of regulations,[225] although they all tend to deal with agriculture. Most notable is Regulation 1200/2009/EC on farm structure surveys and the survey on agricultural production methods.[226] 'Tenure' is used several times in Annex II on the Definitions of the characteristics to be used for the Community farm structure surveys:[227]

> '1.03 | Type of *tenure* (in relation to the holder) and farming system [...]
>
> 1.03.01.01 | | | For owner farming Utilised agricultural area farmed by the holding and which is the property of the holder or farmed by him as usufructuary or heritable long-term leaseholder or under some other equivalent type of *tenure*.'

This provision contains a number of different property rights: ownership, usufruct, and heritable long-term lease. The provision further refers to 'some other equivalent type of tenure'. The provision is a little clumsily formulated. Read together with other language versions, it is easier to distill the meaning of this provision.

222 See for instance Reg. 310/2002/EC concerning certain restrictive measures in respect of Zimbabwe, [2002] *OJ* L 50/4, Art. 1(1).
223 Four regulations, two directives.
224 [1991] *OJ* L 374/7.
225 No results in directives.
226 [2009] *OJ* L 329/1; this Regulation implements Reg. 1166/2008/EC.
227 All under 1.03.

The French version reads:

> 'En faire-valoir direct La superficie agricole utilisée de l'exploitation dont l'exploitant est propriétaire ou pour laquelle il dispose d'un statut équivalent (usufruitier, emphytéote, etc.).'

The German version reads:

> 'In Eigentum Landwirtschaftlich genutzte Flächen des Betriebs, die Eigentum des Betriebsinhabers sind und von ihm bewirtschaftet werden. Hierzu gehören auch Flächen, die vom Betriebsinhaber in Nutznießung, Erbpacht oder in gleichwertigen Besitzformen bewirtschaftet werden'.

The Dutch version reads:

> 'In eigendom tot het bedrijf behorende oppervlakte cultuurgrond die eigendom is van het bedrijfshoofd en door hem wordt geëxploiteerd. Hieronder valt ook de grond die door het bedrijfshoofd uit hoofde van vruchtgebruik, erfpacht en dergelijke wordt geëxploiteerd.'

It is deplorable that a legislative text would contain phrases such as 'some other equivalent type' or 'etc.' for they leave a gap in the provision. Presumably, the property rights mentioned are derived from national property law - they are not given a European-autonomous interpretation here. The Regulation may thus have different meanings in different Member States - a heritable long-term lease is not necessarily the same as an *emphytéose*. The gap will also have to be filled by national law. Looking at the rights already mentioned in the provision, 'some other equivalent type' would have to be a right that grants the holder a right of use similar to that of the owner, for that is also the content of a right of usufruct and of a heritable long-term lease.

A number of regulations mentions the term *tenancy* or *tenancies* in immovable property but none of them define the term.[228] Another regulation mentions tenancies only to exclude them from the scope of application of the Regulation. It is noteworthy that this is the Regulation establishing a European Small Claims Procedure.[229] According to Article 2(2)(g) of the Regulation, a European small claims procedure cannot be brought on matters concerning tenancies of immovable property. There are no directives mentioning tenancy or tenancies.

## 5.4. *Estate/Fee Simple/Freehold/Leasehold*

The search for the term *estate* returned a few hundred results, so the search was modified to reduce the number of results. A search was conducted for 'real estate'

228 See, for instance, the Rome I Regulation and the Brussels I Regulation.
229 Reg. 861/2007/EC, [2007] *OJ* L 199/1.

but that did not render any relevant results. Neither did the search for estate combined with the term land. A sample of the results based on the titles of the regulations and directives, and whether or not they indicate a potential link to property law, showed that the term estate is generally only used in the sense of assets/objects/property, not in the sense of 'an estate in land'. The search for *fee simple* yielded no results; the search for *freehold* only one, namely Regulation 2909/2000/EC on the accounting management of the European Communities' non-financial fixed assets:[230]

> 'Article 7
>
> Land and buildings
>
> 1. The heading "land and buildings" shall comprise property rights and similar entitlements as defined by the national legislation of the country in which the asset is located.
>
> The following shall be regarded as land:
>
> - bare ground,
> - developed land,
> - built-up land.
>
> 2. The following shall be regarded as buildings:
>
> - *freehold* buildings of the Institutions,
> - buildings in shared ownership with co-proprietors,
> - fixtures within the meaning of paragraph 3.'

It is not clear from this provision what is meant with the term freehold; the term is only used but not defined or explained. The German version of the Regulation uses the phrase *Gebäude im vollständigen Eigentum*; the French version reads *les immeubles dont les institutions ont la pleine propriété*, and the Dutch version reads *onroerende goederen die volledig eigendom zijn van de instellingen*.

When searching for the term *lease(hold)*, hundreds of search results came up which contained the term 'release'. These search results were excluded. The remaining results mostly contained the term lease, but there are two regulations that use the term leasehold. See Regulation 1768/95/EC,[231] which is an agricultural regulation:[232]

230 [2000] *OJ* L 336/75.

231 [1995] *OJ* L 173/14.

232 The other Regulation using the term leasehold is Reg. 318/2006/EC, Annex V, Point I: 'For the purposes of this Annex [...](d) "lease of a factory" means the leasehold contract of a technical unit including all the plant required for the manufacture of sugar, with a view to its operation, concluded for a period of at least three consecutive marketing years, which the parties agree not to terminate before the end of the third marketing year, with an undertaking which is established in the same Member State, as the factory concerned, if, after the lease →

'Article 4

The farmer [...]

2. An 'own holding' within the meaning of Article 14 (1) of the basic Regulation shall be considered to be any holding or part thereof which the farmer actually exploits for plant growing, whether as his property or otherwise managed under his own responsibility and on his own account, in particular in the case of *leaseholds*. The disposal of a holding or part thereof for the purpose of exploitation by others shall be regarded as transfer within the meaning of paragraph 1.'

The term *lease* is defined in Regulation 1120/2009/EC[233] - also an agricultural regulation - as follows:

'Article 2

Definitions [...]

(f) "*lease*" means *lease* or similar types of temporary transactions;'

This definition does not tell us much, other than that lease is considered to be a temporary transaction. The French version of this provision reads *bail: le bail ou toute autre transaction temporaire du même type*, the German version reads *Pacht: Pacht oder ähnliche Arten von befristeten Geschäften*, and the Dutch version reads *(ver)huur: (ver)huur en daarmee vergelijkbare soorten tijdelijke transacties*.

The search for these four terms - estate, fee simple, freehold, lease(hold) - shows that, while they are used in EU legislation (with the exception of the term fee simple), they are not given a European-autonomous definition, nor does the context in which they appear provide much information about how they should be interpreted. What can be noted is that the term lease(hold) is used particularly often in regulations on agricultural policy, although it also appears in measures concerning accounting standards or financial institutions.[234]

## 5.5. *Trust/Beneficiary*

Searching for the term *beneficiary* was complicated by the fact that that term is mostly used in the sense of recipient (i.e. the beneficiary of an insurance policy) but not in the sense of a beneficiary of a trust. The term beneficiary was therefore combined with the term trust to limit the search to relevant results. A notable result

takes effect, the undertaking which rents the factory can be considered a solely sugar-producing undertaking for its entire production.'

233 [2009] *OJ* L 316/1.

234 See e.g. Dir. 2006/48/EC relating to the taking up and pursuit of the business of credit institutions (recast), or Reg. 1606/2002/EC on the application of international accounting standards.

was the Brussels I Regulation[235] which uses the term beneficiary in its English law meaning:

> 'Article 5
>
> A person domiciled in a Member State may, in another Member State, be sued: [...]
>
> 6. as settlor, trustee or *beneficiary* of a trust created by the operation of a statute, or by a written instrument, or created orally and evidenced in writing, in the courts of the Member State in which the trust is domiciled;'

The French version uses the terms *fondateur*, trustee, *bénéficiaire* and trust; the German version uses the terms *Begründer*, trustee, *Begünstigter* and trust. Neither seem to be linked to the French or German 'version' of the trust, being the *fiducie* and the *Treuhand*. They are only a translation of the English concepts.

The term *trust* itself can furthermore be found in a number of regulations and directives. One interesting example is the Rome II Regulation on the law applicable to non-contractual obligations:

> 'Article 1
>
> Scope [...]
>
> 2. The following shall be excluded from the scope of this Regulation: [...]
>
> (e) non-contractual obligations arising out of the relations between the settlors, trustees and beneficiaries of a *trust* created voluntarily;'

In this Regulation the term settlor is translated into French as *constituant*, as opposed to *fondateur*, which was the translation used in the Brussels I Regulation. The German version here uses the terms *Verfügenden* and *Treuhändern*, as opposed to *Begründer* and trustees used in Brussels I. These terms used in the French and German versions of Rome II are more in line with the terminology used in French and German law concerning the *fiducie* and the *Treuhand*. The Rome I Regulation uses the same terms as the Rome II Regulation. This means that, of these three principal regulations in the field of EU private international law, Rome I and II are consistent with each other and with national law, but Brussels I deviates from Rome I and II and uses terms that may not be as easy to implement for national legislatures.

## 5.6. *Numerus Clausus and Limited Property Rights*

At the outset, it must be noted that the search for the term *numerus clausus* did not yield any results. The search for specific limited property rights, such as usufruct and emphyteusis, yielded only a few results as far as the limited property rights to

235 Reg. 44/2001/EC.

use are concerned. The term *servitude* cannot be found in any regulation or directive, nor can the term *restrictive covenant*; the term *easement* is mentioned only once, in Directive 88/361/EEC.[236] The term *superficies* was not found in any regulation or directive. The term *usufruct* is used in Regulation 1248/2006/EC[237] and in Directive 88/361. Regulation 1248/2006 amended a previous regulation and, in fact, the term usufruct was added through this amendment. Directive 88/361 states:

> 'EXPLANATORY NOTES
>
> For the purposes of this Nomenclature and the Directive only, the following expressions have the meanings assigned to them respectively: [...]
>
> Investments in real estate
>
> Purchases of buildings and land and the construction of buildings by private persons for gain or personal use. This category also includes rights of *usufruct*, *easements* and building rights.'

The term usufruct is also used in Regulation 1200/2009/EC, which is an agricultural Regulation,[238] and in Regulation 1444/2002/EC, also an agricultural regulation.[239]

Although the term *emphyteusis* as such cannot be found, remarkably, Directive 72/160/EEC[240] speaks of *emphyteutic lease*. This is the only time that this term is mentioned:

> 'Article 5
>
> 1. At least 85% of the utilized agricultural area released by persons benefiting under the measures provided for in Article 2(1)(a) and (b) must either: (a) be leased for a minimum period of twelve years, or convey in absolute ownership or by way of *emphyteutic lease*, to farmers benefiting from incentives given under Article 8 of the Directive on the modernization of farms; [...].'[241]

236 [1988] *OJ* L 178/5.

237 [2006] *OJ* L 227/3, amending Reg. 2342/2002/EC: '29. In Article 116, paragraph 1 is replaced by the following:
'1. Building contracts cover the purchase, long lease, *usufruct*, leasing, rental or hire purchase, with or without option to buy, of land, existing buildings or other real estate.'

238 [2009] *OJ* L 329/1. Annex II, 5.01.01: 'The holder can own the holding outright or rent it or be a hereditary long-term leaseholder or a usufructuary or a trustee.'

239 [2002] *OJ* L 216/1. This Regulation uses the exact same sentence as Reg. 1200/2009; see previous footnote.

240 [1972] *OJ* L 96/9.

241 Dir. 72/160/EEC concerning measures to encourage the cessation of farming and the reallocation of utilized agricultural area for the purposes of structural improvement

In the French version, the equivalent to emphyteutic lease is *emphytéose*. The same French term was used earlier for the English 'heritable long-term lease'.[242]

### 5.6.1. Security Rights

Security rights are mentioned quite a lot more often than limited property rights to use. I will therefore highlight the more interesting examples.

The term *pledge* features, for instance, in Regulation 108/2006/EC amending Regulation 1725/2003/EC adopting certain international accounting standards:[243]

> 'Collateral
>
> 14. An entity shall disclose:
>
> (a) the carrying amount of financial assets it has *pledged* as collateral for liabilities or contingent liabilities, [...] and
>
> (b) the terms and conditions relating to its *pledge*.'

*Hypothec* does not yield any results but *mortgage* does.[244] A particularly striking example can be found in Regulation 2454/93/EC implementing Regulation 2913/92/EC establishing the Community Customs Code:[245]

> 'Article 857
>
> 1. The types of security [...], within the meaning of Articles 193, 194 and 195 of the Code, [...] shall be as follows:
>
> (a) the creation of a *mortgage*, a charge on land, an antichresis or other right deemed equivalent to a right pertaining to immovable property;
>
> (b) the cession of a claim, the *pledging*, with or without surrendering possession, of goods, securities or claims or, in particular, a savings bank book or entry in the national debt register; [...]'

This provision lists a number of security rights in relation to immovable property, as well as in relation to movable property, including claims. The use of the term antichresis (or *antichrèse* in the French version) was unexpected. It used to be a French security right - a charge on land by which the owner of an immovable object transfers the enjoyment of that object to a creditor allowing him to receive the revenues of the immovable up to the point where the value of those revenues repays the debt owed by the owner to the creditor - under Article 2072 of the *Code*

242 See *supra*, section 5.3. *Tenure/tenancy*.
243 [2006] *OJ* L 24/1.
244 In the French version, mortgage is generally translated as *hypothèque*.
245 [1993] *OJ* L 253/1.

*Civil*. It was altered by *Loi* No. 2009-526 of 12 May 2009 and is now called *gage immobilier* (or charge on land).[246]

Another interesting aspect of Article 857 of the Regulation is that it mentions the possibility of pledging goods with or without surrendering possession. It would seem from this provision that the *acquis* accepts not only the traditional possessory pledge but also the non-possessory pledge.

When searching for the term lien, a large number of search results turned out to be irrelevant but nevertheless came up because they contained the term client. After excluding all results containing the word client, only a handful of regulations and directives was left containing the term lien.

The term *lien* can *inter alia* be found in Directive 98/26/EC on settlement finality in payment and securities settlement systems:[247]

> '[W]hereas collateral security is meant to comprise all means provided by a participant [...] to secure rights and obligations [...], including repurchase agreements, statutory *liens* and fiduciary transfers.'

It is furthermore used in all regulations concerning restrictive measures against a particular country.[248]

The term *charge* was difficult to search for, particularly because it can be both a noun and a verb that has a property law sense but also because of its colloquial meaning of either fee or authority. The search was therefore broken down into three sub-searches. EUR-lex was used to search for 'floating charge' and to search for 'fixed charge', neither of which returned any results in regulations or directives. A search in EUR-lex for charge WITH assets, on the other hand, returned too many results. The latter search was therefore repeated in Google. The Google search showed that the term charged is mostly used as 'in charge of' or 'free of charge'. There was only one result which was relevant from a property law point of view, namely Directive 95/18/EC.[249] The Annex to this Directive reads under I:

> '1. Financial fitness will be verified by means of an undertaking's annual accounts [...] Detailed particulars must be provided, in particular on the following aspects: [...]
>
> (e) *charges* on an undertaking's assets.'

246 Art. 2373 French civil code. See also: <http://www.dictionnaire-juridique.com/definition/antichrese-ou-gage-immobilier.php>.

247 [1998] *OJ* L 166/45; Preamble, Recital 9.

248 See e.g. Reg. 965/2011/EU amending Reg. 204/2011/EU concerning restrictive measures in view of the situation in Libya, [2011] *OJ* L 253/8, Art. 1(5): 'Article 8 is replaced by the following: "Article 8 [...]
(a) the funds or economic resources in question are the subject of a judicial, administrative or arbitral *lien* [...] (b) the funds or economic resources in question will be used exclusively to satisfy claims secured by such a *lien*"'.

249 Directive on the licensing of railway undertakings, [1995] *OJ* L 143/70.

In conclusion, Directive 95/18 provides the only information that the *acquis* uses the term 'charge' in a property law sense. The *acquis* does not use floating charge or fixed charge specifically but only pledge, mortgage and lien.

## 5.7. *Movable/Immovable*

Often, when the term immovable (property) is used, it is used to indicate that rights relating to immovable property are excluded from the scope of application of the measure. A good example is Directive 97/7/EC on distance contracts:[250]

> 'Article 3:
>
> 1. This Directive shall not apply to contracts: [...]
>
> - concluded for the construction and sale of *immovable property* or relating to other immovable property rights, except for rental, [...]'

See also Directive 2008/48/EC on credit agreements for consumers,[251] which excludes both credit agreements relating to rights in immovable property as well as credit agreements relating to rights in movable property:

> 'Article 2:
>
> [...] 2. This Directive shall not apply to the following:
>
> (a) credit agreements which are secured either by a mortgage or by another comparable security commonly used in a Member State on *immovable* property or secured by a right related to *immovable* property;
>
> (b) credit agreements the purpose of which is to acquire or retain property rights in land or in an existing or projected building; [...]
>
> (k) credit agreements upon the conclusion of which the consumer is requested to deposit an item as security in the creditor's safe-keeping and where the liability of the consumer is strictly limited to that pledged item; [...]'

The new Timeshare Directive can also be mentioned as an example.[252] Its exclusion of immovable property is a reflection of the fact that, while timeshare has property

250 [1997] *OJ* L 144/19.

251 [2008] *OJ* L 133/66; repealing Dir. 87/102/EEC.

252 Dir. 2008/122/EC, [2009] *OJ* L 33/10. Art. 2 states: 'This Directive is without prejudice to national legislation which: [...] (b) relates to the registration of immovable or movable property and conveyance of immovable property.' See also Dir. 2002/65/EC, [2002] *OJ* L 271/16 concerning the distance marketing of consumer financial services, Art. 6(3): 'Member States may provide that the right of withdrawal shall not apply to:
(a) any credit intended primarily for the purpose of acquiring or retaining property rights in land [...], or
(b) any credit secured either by mortgage on immovable property or by a right related to immovable property.'

law elements particularly under English law, the Directive only regulates the contractual side of timeshare agreements; it does not deal with any property law matters.[253] This is also the reason why it is not discussed in the first part of this chapter on substantial EU property law.[254]

Other interesting examples of EU legislation containing the term *movable* can, *inter alia*, be found in Regulation 2909/2000/EC[255] on the accounting management of the European Communities' non-financial fixed assets,[256] and in Directive 1999/34/EC[257] amending Directive 84/386/EEC on product liability.[258]

## 5.8. *Tangible/Corporeal*

The term (in)corporeal is only used in two directives, one of which is Directive 2005/60/EC on the prevention of money laundering and terrorist financing:[259]

> 'Article 3
>
> For the purposes of this Directive the following definitions shall apply: [...]
>
> (3) "property" means assets of every kind, whether *corporeal or incorporeal* movable or immovable, tangible or intangible, and legal documents or instruments in any form including electronic or digital, evidencing title to or an interest in such assets; [...]'

253 Sagaert 2007, p. 329: 'De richtlijn beheerst enkel de contractuele aspecten, terwijl de goederenrechtelijke aspecten niet aan de orde zijn. Reden hiervoor is dat het juridische karakter van de rechten van deeltijds gebruik sterk verschilt van lidstaat tot lidstaat, en er op dat vlak geen overeenstemming tussen de lidstaten kon worden bereikt.' See also Snijders 2006, p. 158.

254 Apparently, there were three Member States, apart from those that were already familiar with timeshare in their national law, that implemented timeshare as a property right, namely Italy, Spain and Portugal: Rodriguez Murillo 2007, p. 82 and 85. If that were the case, the Timeshare Directive would have made an addition to the *numerus clausus* of those countries. I cannot say with certainty, however, that that was indeed the case. I have no knowledge of the Portuguese language, and while I was able to find the implementing legislation of Italy (*Decreto Legislativo* No. 79, GU No. 129 of 06-06-2011), I was unable to discern with my limited understanding of Italian whether or not this legislative act implemented timeshare as a property right. Spain has implemented the Directive in *Ley* 4/2012, *Boletín Oficial del Estado* (B.O.E.) nr 162/2012 of 07 July 2012 and *Real Decreto Ley* 8/2012, B.O.E. No. 66/2012 of 17 March 2012. My understanding of Spanish is better than of Italian but it was nevertheless not clear – at least to me – from these laws that Spain implemented timeshare as a property right.

255 [2000] *OJ* L 336/75.

256 Art. 7, Land and Buildings, s. 3: 'Any item of *movable* property which is permanently and inseparably attached to a building (such as defined under the first and second indents of paragraph 2) shall constitute a fixture.'

257 [1999] *OJ* L 141/20.

258 Art. 1: 'Directive 85/374/EEC is hereby amended as follows:
1. Article 2 shall be replaced by the following: "[...] For the purpose of this Directive, 'product' means all *movables* even if incorporated into another *movable* or into an *immovable*. 'Product' includes electricity".'

259 [2005] *OJ* L 309/15. Similarly: Dir. 91/308/EEC, [1991] *OJ* L 166/77, Art. 1.

The term (in)tangible is used more often. To reduce the number of search results the combinations 'tangible evidence', 'tangible contribution' and 'tangible criteria' were excluded from the search. Directive 1999/44/EC on the sale of consumer goods[260] uses the term tangible in the following way:

> 'Article 1: Scope and Definitions [...]
>
> 2. For the purposes of this Directive: [...]
>
> (b) *consumer goods:* shall mean any *tangible* movable item, with the exception of:
>
> - goods sold by way of execution or otherwise by authority of law,
>
> - water and gas where they are not put up for sale in a limited volume or set quantity,
>
> - electricity; [...]'

Another interesting example is contained in Regulation 683/3008/EC on the further implementation of the European satellite navigation programmes (EGNOS and Galileo):[261]

> 'Article 8
>
> Ownership
>
> The Community shall be the owner of all *tangible* and *intangible* assets created or developed under the programmes, to which effect agreements shall be concluded with third parties, wherever appropriate, with regard to existing ownership rights.'

The terms tangible/intangible are normally used in English law. The terms corporeal/incorporeal are not used in English law but are translations used by comparative lawyers of the civil law terms *(in)corporel/(nicht)körperlich.* It can be seen in all regulations and directives containing anti-terrorist measures or concerning restrictions against a particular country that (in)tangible and (in)corporeal are used in the same sentence, probably because that sentence contains a catch-all definition of assets. Otherwise, as can be seen from the examples above, the use of the term (in)corporeal is rare – normally the term (in)tangible is used, which is in line with the terminology used in English law.

## 5.9. *Lex Rei Sitae*

The phrase *lex rei sitae* is technically not part of property law but private international law, being the conflict rule that decides the applicable property law. However, since the *lex rei sitae* rule was identified in Chapter 2 as one of the two causes of obstacles to cross-border trade involving matters of property law – the mandatory

260 [1999] *OJ* L 171/12.
261 [2008] *OJ* L 196/1.

nature of substantive property law being the other cause - it has been included in the search conducted for this chapter.

The phrase *lex rei sitae* can be found in two directives,[262] namely Directive 2002/47/EC on financial collateral arrangements and Directive 2001/24/EC on the reorganization and winding up of credit institutions.[263] Directive 2002/47 mentions the *lex rei sitae* rule in its preamble:

> '(8) The *lex rei sitae* rule, according to which the applicable law for determining whether a financial collateral arrangement is properly perfected and therefore good against third parties is the law of the country where the financial collateral is located, is currently recognised by all Member States.'

The EU legislature here recognizes that the *lex rei sitae* rule is adhered to by all Member States and chooses not to deviate from it. In this context, the *lex rei sitae* is the applicable law to determine whether the financial collateral agreement - and the property rights resulting from it - has been validly created. The *situs* is the location of the financial collateral. Directive 2001/24 deals with the *lex rei sitae* rule in a slightly different manner:

> 'Article 24
>
> Lex rei sitae
>
> The enforcement of proprietary rights in instruments or other rights in such instruments the existence or transfer of which presupposes their recording in a register, an account or a centralised deposit system held or located in a Member State shall be governed by the law of the Member State where the register, account, or centralised deposit system in which those rights are recorded is held or located.'

This provision does not deal with the applicable law determining the valid *creation* of a property right but with the applicable law determining the valid *enforcement* of proprietary rights. Article 24 only concerns proprietary rights that have to be recorded in a register of some sort. Whether and how they can be enforced is then governed by the law of the Member State where the register is 'located'. In this context there is no physical *situs* because the objects - the 'instruments' as they are called by Article 24 - are incorporeal.[264]

The *situs*-rule is also adhered to in other legislation, although the literal phrase *lex rei sitae* is not always used. One example is the Insolvency Regulation which states in Article 8 that contracts relating to immovable property 'shall be governed solely by the law of the Member State within the territory of which the immoveable

262 The Insolvency Regulation mentions *lex situs* in its preamble.

263 [2001] *OJ* L 125/15.

264 The definition of these instruments can - in accordance with Art. 2 of Dir. 2001/24 - be found in Section B of the Annex to Dir. 93/22/EEC on investment services in the securities field; [1993] *OJ* L 141/27.

property is situated'.[265] The Insolvency Regulation is especially interesting because it determines what the *situs* of a given object is. According to Article 2(g), the *situs* for tangible property is the Member State within the territory of which the property is situated; the *situs* for property and rights, ownership of or entitlement to which must be entered in a public register, is the Member State under the authority of which the register is kept; and the *situs* for claims is the Member State within the territory of which the third party required to meet them has the centre of his main interests.

## Conclusion

What conclusions can be drawn from all the data collected for this chapter as regards the formation of a system of property law at EU level? The contours of such a system are starting to become visible. Using the elements of the System-Cube as developed in Chapter 1, some search results say something about what are considered to be property *rights* - or rights *in rem* - at the EU level; some results tell us what *objects* can be objects of those property rights under EU law; and some results show us the beginnings of an *operating system* that governs those rights. The picture is still fragmented, but there is more property law to be found at EU level than perhaps initially expected.

A distinction is made between rights *in rem* and rights *in personam*. Rights *in rem* are characterized as relating to a thing and being of an absolute nature, in the sense that they can be invoked *erga omnes*. There is no European-autonomous definition of rights *in rem* but they are functionally described. There are security rights and rights to use and there are specific remedies to protect these rights. Furthermore, a distinction is made between ownership/freehold and other rights/entitlements/forms of tenure. The emphasis throughout EU legislation lies on security rights; rights to use are not often encountered. Apart from a general description of rights *in rem* in general, specific descriptions of property rights are also found. The Insolvency Regulation classifies a floating charge and rights registered by way of *Vormerkung* as property rights. The Late Payments Directive provides a definition of retention of title clauses. The Financial Collateral Directive provides security ownership and a possessory security right (pledge). Security ownership does not exist in all Member States. The Directive has, in that regard, introduced a level of harmonization, albeit restricted to the sector of financial collateral arrangements.[266] The Regulation establishing the Community Customs Code also provides for a possessory and non-possessory pledge, available for both tangible and intangible objects.

The *acquis* also indicates what types of objects can be objects of these property rights. They can be movable or immovable, and immovable property can be

265 Reg. 1346/2000/EC, [2000] *OJ* L 160/1.
266 Sagaert 2007, p. 333.

considered to be included in a measure unless it is explicitly excluded. They can also be tangible or intangible (or in/corporeal). The *acquis* itself introduces a number of new, intangible, objects of property rights, such as the Community Trade Mark, the Community Design, and emission trading rights. By including intangible objects as objects in relation to which one can have a right *in rem*, including ownership, the *acquis* goes further than some Member States. In the Netherlands and in Germany, for instance, ownership of claims is not accepted (although claims can be pledged).

The *acquis* also shows the contours of a system of rules governing these property rights. It is aware that a power to dispose is an essential requirement when transferring ownership -this was seen in the *Möllendorf* judgment. It recognizes that there are different stages in the life of a property right - it distinguishes between the creation and transfer of a property right. It also provides a definition of assignment of claims. Further, it makes a distinction between possessor and holder which resembles the distinction made at national level. The Directive on Financial Collateral Arrangements stipulates that the creditor may keep the collateral in case of non-payment, something which is not usually allowed under national property law. Finally, the EU legislature adheres to the *lex rei sitae* rule.

Rules relating to third party effect can also be seen. The Regulation on the Community Trade Mark stipulates that the acquisition of such a trade mark can have no third party effect without registration. At national level, registration is usually the means by which publicity is achieved. The principle of publicity forms one of the underlying justifications for granting *erga omnes* effect to property rights, the principle of specificity forming the other justification. The Community Trade Mark Regulation also establishes a ranking. The Insolvency Regulation grants property effect to retention of title clauses, in the sense that they can be invoked against third parties, both in the case of insolvency of the buyer as well as in the case of insolvency of the debtor. The Directive on the return of stolen cultural objects restricts third party protection rules. Stolen cultural objects can be retrieved from parties who acquired them in good faith and who would otherwise be protected because they were in good faith.

Finally, it is worth noting that the property law rules and property law terms present in the *acquis* tend to be found in measures on specific issue areas. Property law rules and terms were primarily found in regulations and directives dealing with credit agreements and financial instruments or services, accountancy standards and taxes, insolvency proceedings, environmental issues, restrictions against certain countries or organizations and anti-terrorism measures, agricultural or farming matters, and consumer protection.

These results will be used as a starting point for the next two chapters, in which a framework for the future development of EU property law will be built. These chapters will deal with both form and content of future EU property law respectively. As Chapter 5 will show, a lot of research and discussion has already been devoted to the different forms in which European private law more generally could be shaped (e.g. an optional or mandatory instrument, a Regulation or a Directive, etc). Within this context the form that EU property law might take will be discussed first, in Chapter 5, before turning to content, in Chapter 6. Whereas Chapter 5 builds mainly on the pre-existing discussion concerning the possible forms for future European private law, Chapter 6 provides a new proposal specifically related to the content of future EU property law. It is for that reason that Chapter 6 forms the closing chapter of this study.

Chapter 5

# OPTIONS FOR THE FUTURE DEVELOPMENT OF EUROPEAN UNION PROPERTY LAW

## Introduction

The previous chapters have shown that national rules of property law could, and do, infringe the European internal market rules; to what extent the EU may have the competence to regulate property law; and the extent to which the EU has already created property law. This chapter explores the possible forms in which European Union property law could be shaped in the future, should the European legislature decide to approach this field of law more directly and coherently. The different options include a legislative instrument containing substantive EU property law, an Inter-Institutional Agreement, case law from the CJEU and an international agreement. The possible legislative measures for EU property law are discussed based on the presumption that the EU has the competence to enact them. Whether this is actually the case has already been discussed in greater detail in Chapter 3. Nevertheless, some elements of competence, subsidiarity and proportionality, will be revisited here, now in the specific context of each of the different options for future EU property law as discussed in this chapter. This chapter focuses on the possible forms for future EU property law. What could or should be the content of EU property law will be discussed in the next and final chapter of this study.

It was argued in Chapter 2 that it is not just the differences between the national substantive property law rules that cause obstacles to free movement but that it is the combination with the private international law rule of *lex rei sitae* which leads to these hindrances.[1] Therefore, the discussion of the different forms for future substantive EU property law rules in this chapter will be preceded by an analysis of whether the problems in intra-Union trade could be (partially) solved by changing or replacing the *lex rei sitae* rule.

1 Chapter 2, section 3.4.5.

## 1. Explanation of Terms

The term 'European Union (EU) property law' is used to denote that this study focuses on the European *acquis*. The term 'European property law' sometimes seems to give the impression that this study consists of comparative law research, but comparative law is not the main focus, the *acquis communautaire* is.

Furthermore, a number of terms are used in literature and documents of the EU institutions in relation to harmonisation: full harmonization, maximum harmonization, partial harmonization, targeted harmonization, and minimum harmonization. These terms are not always used in the same way by everyone. For the purposes of this study, these terms are interpreted as follows: minimum harmonization means harmonization laying down a minimum standard, leaving room for the Member States to adopt stricter measures. Maximum harmonization means harmonization laying down a maximum standard, leaving no room for the Member States to adopt stricter measures. This is now often referred to as full harmonization but I would interpret full harmonization as the harmonization of a whole area of law (for instance, property law), as opposed to harmonizing only a part of that area (for instance, only the rules on security rights), which would be partial or targeted harmonization. To avoid the confusion inherent in having two meanings of the term full harmonization, I only use it in the sense of harmonization of a whole area of law.

## 2. The Commission's 2010 Green Paper

The options presented in this chapter for future EU property law are structured along the same lines as the policy options presented by the Commission in the 'Green Paper on policy options for progress towards a European Contract Law for consumers and businesses'.[2] At the end of the chapter, two additional options will be discussed - namely the conclusion of an international agreement, and harmonization through CJEU case law - which were not mentioned in the Green Paper but which are nevertheless worth exploring. While the Green Paper specifically dealt with contract law, it can provide inspiration for this research project in which the options for a future EU property law are explored. The Green Paper listed seven options[3] for a future instrument for European contract law,[4] the first of which

2 COM(2010) 348 final.

3 The Impact Assessment mentions the baseline scenario - maintaining the *status quo* - as option 1, but this option is not listed in the Green Paper; Impact Assessment Accompanying the document 'Proposal for a Regulation of the European Parliament and of the Council on a Common European Sales Law', SEC(2011) 1165 final, section 4.1. The Impact Assessment concludes, as regards the baseline scenario, that transaction costs and opportunity costs would continue, as well as legal complexity for businesses and consumers, and that the practice to refuse to sell cross-border would not decrease: section 5.1.

4 2010 Green Paper, section 4.1.

would be to publish the results of the Expert Group.[5] These results could be a source of inspiration for national and European legislatures and for academic study. However, as the Commission indicated, its lack of formal authority would mean that this option 'could not address the internal market barriers'[6] caused by divergences between the national systems.[7] As a second option the Commission proposed the adoption of an act that would incorporate the results of the Expert Group as a 'toolbox' to be used for future legislation.[8] Such an act could be an inter-institutional agreement.[9] The third option would be for the Commission to issue a Recommendation for the Member States including an instrument of European Contract Law, encouraging the Member States to incorporate the instrument into their national law or make it available as an optional instrument to contracting parties.[10] As a fourth alternative the Commission suggested the adoption of a Regulation setting up an optional instrument.[11] Such an instrument could be beneficial to parties who are currently facing problems when conducting cross-border trade in the internal market but without interfering further with the national systems.[12] From the point of view of subsidiarity and proportionality, therefore, an optional instrument may be a preferable alternative to full harmonization of national laws.[13] The fifth option would be the enactment of a Directive on European Contract Law, 'on the basis of minimum common standards'.[14] However, the downside to minimum harmonization Directives is that they cannot, and do not always, eliminate the obstacles in the internal market caused by diverging national legislation, given that Member States are allowed to maintain stricter rules than the

5 The progress made by the Expert Group and the Draft rules so far developed can be found at: <http://ec.europa.eu/justice/policies/consumer/policies_consumer_intro_en.htm>.

6 2010 Green Paper, p. 8.

7 What these barriers are exactly has been discussed in Chapter 3.

8 2010 Green Paper, p. 8.

9 2010 Green Paper, p. 8. See also *infra*, section 5.1.

10 2010 Green Paper, p. 8-9.

11 2010 Green Paper, p. 9-10.

12 2010 Green Paper, p. 10. Whether there would really be no further interference with the national systems - as the Commission contends - remains to be seen if a Regulation is chosen as the form for an optional instrument. See, for instance, Smits 2002, p. 10: '[A] disadvantage is that the Member State is not able to influence the way the regulation is grafted onto the national legal order. This may very well lead to a problematic relationship between Community law and the national legal system, into which it is directly parachuted.' A similar disadvantage can be encountered with the use of directives, which can lead to the introduction of *Fremdkörper* (Smits 2002, p. 10) into the national systems. The non-interference with the national systems that the Commission speaks of might be a result of the optional nature of the envisaged instrument, but not necessarily of the form of the envisaged instrument, whether regulation or directive.

13 2010 Green Paper, p. 10. For more about subsidiarity and proportionality, see also Chapter 2, section 7.1.

14 2010 Green Paper, p. 10.

minimum level of harmonization.[15] That problem could be circumvented if unification is created by way of a regulation (Option 6).[16] However, opting for a regulation might be more difficult to justify when it comes to subsidiarity and proportionality.[17] These difficulties only increase with Option 7, namely that of adopting a European Civil Code which would cover not only contract law but also other types of obligations and even other areas of private law.[18]

## 3. EU Private International Law - Changing the *Lex Rei Sitae*?

I have argued in Chapter 2 that the *lex rei sitae* rule - by which the proprietary status of an object is determined by the law of the place where the object is situated - is not always suitable in an EU setting where there is free movement of goods and capital.[19] Property rights validly created in relation to an object in the home Member State may be altered or lost when that object crosses the border into another Member State.[20] This situation is called *conflit mobile* or *Statutenwechsel*.[21] The host Member State will either try to adapt the foreign property right into the most similar property right that can be found in its own *numerus clausus* or, if this is not possible, will refuse to recognize the foreign property right.[22] It must be noted, however, that the term 'recognize', when discussing the recognition of foreign property rights, is not always used in the same way. Often, it means recognizing a foreign property right by way of transposing it into a national equivalent. 'Recognize' may in such cases also refer to the vested rights theory under which rights can only be recognized if they have been validly created (vested) under the law of the country

15 2010 Green Paper, p. 10; Basedow *et al.* 2011, p. 24.

16 2010 Green Paper, p. 11: 'A Regulation establishing a European Contract Law could replace the diversity of national laws with a uniform European set of rules'; see also p. 10 of the Green Paper, at footnote 29.

17 2010 Green Paper, p. 11.

18 2010 Green Paper, p. 11.

19 *Cf* Kieninger 2008a, p. 187. Similarly, as Flessner stated about the *numerus clausus*: 'Die strikte Doktrin des Typenzwangs ist im heutigen internationalen Sachenrecht aber schon grundsätzlich fehl am Platz. Sie unterstellt eine Rechtsordnung, die nach außen und in sich geschlossen ist und dadurch ihr Sachenrechtssystem »rein« halten kann. Diese Vorstellung ist unrealistisch und unangemessen in einer Welt, in der internationale Freiheit des Warenverkehrs herrschen soll. Hier kann der einzelne Staat nicht mehr erwarten, dass sich auf seinem Gebiet nur Sachen befinden, die nach seinem geschlossenen System der dinglichen Rechte erworben und belastet wurden'; Flessner 2010, p. 135.

20 This may for instance be the case with liens, which are known to English law but not to Dutch law. Therefore, liens are not likely to be recognized in the Netherlands, because there is no equivalent in the Dutch *numerus clausus*. See also Verhagen 2007a, p. 35 with reference to Wilmowsky 1996.

21 Rauscher 2009, p. 323.

22 A more detailed description of how the *lex rei sitae* rule is interpreted and applied by different countries can be found in Akkermans & Ramaekers 2012b.

where the object was at the time of creation of the right.[23] Such recognition is an essential prerequisite before a property right can be transposed into a national equivalent.[24] It can be debated whether this is truly recognition. Recognition may also mean the recognition of a foreign property right *as such*, i.e. without changing it into a national equivalent.[25] I would consider the latter as a purer form of recognition than the former. Such outright recognition would, for instance, be the case if the internal market concept of 'mutual recognition' were applied to property rights,[26] about which more below.[27] Another example is the Hague Convention on the Law Applicable to Trusts and their Recognition, which entails that a trust validly created under the Convention must be recognized as such in all the countries that ratified the Convention (Art. 11). Whenever the term recognition is used in the following paragraphs, it will be made clear which interpretation of recognition is meant.

Transformation of a foreign property right into the national equivalent may lead to a change in the rights and powers of the holder of the property right; an outright refusal of a foreign property right which has no national equivalent leads to a loss of the property right at the border. A company may, for that reason, choose to no longer conduct cross-border business, to ensure payment of the purchase price through different, more expensive (contractual) means than a property security right,[28] or to increase the price of the object to cover the risk of losing a security right. In every one of these instances, there is an obstacle to the internal market. Either a company no longer trades with businesses in other Member States or its costs increase and therefore potentially also the price of the object, giving the company a competitive disadvantage. Furthermore, a person wishing to acquire immovable property in another Member State is forced to create a right of mortgage or hypothec under the law of that Member State. The unfamiliarity of a foreign mortgage and the additional costs of becoming familiar can form an obstacle to the free movement of capital, given that the acquisition of immovable property in another Member State is considered to be a capital movement.[29]

In principle, the *lex rei sitae* finds its justification, for immovables, in the nature of the object, making it inextricably linked to a State's territory;[30] and for movables, in the protection of third parties who should not be confronted with property rights that could not exist under the law of the country where the object is situated.[31] As

23 Kuipers 2009, p. 75.
24 Polak 2006, p. 128.
25 *Cf* Van der Weide 2006, p. 230.
26 See Chapter 2, section 3.2. *Mutual recognition of property rights?*
27 Section 3.1.5.
28 *Cf* Verhagen 2007a, p. 31.
29 Annex I to Dir. 88/361/EEC, Nomenclature of capital movements, at II: 'Investments in Real Estate'; [1988] *OJ* L 178/5.
30 Verhagen 2007a, p. 7.
31 Kieninger 2002, p. 83. Claims and other intangible objects normally do not have a *situs* and are therefore not subject to the *lex rei sitae* rule; Van der Weide 2006, p. 221. Under the Rome I Regulation, the assignment of claims is governed by the law applicable to the contract be- →

far as movables are concerned, it has been shown in Chapter 2 that third party protection is not always a valid justification for not recognizing a foreign property right.[32] Moreover, an object's current *situs* may be purely a coincidence.[33] Whilst being transported to its country of destination, it may pass through one or several countries with which it has no connection.

Van der Weide, in his doctoral thesis, sees three ways out of the *conflit mobile* problem.[34] The first option would be harmonization or unification of property law.[35] A second option would be to choose a connecting factor for proprietary relationships that is 'immune' to *conflit mobile* problems.[36] Possible alternatives for the *lex rei sitae* are the *lex registrationis,* the *lex destinationis* or the *lex contractus*. A third possibility would be to allow choice of law in property law.[37] The possibilities for harmonization or unification of property law will be discussed in the remainder of this chapter. The possible content of such harmonizing rules will be explored in Chapter 6. The second and third options mentioned by Van der Weide will be discussed hereafter.

## 3.1. *Alternatives to the Lex Rei Sitae Rule*

### 3.1.1. Lex Registrationis

The *lex registrationis* generally seems to be interpreted as the law of the place of registration of the object, as opposed to the place of registration of the property right resting on the object. Several examples illustrate this. The Geneva Convention on the International Recognition of Rights in Aircraft states that certain rights in aircraft must be recognized by the contracting states if these rights have been created in accordance with 'the law of the Contracting State in which the aircraft was registered as to nationality'.[38] The Cape Town Convention on International Interests in Mobile Equipment is also based on the *lex registrationis*.[39] Finally, the Dutch *Wet IPR zee-, binnenvaart- en luchtrecht*[40] designates, in Article 3(2), 'the law of the State where the ship [...] was registered'.[41]

tween assignor and assignee: Art. 14, Reg. 593/2008/EC on the law applicable to contractual obligations (Rome I), [2008] *OJ* L 177/6.

32 Chapter 2, section 7.1 *Proportionality*.

33 Verhagen 2007a, p. 10; Weide 2006, p. 222. Verhagen 2007a, p. 10; Van der Weide 2006, p. 222.

34 Van der Weide 2006, p. 231 *et seq*.

35 Van der Weide 2006, p. 231.

36 Van der Weide 2006, p. 231.

37 Van der Weide 2006, p. 231-232.

38 Geneva Convention of 19 June 1948, 310 UNTS 151, Art. I(1)(i). Polak 2006, p. 126.

39 Polak 2006, p. 126.

40 Private International Law Act relating to maritime law, inland navigation law and aviation law. [translation ER]

41 '[H]et recht van de Staat waar het schip [...] teboek stond.' Van der Weide 2006, p. 231.

Suppose all Member States were to adhere to the *lex registrationis* instead of the *lex rei sitae*. In that scenario, it would be easier for parties to predict which law will apply to their proprietary relationship, namely the law of the place where the object is registered. However, once an object has been registered in a Member State, it is only possible to create property rights in relation to that object under the law of the State of registration. Just as with the *lex rei sitae*, only one national law, i.e. one *numerus clausus* applies. The *lex registrationis* thus provides more predictability for the parties as to what will be the applicable law but it does not provide them with much more choice than the *lex rei sitae*. Parties might choose where to register an object - if that choice is even available - but once the object is registered, the only property rights available to the parties are the ones from the *numerus clausus* of the country of registration.

A next step to solve this problem could be to create a European registry where you would not register the object but the rights created in relation to the object. Rights registered in this European registry would have to be recognized throughout the EU. However, even though such a European registration might provide for recognition of the registered right throughout the EU, the type of right that can be created in the first place will still be determined by either the place where the object is situated or by the place where the object is registered, depending on the national rule of private international law. In other words, the result would be the application of the *lex rei sitae* (or *lex registrationis* of the object) with mutual recognition of the property rights existing in relation to that object throughout the EU, justified through the European registry.

A more effective way in which the *lex registrationis* could solve the problems in the internal market caused by the *lex rei sitae*, in combination with the national *numerus clausus*, would be to create a European registry in which property rights can be registered and to make European law the applicable law as the *lex registrationis* of the property right. The content of the European law, as the applicable law, would have to be a European property right, for instance, a European right of ownership or a European Security Right.

### 3.1.2. Lex Destinationis

The *lex destinationis* is the law of the country of destination of the object.[42] Also here several examples can be mentioned, where the *lex destinationis* is applied instead of the *lex rei sitae*. Article 133(1) of Book 10 of the Dutch Civil Code applies the *lex destinationis* to objects that are being transported.[43] Article 128(2) of Book 10 of the Dutch Civil Code allows parties to agree that the property law consequences of a

42 *Cf* Verhagen 2007a, p. 13.

43 Art. 10:133(1) reads: 'Het goederenrechtelijke regime met betrekking tot een zaak die krachtens een overeenkomst van internationaal vervoer wordt vervoerd, wordt beheerst door het recht van de staat van bestemming.'

reservation of ownership clause are governed by the law of the country of destination, provided that the object is actually imported into that country.[44] This provision allows parties a limited choice of law with which they can deviate from the *lex rei sitae*.[45] The *lex destinationis* can also be found in Article 103 of the Swiss *Bundesgesetz über das Internationale Privatrecht* (IPRG).[46] This Article states: 'Der Eigentumsvorbehalt an einer zur Ausfuhr bestimmten beweglichen Sache untersteht dem Recht des Bestimmungsstaates.'[47] Article 104(1) IPRG goes one step further by stating that parties may subject the acquisition or loss of property rights in relation to movable objects to the law of the country of origin or the country of destination or to the law that governs the underlying agreement (i.e. the *lex contractus*).[48] Article 104(2) takes the bite out of this provision, however, by stating that a choice of law made under 104(1) cannot be invoked against third parties.

### 3.1.3. Lex Contractus

Whenever a property right is created or transferred it would also be a possibility to let the law that governs the underlying contractual agreement also govern the proprietary aspects of the legal relationship. For instance: if two parties conclude a contract of sale, and that contract is governed by English law, then a retention of title clause contained in the same contract could also be governed by English law, even if the goods sold are moved outside of England. The risk involved in this possibility is of course that parties can essentially choose any law to govern their contract and consequentially any law to govern their proprietary relationship. This could certainly be undesirable for courts that would then be faced with having to apply any number of foreign, possibly little-known, property regimes. Whether this would be more undesirable on a global scale than on a European scale remains to be seen.

44 Art. 10:128(2) reads: 'In afwijking van de eerste zin van het eerste lid kunnen partijen overeenkomen dat de goederenrechtelijke gevolgen van een eigendomsvoorbehoud van een voor uitvoer bestemde zaak worden beheerst door het recht van de staat van bestemming indien op grond van dat recht het eigendomsvoorbehoud niet zijn werking verliest totdat de prijs volledig is betaald. De aldus overeengekomen aanwijzing heeft slechts gevolg indien de zaak daadwerkelijk in de aangewezen staat van bestemming wordt ingevoerd.'

45 Van der Weide 2006, p. 222. According to Flessner, this Statute shows that the location of the object as connecting factor is not always an *unüberwindbarer Naturzustand*, but rather a conscious choice by the legislature, a choice that could also be made differently, in favour of choice of law for the parties; Flessner 2010, p. 130.

46 Federal Statute on Private International Law.

47 A reservation of ownership in relation to a movable object meant to be exported is subject to the law of the country of destination. [translation ER]

48 *Die Parteien können den Erwerb und den Verlust dinglicher Rechte an beweglichen Sachen dem Recht des Abgangs- oder des Bestimmungsstaates oder dem Recht unterstellen, dem das zugrundeliegende Rechtsgeschäft untersteht.*

### 3.1.4. Choice of Applicable Property Law

If parties could make a choice of applicable property law - e.g. for the law also applicable to their contract - a *conflit mobile* would no longer arise. As a result, infringements of the freedom of movement would be prevented,[49] and parties would no longer be confronted with the legal uncertainty and unpredictability caused by objective connecting factors.[50] However, as Van der Weide points out, choice of law is generally not compatible with the *numerus clausus* of property rights.[51] Furthermore, it may become difficult for third parties to find out what the content of the rights created under the chosen law is. For instance, if parties create a right of hypothec on a ship under Romanian law, they thereby make a choice for Romanian law as the applicable law to their proprietary relationship. If the ship is then sailed to Germany, how are third parties in Germany to find out about the Romanian hypothec? They could consult the Romanian registry, provided that the hypothec has been registered, but the time and costs involved in travelling to Romania to consult the registry - if the registry is not available electronically - may pose an obstacle to the German third party. Moreover, the registry will probably be in Romanian, which the German third party may not be able to read. These problems could be overcome by making the information in the registry available online, but a translation would be needed. Would the translation be in German? Or in English? These issues are currently being tackled by the EULIS project,[52] which provides access to the land registers of the connected countries.[53] However, until this project is completed, it may not be fair to expect third parties to respect the property rights created by others under foreign law if they cannot know of their existence or content. Swiss law has tried to solve this problem by making such a choice of property law only valid *inter partes*.[54] Van der Weide questions the usefulness of such a choice of law if it cannot be made *erga omnes*.[55] Flessner argues the contrary. He presents a theory according to which the use and protection of a property right must be governed by the *lex rei sitae* but the creation or transfer of property rights should be governed by the law chosen by the parties or by the law that is otherwise applicable to the parties' agreement.[56] I must agree with Van der

49 Flessner 2010, p. 143.
50 Von Wilmowsky 1998, p. 4.
51 Van der Weide 2006, p. 232. See also Polak 2006, p. 124.
52 European Land Information Service at: <http://eulis.eu>.
53 At the time of writing (June 2012) there are 5 connected countries and 15 pending countries.
54 Art. 104 Bundesgesetz über das Internationale Privatrecht (IPRG):
'1 Die Parteien können den Erwerb und den Verlust dinglicher Rechte an beweglichen Sachen dem Recht des Abgangs- oder des Bestimmungsstaates oder dem Recht unterstellen, dem das zugrundeliegende Rechtsgeschäft untersteht.
2 Die Rechtswahl kann Dritten nicht entgegengehalten werden.'
55 Van der Weide 2006, p. 233.
56 Flessner 2010, p. 145. An English version of this contribution has been published as A. Flessner, 'Choice of Law in International Property Law - New Encouragement from Europe' →

Weide, though, that if a choice of property law is only valid between the parties to the agreement and cannot be invoked against third parties, then it only has a limited meaning. Between the parties to the agreement, the choice is meaningful, particularly as long as the debtor does not become insolvent (which is true for most cases). However, if the debtor does become insolvent then the choice of law that he and the creditor have made, to govern a security right created in favour of the creditor, will be of no avail to the creditor if he cannot invoke it against third parties, e.g. other (secured) creditors of the debtor.[57] In any event, it must be noted that choice of law in property law only solves the problems currently caused by the application of the *lex rei sitae* rule if it is accepted in all the Member States.[58] Otherwise, 'limping' proprietary relationships will again arise.[59] One country applying the *lex rei sitae* could negate the choice of property law made by parties under the law of another country which does permit such a choice of property law.

### 3.1.5. Mutual Recognition and Country of Origin Principle

EU law might already provide a conflicts rule that could replace the *lex rei sitae*, namely the country of origin principle. The country of origin principle and the principle of mutual recognition are often discussed together, but it is not entirely clear what these two principles entail. Are they two sides of the same coin or must they be regarded separately? Do the differences in interpretation of these principles stem from a difference in point of view, i.e. do some people interpret them from an EU law point of view and other people from a private international law (PIL) point of view and is that the cause of differing interpretations? Is the country of origin principle a private international law rule or is it an obligation to mutually recognize, which replaces national private international law rules?[60] This study is not the place to go into an in-depth analysis of the discussion on these principles; they deserve a more detailed study in future research. I will try to capture the essence of the debate here, focusing on the main question of this section, which is whether there are viable alternatives to the *lex rei sitae*. The country of origin principle may be such an alternative.

in R. Westrik & J. van der Weide, *Party Autonomy in International Property Law* (München: Sellier, 2011). Other contributions in this publication on choice of law in property law include: J. van der Weide, 'Party Autonomy in Dutch International Property Law'; J. von Hein, 'Party Autonomy in International Property Law: A German Perspective'; and V. Sagaert, 'Party Autonomy in French and Belgian Law'.

57 In the words of Bouckaert, this would be a 'lame duck security'; Bouckaert 2006, p. 189.

58 *Cf* Polak 2006, p. 125.

59 Van der Weide 2006, p. 235: 'hinkende goederenrechtelijke rechtsverhoudingen'. 'Limping' legal relationships are legal relationships that may have a different legal effect in one country than in another, because a different law applies from country to country; *cf* Saarloos 2010, p. 3; Knot 2008, p. 6; Carruthers 2005, p. 199.

60 Heiderhoff 2007, p. 223 at no. 259.

Basedow sees in the concept of mutual recognition a *versteckte Kollisionsnorm* - a hidden conflict of laws rule.[61] The Commission's 1985 White Paper on Completing the Internal Market[62] led him to ask the question whether the programme for the internal market, as expressed through the case law and the policy of the EU institutions, contains hidden conflict of laws rules that set aside the private international law of the Member States as a result of the supremacy of EU law.[63] Mutual recognition - stemming originally from the ECJ's judgment in *Cassis de Dijon*[64] - means having to recognize the regulatory system of another Member State under which a product was marketed, a service was provided, a company established.[65] That also means accepting the existence of foreign legal concepts within the territory of the host Member State.[66] As a result, mutual recognition is a hidden conflict of laws rule that indicates the law of the country of origin as the applicable law.[67] Basedow's analysis does not stop here. According to him, the application of the country of origin principle does not just entail a decision on the applicable law but also the application of a *favor offerentis* or *Günstigkeitsprinzip*: the law of the country of origin of a good or service (or company) has to be respected in the host Member State, unless the law of the host Member State provides more favourable conditions for the good, service or company from the original Member State.[68]

In this view, mutual recognition and the country of origin principle seem to constitute two sides of the same coin. This is logical from an EU law perspective: if Member States are required to recognize the regulatory system of other Member States under which a good, service or company was 'created', then the law of the country where the good, service or company originates must be the applicable law. It is however also possible to view mutual recognition and the country of origin principle separately, which seems to be more of a PIL point of view. They often go together but they are not necessarily inextricably linked to each other. In this view, mutual recognition simply means recognition of the fact that a natural or legal person validly acquired certain rights under the law that was applicable to the acquisition of those rights. In this interpretation of mutual recognition, the applica-

61 Basedow 1995, p. 15.

62 COM(85) 310 final.

63 Basedow 1995, p. 4-5: 'Und hinzu kommt zweitens die Frage, ob nicht das Kriterium für die Auswahl der maßgeblichen Rechtsordnung gerade durch den Grundsatz der gegenseitigen Anerkennung gleichwertiger Lösungen determiniert ist, ob also das in Rechtsprechung und Politik der Gemeinschaftsorgane ausformulierte Binnenmarktprogramm versteckte Kollisionsnormen enthält, die wegen des Vorrangs des Gemeinschaftsrechts das IPR der Mitgliedstaaten verdrängen.'

64 Case 120/78, *Rewe* v *Bundersmonopolverwaltung für Branntwein* (*Cassis de Dijon*) [1979] ECR 649.

65 *Cassis de Dijon*, para. 14. See also Basedow 1995, p. 14; Roth 2003; Kieninger 2002, p. 354; Von Wilmowsky 1998, p. 12.

66 *Cf* Kuipers 2009, p. 68.

67 Basedow 1995, p. 13-15. See also Verhagen 2007a, p. 32.

68 Basedow 1995, p. 16. See also Michaels 2006a, p. 13.

ble law to the enforcement of these rights has yet to be decided.[69] This may well be the law of the country of origin but that is not necessarily so.[70] It could, for instance, also be the law of the country of destination. The term 'recognition' must here be interpreted as meaning that a foreign right will be accommodated by the receiving Member State by being assimilated as much as possible into the law of that State, but the law applicable to its enforcement is in the end the law of destination (or of the forum) and not the law of origin.[71] Interpreted in this way, the country of origin principle could be likened to the vested rights theory, as advanced by Dicey in England and Beale in the United States. As this parallel was drawn in great detail by Ralf Michaels,[72] I will forego discussing it further here. It is noteworthy, though, that Kuipers drew a parallel between the vested rights theory and the concept of mutual recognition, showing once more that it is difficult to draw a strict line between mutual recognition and country of origin.[73] In his interpretation, mutual recognition can function where the vested rights doctrine cannot, in case a natural or legal person has not acquired rights under the law of the home Member State, but still the home Member State's regulatory system must be recognized in other Member States, as is for example the case with tax law.[74]

The last word has certainly not been written about mutual recognition and the country of origin principle.[75] For now, I will focus on the country of origin principle as a potential conflict of laws rule as seen from the EU law perspective, from which it is a necessary consequence of the principle of mutual recognition. In this sense, mutual recognition and country of origin entail that rights lawfully acquired under the rules of one Member State must be recognized and enforced by the receiving Member State without that State's laws imposing any additional burdens or requirements.[76] From an internal market perspective, could the country of origin form an alternative to the *lex rei sitae* so as to reduce obstacles to free movement? Certainly, if mutual recognition and the country of origin principle, as interpreted here, were to be extended to include mutual recognition of property regimes, then that would

69 Michaels 2006a, p. 2 and 22; Kuipers 2009, p. 76.

70 *Cf* Roth 2003, p. 190: '[T]his obligation [of a Member State to recognize a foreign company] presupposes necessarily that the Member State which is deemed to be under the obligation [...] does not regard that company as a company governed by its substantive own law. The obligation of a *duty to recognize* the existence of a foreign company applies to *both* States, and therefore will be of no help as long as we do not introduce a *rule of preference* concerning the relevant connecting factors'. In other words, mutual recognition necessitates a choice for a conflicts rule (e.g. country of origin). Also Tichý 2011, p. 408.

71 *Cf* Michaels 2006a, p. 14.

72 Michaels 2006a.

73 Kuipers 2009, p. 75 *et seq*.

74 Kuipers 2009, p. 80-81.

75 *Cf* Heiderhoff 2007, p. 223.

76 *Cf* Heiderhoff 2007, p. 227; Kuipers 2009, p. 79.

negate the application of the *lex rei sitae* rule.[77] The benefits of using the country of origin as a connecting factor to determine the applicable law is that it provides more legal certainty and prevents additional costs for the seller to compensate for a potential loss of a property right in cross-border trade. The seller will not have to create separate security rights for every Member State that his goods might travel to or through and will not have to make use of alternative means of providing security that will be recognized in other Member States to cover the risk of non-recognition of the original security right of his choice. Of course, courts would be faced with 26 foreign property regimes,[78] with all the difficulties that this entails, although it is a matter of opinion whether this would be more or less problematic than courts facing 26 foreign company regimes as they now do as a result of the CJEU's judgments in *Centros*, *Überseering* and *Inspire Art*.[79]

If the country of origin principle is not accepted as a conflict of laws rule and the *lex rei sitae* rule continues to be applied, then the development of a European property law may nevertheless necessitate a new interpretation of this rule. One could ask the question: what is still the *lex* now that there is so much (directly effective) EU law? The cases of *Van Gend & Loos* and *Costa* v *E.N.E.L.* have established that European law has direct effect within the national legal systems and supremacy over any national law conflicting with European law, provided certain criteria are met.[80] The four freedoms certainly meet those criteria[81] and are therefore part of the national law. Therefore, even if the *lex* (i.e. the applicable law) is national law, the rules on freedom of movement have become part of national law and have to be applied as the *lex rei sitae*. Consequently, national courts - which are after all also Community courts[82] - could no longer just apply national law as the *lex rei sitae* but would also have to apply the rules on free movement, which is not new in

77 Basedow 1995, p. 5: '[...] ob also das in Rechtsprechung und Politik der Gemeinschaftsorgane ausformulierte Binnenmarktprogramm versteckte Kollisionsnormen enthält, die wegen des Vorrangs des Gemeinschaftsrechts das IPR der Mitgliedstaaten verdrängen'. See also Michaels 2006a, p. 13: '[The country of origin principle] would be a challenge only for strictly territorialist conceptions of private international law.' The *lex rei sitae* is of course such a territorialist conception of PIL.

78 In the EU-27.

79 Roth 2003. See also Michaels 2006a, p. 10; Kuipers 2009, p. 68-75.

80 Case 26/62, *NV Algemene Transport- en Expeditie Onderneming van Gend & Loos* v *Netherlands Inland Revenue Administration* [1963] ECR 3; case 6/64, *Flaminio Costa* v *E.N.E.L.* [1964] ECR 1141. Treaty provisions are directly effective where they specifically grant rights or impose obligations on individuals and Member States. The supremacy of EU law follows from the transfer of powers from the Member States to the Union, limiting the Member States' powers and creating a new, supranational legal order.

81 Free movement of goods: case 74/76, *Ianelli & Volpi SpA* v *Ditta Paolo Meroni* [1977] ECR 557, para. 13; free movement of persons and services: case 41/74, *Van Duyn* [1974] ECR 1337, para. 8, and case 33/74, *Van Binsbergen* [1974] ECR 1299, para. 27 respectively; free movement of capital: joined cases C-163/94, C-165/94 and C-250/94, *Sanz de Lera and others* [1995] ECR I-4821, para. 48.

82 Claes 2006, p. 58 *et seq.*

general, it may just be new for property law. In case of a conflict between the free movement rules and rules of national law, the free movement rules must be given priority as a result of the supremacy of EU law. Along similar lines it could be argued that the *situs* is no longer any individual Member State but the entire - boundary-free - internal market.

### 3.2. *Preliminary Conclusions*

Changing the connecting factor from the location of the object to the registration, origin or destination of the object, or to the law governing the underlying contract of a property relationship, would only solve the problems that currently occur in the internal market due to the application of the *lex rei sitae* rule if all the Member States would adopt the new connecting factor. Say, for instance, that Germany and the Netherlands both adhere to the *lex registrationis* rule. If person A registers a car in Germany and then transfers ownership of the car in accordance with German law to person B in the Netherlands, then that transfer would be valid in the Netherlands as well as in Germany under German law as the *lex registrationis*. However, if only Germany applied the *lex registrationis*, but the Netherlands still applied the *lex rei sitae*, then the validity of the transfer of ownership of the car, once the car reached the Netherlands, would be decided under Dutch law, not German law. Uniform use of one connecting factor to decide on the law applicable to transfer and creation of property rights throughout the EU would therefore be necessary. Such a change from the *lex rei sitae* rule to another private international law rule would therefore have to be made through mandatory EU legislation, preferably a regulation.[83] Article 81 TFEU (ex Art. 65 EC) could provide the legal basis for this and speaks of 'measures', leaving it up to the EU legislature to choose between a regulation or a directive. PIL measures may be enacted 'particularly when necessary for the proper functioning of the internal market' (Art. 81(2)). This wording deviates slightly from the wording of Article 65 EC, which stated: 'in so far as necessary for the proper functioning of the internal market'. The new wording seems to suggest that measures based on Article 81 could be enacted for other purposes than the proper functioning of the internal market.[84] Measures taken under Article 81 are however restricted to cross-border situations. The question is whether this is a problem for the creation of rules of private international law. Rules of PIL only come into play in cross-border situations, not in purely internal ones. The fact that Article 81 is limited to cross-border situations should therefore not be problematic for the creation of European rules of PIL. What might however be a problem is the limitation of Article 81 in a territorial sense. The United Kingdom, Ireland and Denmark will only be

[83] Johnston and Unberath point out that 'Regulations are also preferred in private international law'; Johnston & Unberath 2010, p. 91.

[84] *Cf* Basedow *et al.* 2011, p. 17.

bound by measures taken on the basis of Article 81 if they opt into them.[85] As explained above, replacing the *lex rei sitae* rule with another rule of PIL can only solve the problems within the internal market if the new rule is adopted EU-wide. If such a measure is adopted on the basis of Article 81, an EU-wide adoption could be at risk if any of the aforementioned three countries decides not to take part.

Even if all the Member States would adopt one of these new connecting factors, it remains to be seen whether the problems originally caused by the *lex rei sitae* would really be solved. Adhering to the *lex registrationis* would imply recognizing property rights validly created under the *lex registrationis as such*, i.e. without changing them into the nearest equivalent under the receiving Member State's own *numerus clausus*, even if they are foreign. This is exactly what countries are currently unwilling and/or unable to do and why they adhere to the *lex rei sitae*. Having to accommodate property rights from potentially 26[86] foreign legal systems would put an enormous strain on the national courts and can certainly be called undesirable. Applying the *lex destinationis* does not lead to this problem, provided that the parties actually create a property right that is valid under the *lex destinationis*. Furthermore, given that many proprietary issues in relation to transported goods often occur upon delivery of the goods,[87] an added advantage of the *lex destinationis* would be that the court asked to adjudicate these issues can apply its own national law. Other problems may arise, though. A first problem is the interpretation of the *lex destinationis*. If this rule is interpreted in the sense that the property right created by the parties under the *lex destinationis* only comes into existence once the object actually reaches the country of destination then it is unclear what - if any - property right exists in relation to the object if it does not reach the country of destination. The *lex destinationis* could also be interpreted as meaning that the property right created under the *lex destinationis* comes into existence immediately, before the object has actually reached the country of destination. Application of the *lex destinationis* in this manner could, however, be susceptible to fraud. If party A and party B, both living in France, decide to create an Italian right of pledge on a car that will supposedly be exported to Italy, what guarantee is there that the car will actually be exported to Italy?[88] A rule could be made, stating that the property right does not come into being unless and until the object is actually put on transport. Nevertheless, such a rule remains very much open to interpretation. These objections lead to the conclusion that replacing the *lex rei sitae* with the *lex registrationis* or the *lex destinationis* does not necessarily improve the situation within the internal

85 Protocol (No. 21) on the Position of the United Kingdom and Ireland in respect of the Area of Freedom, Security and Justice, [2010] *OJ* C 83/295; Protocol (No. 22) on the Position of Denmark with Annex, [2010] *OJ* C 83/299. See also Basedow *et al.* 2011, p. 18.

86 In an EU-27. There may be more foreign legal systems than there are Member States, given that, for instance, Scottish law differs from English law within the UK.

87 Verhagen 2007a, p. 13-14.

88 *Cf* Carruthers 2005, who signals a similar potential for abuse as regards the *lex rei sitae* rule itself - p. 209.

market. Whether it would be more helpful to replace the *lex rei sitae* with a mutual recognition and country of origin principle remains difficult to say, as long as there is no definitive interpretation of these two concepts.

It must be concluded that if EU measures of PIL are considered as a replacement for the *lex rei sitae* rule, they must be uniformly applied throughout the EU and it must be carefully considered whether the new measure is actually an improvement to the *lex rei sitae*. As was shown above in the discussion of the *lex registrationis*, Europeanization of not just the PIL rules but also of substantive rules of property law may be necessary.[89]

## 4. Cross-Border or Purely Internal Situations[90]

After listing the seven policy options, the Commission went on to consider whether any instrument adopted should be applicable to cross-border situations only or also to purely domestic situations.[91] The Commission differentiates between B2C and B2B contracts. It believes that in B2C contracts, an instrument applicable to both cross-border and domestic situations, 'would impact on consumers who may not wish to venture into the internal market and prefer to preserve national levels of protection'.[92] For B2B contracts, on the other hand, the Commission favours an instrument applicable to both cross-border and domestic situations, as it opens up the possibility for business to trade everywhere in the internal market on the basis of a single set of rules.[93] While the Commission's considerations with regard to consumers are understandable, there may be no need for concern. In the case of an optional instrument (policy Option 4 in the Green Paper), the consumer is left free to choose national law as the applicable law to the transaction, so that he does not have to 'venture into the internal market' if he prefers not to.[94] Furthermore, creating separate instruments for B2B contracts and B2C contracts would mean that businesses could still not trade on the basis of a single set of rules, regardless of whether these instruments applied only to cross-border trade or also to domestic

89 *Cf* Kieninger 2004b, p. 18.

90 This section pertains to the concepts of 'cross-border' and 'purely internal' situations as used in EU law. Private international law also distinguishes between national and international cases but the line drawn by PIL is not necessarily the same as the line drawn by EU law. Furthermore, the EU categories of cross-border and purely internal are redefined regularly by CJEU case law (see fn. 91 below) and will also, for that reason, not always overlap with the PIL categories of national and international. This section is restricted to the EU concepts of cross-border and purely international situations, and does not discuss the PIL distinction between national and international cases.

91 For the difference between cross-border and purely internal (or domestic) situations, see the case law discussed in Chapter 2, section 1. *Cross-border or purely internal situation?*

92 2010 Green Paper, p. 12.

93 Hesselink *et al.* put forth a similar opinion already in 2007: Hesselink, Rutgers & Booys 2007, p. 27. See also Schulte-Nölke 2007, p. 349.

94 See *supra*, note 92.

trade.[95] As Basedow *et al.* point out, '[p]arallel regimes [...] are not only uneconomical from the point of view of legislative technique, but are also a potential source of inconsistencies and contradictions'.[96]

If the decision - whether or not to apply an instrument also to purely internal situations - is left to the Member States, voluntary harmonization[97] might arise among those Member States that make the European option available for purely internal situations, either as an alternative to their own rules or as a replacement for their own rules.[98] One could envisage a situation in which the European rules are the default option for cross-border situations, leaving it up to the parties to opt out of them, and in which the national rules are the default option for a purely internal situation, leaving it up to the parties to opt into the European rules.[99] This could however lead to demarcation problems: it is not always easy to establish when a situation is a cross-border situation or a purely internal situation.[100] These demarcation problems can be avoided by applying the instrument to both situations or, in the case of an optional instrument, by making the European regime available to parties in both situations. That would also prevent instances of reverse discrimination, which would arise if the instrument were only available for parties trading cross-border.

In conclusion, any instrument adopted by the Commission should be applicable to both cross-border and purely internal situations and to both B2B and B2C transactions. Otherwise, both consumers and businesses will be subject to two parallel regimes, something which could greatly reduce the attractiveness of the instrument.[101] The problem of being subject to several regimes was one of the main reasons for drafting an instrument on European contract law,[102] and is a similarly important reason for developing an instrument on EU property law. This problem will not be solved by introducing a new regime that cannot be relied on throughout the entire Union, for all transactions.

## 5. Non-Binding Options

Policy options 1-3 of the 2010 Green Paper are non-binding options of a non-legislative nature. Options 1 and 3 suffer from similar disadvantages. Option 1 -

95 Basedow *et al.* 2011, p. 51; Smits 2011, p. 29.

96 Basedow *et al.* 2011, p. 49. The Commission itself signals this potential problem: p. 11-12 of the 2010 Green Paper.

97 That voluntary harmonization can be successful may be illustrated by the 1988 United Nations Convention on Contracts for the International Sale of Goods (CISG): 'The Convention when it came into force did not represent the law of any nation state. But since 1988 it has been enacted as law in 54 countries'; Watson 2000, at section VI.

98 *Cf* Drobnig 1997, p. 493.

99 *Cf* Wagner 2002, p. 1023. See also *infra* at section 6.3. *Opt-in or opt-out.*

100 See supra note 91. See also Basedow *et al.* 2011, p. 53.

101 Basedow *et al.* 2011, p. 52 at footnote 172, and p. 53.

102 2010 Green Paper, p. 2; Smits 2011, p. 29.

Publication of the results of the Expert Group – is not a very effective option. In general, Option 1 would not help to remove the obstacles in the internal market caused by the divergences of the national laws, given that it would have no formal authority or status.[103] More specifically, the results of the Expert Group in the area of property law are far fewer than in the area of contract law. The most recent achievement – the publication of the feasibility study[104] – does not contain any parts on property law. As far as property law is concerned, therefore, the Expert Group has not yet produced the 'practical and user-friendly text'[105] that could serve as inspiration for legislatures and contracting parties. Indeed, the Commission's Proposal for a Regulation on a Common European Sales Law (CESL),[106] which was adopted in October 2011 as a result of the 2010 Green Paper, does not contain any property law.[107] Option 3 – an instrument of European Contract Law (or Property Law) attached to a Commission Recommendation addressed to the Member States – could either encourage the Member States to replace their national law with the recommended instrument or offer it as an optional regime to contracting parties.[108] Option 3 suffers from a similar deficiency as Option 1, namely that a Recommendation is not binding for the Member States[109] who would be free to choose whether, how and when to implement it. As a result, the discrepancies between the national laws would not be remedied.[110]

Option 2 – an official 'toolbox' for the EU legislature – also has the downside of not being able to remove divergences between national laws.[111] Nevertheless, it is an interesting option in the sense that it could compel the EU institutions to be more consistent and coherent when legislating in the area of European contract law (or property law). Such a toolbox could be adopted in the form of a Communication or Decision, which would make the instrument immediately effective upon adoption by the Commission but it would not have to be considered by the Parliament and Council when proposing amendments.[112] A toolbox binding both the Commission as well as the Parliament and the Council could be laid down in an inter-institutional agreement.[113]

103 2010 Green Paper, p. 8.
104 To be found at: <http://ec.europa.eu/justice/policies/consumer/docs/explanatory_note_results_feasibility_study_05_2011_en.pdf>.
105 2010 Green Paper, p. 7.
106 COM(2011) 635 final.
107 Recital 27.
108 2010 Green Paper, p. 8-9.
109 Art. 288 TFEU: 'Recommendations and opinions shall have no binding force.'
110 *Cf* Basedow *et al.* 2011, p. 14-15.
111 2010 Green Paper, p. 8.
112 2010 Green Paper, p. 8.
113 Basedow *et al.* 2011, p. 10.

## 5.1. *Inter-Institutional Agreement on a 'Toolbox' for European Property Law*

Inter-institutional agreements (IIAs) are a type of soft law within the EU. They are agreements between EU institutions and can form the basis for subsequent hard law.[114] They may be of a binding nature.[115] Whether an IIA containing a 'toolbox' would be binding upon the Institutions would highly depend on the wording.[116] An advantage of using an IIA could be that the Institutions should motivate any deviation from it.[117] Whether they are actually under an obligation to do so is not entirely clear. Article 296 TFEU (ex Art. 25 EC) states that '[l]egal acts shall state the reasons on which they are based and shall refer to any proposals, initiatives, recommendations, requests or opinions required by the Treaties.' It cannot be said with certainty whether the duty to state reasons - in this case the reasons for deviating from the IIA - as laid down in Article 296 TFEU also applies to IIAs as well. The duty to state reasons applies to legal acts, but Article 289(3) TFEU indicates that there is a difference between legal acts and legislative acts: 'Legal acts adopted by legislative procedure shall constitute legislative acts'. An IIA is not a legislative act but it is a legal act. As a result, the duty to state reasons as laid down in Article 296 also applies to IIAs.[118]

An IIA containing a framework of definitions and basic principles could ensure more coherence in future legislation.[119] As was shown in Chapter 4, the use of property law terminology in European legislation is for the moment still very incoherent and inconsistent. Such an IIA may also be an 'adequate follow-up'[120] to the Interinstitutional Agreement on Better Lawmaking. This IIA ensures that the

114 Craig & De Búrca 2008, p. 87 and 129.

115 Art. 295 TFEU.

116 *Cf* Case C-25/94, *Commission* v *Council* [1996] ECR I-1469, para. 49: 'It is clear [...] from the terms of the Arrangement, that the two institutions intended to enter into a binding commitment towards each other.' See also Basedow *et al.* 2011, p. 11; Hesselink, Rutgers & Booys 2007, p. 68.

117 *Cf* European Parliament resolution of 3 September 2008 on the common frame of reference for European contract law, B6-0374/2008, at 10: 'Suggests that, if used as a non-binding legislative tool, the relevant parts of the CFR should be appended to any future legislative proposal or communication made by the Commission which touches on contract law, so as to ensure that this is considered by the Community legislature'.

118 'The ABC of European Union law', a document produced by Klaus-Dieter Borchardt and published on the Eur-Lex website (<http://eur-lex.europa.eu/en/editorial/OA8107147C_002.pdf>) provides clarity in this matter. Under the heading 'The EU Legal Instruments as the Secondary Source of Union Law', p. 82, he writes the following:
'Finally, there is a whole set of "other legal acts" which the Union institutions can use to issue non-binding measures and statements or which regulate the internal workings of the EU or its institutions, such as agreements or arrangements between the institutions or internal rules of procedure.'

119 Karsten & Petri 2005, p. 38-39.

120 Karsten & Petri 2005, p. 39.

legislative institutions shall 'promote simplicity, clarity and consistency in the drafting of laws and the utmost transparency of the legislative process'.[121] An IIA on property law may moreover form an interpretation guideline for the ECJ. It has been suggested on several occasions that the DCFR should be adopted in the form of an IIA.[122] The DCFR - particularly for property law books VIII, IX and X - could certainly provide a basis or source of inspiration to shape the content of an IIA. However, Hesselink, Rutgers and De Booys warn that this may 'raise issues of competence creep'.[123] The DCFR covers such an extensive area that it may go beyond the competences of the EU legislature to enact it as a regulation or a directive. To then enact it as an IIA might be to circumvent the principle of attributed competence (Art. 5 TFEU) through the back door.

Nevertheless, an IIA might be suitable to solve certain problems encountered in the development of EU property law. It could, for instance, be used to shape certain basic property law concepts in a European-autonomous way, such as a European Security Right, or a European concept of ownership. When enacting legislation, the EU legislature would have to adhere to the concepts thus developed or state reasons for deviating from them. This could increase consistency and coherence in future EU property legislation, which is currently lacking.[124] At the moment, there is no formal obligation for the EU legislature to use and define concepts that are repeatedly used in legislative instruments consistently. In the consumer *acquis*, this has, for instance, led to confusion about the term consumer,[125] but also about withdrawal rights and cooling-off periods, which differ from one legislative instrument to the other.[126] The very limited amount of EU legislation in the area of property law provides an opportunity to try and achieve a level of coherence and consistency up front, instead of having to rectify discrepancies in definitions and use of terms *ex post*.

### 5.2. *Legal Basis*

With Option 1 - publication of the results of the Expert Group - the Commission would be fulfilling its obligations under Articles 2 and 12 of Regulation 1049/2001

121 [2003] *OJ* C 321/1, point 2.

122 Summary of responses to the 2003 Action Plan for a more coherent European contract law: <http://ec.europa.eu/consumers/cons_int/safe_shop/fair_bus_pract/cont_law/analyticaldoc_en.pdf>, p. 10.
See also Hesselink 2009, p. 41; Hesselink, Rutgers & Booys 2007, p. 66 and footnote 128, and Karsten & Petri 2005, p. 38.

123 Hesselink, Rutgers & Booys 2007, p. 68.

124 See Chapter 4.

125 Green Paper on the review of the consumer *acquis*, COM(2006) 744 final, at Annex I, 4.1.

126 *Ibidem*, at Annex I, 4.8.

regarding public access to European Parliament, Council and Commission documents.[127]

Option 2 – the creation of a 'toolbox' – could be achieved through a communication, decision or inter-institutional agreement. Communications do not require a legal basis;[128] inter-institutional agreements may be concluded under Article 295 TFEU. A decision is one of the three binding legislative instruments the Union can adopt under Articles 288(1) and 289(3) TFEU. Such a decision, taken by the Commission, would require a legal basis. The Max Planck Research Paper commenting on the 2010 Green Paper does not discuss the issue of a legal basis for a decision on a toolbox, because it views a decision as an 'ill-suited' form for a toolbox.[129] Admittedly, it is not easy to find a legal basis for a decision on a toolbox addressed to the institutions themselves, with the exception, perhaps, of Article 290(1) TFEU, which states that '[a] legislative act may delegate to the Commission the power to adopt non-legislative acts of general application to supplement or amend certain non-essential elements of the legislative act.' Article 114 – the legal basis for measures pertaining to the establishment and functioning of the internal market – cannot be used as a legal basis, even though it provides for the adoption of 'measures', which could include a decision, because a decision on a toolbox would not lead to the approximation of the laws of the Member States.[130] Article 352 – the legal basis of last resort if the Treaty provides no other legal basis – which also provides for the adoption of 'measures', could only be used as a legal basis for a decision on a toolbox, if such action were necessary to attain one of the objectives set out in the Treaties. Both Articles 81 – the legal basis for EU private international law – and 169 TFEU – the legal basis for consumer protection – also provide for the adoption of 'measures'. However, Article 81 again requires approximation of the laws of the Member States, which a toolbox would not do, whereas Article 169 refers back to 'measures adopted pursuant to Article 114', which would also again require approximation of national laws.

Option 3 – a recommendation – could be based on Articles 17(1) TEU and 292 TFEU, regardless of whether it would be meant to replace national laws or create an optional instrument.[131] These provisions provide the Commission with the power to

127 [2001] *OJ* L 145/43. Art. 2(1): 'Any citizen of the Union, and any natural or legal person residing or having its registered office in a Member State, has a right of access to documents of the institutions'; Art. 12(1): 'The institutions shall as far as possible make documents directly accessible to the public in electronic form or through a register in accordance with the rules of the institution concerned.' See also Basedow *et al.* 2011, p. 7.

128 Basedow *et al.* 2011, p. 7.

129 Basedow *et al.* 2011, p. 7.

130 See *infra*, section 6.1. *Legal basis.*

131 Basedow *et al.* 2011, p. 8.

issue recommendations on areas covered by the Treaties where it deems it necessary to do so.[132]

## 6. Optional Instrument

A noteworthy difference between an optional instrument and a mandatory instrument is that an optional instrument - contrary to a mandatory instrument - does not replace the national systems but exists next to it, as a so-called 28th system.[133] Schulte-Nölke feels that, in this way, the 'national laboratories of legal development'[134] continue to be a source for comparative research and to provide examples of how different legal systems solve a particular problem. It would no longer be possible to draw inspiration from the different national legal systems if they were all replaced by one harmonized European system. Furthermore, according to Weatherill, '[a] harmonized private law will not display the susceptibility to local preference that is the preserve of a more decentralized system'.[135] Whether this is true can be debated. European rules which aim to harmonize will still be woven into the national system somehow and will not be applied uniformly throughout the EU. Local preferences could still be visible through the way in which the harmonized rules are incorporated into the national system. However, the use of an optional instrument instead of harmonized rules could show, through choices made by consumers and businesses for either the optional instrument or their own national law, whether the local preference is for the national rule or for the European rule.[136] This could form an indication about the attractiveness and quality of the European rule for the end-users (which could be multi-nationals, SMEs or consumers, depending on the content of the instrument), an indication which you could not get when implementing harmonized rules.[137] Furthermore, providing the possibility to opt for this 28th system as an alternative to a national system means that courts would only have to apply either their own domestic law or the European optional law.[138] This may be an advantage over a country of origin principle in

132 Craig & De Búrca 2008, p. 86.

133 In an EU with 27 Member States. Technically, for property law it could even be a 29th system or more, given that within some Member States more than one system applies (e.g. within the UK, Scotland has its own system of property law, separate from England and Wales, and Northern Ireland); see Smits 2009b, p. 1731. See also Kieninger 2002, p. 369-371; in the context of property law, several projects on optional property law have been started in the past, for a European Security Right on movables and for a European hypothec or mortgage, but they have not been successful so far.

134 Schulte-Nölke 2010, p. 140.

135 Weatherill 2004b, p. 647.

136 Smits 2006b, at no. 27.

137 Such an indication would be the result of regulatory competition between the European rule and the national rule; see *infra*, section 6.4.

138 Schulte-Nölke describes this as the 'blue button' option: Schulte-Nölke 2010, p. 142 and Schulte-Nölke 2007, p. 348-349.

combination with mutual recognition, which would confront the courts with 26 foreign systems of law, rather than just one European law.[139] In the Commission's view, an optional instrument could facilitate the functioning of the internal market for two main reasons: such a non-national regime would be specifically adapted to cross-border transactions and it may be 'an acceptable and adequate solution'[140] for both the economically stronger and weaker parties.

Having a 28th system only works if private individuals can choose this option as the applicable law to their legal relationship. However, traditionally, choice of law is not an option in property law. It may therefore be pointless to devise an optional instrument directed at private parties if they cannot choose it. Instead, the instrument would have to be directed at the Member States, who would be obliged to make the optional regime available next to their own national law, thereby providing a choice of law for private parties.[141] Member States could also choose to incorporate the rules from the optional model into their own national system, thereby avoiding the issue of whether or not to grant choice of law in property law to private parties. The question for the Member States then becomes whether it would put less of a burden on their national system to have to allow individuals to choose between the national and the European regime or to adapt the national system to the European regime. If the European regime will be applicable to cross-border situations only, then it can simply exist as an available option next to the Member States' own national systems. If on the other hand the European regime becomes applicable also to purely internal situations, then the competition with and the pressure on the national system may increase. This in turn may lead a national legislature to decide to adapt the national system to the European system, instead of maintaining both regimes next to each other.

The Proposal for a Common European Sales Law, which was adopted as a result of the Commission's 2010 Green Paper, proposes a Regulation that will add a second national regime next to the already existing national regimes, thereby implementing the CESL at the national level as opposed to the European level.[142] This would mean that, once the rules of private international law have indicated the applicable national law to a contract, within the applicable national law parties can choose between the national law that is of national origin and between the national law that is of European origin. The reason for introducing the CESL in this way seems to have been to meet the 'approximation' requirement of Article 114, which

139 See *supra* section 3. *EU Private International Law.*

140 Communication from the Commission to the European Parliament and the Council - A more coherent European contract law - An action plan, COM(2003) 68 final, *OJ* C 63/1, at 90. See also Hesselink, Rutgers & Booys 2007, p. 14.

141 *Cf* 2010 Green Paper, p. 9: 'A Regulation could set up an optional instrument, which would be conceived as a "2nd regime" in each Member State, thus providing parties with an option between two regimes of domestic contract law.'

142 Proposal for a Regulation on a Common European Sales Law, COM(2011) 635 final, p. 8-9.

has been chosen as the legal basis for the CESL.[143] We will have to wait and see whether this manner of introducing optional European private law will be accepted by the Parliament and Council during the legislative procedure and how it will work in practice if the Regulation containing the CESL is indeed introduced this way.

### 6.1. *Legal Basis*

Should the Commission decide in the future to enact rules of property law by way of an optional instrument, then the legal basis must be chosen carefully.[144] Several authors point out that Article 114 TFEU (ex Art. 95 EC) would probably not be the correct legal basis, given that an optional instrument does not lead to 'approximation', as is required by Article 114.[145] An optional instrument containing new rules or European concepts would exist next to the national systems, without changing them. Such instruments, according to the ECJ, are not 'measures for the approximation'.[146] Article 352 TFEU (ex Art. 308 EC) would offer an alternative legal basis but requires unanimity in the Council, which may be very difficult to achieve. Moreover, involvement of the European Parliament is limited under Article 352; its consent needs to be obtained but it is not part of the legislative procedure as it normally is under the codecision procedure. Given that the EP has specifically indicated that it feels that codecision is required when legislation is drafted in the

143 See Chapter 6, Part II at 3.1. *Legal basis revisited.*

144 Unfortunately, the Commission does not address the matter of legal basis in its 2010 Green Paper: Basedow *et al.* 2011, p. 16. With regard to EU property law, the Commission does address legal basis (although more the principles of subsidiarity and proportionality than legal basis itself) in its Proposal for a Directive on credit agreements relating to residential property, COM(2011) 142 final, p. 7.

145 See *inter alia* Basedow *et al.* 2011, p. 19; Weatherill 2010b, p. 67; Hesselink, Rutgers & Booys 2007, p. 47-50.

146 Case C-436/03, *European Parliament* v *Council* [2006] ECR I-3733, paras. 43-46: 'Finally, it is apparent [...] that the European cooperative society is a form which coexists with cooperative societies under national law. In those circumstances, the contested regulation, which leaves unchanged the different national laws already in existence, cannot be regarded as aiming to approximate the laws of the Member States applicable to cooperative societies, but has as its purpose the creation of a new form of cooperative society in addition to the national forms. That finding is not affected by the fact that the contested regulation does not lay down exhaustively all of the rules applicable to European cooperative societies and that, for certain matters, it refers to the law of the Member State in the territory of which the European cooperative society has its registered office, since, as pointed out above, that referral is of a subsidiary nature. It follows from the above that Article 95 EC could not constitute an appropriate legal basis for the adoption of the contested regulation, which was correctly adopted on the basis of Article 308 EC.'

area of civil law,[147] it may object to the use of Article 352 as a legal basis for an optional instrument in property law.

Article 169(2) TFEU is not likely to be a suitable legal basis. An instrument based on this provision would be restricted to consumer law, thereby excluding B2B- and C2C transactions and the protection of SMEs.[148] In the area of property law, many of the barriers to intra-Union trade are experienced by companies who lose their security rights when transporting goods across Member States' borders.[149] It would therefore not make sense to create an instrument of EU property law that does not apply to B2B-transactions.

Article 81 TFEU may serve as a legal basis, although it is debated whether it can be used for measures containing substantive private law or whether it can only be used for measures containing private international law rules.[150] Notwithstanding the outcome of that debate, Article 81 can in any event only be used for instruments that apply to cross-border situations, not for instruments that also apply in purely internal situations. Given that I would be in favour of an instrument of EU property law that can also be used in purely internal situations,[151] I would not propose to base such an instrument on Article 81 TFEU.

In conclusion, even though there are some procedural hurdles attached to the use of Article 352 TFEU, it nevertheless seems to be the most suitable legal basis for an instrument on EU property law.[152]

### 6.2. *Regulation or Directive*

Regulation 593/2008/EC on the law applicable to contractual obligations (Rome I) only allows parties to choose the law of a State as the applicable law to their legal relationship.[153] The proposal for this Regulation envisaged a provision making it possible for parties to choose a non-State body of law - including a future optional

147 European Parliament resolution on the approximation of the civil and commercial law of the Member States, [2002] *OJ* C 140E/538, at 21: 'Insists that the codecision procedure involving the full participation of the European Parliament must in principle be used when adopting legislation in the field of civil law'.

148 Basedow *et al.* 2011, p. 25.

149 This is a result of the private international law rule of *lex rei sitae*, which makes it impossible for parties to choose the law applicable to their proprietary relationship, and of the closed system of property rights (*numerus clausus*), which will not accept the 'import' of a foreign property right into the national list of property rights. The EU Member States generally adhere to both these rules.

150 Basedow *et al.* 2011, p. 17.

151 See *supra* at section 4. *Cross-border or purely internal situations.*

152 Basedow *et al.* even state that '[f]or such an instrument [an optional instrument which covers both domestic and cross-border transactions], it is also the only possible legal basis'; Basedow *et al.* 2011, p. 27.

153 This is not explicitly stated in the Regulation, but can be deduced from the wording of Art. 3(3): 'the country whose law has been chosen'. See also Smits 2011, p. 25.

instrument[154] - but this provision has not become part of the final version. However, this possibility is still mentioned in the Preamble to the Rome I Regulation:

> '(13) This Regulation does not preclude parties from incorporating by reference into their contract a non-State body of law or an international convention.
>
> (14) Should the Community adopt, in an appropriate legal instrument, rules of substantive contract law, including standard terms and conditions, such instrument may provide that the parties may choose to apply those rules.'

As a result, a future European optional instrument - even though it would not constitute a State's law - may provide that parties can choose it as the applicable law to their legal relationship, in deviation from the Rome I Regulation.[155] I would agree with Lagarde that one can only deviate from a regulation with another regulation, not with a directive.[156] Therefore, a future optional instrument should be laid down in a regulation, not a directive. This is indeed the case with the proposed Common European Sales Law,[157] although this proposal works around Recital 14 of the Rome I Regulation by introducing the Common European Sales Law as a second national law, rather than a European law.

Is it a problem for property law that the Preamble to Rome I only envisages the adoption of 'rules of substantive contract law' in an optional European instrument? The answer to that question would seem to depend on whether this phrase is interpreted narrowly or widely. Rome I does not treat rights *in rem* separately, as it does trusts.[158] It recognizes that a contract will be the origin of the creation or transfer of a right *in rem*: it always uses the phrase 'contract relating to a right in rem'.[159] Currently, it refers contracts relating to a right *in rem* to the *lex rei sitae*, in other words it does not provide for a choice of applicable law to a contract

154 'To further boost the impact of the parties' will, a key principle of the Convention, paragraph 2 authorizes the parties to choose as the applicable law a non-State body of law. The form of words used would authorize the choice of [...] a possible future optional Community instrument'; Proposal for a Regulation of the European Parliament and the Council on the law applicable to contractual obligations (Rome I), COM(2005) 650 final, Art. 3. See also Lagarde 2009, p. 282-3.

155 Synthesis of the Fifth Meeting of the Expert Group on a Common Frame of Reference in European Contract Law, Brussels, 5 October 2010, p. 1; to be found at: <http://ec.europa.eu/justice/policies/consumer/docs/cfr_report_10_10_01_09_30_en.pdf>.

156 Lagarde 2009, p. 284: 'Il ne peut s'agir à mon sens que d'un instrument ayant la même force que le règlement Rome I. Ce que le règlement Rome I a fait, un autre règlement peut évidemment le défaire.'

157 COM(2011) 635 final, p. 6.

158 Art. 1(2)(h) of Rome I.

159 See e.g. Art. 4(1)(c).

relating to a right *in rem*.[160] The Proposal for a Common European Sales Law states in Recital 27 that

> '[a]ll the matters of a contractual or non-contractual nature that are not addressed in the Common European Sales Law are governed by the pre-existing rules of the national law outside the Common European Sales Law that is applicable under Regulations (EC) No 593/2008 [Rome I] and (EC) No 864/2007 [Rome II] or any other relevant conflict of law rule. These issues include [...] property law including the transfer of ownership.'[161]

The wording of this Recital suggests only that certain contractual and non-contractual issues - such as property law - have not been addressed by the proposed CESL, but that does not necessarily mean that they could not have been addressed or be addressed, in another optional instrument.

### 6.3. *Opt-In or Opt-Out*

An optional instrument can provide for the possibility to opt-in or to opt-out of it. In the first instance, the instrument is only applicable if specifically elected. In the second instance, the instrument is applicable by default unless opted out of. The question, whether an optional instrument should contain an opt-in or an opt-out regime, can be asked at three different levels. One could ask, whether the Member States should be given the opportunity to opt into or out of an optional instrument, in the sense that they can decide whether or not to make the European regime available next to their national regime. This can happen in two ways. First, the United Kingdom and Denmark have opted out of the application of certain provisions of the TEU and TFEU through Protocols Nos. 15 and 16, which are attached to those treaties. One could call this Treaty-based opt-out. Second, an optional regime laid down in a regulation or directive based on a Treaty provision not excluded in Protocol No. 15 or 16 could provide the Member States with the choice whether or not to implement this optional regime. At this level, I would be in favour of an opt-out regime, otherwise - with an opt-in regime - the risk may be too great that too few Member States make the European option available for it to actually be useful for parties.[162] An optional instrument with an opt-in regime for the Member States would practically amount to the same as Option 3(b) of the 2010 Green Paper - A Commission Recommendation for an optional regime - with regard to which the same objection was made.[163]

160 To clarify: the law applicable to the contract as such can still be chosen under Art. 3 of the Rome I Regulation, but parties cannot choose the law applicable to the creation or transfer of a property right envisaged by the contract.

161 Recital 27 in the Preamble.

162 An optional instrument with an opt-in regime resembles the process of enhanced cooperation; enhanced cooperation will be discussed below, at section 8.1.

163 See *supra*, at section 5. *Non-binding options*.

One could also ask whether private parties should be given the opportunity to opt into or out of an optional instrument. At this level, there is a pre-supposition that the European regime is available next to the national regimes. In this scenario, there is no longer a choice for the Member States whether or not to make the option available, but there is now a choice for parties whether or not to make use of the European option. At this level, I would be in favour of an opt-in regime. An opt-out regime can become *de facto* binding,[164] given that it will be the default regime unless explicitly rejected by the parties. An optional instrument containing an opt-out regime will therefore come much closer to a mandatory instrument, whereas an optional instrument containing an opt-in regime will be more 'truly' optional, leaving the choice with the parties rather than making it for them. I would agree with Smits that the legitimacy of an optional instrument lies primarily in the choice that parties make for it.[165] An opt-in regime provides parties with that possibility to choose.

### 6.4. *Optional Instrument and Regulatory Competition*

Much has been written about regulatory competition in the context of harmonization of private law in the EU,[166] the idea being that an optional instrument could compete with the national systems and that parties would choose the rules which best suit their wishes. In this way, the European rules could prove their quality. It must be noted, however, that many of these writings concern harmonization of contract law, not property law. Regulatory competition can only take place if parties can choose between different regimes. Choice of law is common in contract law. It would thus not be problematic to introduce another - European - option into the range of options already available to the contracting parties.[167] By contrast, choice of law is not normally accepted in property law.[168] The national systems of property law lay down mandatory rules that cannot be deviated from.[169] This is inherent to this area of law and is only logical given the *erga omnes* effect that distinguishes property rights from contractual rights.[170] Given that the applicable property law

164 Hesselink, Rutgers & Booys 2007, p. 17.

165 See Smits 2011, p. 31-32 and Smits 2006b at 29: '[I]n geval van een optionele code ligt de legitimering primair in de keuze die door partijen daarvoor wordt gedaan.'

166 See, *inter alia*, Smits 2009a, p. 35 with reference to Charles Tiebout who developed the theory of 'jurisdictional competition'; Michaels & Jansen 2006, p. 863-864; Weatherill 2004b, p. 653 *et seq.*; Wagner 2002, p. 1002; Kieninger 2002.

167 Although Kenny sees this as a risk: introducing a 28th system of contract law as yet another choice in cross-border trade could lead to even more legal fragmentation than is currently already the case; Kenny 2006, p. 781. This risk is less prevalent for a European system of property law, as it would technically not constitute a 28th system but only a 2nd system next to each of the Member States' systems.

168 Van Erp 2011a, p. 1.

169 *Cf* Smits 2009a, p. 36; Kieninger 2002, p. 83.

170 Van Erp 2006a, p. 1051-1053.

will always be the *lex rei sitae*, the only way in which parties could choose the applicable law, when creating or transferring a property right, is to make sure that the object in relation to which they want to create or transfer the right has first been brought to the country whose law they wish to be applicable.[171] Obviously, this is only possible for movable objects, not for immovables. And even then, this only works as long as the object stays within that country. As soon as the object is moved across a border, the *situs* changes and, with that, the applicable law also changes.[172] Regulatory competition between an optional set of European rules of property law and each of the Member States' systems of property law is therefore only possible if the Member States are obliged to offer their citizens the European option next to their national law.[173] It must be kept in mind that this would still only lead to a competition of two legal systems, namely between a Member State's national property law and the European property law, as opposed to the competition of 28 (or more) legal systems that could take place if a European contract law were introduced next to the 27 existing Member States' contract laws.

## 6.5. *Preliminary Conclusions – an Optional Instrument for EU Property Law?*

In this section I have focussed on one of the policy options formulated by the Commission in its 2010 Green Paper, namely that of a Regulation setting up an optional instrument (Option 4). While the Commission's Green Paper is concerned with European contract law, I have used it as a starting point to draw a parallel with the option of an optional instrument for EU property law.

A preliminary matter is that of legal basis. What would be the legal basis for an optional instrument? Article 114 TFEU might be used, but the objection could be raised that an optional instrument does not actually lead to 'approximation' of national laws, as is required by Article 114. In accordance with the CJEU's case law, an instrument containing new rules or European-autonomous concepts – which an optional instrument does – should rather be adopted on the basis of Article 352 TFEU. While this may formally be a more appropriate legal basis, it raises several practical problems: unanimity is required, which may be difficult to reach with 27 Member States; and the Parliament's involvement would be limited, to which the Parliament may object.

An optional instrument is only useful if parties can actually choose it as the applicable law to their legal relationship. However, whereas choice of law is common in contract law, it is not generally accepted in property law. Therefore, if an optional instrument containing rules of EU property law were to be drafted, Member States should be obliged to make it available next to their national system

171 *Cf* Kieninger 2002, p. 83.
172 See, *inter alia*, Strikwerda 2008, p. 151; Van der Weide 2006, p. 34; Kieninger 2004b, p. 17.
173 *Cf* Basedow *et al.* 2011, p. 43.

so that parties can choose between the two regimes. Both the 2010 Green Paper and the Max Planck Institute (MPI)'s comments on the Green Paper indicate that the optional instrument is not meant to be optional for the Member States but optional for the contracting parties. This follows from the Green Paper's proposal to implement such an optional instrument by way of a regulation; it also follows from the MPI's comment that 'option [3(b): Recommendation of an optional regime] is fundamentally different from option 4 [Optional instrument] in that the "optional regime" of option 3(b) would not be available in all Member States'.[174]

I would be in favour of an opt-in instrument which parties can choose for both purely internal situations and cross-border situations. This approach makes regulatory competition possible between, on the one hand, the Member States' national systems and, on the other hand, the European regime. The fact that parties choose the European regime would legitimize the optional instrument and provide an indication of its quality and attractiveness.[175] It could verify or falsify the hypothesis that differences in national law (actually or potentially) hinder intra-Community trade,[176] a hypothesis which may otherwise be difficult to test empirically.[177] Time would have to tell whether or not the optional instrument would be a success. Finally, an optional instrument would mean less interference with and fragmentation of the national system of property law than harmonization.[178] This may make the instrument more attainable than harmonization would be.[179]

## 7. Binding Instrument

Policy options 5, 6 and 7 in the 2010 Green Paper all propose a binding instrument, although with differing scopes of application: Option 5 – a Directive on European Contract Law on the basis of minimum common standards; Option 6 – a Regulation establishing a European Contract Law; and Option 7 – a Regulation establishing a European Civil Code.

Harmonization or unification through a binding, mandatory instrument has advantages and disadvantages. An important advantage over an optional instrument would be that it would be meant to apply in the same way in all the Member States. This would not necessarily be the case with an optional instrument, in which case the discrepancies between the Member States might remain, depending on how the optional instrument would be implemented. As described above,[180] it is possible to create an optional instrument which provides the Member States a choice

174 Recommendations are not binding for Member States and they can therefore choose whether or not to implement them.

175 *Cf* Keirse & Veder 2010, p. 89.

176 Keirse & Veder 2010, p. 56.

177 *Cf* Heiderhoff 2007, p. 11.

178 *Cf* Snijders 2006, p. 160; Bouckaert 2006, p. 191.

179 Keirse & Veder 2010, p. 56.

180 Section 6.3.

whether to opt into or out of the instrument. If the Member States are not obliged to make the optional instrument available for parties to choose as the applicable law to their legal relationship, then a situation may arise whereby some Member States do participate in the optional instrument but others do not. In that case, the former discrepancies between the national laws of the Member States would be replaced by new discrepancies, this time between the participating and non-participating Member States. These discrepancies showed a need for harmonization in the first place. Therefore, a binding instrument in the form of a regulation may also be preferable over a directive, given the direct applicability of regulations without any need for implementing measures.[181] This will be explored below.[182]

### 7.1. *Legal Basis*

As mentioned before under the heading of a legal basis for an optional instrument,[183] Article 114 TFEU requires approximation of national laws if it is to be used as a legal basis. While this requirement rendered Article 114 an unlikely legal basis for an optional instrument, it will probably not be an obstacle in relation to options 5-7 of the Green Paper, which provide for a binding instrument. A measure based on Article 114 must have as its objective the establishment and functioning of the internal market. According to the ECJ's well-known *Tobacco* judgment, a mere discrepancy between national laws is insufficient to merit regulation of the internal market.[184] Rather, it must be shown that this discrepancy actually causes obstacles to intra-Union trade and that the proposed legislation will actually remove these obstacles, be they present or future.[185] I refer to Chapter 3 for a more elaborate discussion of whether this is actually the case as regards diverging national property laws.[186] The main argument - and an important difference to contract law - is that parties are unable to circumvent diverging national property laws because choice of law is in principle not allowed in property law. It is therefore the mandatory nature of property law that causes obstacles to intra-Union trade. Depending on the exact content, a binding instrument providing rules of property law that can be relied on throughout the EU could remove such obstacles.

Article 81 TFEU can only be used for measures regulating cross-border trade, not for measures that also apply to purely internal situations.[187] Given that I have argued that I would advocate a measure that also applies to purely internal

181 Art. 288 (ex Art. 249 EC). *Cf* Schulze 2009, p. 67; Müller-Graff 2004, p. 87.
182 Section 7.2. *Regulation or Directive.*
183 Section 6.1.
184 Case C-376/98, *Germany* v *Parliament and Council* ("Tobacco I") [2000] ECR I-2247.
185 See Chapter 3, section 8. *Legal basis.*
186 Chapter 3, section 8.
187 See *supra*, section 6.1. *Legal basis.*

situations,[188] I would not be in favour of using Article 81 as a legal basis for a binding instrument.

Article 169(2) TFEU can only be used for measures regulating B2C transactions.[189] As indicated before, the majority of cross-border problems in property law are experienced in B2B transactions.[190] I would therefore also not propose to use this Article as a legal basis for a binding instrument in the area of property law.

Article 352 TFEU can only be used if action by the Union is necessary to attain one of the objectives set out in the Treaties.[191] One of the Treaties' primary objectives is the establishment or functioning of the internal market.[192] Options 5 and 6 of the 2010 Green Paper might fulfil that requirement but Option 7 - a European Civil Code - would contain other rules that are not necessarily aimed at regulating free movement or competition and would thus go beyond the pursuit of the establishment or functioning of the internal market.[193] Furthermore, as a point on subsidiarity, Article 352 may only be used if the Treaty provides no other legal basis. Given that Article 114 is already a likely legal basis for a binding instrument - provided that the requirement of approximation is fulfilled - Article 352 may not serve as a legal basis for such an instrument.

Consequently, Article 114 seems to be the most suitable legal basis for a binding instrument as envisaged under options 5-7 of the 2010 Green Paper. For options 5 and 6, Article 352 may form an alternative legal basis, in case the requirements of Article 114 are not met, but this is not a possibility for Option 7 of the Green Paper, as a European Civil Code would include rules that pursue other objectives than the ones set out by the Treaties.

### 7.2. *Regulation or Directive*

Policy Option 5 entails a minimum harmonization directive; policy Option 6 entails a regulation replacing national laws with a uniform set of European rules. As stated in the introduction, a regulation may be preferable over a directive, for a regulation would apply uniformly throughout the EU and be directly applicable. Not only would this circumvent the private international law problems encountered by an optional instrument,[194] but it would also remove the discrepancies between the laws of the Member States. Due to differences in implementation of a directive, new discrepancies between the laws of the Member States might arise. A study performed by Vogenauer and Weatherill on the perceived effects of differing national legislation in the area of contract law on cross-border trade shows that this can be a

188 See *supra*, section 4. *Cross-border or purely internal situations.*
189 See Chapter 3, section 8. *Legal basis.*
190 See Chapter 3, *Final conclusions.*
191 Art. 352 TFEU.
192 Art. 3(3) TEU and Art. 26 TFEU.
193 Basedow *et al.* 2011, p. 26.
194 *Supra*, sections 6 and 6.3. See Basedow *et al.* 2011, p. 28.

real problem. This study, in which Vogenauer and Weatherill acted as 'academic advisors' to Clifford Chance,[195] was conducted as a follow-up to the consultation process started by the Commission with its 2001 Communication on European Contract Law.[196] In their opinion, by 2005, the questions resulting from the Commission's consultation process were not yet sufficiently answered. The Clifford Chance study was a renewed attempt to provide answers to these questions. One of these questions was whether

> 'the existing piecemeal approach to European legislation in contract law [was] sufficient to remove such obstacles [to cross-border trade], or [whether] it rather [created] further difficulties, such as an inconsistent application of European law in the various Member States'.[197]

The results of the survey showed the following:

> 'Six out of ten respondents had experienced significant differences in the implementation and interpretation of directives across the Member States. [reference omitted] Almost two-thirds of those who had experienced such differences did not think that they impinged on their ability or desire to conduct cross-border trade. That still leaves approximately a third who are concerned by the issue, and even more so in Germany and in the UK [reference omitted].'[198]

Granted, this was a study on contract law, not property law, but there is no reason to assume that differing implementations of directives containing property law rules would not lead to similar problems.

On the other hand, directives have some advantages over regulations. Leaving a margin of discretion to the Member States as to how to achieve the ends of the directive may make it easier for them to incorporate it into their national system.[199] A regulation may have a more disruptive effect on the coherence of the national system due to its direct application. As was shown in Chapter 2, when it comes to rules of European Union private law, Member States are protective of the coherence of their national system. Particularly in the area of property law, European Union rules may put pressure on the national *numerus clausus*, for instance, by introducing new, European-autonomous property rights. If such European property rights were introduced through a regulation, they would enter the national system of property law without the possibility for the Member States to incorporate them in the national *numerus clausus*. The Member States would have that possibility if the European property rights were introduced by way of a directive. Therefore, from a point of view of proportionality, directives may be preferred over regulations as the

195 Vogenauer & Weatherill 2006, p. 117.
196 COM(2001) 398 final.
197 Vogenauer & Weatherill 2006, p. 113.
198 Vogenauer & Weatherill 2006, p. 128-129.
199 Johnston & Unberath 2010, p. 85-86.

'less intrusive legislative device'.[200] It must be noted, however, that the Protocol on the application of the principles of subsidiarity and proportionality to the Lisbon Treaty no longer mentions that directives should be preferred over regulations, as it did in the wording attached to the Amsterdam Treaty.[201] Nevertheless, it must be taken into account that the costs of adapting various types of transactions - most of which will remain purely domestic - to the regulation may not outweigh the reduction of transaction costs envisaged by the regulation. Furthermore, a uniform regime would make regulatory competition impossible and would take away parties' possibility to choose the law applicable to their transaction.[202]

Schulte-Nölke proposes a general framework directive on (consumer) contract law which would contain 'a legislative reservoir of definitions and general rules'.[203] Such a framework directive would form the basis for any future sector-specific directives. These directives - regardless of their specific content - would have to be based on the general definitions and rules laid down in the framework directive, thereby minimizing the patchwork of separate directives that currently exists in European private law. Such a framework directive could help create a more coherent European private law. In relation to property law, a framework directive could lay down certain principles and ground rules, such as the principle of *numerus clausus* or the *nemo dat* rule.[204] It could also reflect some fundamental choices made by the EU legislature regarding rules on, for instance, the creation and transfer of property rights.[205] With such a framework directive in place, future EU legislation creating, for instance, a European right of mortgage has a foundation to build on. It would be clear to Member States and private parties that European-autonomous property rights would always have to be created or transferred based on the system as opted for in the framework directive. Yet, in spite of these potential advantages of a framework directive, there are three disadvantages to it: firstly, as with any directive, it would be directed at the Member States who would be responsible for its implementation. Given the closed and mandatory nature of property law, and the sometimes substantial differences between the Member States' property laws, implementation may result in a different application of the directive in different Member States. Secondly, the introduction of a framework directive on EU property law would undoubtedly spark a discussion on whether such a directive should entail minimum or maximum harmonization. The problems encountered around this issue during the drafting process of the new Consumer Rights Directive[206] would undoubtedly also arise with regard to a framework directive on property law. Thirdly, and perhaps most importantly, the creation of

200 Hesselink, Rutgers & Booys 2007, p. 45-46.
201 Basedow *et al.* 2011, p. 24.
202 Basedow *et al.* 2011, p. 29.
203 Schulte-Nölke 2010, p. 141.
204 *Cf* the 'classical model of property law' as developed by Van Erp; Van Erp 2009b.
205 See Chapter 6, Part II at 4. *Operating rules and definition of terms.*
206 See *infra*, section 7.2.1. *Minimum or maximum, partial or full harmonization.*

EU property law by way of a framework directive and subsequent directives could lead to a fragmented approach to EU property law. Given that the property law *acquis* is already extremely fragmented,[207] a more coherent approach to its future development would be preferable, if not strongly advisable.

### 7.2.1. Minimum or Maximum, Partial or Full Harmonization

If a choice were to be made to enact rules of European Union property law in the form of a directive, a choice must be made between minimum and maximum harmonization.[208] Several authors have argued in favour of maximum harmonization.[209] In the case of minimum harmonization, there is still an option for the Member States to go beyond the rules laid down by the European legislature, as long as they fulfil the minimum requirements imposed upon them. Even though, at the minimum level, the rules will be the same throughout the EU, beyond that level there will again be discrepancies. Minimum harmonization would therefore not solve the problems caused by differing national laws, as it does not take away these differences.[210] Even though, in its 2010 Green Paper under policy Option 5, the Commission proposes a minimum harmonization directive, it does recognize the problem that minimum harmonization 'would not necessarily lead to uniform implementation and interpretation of the rules'.[211] On the other hand, the new consolidating the consumer *acquis* was originally proposed as a maximum harmonization directive[212] but came under pressure for this reason from MEPs and a number of Member States.[213] This pushed the discussion towards so-called targeted maximum harmonization.[214] The end result was that the Consumer Rights Directive does entail maximum harmonization,[215] but it only replaces Directive 85/577/EEC

207 See Chapter 4 of this study.

208 See *supra*, section 1. *Explanation of terms.*

209 In general, not only for EU property law.

210 Roth 2009, p. 41.

211 2010 Green Paper, p. 10. The Commission also expressed this in earlier documents. See, for instance, Commission 2007 Green Paper on the Review of the Consumer Acquis, COM(2006) 744 final, p. 7; Commission Communication on Consumer Policy Strategy, 2002-6, COM(2002) 208, para. 3.1.2.2.: 'For these directives, one of the key priorities for the Commission would be to propose full harmonization in order to minimize variations in consumer protection rules across the EU that create fragmentation of the internal market to the detriment of consumers and business.' See also Basedow *et al.* 2011, p. 28.

212 Maximum harmonization as meant in this Chapter: see section 1. *Explanation of terms.* Referred to by the European Parliament as 'full harmonization': Press Release of 17-03-2010, ref. no. 20100317IPR70798, to be found at: <http://www.europarl.europa.eu/sides/getDoc.do?language=nl&type=IM-PRESS&reference=20100317IPR70798>.

213 European Parliament Press Release of 17-03-2010, ref. no. 20100317IPR70798.

214 See an online post by Hector L. MacQueen, Eric Clive and Laura Macgregor of 16 January 2011 in 'European Private Law News', to be found at: <http://www.law.ed.ac.uk/epln/blogentry.aspx?blogentryref=8557>.

215 Dir. 2011/83/EU on consumer rights, [2011] *OJ* L 304/64, Art. 4.

on contracts negotiated away from business premises and Directive 97/7/EC on distance contracts. It does not replace Directive 93/13/EEC on unfair terms in consumer contracts and Directive 1999/44/EC on consumer sales, as was originally intended.[216]

Furthermore, a choice will also have to be made between full harmonization and partial harmonization,[217] meaning that only certain aspects of property law are regulated (e.g. only the rules on security rights) rather than the whole of property law.[218] On the one hand, it might be easier to find a proper legal basis for the harmonization of only a certain area, as opposed to an all-encompassing instrument, covering the whole area of property law. On the other hand, partial harmonization may disrupt the national system of property law more than a full harmonization of the area of property law would, given that it would replace only a part of the system, leaving the rest of the system to adapt to the new, European elements.[219]

## 7.3. *European Civil Code*

In theory, a binding instrument could also take the form of a European Civil Code, thereby fully unifying not just property law but also other areas of private law. The Green Paper discusses this as policy Option 7: Regulation establishing a European Civil Code.[220] However, the feasibility and acceptability of such a Code is doubted for several reasons, as was *inter alia* indicated in the Max Planck Research Paper on the 2010 Green Paper:

> 'A comprehensive European civil code appears to be practically unrealistic. Especially in relation to areas of the law that lack an internal market link, the competence issue arises. Preliminary work establishing a common European core in fields such as property, family law and the law of succession is far less advanced than with regard to contract law, or even entirely absent. Furthermore, political opposition from the Member States against a comprehensive civil code appears to be insurmountable. The Commission itself recognizes in its Green Paper that the justification for such a far-reaching harmonization has not yet been established.'[221]

216 MacQueen, Clive and Macgregor in 'European Private Law News', available at: <http://www.law.ed.ac.uk/epln/blogentry.aspx?blogentryref=8557>.

217 See *supra*, section 1. *Explanation of terms*.

218 Van Gerven 2004, p. 508 where he summarizes the different harmonization methods.

219 Full harmonization of the entire area of property law could still lead to disruptions where property law connects to other areas of law, such as insolvency law, matrimonial property law or the law of succession. The question then becomes whether disruptions at these border areas are more or less severe than disruptions within an area, in this case the area of property law. This will depend on the national system and how these different areas are linked to each other.

220 2010 Green Paper, p. 11.

221 Basedow *et al.* 2011, p. 28; see also Schulte-Nölke 2010, p. 140: '[P]olitical and academic discussion shows that in many countries lawyers, businesses and consumers are not ready to →

First, the EU may not have the competence for the kind of all-encompassing unification that a European Civil Code would be.[222] Second, even if such a competence existed, a proposal to draft a European Civil Code would probably not pass the subsidiarity and proportionality tests.[223] Third, the costs of unification through a European Civil Code may not outweigh its advantages and will not necessarily be less than the costs of maintaining the status quo.[224] The 'academic, political, administrative and judicial efforts to prepare, adopt, implement and apply comprehensive legislation'[225] may lead to higher costs than the original costs one was trying to reduce or eliminate through harmonization in the first place. On the other hand, the costs of transitioning to a European Civil Code are of a temporary nature; the question in the end is whether the long term reduction in information costs and transaction costs of cross-border trade envisaged by a unification of private law in the EU can be offset against the costs of maintaining the status quo.[226] The Impact Assessment accompanying the Proposal for a Common European Sales Law answers this question in the negative: 'Therefore from a holistic perspective, taking all the costs (monetary or otherwise) into account these cost outweigh by far the benefits of the instrument.'[227]

## 8. International Agreement

A possibility for the future development of EU private law – be it contract or property law – not mentioned by the 2010 Green Paper is the possibility for Member States to conclude an international agreement in this area. Technically speaking, this would not be EU property law but European property law (or international property law, depending on the countries involved) since it would not originate from the EU. In that sense, it is not surprising that this was not mentioned as a policy option in the Green Paper.

In case there would not be a legal basis to enact European rules of property law, an international agreement may be the only way to enact uniform measures.[228]

give up their national laws in favour of a European code. Usually trust in national law, even if it is essentially just a transposition of European law, is much higher than in the case of directly applicable European legislation.' See also Watson 2000, at para. VIII: '[I]t will be objected against a code of private law for the European Union that national pride and identity is much tied up with a system of national law. I understand. But then I would point out how much of a nation's law – rules, institutions, concepts, structures – results from borrowing.'

222 Keirse & Veder 2010, p. 6; Kenny 2006, p. 777; Van Gerven 2002, p. 157; Drobnig 1997, p. 492.

223 2010 Green Paper, p. 11; Impact Assessment accompanying the Proposal for a Common European Sales Law, p. 51 – Policy option 5a; Keirse & Veder 2010, p. 52.

224 Van Gerven 2002, p. 163.

225 Van Gerven 2002, p. 163.

226 Strese 2006, p. 200-201.

227 SEC(2011) 1165 final, section 6: Comparative assessment of options.

228 Van Gerven 2002, p. 173.

However, there is one possible, significant disadvantage to harmonizing European property law or indeed European private law in this way. I would agree with Müller-Graf, that:

> '[T]here is no basic obligation of any State to take part in any treaty-project to harmonize the national private law with a model set of rules. In consequence, the composition of the group of participating States may vary from convention to convention, thereby creating a complex and badly arranged private law situation when looked upon from the viewpoint of a common private law in the Community.'[229]

In other words, unless such an international agreement is concluded by the EU as a whole, the result will be a fragmented and unsystematic European property law. Another matter would be the interpretation of such a convention or conventions. Van Gerven suggests that any agreement concluded should contain a preliminary ruling procedure before the CJEU.[230] While I would agree that that could ensure coherent interpretation of the international agreement(s), the practical execution may be problematic. The Courts already have a significant caseload to deal with without adding the task of interpreting international agreements concluded between Member States. Solving this problem by, for instance, creating a new court or extending the current courts would require a lot of resources,[231] which Member States who do not participate in the international agreement may not be willing to provide.

A treaty concluded between France and Germany in 2010 shows that the creation of 'European' property law through international agreements may, in spite of the concerns just mentioned, nevertheless be an attractive option. Under the treaty, entitled *Abkommen zwischen der Bundesrepublik Deutschland und der Französischen Republik über den Güterstand der Wahl-Zugewinngemeinschaft*,[232] a model matrimonial property regime can be chosen if the law of either Germany or France would apply to the matrimonial property regime.[233]

## 8.1. *Enhanced Cooperation*

The Treaties offer a potential framework for an agreement between the Member States, namely that of enhanced cooperation.[234] Title III of Part Six TFEU and Article 20 TEU stipulate the procedure that Member States must follow to establish enhanced cooperation. The result is what is often termed a 'Europe of two

229 Müller-Graff 2004, p. 84.
230 Van Gerven 2002, p. 173.
231 Van Gerven 2002, p. 173.
232 To be found at: <http://www.bmj.de/SharedDocs/Downloads/DE/pdfs/Abkommen_zwischender_Bundesrepublik_Deutschland_und_der_Franzoesischen_Republik_ueber_den_Wahl_Gueterstand.pdf?__blob=publicationFile>.
233 Article 1 of the agreement. See also Van Erp 2010b, p. 15.
234 Formerly called closer cooperation: Usher 2002, p. 97.

speeds'.[235] Some Member States move forward in a particular area where other Member States do not wish to participate or are not yet able to participate. Closer cooperation, as introduced by the Treaty of Amsterdam,[236] was never used as such but it does feature in the Protocol on the Schengen *Acquis*.[237] Article 1 of the Protocol provides that the Member States to the Schengen *Acquis* 'shall be authorized to establish closer cooperation among themselves in areas covered by provisions defined by the Council which constitute the Schengen *acquis*'. Furthermore, a form of closer cooperation can be seen in the context of Economic and Monetary Union (EMU). However, where closer cooperation is open to all Member States at any time on an opt-in basis,[238] the EMU is in principle binding on all the Member States but they have the possibility to opt out for various reasons. These Member States are then referred to as 'Member States with a derogation'.[239] With the Treaty of Nice, the possibility for a Member State to veto closer cooperation was removed.[240]

Creating a 'European' property law by way of enhanced cooperation could have the disadvantage that it fragments the internal market.[241] Article 326 TFEU stipulates that enhanced cooperation shall not undermine the internal market, constitute a barrier to trade or distort competition between the Member States.[242] In the context of Article 114 as legal basis it is often argued that differences between national laws hinder intra-Union trade or distort competition and that harmonizing measures enacted on the basis of Article 114 are therefore justified. At first instance it would thus seem that enhanced cooperation could hinder intra-Union trade or distort competition since it leads to different rules for those Member States who participate and those who do not. However, the ECJ stated in its *Tobacco* judgment that not all differences in national laws amount to a hindrance of trade or a distortion of competition and that legislative action is only allowed if such a hindrance or distortion becomes 'appreciable'.[243] It could be deduced from this that enhanced cooperation would only breach Article 326 if the resulting differences in national laws had an appreciable effect on the internal market.

235 E.g. Curtin 1995 as quoted by Weatherill 2010a, p. 628; Scharpf 2002, section 5.1.

236 Usher 2002, p. 97.

237 Protocol (No 19) to the Lisbon Treaty on the Schengen *Aqcuis* integrated into the framework of the European Union. See Usher 2002, p. 102.

238 Art. 328(1) TFEU.

239 Art. 140 TFEU; Usher 2002, p. 102-103.

240 Usher 2002, p. 110-111. Art. K.12(2) of the Treaty of Amsterdam stated: 'If a member of the Council declares that, for important and stated reasons of national policy, it intends to oppose the granting of an authorization [for closer cooperation] by qualified majority, a vote shall not be taken. The Council may, acting by qualified majority, request that the matter be referred to the European Council for decision by unanimity.'

241 *Cf* Scharpf 2002, section 5.1.

242 *Cf* Curtin, who submits that enhanced cooperation should not be used for the so-called 'hard core' of Union law, 'in particular not those policy areas which might impair the cohesion of the internal market'; Curtin 1995 as quoted by Weatherill 2010a, p. 630.

243 Case C-376/98, *Germany* v *Parliament and Council* [2000] ECR I-8419, para. 29; Usher 2002, p. 99.

Despite the disadvantage of leading to a fragmented internal market, enhanced cooperation may be the only remaining option to move forward in a certain area. This may be the case if no legal basis is found and/or there is no political will amongst all the Member States to create an optional or binding instrument as described above. In time, this form of cooperation may lead to participation by most or all Member States. Some of the Member States may initially be sceptical, but the way in which the other Member States move forward under enhanced cooperation may ease some of that scepticism and lower the threshold for the others to join.

It is not easy to determine whether enhanced cooperation in the area of property law would actually impair the cohesion of the internal market because, as stated above, enhanced cooperation has never really been used before.[244] It is only now - at the time of writing[245] - that enhanced cooperation is being used for the first time, in two separate instances. Remarkably, one of those instances[246] is an area related to general property law, namely international divorces.[247] Fourteen Member States requested the Commission to propose legislation in this area, which it did, and on 20 December 2010 the Council approved the Commission's proposal and adopted Regulation 1259/2010/EU implementing enhanced cooperation in the area of the law applicable to divorce and legal separation.[248] Countries wanting to join at a later stage are free to do so. The Regulation stipulates, among other things, that it has universal application, meaning that '[T]he law designated by this Regulation shall apply whether or not it is the law of a participating Member State.'[249] This means that the Regulation could have consequences even for those Member States who are not currently participating in the enhanced cooperation.

This agreement on enhanced cooperation in international divorces was followed by proposals from the Commission for EU-wide rules to clarify the proprietary situation of international couples, yet another step closer to matters of general property law.[250] The Commission's 2010 EU Citizenship Report contains a

244 Weatherill 2010a, p. 635; Scharpf 2002, section 5.1.

245 May 2011.

246 The other instance where enhanced cooperation is being used is the so-called unitary patent protection: see the Proposal for a Regulation of the European Parliament and of the Council implementing enhanced cooperation in the area of the creation of unitary patent protection, COM(2011) 215 final. For more information see also: <http://ec.europa.eu/internal_market/indprop/patent/index_en.htm>.

247 Press Release of 20 December 2010, 'European Commission proposals to bring legal certainty to couples in cross-border marriages approved by EU ministers', MEMO/10/695, to be found at: <http://europa.eu/rapid/pressReleasesAction.do?reference=MEMO/10/695&format=HTML&aged=0&language=EN&guiLanguage=en>.

248 [2010] *OJ* L 343/10, Preamble, Recital 6.

249 Reg. 1259/2010, Art. 4.

250 Press Release of 16 March 2011, 'Commission proposes clearer property rights for Europe's 16 million international couples', IP/11/320, to be found at: <http://europa.eu/rapid/press ReleasesAction.do?reference=IP/11/320&formate=HTML&aged=0&language=EN&guiLanguage=en>; 'Today's proposals are the logical next step following the swift agreement last year on EU legislation to determine which country's rules apply in cross-border divorce cases'.

list of 25 Actions to Improve the Daily Life of EU Citizens. Number 1 on the list states that the Commission 'will make it easier for international couples [...] to know which courts have jurisdiction and which law applies to their *property rights* (e.g. a jointly owned house) by proposing a legislative instrument in 2011' [emphasis added].[251]

In this instance, enhanced cooperation seems to have been a stimulant for further legislative action. According to a Press Release of 16 March 2011, the Commission will, amongst others, 'enable married international couples to *choose the law that applies* to their joint property in case of death or divorce' [emphasis added].[252] Given that, in general, choice of law in property law is not permitted, or only to a very limited extent, it would be a very interesting development if the Commission proposals would go in that direction. This is indeed the case with the Regulation on international successions, which provides a person with a choice of law to govern his or her succession.[253]

## 9. Harmonization through Case Law

Harmonization of European property law through case law of the CJEU is certainly an option,[254] although its desirability could be questioned. The method applied by the CJEU to solve cases when EU law does not provide an adequate solution is discussed in detail in Chapter 1. Its functional approach (i.e. 'looking for common *solutions*'[255] rather than common rules) makes it possible to overcome some of the differences that exist at the national level. Furthermore, the way in which judgments are prepared shows that the Court does not operate in a vacuum. Before the Court gives a judgment, its research department will prepare internal memoranda, thoroughly analysing the national legal systems.[256] Moreover, extensive (comparative) research also tends to go into the Advocate General's Opinion.[257] These preparatory works can ensure that the judgment given by the Court in the end will not unnecessarily upset the national legal systems but will rather fit into them relatively easily.

251 EU Citizenship Report 2010: Dismantling the obstacles to EU citizens' rights, Brussels 27.10.2010, COM(2010) 603 final, p. 24.

252 Press Release entitled 'Commission proposes clearer property rights for Europe's 16 million international couples'; doc. no. IP/11/320.

253 Reg. 650/2012/EU,[2012] *OJ* L 201/107, Art. 22(1): 'A person may choose as the law to govern his succession as a whole the law of the State whose nationality he possesses at the time of making the choice or at the time of death.'

254 See e.g. Hartkamp 2011.

255 Van Gerven 2004, p. 516. Van Gerven is optimistic: 'Because of the multi-national composition of the Community Courts, it is very likely that they will succeed in "fashioning" an underlying principle which fits sufficiently well with the legal systems of the Member States, even those where the principle was unknown, or differently formulated.'

256 Van Gerven 2004, p. 518.

257 Van Gerven 2004, p. 518-519.

A downside to harmonization through judgments of the CJEU is that the Court will have to wait until a relevant case comes up or until it is asked for its opinion. When a case does come up, it is limited to its particular circumstances and it may therefore be difficult to formulate general rules or principles.[258] Overall, harmonization through case law is more likely to be piecemeal than to be coherent, even if the Court would wish to build a coherent system.[259] The CJEU will only create European private law where it has the authority to do so based on the Treaties.[260] Harmonization through case law will thus only occur within the limitations of the Treaties. The Treaties do not contain a general competence for the Union in the area of private law[261] and so the CJEU is limited in its judgments to the specific issue-areas with regard to which it has been established that the Union has competence.[262] Particularly in light of the argument often voiced by national property lawyers and Member State governments that European property law rules could damage the coherence of the national system,[263] harmonization through case law may not be the best option because it does not offer a coherent system.

## Final Conclusions

This chapter explored the possible forms in which future EU property law could be shaped. The chapter has been structured along the same lines as the Commission's 2010 Green Paper on policy options for progress towards a European Contract Law for consumers and businesses. As argued in Chapter 3 of this study, it is not just the differences between the substantive rules of property law of the Member States that cause obstacles to the internal market but, in particular, the combination of these differences with the private international law rule of *lex rei sitae*. This chapter therefore first addressed the possibility of replacing the *lex rei sitae* with a different PIL rule in order to find out whether some of the internal market problems could be solved in this way, before looking at the different options for the creation of substantive EU property law. I concluded that if EU measures of PIL are considered as a replacement for the *lex rei sitae* rule, they must be applied uniformly throughout the EU. Even then, a change of the PIL rules in itself cannot solve all the hindrances to free movement that occur when property rights (or the people or companies holding them) cross borders. Additional, substantive rules of EU property law are necessary.

A preliminary point that must be discussed for any instrument - and is discussed by the Commission in the Green Paper as well - is the question whether the

258 *Cf* Micklitz 2009, p. 46.
259 Van Gerven 1998, p. 92.
260 Van Erp 2001, section 4 'Comparing and concluding remarks'.
261 *Ibidem.*
262 Art. 5(2) TEU (ex Art. 5 EC) lays down the principle of conferral.
263 See on this argument concerning the coherence of the national system of property law Chapter 2, section 7. *Justification grounds.*

instrument should only apply in cross-border situations or also in purely domestic situations. I would submit that it should be available in both situations. If it were available for cross-border situations only, a situation of reverse discrimination would arise: parties doing cross-border business would be able to make use of a European regime that would not be available for parties doing business in a purely internal situation. Furthermore, parties doing business both in a purely internal setting as well as cross-border would still be subject to two different legal regimes, a situation which any future instrument of EU property law would be meant to remedy.

Next to the three soft law options from the Commission's 2010 Green Paper, there are two other non-legislative forms: future EU property law could be shaped by way of an international agreement - possibly in the form of enhanced cooperation - or through case law of the CJEU. While these options may be less intrusive from the point of view of the national systems of law than the hard law options, they all share the disadvantage of not removing the discrepancies between the national laws that cause hindrances to the internal market. The hard law, legislative options for EU property law can lead to one of two scenarios: either the legislation is binding and replaces national property law or it is optional and exists next to the national systems of the Member States. In the latter case, the European legislation would constitute a 28th system of property law next to the national systems,[264] or, from the point of view of property law, a second system next to a party's own national system. In property law, choice of law is not generally possible, meaning that parties cannot choose the law of another Member State as the applicable law. With an optional instrument, the choice would therefore be between either the party's own national law or the European regime.

The option of introducing binding legislation is subdivided in the Green Paper in three versions: a minimum harmonization directive; a regulation; or a European Civil Code. Article 114 could form a legal basis for a directive or a regulation but not for a European Civil Code. An all-encompassing code would go beyond the scope of the Treaties. A minimum harmonization directive is not to be recommended because it would not remove the discrepancies that currently exist between the Member States' laws and that cause the obstacles to the internal market. In that regard, a regulation would be the better option. It must be noted, however, that a regulation would completely replace the national rules, which could be a highly costly operation and possibly an unnecessary one, given that the majority of transactions will remain purely internal and can be concluded on the basis of national law. A framework directive may be a better alternative. Such a framework directive could contain general principles of property law and systematic choices about rules such as those concerning the creation and transfer of property rights. The Member States would implement the framework directive, after which the EU

264 As indicated above, it would actually be a 29th system or more, given that several Member States contain more than one national legal system; see *supra*, at note 86.

legislature could use it as the basis for future rules of EU property law, such as the creation of a European right of mortgage or pledge.

Policy Option 4 of the Green Paper - a regulation containing an optional regime as an alternative to the national regimes - is currently the preferred option.[265] The proposed Regulation for a Common European Sales Law will, if it becomes law, constitute an optional instrument which can be chosen by parties as an alternative to national contract law. The most suitable legal basis for such an optional instrument would seem to be Article 352, although the proposed Regulation on a CESL has been based on Article 114. It is not completely certain that Article 114 can be used, however, because an optional instrument does not lead to approximation of the laws of the Member States.

From the point of view of proportionality, an optional instrument may be the less far-reaching measure as opposed to a mandatory instrument.[266] It leaves the national systems intact and provides an alternative to contracting parties. The introduction of an optional instrument could help to establish whether there is truly a need for European legislation for cross-border transactions involving property law. How often the instrument would be chosen as the applicable law could be an indication of its quality and its attractiveness to the end-users. Moreover, the parties' choice for this instrument would provide it with a degree of legitimacy which a binding instrument, 'forced' upon the parties, might not have. There are already some examples of optional instruments that illustrate how optional regimes work, such as the Societas Europaea[267] and the Community trade mark[268] and Community designs.[269]

In conclusion, the optimal form for the development of future EU property law would be the following: first of all, the implementation of a framework containing basic principles, definitions of property law concepts and ground rules. Thereafter, an optional EU regime of property law, available for both cross-border and internal situations, could be embedded within this framework. The fact that

265 Basedow *et al.* 2011, p. 71.

266 Schulte-Nölke 2010, p. 144.

267 Reg. 2157/2001/EC on the Statute for a European company (SE), [2001] *OJ* L 294/1, Preamble at 6: '[P]rovision should be made for the creation, side by side with companies governed by a particular national law, of companies formed and carrying on business under the law created by a Community Regulation directly applicable in all Member States.'

268 Reg. 207/2009/EC on the Community trade mark, [2009] *OJ* L 78/1, Preamble at 4: 'In order to open up unrestricted economic activity in the whole of the internal market for the benefit of undertakings, trade marks should be created which are governed by a uniform Community law directly applicable in all Member States.'

269 Reg. 6/2002/EC on Community designs, [2002] *OJ* L 3/1, Preamble at 4 and 5: 'The effect of design protection being limited to the territory of the individual Member States [...] leads to a possible division of the internal market [...] and hence constitutes an obstacle to the free movement of goods. This calls for the creation of a Community design which is directly applicable in each Member State'.

such a regime would be directly applicable in all the Member States would greatly reduce the need to change the PIL rule of *lex rei sitae*.

The next and final chapter will be devoted to the content of future EU property law. The first part of the chapter will summarize the existing EU property law, based on the results of the research conducted for Chapter 4. The System-Cube, as developed in Chapter 1, will be used to visualize the status quo of EU property law. The second part of the chapter will take as its starting point the conclusion reached in Chapter 5 that an optional instrument would be the best way forward to develop EU property law. A proposal will be made in the final chapter as to what the content of such an optional instrument could and should be, encompassing issues like the creation of European-autonomous property rights and the development of a European operating system governing those rights.

Chapter 6

# A FRAMEWORK FOR EUROPEAN UNION PROPERTY LAW

## Introduction

The purpose of this study has been twofold: mapping out the landscape of the *acquis communautaire* in the field of property law, in other words EU property law,[1] and proposing a framework for its future development. The reasons for conducting this research were first of all that the differences between the national systems of property law and their closed nature cause, or have the potential to cause, obstacles to the internal market,[2] and secondly that the (lack of) developments in EU property law were significantly out of step with the rest of EU private law, in particular with EU contract law.[3] Chapter 1 set out how the research was going to be conducted: by developing a standardized model – which I have called the System-Cube model – which describes the characteristics of a system of property law and by using that model to demarcate the field of EU property law. Chapter 2 showed in what way the differences between the national systems of property law (potentially) create obstacles to the internal market and how the four freedoms[4] affect national property law. Given the potential obstacles to the internal market, the EU may have the competence to enact legislation to remove these obstacles. Chapter 3 explored whether and to what extent the EU has the competence to legislate in the area of property law, paying particular attention to Article 345 TFEU which, at first glance, seems to preclude legislative action in the field of property law. Chapter 4 showed to what extent the EU has already legislated in the area of property law. It covered not only substantive EU property law but also whether and to what extent the EU

1 For the difference between EU property law and European property law, see Chapter 1, *Introduction*.
2 See Chapter 2 for a detailed explanation how these obstacles flow from the different national systems of property law, and what these obstacles consist of.
3 See for a more detailed description of the reasons for conducting this study Chapter 1, section 1, *Reasons for the development of property law by the European Union*.
4 Free movement of persons, services, goods and capital.

legislature uses property law terminology. The research conducted for Chapter 4 showed that the substantive rules of EU property law are scattered over a number of instruments, which do not primarily purport to deal with property law but with different topic areas such as the return of stolen cultural objects or combating late payments. This is mainly caused by the competence-driven nature of European legislation.[5] Chapter 4 also showed that the use of property law terminology by the EU legislature has so far been inconsistent and incoherent and often heavily reliant on national law for the interpretation of these terms. Chapter 5 explored the different options for the future development of EU property law. These options range from soft law, such as a Commission Recommendation, to hard law, such as a regulation replacing national laws with a uniform set of European rules. The conclusion of that chapter was that an optional instrument would be the best way forward for EU property law.

This chapter proposes a framework for future EU property law, laid down in a regulation as an optional instrument and consisting of three elements: operating rules[6] for the creation and transfer of European property rights; substantive rules on European property rights which function within the operating rules created for that purpose;[7] and a list of definitions of key terms, such as ownership, (im)movable, transfer. This chapter takes as a starting point the System-Cube model as developed in Chapter 1. The 'blank' version of this model shows the characteristics of a system of property law but it has not yet been filled in with information from any specific system of property law. In Chapter 1, this blank version of the model was filled in with information from several national systems to show how it functions and how it can be used. In this chapter, I again start with the blank version of the System-Cube model which is then filled in with the results from the research conducted for Chapter 4. This will show the status quo of EU property law. From there on, the optional instrument on EU property law can be developed.

Certain parts of the optional instrument will be inspired by national property law. The choice for three European-autonomous property rights is one example.[8] This trichotomy will be founded on the functions fulfilled by national property rights. Other parts of the optional instrument will be based on existing EU property law and international property law, such as the Cape Town Convention on international interests in mobile equipment. When developing EU property law, national property law from the Member States is a useful source of inspiration. There is no need to deviate completely from national property law at EU level unless there is a specific reason for doing so, for instance, where the interests of the internal market would not be best served by staying too closely to national concepts

5 Chapter 1 at 2. *The acquis method: defining EU property law.*

6 The term 'operating rules' was developed in Chapter 1 to describe those rules in property law that determine what one can and cannot do with a property right, how a property right can be created and transferred, etc. See Chapter 1, sections 2.2.1. and 2.2.2.

7 *Cf* Kieninger 2004a, p. 666.

8 See *infra*, Part II, section 2.

of property law. Developing EU property laws that resemble national property laws can only help their acceptance by Member States. Having said that, EU property law will inevitably serve different purposes than national property law and is therefore likely to encompass new and different rules and concepts.

## Part I - Status Quo of European Union Property Law

### 1. The System-Cube

Chapter 1 presented a method which makes it possible to establish what belongs to the European property law *acquis* and what does not. This method made use of the System-Cube model. The elements of the model were derived from comparative studies of national systems of property law in Europe.[9] The practical application of the model was illustrated by filling it in with examples drawn from several national systems of property law.[10] Subsequently, the model was used to select European legislation that dealt with property law, either substantially or terminologically. This legislation was thereafter described and analysed. In this chapter, the System-Cube model will be revisited to show the outcome of the analysis conducted in Chapter 4.[11] Starting with a blank model (Fig. 1), the model will be filled in on the basis of the results from the search conducted with the list of search terms[12] to show what the European system of property law currently looks like (Fig. 2). To clarify up front: the model is fed with the results from the search for terminology and substantive property law in the Lisbon Treaty and in secondary legislation as carried out in Chapter 4. The four freedoms as discussed in Chapter 2 cannot contribute to the EU version of the System-Cube, because they only affect national law. In other words, even though they are likely to affect the System-Cube model at the national level - as demonstrated in Chapter 2[13] - they do not themselves contain new, European-autonomous, rules or concepts that could be reflected in the EU version of the System-Cube.

9 Van Erp & Akkermans 2012; Van Erp 2009b; Hinteregger & Borić 2009; Akkermans 2008; Faber & Lurger 2008; Gretton 2007; Drobnig, Snijders & Zippro 2006; Van Erp 2006a; Van Erp & Akkermans 2006; Von Bar 2000; Merrill & Smith 2000-2001; Van Vliet 2000; Rutgers 1999; Herfurth 1998; Kieninger 1996; Ginossar 1979; Honoré 1961; Hohfeld 1916-1917.

10 See Chapter 1, section 2.2.3. *Practical application of the System-Cube.*

11 An overview of the results is also included in the Conclusion to Chapter 4.

12 See Chapter 4 at Part II, section 3. *Searching for property law terms.*

13 Under the headings entitled The effect of the free movement of [...] on national property law.

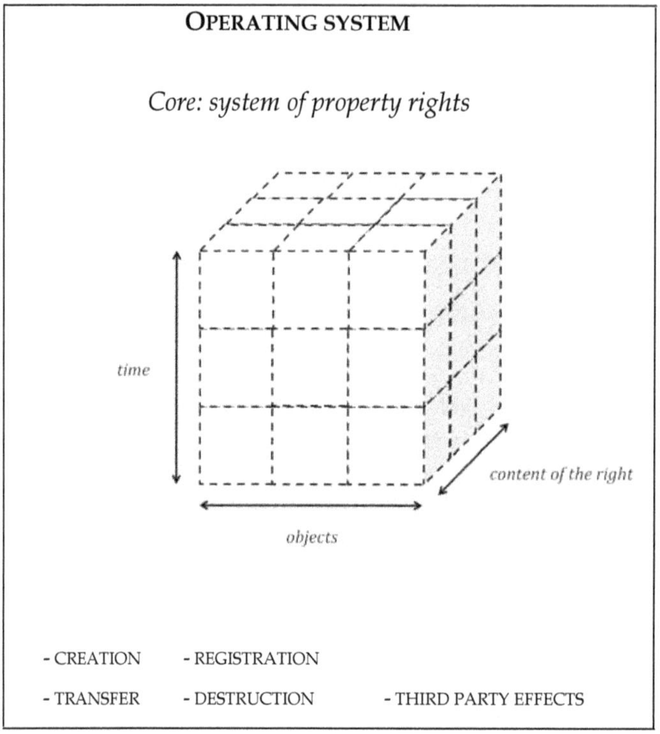


*Figure 1. Blank System-Cube*

Before filling in the model with the data acquired through the research done for Chapter 4, let us first briefly revisit the different elements that make up the System-Cube model. The model consists of a core - represented by the cube - and a framework of rules surrounding that core, which I have called the operating system. The operating system consists of the rules that govern property rights: rules on creation, transfer, registration and destruction and rules concerning the effects property rights have on third parties. The core consists of the system of property *rights*. The core and the framework together represent the system of property *law*. Whether or not a right is a property right is determined by the principle of *numerus clausus*. According to this principle the list of property rights available to parties is closed. Rights featuring in the *numerus clausus*, and which are thus property rights, all share the characteristics that they are rights in relation to an object, which can be invoked *erga omnes*. Rights that do not pass through the filter of the *numerus clausus* - i.e. that do not have these characteristics - are not property rights.[14] Once it is established that a right is a property right, the System-Cube can be applied to show

14 Akkermans 2008, p. 402; Van Erp 2006b, p. 13-14.

what the right looks like and what the operating system looks like within which it functions.

Every property right has three dimensions. The first dimension is the content of the right. This dimension gives information on the powers of the rightholder, whether they are extensive as, for instance, in the case of a right of ownership or whether they are more limited as, for instance, in the case of a right of pledge. The second dimension is the object in relation to which the property right can be held. Three different categories of objects are distinguished: immovables, movables and intangibles. Some property rights can be held in relation to each type of object, whereas other property rights can only exist in relation to one or two types of objects. The third dimension is the dimension of time. This dimension reflects the fact that property rights can be limited in time, as is, for instance, the case with a right of usufruct connected to the life of the usufructuary. It also reflects the fact that objects can be limited in time, as is, for instance, the case with emission rights, a new object of property law that was introduced by EU legislation.[15]

The following sections describe the status quo of EU property law using the System-Cube model. They start with the three dimensions of the core of the model and continue with the operating system that surrounds the core.

## 1.1. *Dimension One: Content of Property Rights*

EU legislation seems to maintain a list of property rights, and the distinction between more/most extensive rights and lesser/limited rights is there. One can see examples of the use of freehold or ownership of security rights, such as a right of pledge, and of rights of use such as a right of usufruct. In contrast to the dimension of objects, however,[16] EU legislation seems to be borrowing heavily from national law. The content of rights is never defined and is thus left to be interpreted by the national implementing legislation. Only a functional description of 'rights *in rem*' is provided but there are no definitions of any specific rights *in rem* (i.e. no European definition of a pledge, a usufruct, a servitude etc.). How rights are dealt with depends on the context, the issue area of the measure, in which the right is mentioned. The measure may, for instance, be an agricultural, taxation, or anti-terrorism measure. The purpose of anti-terrorism measures is, for instance, to prevent black-listed persons from acquiring assets. In those measures it makes sense that rights *in rem* are defined as being capable of existing in relation to any type of object so that people suspected of terrorism cannot acquire or transfer rights *in rem* in relation to any assets. It can be said that the contours of a list of property rights are there, but the content of those rights cannot be established in a European-autonomous way with the information that is currently available in the *acquis*.

15 Dir. 2003/87/EC establishing a scheme for greenhouse gas emission, [2003] *OJ* L 275/32.

16 See *infra*, section 1.2. *Dimension two: Objects of property rights*.

### 1.2. *Dimension Two: Objects of Property Rights*

EU legislation distinguishes between movable and immovable property and accepts both as being capable of forming the object of property rights. It also includes intangible property as an object of property rights. There seems to be a functional approach: as long as things or assets have an economic value, they are deemed capable of forming the object of property rights, both of a right of ownership or freehold, as well as of limited property rights, most notably security rights. EU legislation also introduces new objects of property rights, often of an intangible nature, such as emission trading rights or the Community trade mark.

### 1.3. *Dimension Three: Time*

Given that the content of property rights is not defined in a European-autonomous way, it is difficult to say anything about the element of time in these rights. European legislation mentioning property rights relies on national law to fill in the content of these rights. Therefore, whether or not these rights are limited in time also depends on how these rights are defined by national law. As far as objects are concerned, however, EU legislation has introduced an object which is by nature limited in time, namely emission trading rights. Once emission trading rights have been used up - in other words, once the greenhouse gases that were allowed to be emitted under such a right, have been emitted - they seize to exist.

In light of the above, the European version of the core of the System-Cube, depicting the European system of property rights, looks like this:

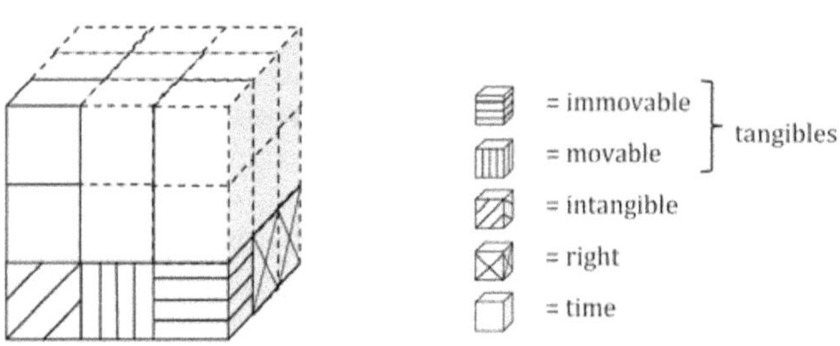


*Figure 2. EU System-Cube*

The dotted lines indicate the areas that have not yet been filled in or are insufficiently defined by the *acquis* to draw any definite conclusions.

## 2. The Operating System

The *acquis* currently only shows the very earliest beginnings of an operating system. The following sections describe to what extent there already are operating rules and what is still lacking.

## 2.1. *Creation*

There are examples in EU legislation that property rights *can* be created and a distinction is made between creation and transfer. There are no examples as to *how* they must be created, although it is recognized that a power to dispose is required to be able to create and transfer property rights.[17]

## 2.2. *Transfer*

Different types of transfer can be seen in EU legislation, e.g. full transfer or fiduciary transfer. Furthermore, the wording of the legislation shows that the European legislature has not only considered the right of ownership to be transferable but also other rights. However, there is no indication of any system of transfer, like a consensual or tradition system. A difference is made in EU legislation between possessor - someone physically holding an object on his own account - and holder - someone physically holding an object for a third party.[18] This difference is important in some national systems where delivery is necessary for the transfer of a property right and where only possessors can deliver, not holders.[19] The distinction is basically eliminated by EU law which treats possessors and holders in the same way. It simply makes the distinction to make sure that both possessors and holders fall within its scope, regardless of how they are classified under national law.

The term assignment - transfer of claims - is defined in Article 14(3) of the Rome I Regulation: 'The concept of assignment in this Article includes outright transfers of claims, transfers of claims by way of security and pledges or other security rights over claims.'

The term assignment is also used in other measures, although without being defined. The same is true for the term cession, which is an alternative to the term assignment. Even though there is a definition of assignment in the Rome I Regulation, nowhere is it stated how such an assignment should take place. The search for the term convey - the term generally used in English law for a transfer of land - also did not yield any results that indicated a system of conveyancing (or transferring) land or for that matter any other object.

## 2.3. *Registration*

The Regulation on the Community trade mark was the only clear example where registration was relevant. A Community trade mark cannot be invoked against

17 See the discussion of the ECJ's Möllendorf judgment in Chapter 4, Part I section 2.1. *Regulation 881/2002/EC imposing certain specific restrictive measures directed against certain persons and entities associated with Usama bin Laden, the Al-Qaida network and the Taliban.*

18 Art. 1 of Dir. 93/7/EEC on the return of stolen cultural objects, [1993] *OJ* L 74/74.

19 This is for instance the case in Dutch law: see Artt. 84(3), 90, 111 and 114 of Book 3 of the Dutch civil code. Translation can be found in Kiiver & Kornet 2010.

third parties unless it has been registered. Otherwise, no examples were found where registration played a relevant role from a property law point of view. The Community design, while in many ways similar to the Community trade mark, can also be relied upon against third parties if it has been disclosed in ways other than registration.[20] Registration therefore plays a less prominent role as regards the Community design than it does with regard to the Community trade mark.

### 2.4. *Destruction*

The only example that relates to the destruction or extinction of a property right can be found in the Directive on Financial Collateral Arrangements: it allows the creditor to keep the collateral for himself in case of non-payment by the debtor.[21] In this way, the debtor's property right in relation to the collateral is removed from him in favour of the creditor. Otherwise, nothing has been found in EU legislation concerning the destruction or extinction of property rights.

### 2.5. *Third Party Effects*

See the aforementioned example of the Community trade mark under 2.3 *Registration*. The Community trade mark Regulation also establishes a ranking.[22] The Insolvency Regulation grants property effect to retention of title clauses – they can be invoked against third parties.[23] The Directive on the return of stolen cultural objects restricts the scope of national third party protection rules.[24] Under this Directive stolen cultural objects can be retrieved from parties who acquired them in good faith and who would otherwise be protected because they were in good faith.

## Concluding Remarks to Part I

At this moment, EU property law is still in its earliest stages of formation. There is a small core of rules and definitions which are European-autonomous, but most of EU property law still consists of scattered fragments circling around the core. The formation – or systematization – of this area of law is far from complete and it is not easy to predict which parts will eventually form a whole.

When it comes to establishing what kind of objects can be objects of property rights the *acquis* is consistent and takes a functional approach. All types of objects, whether movable, immovable or intangible, are accepted by the *acquis* as objects of

20 Artt. 1(2) and 7 of Reg. 6/2002/EC on Community designs.
21 Dir. 2002/47/EC on financial collateral arrangements, Art. 5.
22 Reg. 207/2009/EC on the Community trade mark (codified version), Art. 29(2).
23 Reg. 1346/2000/EC on insolvency proceedings, Artt. 7(1) and (2).
24 Dir. 93/7/EEC on the return of stolen cultural objects, Art. 5.

rights *in rem*.[25] The criterion seems to be that as long as an asset is capable of representing an economic value it can be an object of rights *in rem*. It makes sense in an internal market, which is primarily geared towards economic integration, to accept rights *in rem* over all objects as long as they represent some economic value, so that at least from that perspective they are all equally easily tradable. However, as far as the content of the rights *in rem* is concerned, which could be created in relation to these objects, there is barely a system whatsoever. In this respect the *acquis* borrows heavily from the national systems.[26] Property rights such as ownership, usufruct or pledge are mentioned in EU legislation but are not given a European-autonomous definition. It is therefore up to the Member States to define them, resulting in differences in implementation of the European legislation. As far as the operating system is concerned, the *acquis* does contain some operating rules but none in the key areas of creation and transfer of property rights.[27]

Now that we have seen what EU property law currently looks like, the next question is how to proceed in further developing this area of EU law. The positive side of the fact that EU property law is still so sparse is that there is a lot of room to develop a coherent and consistent system, one that is truly European.[28] Such a system would involve the drafting of operating rules on matters such as creation and transfer of property rights. It would furthermore involve the creation of European property rights. These rights would be able to function within the operating rules drafted for this purpose. Finally, this system of operating rules and European property rights would have to be accompanied by a standardized list of European-autonomous definitions of property law concepts that will be the same for any and all (future) legislation in the field of EU property law.[29] This system should be laid down in an optional instrument,[30] providing parties the option to choose between using a national property right or a European one. If they chose to use the European property right, they would have to follow the rules laid down in the optional instrument for the creation, transfer etc. of these European property rights. The second part of this chapter is devoted to each of the elements that would have to be contained in an optional instrument on EU property law.

25 See *supra*, section 1.2. *Dimension two: Objects of property rights*.

26 See *supra*, section 1.2. *Rights*.

27 See *supra*, section 2.1. *Creation* and section 2.2. *Transfer*.

28 *Cf* Goode 1998, p. 462: 'The task [of overcoming doctrinal differences between legal systems] is easier where [...] a new type of interest is being fashioned as an international interest by the [constitutive instrument] itself, for since this does not derive from national law it need not carry with it the accumulated baggage of national law rules and concepts.'

29 *Cf* Gambaro 1997, p. 500.

30 The reasons for choosing an optional instrument were set out in detail in Chapter 5, section 6. *Optional instrument* and will be briefly revisited *infra*, Part II, section 3.2. *Advantages of an optional instrument*.

## Part II - Where to?

## 3. An Optional Instrument for EU Property Law

A proposal is set out here for the development of European property rights and European rules of property law governing those rights by way of an optional instrument, laid down in a European Regulation. The reasons for choosing an optional instrument as the form in which to shape EU property law were set out in detail in Chapter 5.[31] An optional instrument can achieve its purpose of facilitating cross-border property transactions without it being necessary to replace the national systems of property law with a European system.[32] The majority of transactions will still take place between parties with the same nationality, residing in the same country, creating and transferring rights in an object that is, and will stay, within that country. In such purely internal situations, none of the problems with free movement arise that might otherwise call for a European system to take over from the national system. In other words, if a Belgian person wants to sell his Belgian car or his house in Antwerp to another Belgian person, there is no reason why such a transfer should not be concluded under Belgian law. The most important exception to this is, of course, the following: if the parties themselves find Belgian property law unsuitable for their wishes, they may want to be, and should be able to resort to an alternative.[33] A European system of property law would provide such an alternative. The European system would have to be set up in such a way that the Member States would be obliged to make it available next to their own national law.[34] The European legislature could ensure this by laying down the European rules in a Regulation. They would then become directly applicable in all Member States.[35] This would provide parties with a choice of law, namely the choice between the national and the European system.

While the European regime should also be available for purely internal situations,[36] it would make its most significant contribution in cross-border situations. Cross-border situations ask for a different approach than purely domestic situations. Persons or companies doing business in, or wanting to establish themselves in, more than one country face several regulatory systems that they must comply with. This increases information and compliance costs and could therefore pose an obstacle for these persons and companies to enjoy their freedom of move-

31 Chapter 5, section 6. *Optional instrument.*

32 *Cf* Wehrens 2004, p. 773; Drobnig 1997, p. 492; Kreuzer 1990, p. 638.

33 *Cf* Kieninger 2004a, p. 666.

34 See Chapter 5, section 4.

35 Art. 288 TFEU.

36 *Cf* Wehrens 2004, p. 773. It has become more and more difficult to distinguish between wholly internal and cross-border situations: see Chapter 5 at 4. *Cross-border or purely internal situations.*

ment.[37] It would seem from the literature and case law regarding cross-border property transactions that the problems encountered in such transactions mostly have to do with non-recognition of security rights (or transfers for security purposes), leading to a change of the content of the security or to a complete loss of the security.[38] However, scenarios can also be conceived in which there are problems with the recognition of a right of use, such as a right of usufruct but there do not seem to be many practical examples, with the exception of those to be found in the law of succession.[39] Nevertheless, so far the attention that has been paid by the EU to cross-border property cases primarily concerned security rights.[40] See, for instance, the Commission's 1973 Draft Directive on the mutual recognition of non-possessory securities in movables[41] (hereafter: the 1973 Draft Directive), the retention of title clause in the Late Payments Directive or the discussion on the creation of a Euromortgage.[42] Cross-border security rights have also received attention in other contexts, outside the EU. Examples are Article 9 of the Uniform Commercial Code (UCC) in the United States and the UNIDROIT Convention on International Interests in Mobile Equipment[43] (hereafter referred to as the Cape Town Convention). For the development of a European Security Right inspiration could be drawn from these international attempts to provide property rights that can be used in cross-border situations. Moreover, lessons can be learned from past attempts by the EU to introduce mutual recognition of security rights in movables,[44] and to introduce a Euromortgage or Euro-hypothec.[45]

### 3.1. *Legal Basis Revisited*

The possible legal bases for an optional instrument were discussed in Chapter 5[46] and will be briefly revisited here. As far as an optional EU property law as an alternative to the national systems is concerned, there is a risk that Article 114 TFEU will not be accepted as a legal basis because there would be no 'approximation' of the laws of the Member States. It might therefore seem surprising that the Commission has chosen Article 114 as the legal basis for its legislative proposal on a Common European Sales Law (CESL) which, at first glance, would also appear to

37 Wagner 2002, p. 1013.
38 See *inter alia* Akkermans & Ramaekers 2012a; Sagaert 2007, p. 316; Kieninger 2004b, p. 20.
39 *Cf* Bouckaert 2006, p. 183. See Chapter 2, section 6. *Free movement of persons.*
40 *Cf* Hunter 1976, p. 322.
41 DG Internal Market, Document XI/466/73-E.
42 Green paper on Mortgage Credit in the EU, COM(2005) 327 final.
43 <http://www.unidroit.org/english/conventions/mobile-equipment/main.htm>.
44 1973 Draft Directive concerning the recognition of securities on movables without dispossession and of the terms relating to the transfer of ownership, Commission DG Internal Market, Document XI/466/73-E.
45 Commission Green Paper Mortgage Credit in the EU, COM(2005) 327 final.
46 Chapter 5, section 6.1. *Legal basis.*

be an optional instrument in European private law.[47] However, the proposed CESL would not be an optional instrument in the sense that parties could choose between national law and European law. Rather, it would harmonize national contract law by introducing a second contract law regime within each Member State's national system of law.[48] This would mean that, once the rules of private international law have indicated the applicable national law to a contract, within that national law, parties can then choose between the national law that is of national origin and between the national law that is of European origin. It remains to be seen during the legislative process whether this interpretation of Article 114 will be accepted so that it can indeed form the legal basis for the CESL.

Article 352 TFEU may be a more suitable legal basis, given that it does not require approximation. However, unanimity would be required, which may be very difficult to achieve and the European Parliament would only have to consent but would not be part of the legislative process. Nevertheless, this Article has been used as legal basis in the past to create new, European-autonomous concepts.[49] As Hesselink *et al.* put it:

> 'The features of these instruments are similar to the likely features of the optional instrument under consideration here. First, they all concern private law institutions on a European community level. Secondly, they exist in addition to the various national types. Thirdly, the parties have a choice between the national instrument and the European one. Finally, they were all introduced on the basis of regulations.'[50]

With regard to the creation of a European Security Right that could be used to acquire immovable property in another Member State Article 50(2)(e) could serve as the proper legal basis.[51] The ordinary legislative procedure could then be followed. The downside to this Article is that it can only be used for the enactment of directives, whereas the preferable measure for an optional instrument is a regulation.

47 COM(2011) 635 final.

48 Proposal for a CESL, p. 8-9.

49 See, for instance, the Societas Europaea, Reg. 2157/2001/EC, *OJ* L 294/1, and the Community trade mark, Reg. 207/2009/EC, *OJ* L 78/1.

50 Hesselink, Rutgers & Booys 2007, p. 62.

51 Art. 50 TFEU states: '1. In order to attain freedom of establishment as regards a particular activity, the European Parliament and the Council, acting in accordance with the ordinary legislative procedure and after consulting the Economic and Social Committee, shall act by means of directives.
2. The European Parliament, the Council and the Commission shall carry out the duties devolving upon them under the preceding provisions, in particular: […]
(e) by enabling a national of one Member State to acquire and use land and buildings situated in the territory of another Member State, in so far as this does not conflict with the principles laid down in Article 39(2)'.

### 3.2. *Advantages of an Optional Instrument*

I explained in Chapter 2 that mutual recognition works as a default solution where there are no harmonizing measures yet or where they are not deemed to be necessary. While I am of the opinion that mutual recognition should be extended to property rights validly created in another Member State, I also realize that this potentially confronts a national court with 26 foreign lists of property rights, which can lead to an unworkable situation.[52] Therefore, the sooner European versions of these property rights can be developed, the better. Using European-autonomous property rights makes it possible to sidestep the issues of recognition that are otherwise encountered in cross-border trade.[53] To clarify: if a German company exporting goods to the Netherlands can make use of a European Security Right, of which it is assured that it will be valid and recognized and can be used in the same way in both Germany and the Netherlands, it does not run into the cross-border problems that it may otherwise run into when using a German security right. Moreover, a Dutch court may be faced with the European Security Right next to the Dutch security rights but not with a German - or any other foreign - security right. It may be a bit of a compromise in the sense that the German company cannot make use of the rights available under the German *numerus clausus* when trading cross-border, but I nevertheless think that this would be a win-win situation for the German trader who will not lose his property right when selling goods across a border, and for the Member States who are not faced with 26 foreign lists of property rights, while at the same time balancing the interests of the EU and resulting in a better functioning internal market.[54] I agree with Flessner's observation:

> 'Am fernen Horizont steht ein einheitliches "Europäisches Sicherungsrecht". Es wird den Parteien als Option zu den mitgliedstaatlichen Sicherungsrechten angeboten werden. Den Rechtsverkehr würde es von der Qual der Wahl zwischen den mitgliedstaatlichen Rechten entlasten, würde aber durch seinen optionalen Charakter auch zeigen, dass Rechtswahl im Sachenrecht ein gangbarer Weg ist. Er ist der allein realistische in der Welt, in welcher die wirtschaftlichen Akteure, ihre Waren und ihr Geld sich tatsächlich und - in der Europäischen Union - rechtlich garantiert frei im internationalen Markt und über die lokalen Rechtsgrenzen hinweg bewegen.'[55]

52 *Cf* Schulte-Nölke 2010, p. 139; Wagner 2002, p. 1011.
53 *Cf* Kreuzer 1990, p. 638.
54 *Cf* Kreuzer 1990, p. 640.
55 'A uniform "European Security Right" is on the far horizon. It will be offered to parties as an alternative to the Member States' security rights. It would lift the burden of choice between the laws of the Member States from those engaging in legal transactions, but it would also, because of its optional character, show that choice of law in property law is a viable possibility. It is the only realistic one in a world in which the economic actors, their goods and their money, actually and - within the European Union - legally endorsed, move freely within the international market and across local legal boundaries.' Flessner 2010, p. 146.

Furthermore, an optional instrument does not replace national law but merely provides an alternative that can exist next to national law. This provides the European legislature with the room to develop 'innovative concepts'[56] which are not necessarily based on the same doctrinal legal theories that underpin national concepts.

### 3.3. *Interpretation of the Optional Instrument*

The optional instrument proposed below should be interpreted in a European-autonomous manner, not in accordance with national theory or concepts of property law.[57] The European Court of Justice would have to have the final say about the meaning of or intention behind these European rules of property law. I would agree with Goode that in an international instrument which provides for property rights that can be used in a cross-border setting it is better to strive for simplicity, not complexity.[58] In the style of Article 9 UCC, the Cape Town Convention, and Book IX DCFR, which will all be discussed in more detail below, it would be possible to explain the rationale behind each provision contained in the optional instrument in a detailed commentary – or the *travaux préparatoires* – to which courts and parties could resort if a provision or definition were unclear.

## 4. Operating Rules and Definition of Terms

### 4.1. *Operating Rules*

Rules in the operating system are a reflection of underlying principles, such as the principle of transparency.[59] The value that the EU attaches to such principles needs to be reflected in the choices it makes for operating rules.[60]

Rules governing the *creation* of European property rights would need to be established. These should clearly state all the requirements that must be fulfilled to create a European property right. These rules would apply to the creation of European property rights only, as they would have been specifically developed for them. They could not be used for the creation of national property rights. The creation and transfer of European property rights cannot be left to national law.

56 Kieninger 2004a, p. 669.

57 *Cf* Goode 2008, p. 19.

58 Goode 1998, p. 463 in general, and p. 464 specifically about the EBRD Model Law on Secured Transactions, the simplicity of which is 'one of [its] great merits'.

59 The principle of transparency can be further subdivided into the principle of specificity and the principle of publicity. See Van Erp 2009b.

60 Compare in that regard for instance the Cape Town Convention – about which more below – which is governed by five underlying principles: practicality, party autonomy, predictability, transparency and sensitivity. Goode 2008, p. 18. See also Van Erp 2008b, p. 22 and 32.

Otherwise, problems of recognition as outlined in Chapter 2 would again arise[61] – an Italian might still ask whether the European property right was validly created or transferred under Spanish law. The whole purpose of creating EU property law is to circumvent such issues. Therefore, European property rights need to be able to function within a European set of rules on creation and transfer.

Rules governing the *transfer* of European property rights would need to be established. The EU could design its own transfer system but, if it wanted to draw inspiration from the Member States, research shows that there are three systems to choose from: the causal consensual system, the causal tradition system, and the abstract tradition system.[62] Different transfer systems protect different interests. Causal transfer systems tend to protect owners, whereas abstract transfer systems tend to protect third parties in the interest of commerce.[63] Under national law, rules are usually in place that counterbalance the transfer system to prevent over-protection of one particular interest. In causal systems this counterbalance is provided by third party protection rules; in abstract systems this is, for instance, a doctrine such as *Fehleridentität* which can be found in German law. This doctrine protects the original owner in cases of serious defects of consent.[64] When developing a transfer system for EU property law a policy choice would need to be made about what interests to protect by the transfer system and how to counterbalance this protection.

Transfer systems tend to be matched with a registration system: causal transfer systems with a negative registration system, abstract transfer systems with a positive registration system. The EU should develop a *registration system* that functions well together with the transfer system it develops. This would also involve setting up a European registry for the registration of European property rights.[65] Registering European property rights in a European registry would provide publicity and establish a ranking among the registered rights. Registration in national registers would not provide adequate protection for third parties, for they might not know the country of origin of an object of which they are trying to find

61 *Cf* Goode 2008, p. 13: 'Traditional conflict of laws rules apply the *lex rei sitae* as the law governing proprietary rights, but such a principle is unsuited to items of mobile equipment which are constantly moving from one country to another [...] Hence the need for an international set of rules governing security, title-retention and leasing interests in such equipment which will provide creditors with the necessary safeguards, while at the same time incorporating measures for the protection of debtors.'

62 Van Vliet 2000.

63 Van Erp 2008b, p. 29.

64 Van Erp 2008b, p. 29.

65 Such a registry was also foreseen in Book IX DCFR. See Art. IX. - 3:301 on a European register of proprietary security. It was also envisaged by Kreuzer in his proposal for a European security right; Kreuzer 1990, p. 639. See further Van Erp 2004, p. 108.

out whether it has been burdened with a European property right.[66] They would therefore not know in which Member State's registry to look for information. It would moreover be inappropriate to register European-autonomous property rights in any registry that was not also European-autonomous.

A decision would have to be made whether registration would be a constitutive element for the creation and transfer of European property rights, or whether it would only be necessary for publicity purposes (i.e. makes the creation/transfer valid as against third persons rather than only *inter partes*), or whether registration is not necessary at all for the valid creation of a European property right. A choice to make registration a constitutive element for the creation of a European property right would imply a strict adherence to the principle of publicity, one of the leading principles of property law.[67]

The European Registry could be *asset-based or debtor-based*. The latter would mean registration against the debtor of a claim secured by a European Security Right or registration against the grantor of a European Use Right.[68] An asset-based system might not be feasible for the registration of European property rights on assets that are not easily identifiable, which is likely to be the case with most movable property. A debtor-based registry might for that reason be preferable.[69] A debtor-based registry would of course require the registration of certain information concerning the person of the debtor. To respect the debtor's right to privacy, the European Data Protection Directive[70] should be applied to registrations made in the European Registry. Use of the European Registry could furthermore be limited to persons with a legitimate interest to access the data recorded in the Registry.[71] Registration of immovable assets could continue to also be asset-based by linking the European Registry to the national cadastres. It can be observed that 'once the average values and/or durability of movable assets crosses a certain threshold the relative cost of registration declines enough to justify the initial investment into the setting up of a registration system'.[72] This would seem to be the case with the Cape

66 See the Report of the Meeting of the Subcommittee on Private International Law; Doc. XI/151/74-E of Commission DG Internal Market, 13-15 February 1974, p. 6; Report of the same Subcommittee, Doc. XI/526/74-E, 1-2 October 1974, p. 5.

67 Erp 2009b; Erp 2004, p. 107. Van Erp 2009b; Van Erp 2004, p. 107.

68 The European Security Right and European Use Right are discussed hereafter.

69 *Cf* Kieninger 2004a, p. 670.

70 Dir. 95/46/EC on the protection of individuals with regard to the processing of personal data and on the free movement of such data, [1995] *OJ* L 281/31.

71 In contrast: the International Registry set up under the Cape Town Convention is open to everyone wanting to conduct a search, and can be accessed at: <https://www.international registry.aero/irWeb/Controller.jpf>. Those wanting to make an entry in the International Registry have to be approved before they can do so. The fact that the International Registry is asset-based means that it is not necessary to register potentially sensitive data about the debtor. It is therefore less problematic to open it up for everyone. See also Van Erp 2004, p. 100-1.

72 Bouckaert 2006, p. 181. See also Van Erp 2004, p. 92.

Town Convention[73] under which an International Registry has been set up for the registration of international interests, created in accordance with the Cape Town Convention in relation to high-value movable assets such as railway rolling stock.[74] With all the possibilities that present-day internet and software have to offer us, and with e-signatures and timestamps providing legal validity to digital documents,[75] it becomes simpler and less costly to set up a registration system for European property rights.[76] In that sense, much has changed since the 1973 Draft Directive on mutual recognition of securities on movables[77] when the establishment of a Community register was still considered to be too costly.[78] A milestone in technological developments as regards their impact on legal developments was the first Cross Border Electronic Conveyancing (CROBECO) mortgage deed, sent electronically on 31 May 2012 by a Dutch notary to the Spanish Land Registry.[79]

The European Registry could be a *title registry, a deeds or documents registry, or a mere notice-filing system.* A title registry is a registry in which property rights themselves are registered, whereas a deeds or documents registry is a registry which only records documents relating to property rights.[80] Registration systems within Europe vary from country to country, with some countries (such as France)[81] using a deeds registry, other countries (such as Germany)[82] using a title registry and yet other countries using a system that has characteristics of both.[83] Countries such as the Netherlands and France seem to employ a deeds registry that converges towards a title registry.[84] A notice-filing system is the simplest form of registration

73 More about the Cape Town Convention *infra,* section 5.2.1. *Past proposals and existing cross-border security rights.*

74 Artt. 1(p) and 16 of the Convention.

75 See Dir. 1999/93/EC on a Community framework for electronic signatures, [2000] *OJ* L 13/12.

76 *Cf* Sigman 2004, p. 76: 'The filing systems in the US are in the process of changing from paper-based to electronic filing [...] In Canada, electronic filing is the norm [...] Any jurisdiction adopting a notice filing regime today no doubt would be fully computerized and likely would function solely on an electronic filing basis. Such a system not only is virtually error-free, but also is not expensive to establish, is extremely efficient, and is financially self-sustaining.' See further Honnebier 2006, p. 24; Kreuzer 1990, p. 639. *Cf* also the European Registry of Internet Domain Names (EURid), managing the .eu top-level Internet domain name: <http://www.eurid.eu/en/about>.

77 More about the 1973 Draft Directive *infra,* sectiont 5.2.1. *Past proposals and existing cross-border security rights.*

78 See the Report of the Meeting of the Subcommittee on Private International Law in which the 1973 Draft Directive was discussed; Doc. XI/151/74-E of Commission DG Internal Market, p. 6.

79 For more information on the CROBECO project, see Van Erp & Akkermans 2013.

80 Van Erp & Akkermans 2012, p. 907.

81 Van Erp & Akkermans 2012, p. 892 *et seq.*

82 Van Erp & Akkermans 2012, p. 866 *et seq.* at II.A.2.e *Registrable rights and interests.*

83 Zevenbergen 2002, p. 61-62.

84 Zevenbergen 2002, p. 57-59.

and is, for instance, used under Article 9 Uniform Commercial Code (UCC).[85] Such a filing system purely provides publicity of the fact that a security right has been created and nothing else. Just how simple notice-filing can be is illustrated in Sigman's commentary on Article 9 UCC, stating that a single sentence such as the following would suffice:

> 'Debtor grants a security interest to Secured Party in all of Debtor's inventory, wherever located, whenever acquired, to secure all of Debtor's present and future obligations, of whatever nature, whenever and however arising in favor of Secured Party.'[86]

A title registry provides the most legal certainty, which may be desirable for European property rights but it can only function properly if the correctness of its contents can be guaranteed.[87] The question then becomes: who will provide that guarantee? In a national setting, this guarantee is provided by the government, as the registry is a civil service. With regard to the EU it may not be so self-evident which institution would fulfil this role. Guaranteeing the correctness of the European Registry would also mean that the guarantor would have to assume liability for errors in the registry. This may mean an increase in the costs of registration.[88] On the other hand, as we saw before, it has become technologically simpler to register a variety of information concerning an object, a debtor, or a property right. This in turn reduces the costs of registration. Arguably, the costs of registration are also affected by the number of different property rights that can be registered. Given that there would only be three European property rights that could be registered in the European Registry, costs of registration would again be reduced. Therefore, costs or practical difficulties as such should not pose an obstacle to title registration in the European Registry. Whether the EU would want to assume liability for errors in the registry remains a policy choice. If it does not, then a deeds registry may be a better option. It is worth noting that neither Article 9 UCC nor the Cape Town Convention uses title registration.

Rules would be needed to establish a *ranking* amongst the different European property rights and amongst European property rights and national property rights. There are three possibilities to establish where a European property right should rank in relation to other European property rights and in relation to national property rights created in relation to the same object. Usually, ranking is based on the *prior tempore* rule: a property right that was created earlier - and registration may be a requirement for creation - has priority over later created property rights. This same rule could also be applied to European property rights. It may, however,

85 Sigman 2004, p. 77-78. For an extensive discussion of the characteristics and (dis)advantages of different registration systems see Zevenbergen 2002.

86 Sigman 2004, p. 64.

87 Zevenbergen 2002, p. 60-61.

88 Zevenbergen 2002, p. 61.

prove difficult to establish whether a European property right was created earlier or later than a national property right, depending on whether and how a European property right is registered and whether and how national property rights are registered. Alternatively, European property rights could be granted priority over all national property rights, regardless of the moment of their creation. This option would however not likely be in line with the principle of proportionality, according to which a European rule cannot go beyond what is necessary to achieve the goal for which it was implemented. The simple creation of European property rights suffices to achieve the goal of enabling cross-border trade, without granting them a 'super-priority' over national property rights. Finally, in theory, national property rights could be granted priority over European property rights, meaning that a holder of a European property right would have priority only over unsecured creditors. This option on the other hand would conflict with the principle of supremacy of EU law over national law.

The *prior tempore* rule therefore seems to provide the best means to establish a ranking. It can furthermore be seen as a ground rule shared by the Member States' national systems of property law.[89] In this instance it is advisable that this commonly shared ground rule of property law is also taken over as a ground rule of European property law.[90]

The Cape Town Convention also follows the *prior tempore* rule. Article 29 of the Convention states that: '[a] registered interest has priority over any other interest subsequently registered and over an unregistered interest'.[91] For a national interest to become a registered interest for the purposes of Article 29 - and thus to acquire an 'international' ranking, so to speak - it is necessary that the International Registry receives notice that a national interest has been created.[92] This system could also be applied to determine the relationship between European property rights and national property rights. Ranking would then be established on the basis of the *prior tempore* rule: earlier registered rights have priority over later registered rights. It should be made possible to notify registration of national property rights to the European Registry, so as to simplify a ranking between European rights and

89 Van Erp 2009b.

90 To compare, see the Text of Forum Group Report Recommendations attached in Annex II to the Commission's 2005 Green Paper on Mortgage Credit, which, at no 30, states: 'The Commission should ensure that:
- all charges affecting real estate must be registered in a Public Register in order to be binding on and take effect against third parties, regardless of their nature
- the creation, modification or extinction of a charge on real property shall become effective vis-à-vis third parties only at the point of registration in the Public Register; and
- registered charges on real property in relation to the same estate *shall rank in the order of priority* disclosed in the Public Register.' [emphasis added]

91 See also Honnebier 2006, p. 24.

92 Art. 1(t) and (cc); Goode 2008, p. 223.

national rights.[93] The International Registry set up under the Cape Town Convention itself and also the European Union Land Information Service (EULIS) project[94] show that it should be possible to link national registries to a European registry (and vice versa). Notice of registration of national property rights could in that way be made automatic, thus enhancing the application of the *prior tempore* rule to the ranking between European property rights and national property rights.[95]

The topic of registration will be revisited briefly below, when the European Security Right is discussed, to draw a parallel with other international registration systems that have been set up for the registration of international security rights.

A European property right should have *effect in insolvency proceedings* if it was registered prior to the opening of the proceedings. If registration is a constitutive element for the valid creation of a European property right then any European property right existing at the moment insolvency proceedings are opened will have been registered. 'Effect' means that the holder of a European property right has priority over unsecured creditors.[96] In the absence of substantive EU rules on insolvency law - the Insolvency Regulation primarily governs matters of private international law[97] - European property rights will somehow have to be made to fit into the national systems of insolvency law. This is not an ideal situation.[98] The ECJ

93 In that sense, the proposal in this chapter would go a step further than Veder's suggestion that every national system indicates where it places a European Security Right; Keirse & Veder 2010, p. 185 *et seq*. See also Smits 2010, p. 430: 'Om dat recht overal in Europa dezelfde plaats te geven ten opzichte van locale rechten [...] is een utopie, zoals Veder terecht schrijft. Maar dat is ook niet nodig: als bekend is hoe elk nationaal recht een dergelijk Europees recht plaatst in de nationale rangorde, kan al belangrijke winst worden geboekt.'

94 The project links together several national digitized databases containing information on land, for instance national land registries and national cadastres. It can be found at: <http://eulis.eu/>. EULIS is supported with funding by the Commission: see the Commission's 2005 Green Paper on Mortgage Credit in the EU, COM(2005) 327 final, p. 12 at 45. For more information about EULIS see Ploeger & Loenen 2004.

95 Kreuzer, when he proposed the creation of a European Security Right in 1990, argued that ESRs and national security rights should be separated more strictly: it should not be allowed to cumulatively create both ESRs as well as national security rights in relation to the same object, but only to create either ESRs or national security rights in relation to the same object; p. 638. However, with the present-day possibilities for electronic registration, it should be possible to create ESRs and national security rights in relation to the same object, if parties so wish, and still maintain a high level of publicity and accessibility to information about registered rights.

96 *Cf* Goode 2008, p. 231-232 on Art. 30 of the Cape Town Convention on Effects of Insolvency. The principal purposes of (corporate) insolvency proceedings are to seize and realize (or take possession and sell) the bankrupt company's assets, and to rank the claims of creditors and meet their claims from the proceeds of the sold assets in order of priority. Holders of security rights that are effective in insolvency proceedings will have their claims met in priority over unsecured creditors. McKendrick & Goode 2010, p. 907.

97 See Chapter 4, Part I at 1.3. *Regulation 1346/2000/EC on insolvency proceedings.*

98 It would be more ideal to have European substantive insolvency law complement EU property law. Similarly Kreuzer 1990, p. 633.

case of *Krantz*, which is discussed at length in Chapter 2, shows that national rules of insolvency law or tax law may overrule the priority which the holder of a security right would otherwise have had (in the case of *Krantz* it became clear that under Dutch law the tax authorities are allowed to seize goods that are found on the premises of a taxpayer even if those goods have been delivered under a retention of title clause and are therefore not yet owned by the taxpayer but by the seller). It would be preferable to have European substantive regulation of insolvency law as well as EU property law. However, as long as such regulation is not in place, national courts, when applying national insolvency law, will still have to abide by the EU's *effet utile* principle. If the intention of the European legislature is that European property rights have effect in insolvency proceedings then national courts must ensure this effectiveness. Furthermore, as was explained in detail in Chapter 2, the application of national law may not lead to obstacles to free movement within the internal market. However, given that the starting point of national insolvency law is generally to recognize property rights validly created before insolvency proceedings commence, it should not be too problematic to recognize the effectiveness of European property rights in insolvency where they have been validly created and registered prior to the insolvency proceedings.[99]

Rules governing the *destruction* (or extinction) of European property rights would have to be established. A property right is destroyed if the object on which it rests ceases to exist (destruction of subject-matter) or if the right itself ceases to exist (destruction of right).[100] Destruction of subject-matter can be as straightforward as a burnt-out car, but it also occurs when a loan is repaid, destroying the right of pledge resting on it,[101] or in the case of accession, when one thing becomes physically attached to another leading to a loss of the right on the minor thing.[102] Destruction of the right itself can, for instance, occur through acquisitive prescription, when a non-owner has been in possession of an object for a period of time after which the law grants ownership to this person, thereby destroying the right of the original owner.[103] Destruction of the right itself can also occur when the rightholder abandons his right, although whether abandonment actually leads to destruction depends on whether the object is movable or immovable and whether the return of the right to the State – if this happens – is considered to be creation of a new right or transfer of the existing right.[104]

The question for EU property law would be whether or not European property rights can be extinguished in the same manner by which they were created. If registration is a constitutive requirement for the creation of a European property

99 Goode 1998, p. 464.
100 Van Erp & Akkermans 2012, p. 1008.
101 See e.g. a Dutch judgment from the Hoge Raad, 17 February 1996, *Mulder qq* v *CLBN NJ* 1996, 471 as excerpted in Van Erp & Akkermans 2012, p. 914-915.
102 Van Erp & Akkermans 2012, p. 980 *et seq.*
103 Van Erp & Akkermans 2012, p. 1009.
104 Van Erp & Akkermans 2012, p. 1009-1010.

right, then it should also be a constitutive requirement for the destruction of a European property right.

A decision must be made whether it will be allowed to use the European Use Right - about which more hereafter - as security, in other words whether a European Security Right can be created on a European Use Right. This involves the stacking[105] of property rights. There is no reason why a European Security Right should not be able to be created in relation to a European Use Right. A European Use Right would be an intangible asset - a right representing an economic value for the rightholder. The rightholder of the European Use Right should be able to provide that right as collateral for a loan secured by a European Security Right.

The operating rules should state in relation to what *objects* European property rights can be created. The *acquis* already clearly distinguishes three categories of objects as objects of property rights, namely immovable, movable and intangible objects. This should be consolidated in the optional instrument on EU property law. What are still needed are definitions of these three categories. These would have to be included in the list of definitions in the optional instrument.

European-autonomous property *rights* should be drafted. Examining the different national property rights that have developed over centuries leads to the conclusion that they all fulfil one or both of two basic functions: to enable the use and benefit of an object; or to have the power to dispose over an object for security purposes.[106] At national level, limited property rights contain one of these functions, whereas the primary right (which is either ownership, fee simple, or title) contains both of them.[107] Therefore, at European level, it would suffice to create three types of property rights: a primary right, a security right and a use right. This trichotomy is based on what is known about national property rights and about the functions they fulfil but the content of these European property rights will be influenced by both national and existing EU property law, and by other international property rights. I have decided to name these European property rights after the function they fulfil and not to use terms such as 'ownership' and 'limited property rights'. This terminology is connected to national property law concepts and to theories regarding the relationship between limited/lesser property rights and more extensive/the most extensive property right within a property law system. These theories are meant to explain where the limited property rights come from, whether and how they burden the primary right and whether or not they are carved out of the primary right. As will be discussed further below, these theories do not necessarily need to underlie EU property law. It is therefore useful, when describing the development of European property rights, to use 'system-neutral terminolo-

105 Akkermans 2008, p. 401.
106 Van Erp & Akkermans 2012, p. 425. See also Akkermans 2008, p. 412.
107 Akkermans 2008, p. 418.

gy'.[108] The terms primary right, security right and use right are system-neutral (as opposed to, e.g., freehold title, *Grundschuld* or *usufruit*) and functional.

The primary right would be the most extensive property right a person could hold under EU property law.[109] With regard to the security right and the use right, two approaches can be taken: a uniform approach, in which all types of use rights are subject to the same set of rules[110] (and in which all types of security rights are subject to the same set of rules - this is the approach taken in Article 9 Uniform Commercial Code on Secured Transactions,[111] in the Cape Town Convention,[112] and to a large extent in Book IX of the Draft Common Frame of Reference;[113] it was also the approach suggested by Kreuzer when he first proposed a European Security Right);[114] or a fragmented approach, in which different rules apply for each type of use right and for each type of security right.[115] Under the latter approach, different rules would, for instance, apply to rights on movables than those that would apply to rights on immovables. I would propose to follow the uniform approach for the creation of European-autonomous property rights. The fragmented approach which currently exists at Member State level is sometimes the result of historical developments rather than of deliberate choices based on consistency and coherence.[116] Given that there is still so little EU property law, there is no need to build on an existing system that developed long ago and under different circumstances and there is room to make consistent and coherent choices.[117] A uniform approach would make the European list of property rights simpler, more efficient and more transparent: it would only need to contain a European Primary Right (EPR), a European Security Right (ESR) and a European Use Right (EUR). The fewer property rights can be created, the simpler registration of these rights becomes and the easier it becomes for third parties to find out about the existence of those rights.[118] This in turn reduces information costs and increases legal certainty.[119] Should specific rules be necessary in addition to the general rules governing these European property rights - for instance, to provide protection for consumers in the case of a B2C transaction - then they can be included.[120]

108 Akkermans 2008, p. 410-412. See also Gretton 2007, p. 851.
109 *Cf* Van Erp 2008b, p. 25-26.
110 *Cf* Füller 2006, p. 560-1 as quoted in Akkermans 2008, p. 465-466.
111 Sigman 2004, p. 56 and 58.
112 Van Erp 2004, p. 93.
113 Van Erp & Akkermans 2012, p. 1067-1070.
114 Kreuzer 1990, p. 638. See also Kieninger 2004a, p. 669, who also proposes a uniform approach.
115 *Cf* Sagaert 2006, p. 31.
116 *Cf* Akkermans 2008, p. 486; Van Erp 2008b, p. 22; Van Erp 2006c, p. 8-9; Sagaert 2006, p. 46-47; Füller 2006, p. 560-561 as quoted in Akkermans 2008, p. 466. See also Kreuzer 1990, who refers to the current landscape of security devices in Europe as a *Flickenteppich*; p. 637.
117 *Cf* Van Erp 2008b, p. 33.
118 Sagaert 2006, p. 42.
119 Sagaert 2006, p. 42. See also Merrill & Smith 2000-2001, p. 26.
120 A similar approach is taken in Art. 9 UCC: Sigman 2004, p. 56.

A person wanting to create an ESR or EUR in relation to an object should have the *power to dispose* over that object. According to national law the power to dispose over an object normally flows from holding the primary right (e.g. ownership) in relation to that object. The security right or use right is then either derived from that primary right or seen as burdening the primary right. The former is referred to as the method of *démembrement* (or subtraction) by which a limited property right is created by transferring parts of the primary right to another party, in whose hands they will form a new property right.[121] The latter is referred to as the limitation method by which a limited property right is created separately from the primary right. It will not involve the separation of certain parts of the primary right, as is the case with *démembrement* but its existence does limit the holder of the primary right in his exercise of that right.[122] It could be decided in the optional instrument on EU property law that one only has the power to create an ESR or EUR if one is already the holder of an EPR. In that case, the existence of an ESR or EUR would be dependent on the existence of an EPR. It is however not necessarily required to create an EPR for this purpose as the decision whether someone has the power to dispose over an object could also be left to national law. In that case, if someone has the power to dispose over an object because that person is the rightholder of a national primary right in relation to that object then that could be sufficient to allow him to create an ESR or EUR.

The need for the creation of an EPR alongside the ESR and EUR in the optional instrument therefore rests on different reasons. It would enable parties to acquire property in another Member State with the certainty that the content of their primary right would not be dependent on the current or future location of the property. This could, for instance, be interesting for someone wanting to buy immovable property in another Member State or for a company wanting to establish a base in several Member States.[123]

An issue that would need to be taken into account with regard to the EUR is whether or not it could exist 'in gross'. Within national systems of property law it can be observed that most use rights in relation to immovable property can exist 'in gross', or without a dominant tenement, but some cannot. For some use rights in relation to immovable property it is required that the grantee of the use right, the rightholder, must own immovable property himself and that the immovable property must directly benefit from the use right.[124] This is, for instance, the case for civil law servitudes and English easements and restrictive covenants but not for English profits a prèndre.[125] Sagaert describes this with the terms 'active side'

121 Akkermans 2008, p. 413.
122 Akkermans 2008, p. 413.
123 *Cf* Bright & Bright 1998, p. 372.
124 Akkermans 2008, p. 423; Sagaert 2005 at No. 41.
125 Van Erp & Akkermans 2012, Chapter 3, Note 2 under excerpt 3.85 (E&W), Note 1 under excerpt 3.94 (E&W), Note under excerpt 3.98 (E&W), and section II.A.7. *Profits a prèndre*. See also Sara 2011, p. 239; French 2000-2001, p. 231.

(*actiefzijde*) and 'passive side' (*passiefzijde*) of patrimonial rights (*vermogensrechten*).[126] The active side is the person holding the property right to use, the grantee or rightholder; the passive side is the grantor of the property right to use, the person whose ownership of an immovable is limited by this use right. For use rights such as profits, usufruct, emphyteusis and superficies only the passive side needs to have a right of ownership over an immovable object that 'serves' the use right that rests on it (i.e. servient tenement). For these rights it is not necessary that the active side owns immovable property that benefits from the use right. The fact that, for servitudes and easements, it is required that the active side own immovable property, and that that property directly benefit from the use right, makes those rights a-typical in comparison to other use rights.

Given that there would only be one European Use Right, a decision would have to be made whether or not that use right can exist without the need for a dominant tenement owned by the active side, or rightholder, of the EUR, that benefits from the EUR.

### 4.2. *Definition of Terms*

The operating rules would have to be accompanied by a list of definitions of property law terms used in the optional instrument on EU property law and in future legislative measures using property law terms.[127] Such a list is necessary for a number of reasons. It is meant to promote coherence and consistency in the use of property law terms in EU legislation. This in turn will prevent uncertainty about the meaning of terms for those implementing and relying on the legislation.[128] This should decrease the need to resort to the ECJ to obtain an authoritative interpretation. These definitions should also be used in legislation which regulates an area of law other than property law but which nevertheless uses property law terminology. The research culminating in Chapter 4 showed that many of the property law terms are found in legislation which deals with a different issue area than property law. Nevertheless, it is also important for those instruments that if and when property law terminology is used it is used consistently. Inconsistent use of property law terminology in EU legislation leads to inconsistent implementation at national level, neither of which is helpful for a proper understanding of EU property law. If a different definition is required, there should be a clear statement why and how it deviates from the standard definition.

126 Sagaert 2005 at No. 39.

127 The need for definitions is not just felt in the area of property law: the proposed consumer rights Directive also aims to harmonize core concepts of consumer law to create more legal certainty for consumers and companies; see Keirse & Veder 2010, p. 32. *Cf* also Schulte-Nölke 2007, p. 342: 'A core task could be coherence of terminology.'

128 In a similar context Harry C. Sigman, member of the Drafting Committee that revised Art. 9 UCC, stressed the importance of the definitions contained in Art. 9 UCC: Sigman 2004, p. 55.

It is impossible to reach purely European-autonomous definitions on the basis of existing European legislation only: the existing property law *acquis* simply does not provide the foundation for it. Comparative research will often be necessary to come to a definition, which is however not to say that such definitions cannot be constructed in such a way as to accommodate the needs and requirements of the European Union.[129]

Looking at the list of terms drawn up for the terminological research conducted in Chapter 4,[130] there are only four terms defined in the *acquis*, namely rights *in rem*, property/assets, possessor, and assignment.[131] The other terms in the list do not yet have a European-autonomous meaning. These definitions still need to be filled in. As said, comparative research could play a role here. In order to formulate these definitions, inspiration might also be drawn from the definitions drafted in the context of the DCFR. The DCFR contains three books on property law: Book VIII on Acquisition and loss of ownership of goods; Book IX on Proprietary security in movable assets; and Book X on Trusts. The property terminology used in these books - and in some of the other books - has been defined in the Annex to the DCFR.[132] The DCFR is currently the only comprehensive study which provides definitions of property law terms that might be used at European level. There is, for instance, no property law equivalent to the Principles on European Contract Law (PECL) or the Principles on European Tort Law (PETL) in which definitions of property law terms have been developed. Nevertheless, while the DCFR definitions may provide inspiration for creating European definitions of property law terms, the DCFR definitions must be used with some caution. First of all, the DCFR books on property law are incomplete: they focus primarily on movables and they only deal with limited property security rights but not with limited property rights to use. Secondly, they were developed under great time pressure, which may have had an impact on their quality.[133] These two issues may also be reflected in a negative sense in the DCFR's list of definitions.

129 *Cf* Kieninger 2002, p. 371: 'Ein kraftvoller Ideenwettbewerb zwischen mitgliedstaatlicher und europäischer Ebene [...] [ist] allerdings nur dann zu erwarten, wenn der Gemeinschaftsgesetzgeber die Schaffung europäischer Rechtsformen nicht [...] nur als Suche nach einem Kompromiβ zwischen den vorhandenen mitgliedstaatlichen Rechtsordnungen begreift, sondern den Mutt zu eigenständigen und innovativen Lösungen findet, die in möglichst geringem Umfang auf das nationale Recht der Mitgliedstaaten rekurrieren.'

130 Chapter 4, Part II section 3.

131 See Chapter 4, Part II section 4. *Defined property law terms.*

132 Relevant terms as regards property law are the following: Acquisition finance device, Act of assignment, Assets, Assignment, Beneficiary, Co-ownership, Corporeal, Delivery, In/Dependent personal security, Direct physical control, Global Security, Goods, Immovable property, Incorporeal, Indirect physical control, Intangibles, Interest, Keeper, Lease, Limited proprietary rights, Limited-right-possessor, Movables, Owner-possessor, Ownership, Physical control, Possession, Possessory security right, Property, Proprietary security, Retention of ownership device, Security right in movable asset, Trust, Trustee, Truster.

133 Comments to Book X DCFR, p. 5669. See also Van Erp, Akkermans & Ramaekers 2012, p. 7.

To illustrate how the DCFR definitions could be used as inspiration for the development of property law definitions for an optional instrument on EU property law, let us look at the term *ownership*. According to the DCFR, ownership means:

> '"Ownership" is the most comprehensive right a person, the owner, can have over property, including the exclusive right, so far as consistent with applicable laws or rights granted by the owner, to use, enjoy, modify, destroy, dispose of and recover the property.'

Ownership has not been given a European-autonomous definition in the *acquis*. There is no EU legislation which states what the right of ownership entails. EU law does however tell us what can be owned. According to the DCFR, one can have ownership over property. *Property* is defined as: '"Property" means anything which can be owned: it may be movable or immovable, corporeal or incorporeal.'

This definition is comparable to definitions of property found in the *acquis*. Definitions of property and assets found in the *acquis* cover movables and immovables, corporeals and incorporeals. The *acquis* recognizes that one can have rights *in rem* - including ownership - over all these types of objects. The definition of *assets* in the DCFR is somewhat puzzling: '"Assets" means anything of economic value, including property; rights having a monetary value; and goodwill.'

Having just seen the definition of property, it is difficult to imagine anything of economic value that would be considered an asset but would not fall under the definition of property. The definitions overlap and it is not clear why it is necessary to have these two separate definitions. The same is true for the *acquis*: property and assets essentially mean the same thing.[134]

The list of terms that would need to be defined in the optional instrument on EU property law could be somewhat shorter than the list of terms used in Chapter 4 of this study. If the EU were to create only three European property rights, namely a European Primary Right, a European Security Right and a European Use Right, then there would be no need for definitions of terms such as servitude, mortgage or usufruct.

## 5. EU Property Rights

This section is devoted to the issues and policy questions that must be addressed when developing European property rights.

### 5.1. *European Primary Right*

The European Primary Right (or EPR) could be used by parties as an alternative to their national primary rights (i.e. ownership, fee simple, title...). Transferring an

[134] See Chapter 4, Part II section 4.2. *Property/assets/things/objects*.

EPR from one party to another would be done in accordance with the rules laid down in the optional instrument. The question then remains where the 'first' EPR comes from; how it is created. For the European Security Right and European Use Right this question is easily answered: if someone has the power to dispose over an object that person can create limited property rights in relation to that object. As was discussed above, the power to dispose could be derived from having an EPR or it could be determined by national law (under which the power to dispose over an object normally also derives from having a primary right such as ownership). This however does not explain how one acquires an EPR. Suppose a person has a fee simple estate on a plot of land in England and that person wants to sell that land to an Italian but not by granting him the fee simple estate but by granting him an EPR on the land. Since there cannot be two persons holding two primary rights in relation to one and the same object,[135] the fee simple estate would have to come to an end once the Italian acquires the EPR, otherwise the Englishman (or someone else for that matter) could continue to hold the fee simple estate while the Italian held the EPR. I would therefore propose to regulate in the optional instrument on EU property law that a national primary right would first have to be converted into an EPR before the EPR could be transferred to someone else. This conversion would extinguish the national primary right. Conversely, it should be possible to convert an EPR back into a national primary right if someone so wished. Such conversion ought to be registrable. Information on which rights constitute primary rights in national property law could be drawn from comparative research.

An important point that would have to be addressed, if this method of conversion were introduced, is what happens to limited property rights that already existed before the primary right - on whose existence they depend - is converted and then transferred to someone else. This requires a consideration of the concepts of original and derivative acquisition of property. In the case of *original acquisition*, one receives 'a right which did not previously exist, which originates in the hands of the new owner or holder of the right'.[136] In the case of *derivative acquisition* on the other hand, one receives 'a right which previously belonged to someone else'.[137] Going back to our earlier example above, the Englishman would convert his English fee simple estate into an EPR and then transfer the EPR to the Italian. The transfer of the EPR between the Englishman and the Italian would constitute a form of derivative acquisition, as the Italian would be acquiring an EPR that previously belonged to the Englishman. In this instance, the *nemo dat* rule - according to which a person cannot transfer more rights than he or she has[138] - prevents any other rights than the fee simple estate burdening the land from disappearing when the land is transferred to the Italian. This of course presupposes that the *nemo dat* rule

135 Akkermans 2008, p. 418.
136 Van Erp & Akkermans 2012, Chapter 7, p. 617.
137 Van Erp & Akkermans 2012, Chapter 7, p. 617.
138 Van Erp 2009b, p. 11.

would be part of EU property law. In my view, it should be since it is a ground rule generally underlying any system of property law.[139] The remaining question is whether the conversion of the English fee simple into an EPR itself could cause any limited property rights resting on the land to be lost. Is an EPR a right which did not previously exist or is it a right which previously belonged to someone else?

The argument could go both ways. It could be said that conversion creates a new EPR, which is a right that did not previously exist. In that case, conversion would resemble original acquisition. It is important to keep in mind that original acquisition normally means that previously existing limited property rights are lost because the primary right on which their existence depended has been lost as a result of the original acquisition. It would therefore be dangerous to equate conversion with original acquisition because it could lead to abuse and fraud: a person could get rid of any number of limited property rights simply by converting his or her national primary right into a European Primary Right. This could and should not be the result of a European system of property law.

It could also be argued that an EPR is a right which did exist before but which is simply a conversion of a national primary right into a European Primary Right. In that case, conversion would more closely resemble derivative acquisition, meaning that conversion would not lead to a loss of the limited property rights that burdened the original national primary right.

A decision would have to be made whether or not the primary right can be used for management purposes (like the English trust and certain forms of the German *Treuhand*[140] and the French *fiducie*)[141] and for security purposes (like fiduciary transfers such as the German *Sicherheitsübereignung*[142] and retention of title clauses). In that regard it must be noted that the Financial Collateral Directive has introduced security ownership. This can be taken as an indication that the use of the primary right for security purposes is a concept already known to the *acquis communautaire*. As regards the use of the primary right for security purposes by way of a retention of title, a decision would have to be made whether this could only be a simple retention of title, as is currently provided for under the Late Payments Directive,[143] or whether it could also be an extended retention of title similar to a German *Verarbeitungsklausel*, which extends the title retention to products manufactured from the original goods.[144]

139 Van Erp 2009b, p. 19.
140 Van Erp & Akkermans 2012, Chapter 6 at I.B *The Fiduziarische Treuhand*.
141 Van Erp & Akkermans 2012, Chapter 6, Note 7 under excerpt 6.7 (FR).
142 Van Erp & Akkermans 2012, Chapter 5, Note 2 under excerpt 6.76 (DE).
143 Dir. 2000/35/EC. See Chapter 4, Part I section 1.7.
144 Van Erp & Akkermans 2012, p. 499-505.

### 5.1.1. Ownership in the Euratom Treaty

A primary right may already exist within EU law. The Lisbon Treaties do not contain any definition of ownership, nor do any measures of secondary legislation, but the 'Community's right of ownership' is explicitly mentioned in the Treaty establishing the European Atomic Energy Community (Euratom).[145] The question is whether or not this 'right of ownership' is a primary right such as the French *droit de propriété*, the German *Eigentum*, the Dutch *eigendom*, the English fee simple, etc. The first important feature of the Euratom Community's ownership is that title to nuclear materials is vested in the Community, whereas Member States, persons and undertakings have unrestricted rights of use and consumption.[146] Strictly speaking, this division between formal title and economic ownership is already a deviation from the unitary concept of ownership as adhered to by Member States with a civil law system.[147] The Community's title to nuclear materials has no economic content: Euratom cannot profit or lose from changes in value of nuclear materials.[148] It cannot possess, use or dispose over nuclear materials and any liability for damages caused by nuclear materials falls on the holder of those materials (i.e. a Member State, person or undertaking - Article 87 Euratom), not on the owner.[149] In fact, the only reason that 'ownership' of nuclear materials has been vested in the Community is so that it can execute safety control over these potentially very dangerous materials. It follows from Article 86(2) Euratom that the Community's ownership of nuclear materials is dependent on the existence of safety control.[150] This safety control is executed through the Agency.[151] As soon as nuclear materials enter Euratom territory, the Community automatically acquires ownership of them.[152] The Agency then controls all consumers' supply and demand and has a right of option with regard to all nuclear materials produced within the Community.

The Euratom Community's right of ownership under the Euratom Treaty is consequently very limited in terms of capacity (no capacity to transfer or otherwise dispose over nuclear materials) and content (no use or consumption).[153] It may be a primary right in the formal sense but it does not constitute a European Primary Right as envisaged in this chapter.

145 [2010] *OJ* C 84/01, Art. 86: 'Special fissile materials shall be the property of the Community. The Community's right of ownership shall extend to all special fissile materials which are produced or imported by a Member State, a person or an undertaking and are subject to the safeguards provided for in Chapter 7.'

146 Art. 87 Euratom.

147 Böhm 1962, p. 175-176.

148 Böhm 1962, p. 172.

149 Böhm 1962, p. 177.

150 Böhm 1962, p. 174 and 178.

151 Artt. 53 *et seq*. Euratom.

152 Böhm 1962, p. 171.

153 *Cf* Böhm 1962, p. 178: 'Euratom can be the owner of special nuclear materials only under the ownership provisions in force at the place where such materials are located.'

## 5.2. *European Security Right*

When considering an ESR we can benefit from the example of a number of past attempts - some successful, some unsuccessful - to create a cross-border security right. It was not possible to discuss all examples at length here. I have therefore chosen to focus on five examples, for reasons described below. Examples not included are, for instance, the European Bank for Reconstruction and Development's Model Law on Secured Transactions and the UNCITRAL Legislative Guide on Secured Transactions.[154] The EBRD's Model Law was drafted with a very specific objective in mind, namely to assist the development of rules on secured transactions in post-communist countries in central and eastern Europe.[155] Given that this objective is quite different from the objective of drafting a European Security Right that can be used throughout the EU, the EBRD has not been used as an example here for the development of such a European Security Right.

Previous attempts by the EU itself as regards cross-border security rights were the 1973 Draft Directive on mutual recognition of security rights in movables and the Green Paper on a Euromortgage. Neither of those instruments eventually came into being but they are revisited here to see whether they nevertheless contain elements that can be taken over for an ESR and where improvements could be made to increase the likelihood that an ESR would make it into legislation the next time round. Article 9 of the United States Uniform Commercial Code (UCC) and the Cape Town Convention creating an international interest in mobile equipment are both successful examples of international instruments providing for a cross-border security right. Finally, Book IX of the Draft Common Frame of Reference (DCFR) on proprietary security rights in movable assets is taken into account because it was modelled after Article 9 UCC. A further reason for including Book IX DCFR is that it was developed by the Study Group on a European Civil Code as a proposed law for the whole of the European Union.

Below, each of these five instruments is introduced briefly. They are thereafter used as supporting material for the discussion on the different elements of a European Security Right.

### 5.2.1. Past Proposals and Existing Cross-Border Security Rights

*1973 Draft Directive on mutual recognition of securities on movables*

In 1973 the Commission proposed a Draft Directive concerning the recognition of securities on movables without dispossession and of the terms relating to the

[154] For more information about these two instruments, see Van Erp & Akkermans 2012, Chapter 10 at sections V.B and V.C.

[155] EBRD Model Law on Secured Transactions, Introduction. To be found at: <http://www.ebrd.com/downloads/research/guides/secured.pdf>.

transfer of ownership[156] (hereafter 'the 1973 Draft Directive'). The Commission was concerned about hindrances to the functioning of the internal market resulting from the fact that security rights on movables differ greatly from Member State to Member State and that mutual recognition of those rights was (and still is) not guaranteed.[157] In the note preceding the Draft Directive the Commission pointed out that the problems with recognition of foreign security rights and reservation of ownership clauses cannot be solved through conflict of laws rules alone.[158] The essence of the Draft Directive was therefore to facilitate mutual recognition of security devices by having these security devices be registered in a central European registry.[159] The secured party would thereafter obtain the rights which it would have as a pledgee under the law of the host Member State.[160] The Draft Directive contained three alternatives for setting up a registration system. In the end, the Directive never came into being because of the inability of the Member States to reach an agreement on a registration system.[161]

Even if the Directive had come into being, it is questionable whether it would have had any real effect. According to the discussion by the Subcommittee on Private International Law,[162] the term recognition, as used in the Directive, should be interpreted as follows: 'Recognition is restricted to the "validity" of the security and does not cover the "effects", which will be governed by another law'.[163] What is more, the Subcommittee wondered whether an exception should be made allowing Member States to refuse recognition where it 'would affect the conditions of trade or competition in the country recognizing the security'.[164] Experts taking part in the discussion observed that mandatory law should in any event be adhered to.[165] In other words, Member States would, under the Directive, only have had to recognize the validity of a foreign security right. They would not have had to recognize it *as such*, meaning that it would still be transposed into the nearest national equivalent.[166] They could moreover choose not to recognize it at all if it conflicted with

156 DG Internal Market, Document XI/466/73-E.

157 Kreuzer 1991, p. 92 at footnote 211.

158 Doc. XI/466/73-E, p. 2. See to the same extent Kreuzer 1990, p. 614, and with regard to the Euromortgage Wehrens 2004, p. 779.

159 Doc. XI/466/73-E, p. 3.

160 Artt. 3 and 4 of the proposed Directive. See also Kieninger 2004b, p. 22.

161 Bouckaert 2006, p. 187; Kieninger 2004b, p. 22. See also Goode 1998, p. 454. The Report of the meeting of the Subcommittee on Private International Law of the Commission's DG for the Internal Market, Doc. XI/526/74-E, 102 October 1974 does not contain a final decision on a registration system.

162 A subcomittee of the European Commission's DG Internal Market.

163 Report of the Meeting of the Subcommittee, Doc. XI/151/74-E of Commission DG Internal Market, p. 11.

164 *Ibidem.*

165 Report of the Meeting, p. 12.

166 See also the discussion concerning Art. 3 of the Draft Directive, which places the enforcement of a security right under the *lex rei sitae* at the time of enforcement and provides 'assimilation →

their mandatory law. Given that essentially all rules of property law are deemed to be mandatory, a Member State could practically always refuse to recognize a foreign security right. By having been drafted the way it was, the Directive barely stood a chance of lifting the barriers to trade caused by non-recognition of foreign security rights.[167]

The Report of the meeting of the Subcommittee on Private International Law of 1-2 October 1974[168] briefly mentions that the Subcommittee was invited by the Secretary-General of the Hague Conference to consider the creation of a European Security Right.[169] The Subcommittee however does not address this option at all.

*Euromortgage*

A report drafted for the European Commission by London Economics in 2005 on the Costs and Benefits of Integration of EU Mortgage Markets names as an important, and potentially substantial, benefit of integration the increase of supply and consumption of housing: 'The primary means by which we expect mortgage integration to benefit the EU is by increasing the supply and consumption of housing. [...] The increase in the total EU housing stock, at 3.7%, is fairly substantial.'[170]

The Commission's 2005 Green Paper on Mortgage Credit in the EU[171] presented the idea of a Euromortgage (*Eurohypothèque/Euro-Hypothek*).[172] The Euromortgage would be a security right that could be used throughout the EU. It would be presented in the form of a 28th system. The main element of the Euromortgage would be a decoupling of the security right - the Euromortgage - from the underlying claim that it secured. In other words, the accessority (*principe d'accessoirité/Akzessorietät*) between the security right and the secured claim would

rules' which provide how foreign security rights are to be transformed into an equivalent in the host Member State; Report of the Meeting, p. 14.

167 For more about what these obstacles are and how they are caused by non-recognition, see Chapter 2, section 3.4.5. *The obstacles to free movement of goods: loss of property right and increase in costs*. *Cf* Honnebier 2006, p. 26, who criticises the 1948 Geneva Convention on the International Recognition of Rights in Aircraft for only containing rules on mutual recognition but no substantive property law rules.

168 Commission DG Internal Market, Doc. XI/526/74-E.

169 P. 5.

170 *The Costs and Benefits of Integration of EU Mortgage Markets*, Report for European Commission DG Internal Market and Services by London Economics, August 2005, to be found at: <http://ec.europa.eu/internal_market/finservices-retail/docs/home-loans/2005-report-integration-mortgage-markets_en.pdf>. See also Snijders 2006, p. 156.

171 COM(2005) 327 final.

172 2005 Green Paper, p. 13 at 47, 48. This was not the first time. The idea for a Euromortgage had already been introduced in the 1966 Segré Report on The development of a European capital market; to be found at: <http://ec.europa.eu/economy_finance/emu_history/documentation/chapter1/19661130en382develeurocapitm_a.pdf>. See also Wehrens 2004, p. 769-770.

be weakened.[173] Whether or not a European Security Right should be accessory to the underlying claim is discussed in more detail below.[174] Suffice it to say, the Euromortgage was never introduced. It disappeared from view after the Commission's White paper on the integration of EU mortgage credit markets[175] no longer made any mention of it.[176]

According to Wehrens, if the Euromortgage had come into being, its creation would have depended 'on the composition of the respective national system of land registration'.[177] In other words, national rules on the role of notaries and land registries in the creation of a right of mortgage would also have applied to the creation of the Euromortgage. In my opinion, this would have weakened the effectiveness of the Euromortgage. The reason that I, in this Chapter, propose a European Security Right that must be created in accordance with European rules on the creation of property rights is that any party would be able to use the ESR on the basis of the same set of rules, everywhere in the EU, so as to eliminate obstacles to, in particular, the free movement of capital, which result from the differing national rules on the creation of security rights. By making a Euromortgage dependent on national rules concerning creation and registration, these obstacles to the internal market would not have been sufficiently reduced.

*Article 9 of the Uniform Commercial Code (UCC)* deals with secured transactions. It has been implemented by all the states of the USA. It provides for a security interest, enforceable throughout the United States, which can be created in relation to movables, both tangible and intangible.[178] It is a functional piece of legislation, concerned more with practicality and less with theory.[179] According to section 9-109(a)(1), Article 9 UCC applies to any transaction 'regardless of its form, that creates a security interest in personal property'. This means any agreement creating a security interest, whether or not it is denominated by the parties as such.[180] This makes the Article 9 UCC security interest a self-standing one which is not dependent on a previously created national property right which is then converted into an Article 9 UCC interest.[181] Apart from the agreement that creates the security

173 See also the Text of Forum Group Report Recommendations attached as Annex II to the 2005 Green Paper which, at no 36, recommends that the Commission 'should ensure that links between mortgage debts and the collateral security are made more flexible'.

174 Section 5.2.2.4. *Accessory or non-accessory security right.*

175 COM(2007) 807 final.

176 For a more detailed overview of the origins of and developments around the Euromortgage, see Van Erp & Akkermans 2013.

177 Wehrens 2004, p. 775.

178 S 9-109. The UCC can be found at: <http://www.law.cornell.edu/ucc>.

179 Van Erp & Akkermans 2012, p. 430; Sigman 2004, p. 55 and 57; Goode 1998, p. 458.

180 UCC: Official Text and Comments 2008 Edition, Official Comment 2 at p. 875; Sigman 2004, p. 64.

181 *Cf* UCC: Official Text and Comments 2008 Edition, Official Comment 3(b) at p. 854: 'Whether an agreement creates a security interest depends not on whether the parties intend that the →

interest, three elements are required for the security interest to 'attach', i.e. to become enforceable against the debtor and third parties. These have been listed in section 9-203. Perfection is furthermore necessary to establish priority of a security interest. Some security interests are perfected upon attachment[182] but for others either filing, possession or control are required.[183] Because every State has its own filing system, a conflicts rule laid down in section 9-301(1) determines that the law of the location of the debtor governs perfection and priority of a security interest.

*Cape Town Convention*

The Cape Town Convention on International Interests in Mobile Equipment was promulgated in 2001. Its preamble tells us what the essential characteristics and goals of the Convention are: it first of all recognizes the need to ensure that interests in mobile equipment are recognized and protected universally; secondly, it promotes the autonomy of the parties necessary in asset-based financing and leasing transactions; and thirdly, it recognizes the need to establish a legal framework for international interests in mobile equipment and for that purpose to create an international registration system for the protection of such international interests.

The Cape Town Convention provides for an 'international interest'.[184] The international interest must be created in accordance with the requirements laid down in Article 7 of the Convention.[185] An international interest can take the form of a security agreement, a retention of title agreement or a leasing agreement. The international interest is self-standing in the sense that it derives from the Convention, not from national law.[186] This means that an international interest is created if the requirements of Article 7 are met, regardless of whether this would also constitute such an interest under the otherwise applicable (national) law or whether such an interest is known to that law.[187] The Convention does however leave certain aspects to national law. For instance, the validity of an agreement which purports to create an international interest is to be determined in accordance with the applicable national law.[188] Furthermore, whether the international interest

law *characterize* the transaction as a security interest but rather on whether the transaction falls within the definition of "security interest" in Section 1-201.'

182 S 9-309.

183 S 9-310 - 9-314.

184 Art. 2(1) of the Convention.

185 Art. 7 reads: 'An interest is constituted as an international interest under this Convention where the agreement creating or providing for the interest:
(a) is in writing;
(b) relates to an object of which the chargor, conditional seller or lessor has power to dispose;
(c) enables the object to be identified in conformity with the Protocol; and
(d) in the case of a security agreement, enables the secured obligations to be determined, but without the need to state a sum or maximum sum secured.'

186 Goode 2008, p. 175; Honnebier 2006, p. 26; Goode 1998, p. 460.

187 Goode 2008, p. 175; Honnebier 2006, p. 26; Goode 1998, p. 460.

188 Goode 2008, p. 15, 35, 176.

is to be classified as a security agreement, a retention of title agreement or a leasing agreement also depends on the applicable national law.[189] For reasons set out above, a European Security Right should function within a European framework that includes rules on creation so as not to be dependent on national law.[190] The proposal for an ESR as laid down in this chapter purports to provide a self-standing interest which does not rely on classifications of security rights under national law.

*Book IX of the Draft Common Frame of Reference*

The Draft Common Frame of Reference (DCFR) is an academic study, conducted and published by the Study Group on a European Civil Code and the Research Group on Existing EC-Contract Law, also known as the *acquis* group. It is a large body of model rules on European private law. In 2010 the drafters of the DCFR published the final edition, along with their notes and comments on the provisions contained in it. The DCFR consists of ten books. Book IX deals with Proprietary security in movable assets. It has been based on Article 9 UCC.[191] Book IX takes a semi-functional approach: it covers all security devices, both limited security rights and ownership for security purposes, but unlike Article 9 UCC it still denominates these devices along the lines of national concepts of security rights.[192] Article IX. – 1:101 reads:

> '(1) This Book applies to the following rights in movable property based upon contracts for proprietary security:
>
> (a) security rights; and
>
> (b) ownership retained under retention of ownership devices.'

Articles IX. – 1:102 and 1:103 then continue to further define what a security right is[193] and what a retention of ownership device is. Book IX DCFR provides rules for the creation of the security devices covered by it,[194] so that it is not necessary to depend on national rules for the creation of limited property security rights.[195]

189 Art. 2(4) of the Convention; Goode 2008, p. 33.
190 *Cf* Wehrens 2004, p. 775.
191 Van Erp & Akkermans 2012, p. 1070.
192 Van Erp & Akkermans 2012, p. 430. For a general overview of Book IX DCFR see Erp, Akkermans & Ramaekers 2012, p. 90-91.
193 This includes 'especially the pledge' – Art. IX. – 1:102(2)(a).
194 Artt. IX. – 2:101 and 2:102.
195 Van Erp & Akkermans 2012, p. 1070.

### 5.2.2. Characteristics of the European Security Right

A decision would have to be made regarding each of the following characteristics:[196] a) whether the ESR is a possessory or (also) a non-possessory security right; b) in relation to what type of objects the ESR can be created (i.e. movable/immovable, tangible/intangible); c) whether it is a general or specific security right, i.e. must the objects on which it rests be specified or can the ESR be created in relation to a group of (undefined) assets or future assets; d) whether it should be an accessory or a non-accessory security right; and e) whether registration is required and if so, in what form.

#### *5.2.2.1. Possessory or Non-Possessory Security Right*

Non-possessory security rights have increased in popularity over the last decades.[197] French law, for instance, went with the legal reforms of 2006 from a very specific non-possessory pledge on cars to a general non-possessory pledge, now laid down in Article 2337 of the *Code Civil*.[198] Conventional possessory security rights fail where the debtor needs the encumbered assets in the course of his business to generate the proceeds necessary to repay his loan.[199] Non-possessory security rights, such as the Dutch silent pledge (*stil pandrecht*) or the Italian hypothec on motor vehicles (*ipotecha sul autoveicolo*) do not have that downfall and have thus become more common. For the same reason Article 9 UCC also provides for a non-possessory interest; it facilitates 'efficient financing'.[200] The same was already true for the European Commission's Draft Directive on the recognition of securities on movables without dispossession[201] and is also true for Book IX DCFR. The latter provides that '[u]nless otherwise agreed by the parties, the creation of a security right by contract does not require possession of the encumbered asset by the secured creditor'.[202] AN ESR should follow this trend and should in any case be available as a non-possessory security right. If parties want to agree to use the ESR as a possessory security right after all then this option could be made available to them in the European Regulation providing for the ESR.

196 *Cf* Snijders 2006, p. 157 and 163; Kieninger 2006, p. 166.

197 *Cf* Van Erp 2008b, p. 18; Kieninger 2004a, p. 653; Goode 1998, p. 458.

198 Art. 2337 *Code Civil*: 'A pledge is effective against third parties due to the compliance with the publicity attached to it. That is also the case by surrendering of its object into the possession of the creditor or a third party upon which they agreed.' Van Erp & Akkermans 2012, p. 446 and 449.

199 Akkermans 2008, p. 429.

200 Sigman 2004, p. 59.

201 DG Internal Market, Document XI/466/73-E.

202 Art. IX. - 2:103.

#### 5.2.2.2. *For what Type of Objects?*

Given that there would be one all-encompassing EU security right, that right should be able to be created in relation to all types of objects: immovable, movable and intangible.[203] The international interest stemming from the Cape Town Convention can only be created in relation to tangible movable objects. They are however registered movable objects of great value and are therefore similar to registered immovable property which normally also has a high value. The security interest from Article 9 UCC can only be created in relation to movables, both tangible and intangible; and Book IX of the DCFR also only applies to movable property, both tangible and intangible. The ESR, however, should also be able to be used for immovables. Otherwise its goal – improving the functioning of the internal market – cannot be achieved fully. If the ESR were applicable to movables only, it might improve the free movement of goods but not the free movement of capital. As was explained in Chapter 2, property law issues involving the free movement of capital concern mostly the acquisition of immovable property in another Member State.[204] The free movement of capital would therefore benefit from an ESR that can also be used for immovable property. Furthermore, because immovable property is still the most common collateral to secure repayment of a loan, having an ESR that can be created on immovable property may increase the importance and volume of cross-border mortgage lending.[205]

Intangible objects should also be included as possible objects of an ESR. It follows from the research conducted for Chapter 4 on property law in EU secondary legislation that the *acquis* already accepts that rights *in rem* – as is the term used in the *acquis* – can exist in relation to all types of objects, as long as they represent an economic value. Given that the development of an ESR would build on the existing property law *acquis*, it should be able to be created in relation to movables and immovables, both tangible and intangible.

#### 5.2.2.3. *General or Specific Security Right*

Should the ESR be a general or specific security right? A specific security right can only be created in relation to a specified object, whereas a general security right can be created in relation to (groups of) specifiable objects or in relation to unspecified objects. The Cape Town Convention only allows the creation of an international interest in relation to a specified object. This prerequisite of specification is linked directly to the fact that the registration system set up under the Convention is asset-based.[206] Registration of an international interest is not possible if the asset is not

[203] *Cf* Kreuzer 1990, p. 639.

[204] Chapter 2, section 4.3. *Obstacles to the free movement of capital.*

[205] Wehrens 2004, p. 770.

[206] Goode 2008, p. 51: 'Registration is against the individual object, not against the debtor; hence the requirement that the object must be uniquely identifiable'. See also Goode 1998, p. 460-1, →

identified. General security rights have become more popular, however, over the last few decades. See, for instance, the English floating charge,[207] the Belgian *gage sur fonds de commerce* or *pand op de handelszaak*,[208] or the case law of the Dutch supreme court (*Hoge Raad*) which permits pledging of groups of (future) claims by way of a *verzamelpandakte* (collective deed of pledge).[209] General security rights allow the creation of a security right over classes of assets or future assets, without having to create a new security right for each individual asset. This makes general security rights cost-effective.[210] The security interest that can be created under Article 9 UCC is a general security right or 'floating lien', as it is referred to.[211] Book IX DCFR has not entirely followed this trend; Article IX. – 2:102 requires *inter alia* that the asset exists. At first sight, this seems to mean that the creation of a security device in relation to future assets is not possible. However, according to the comments to the DCFR, what this provision means is that a security agreement has no proprietary effect, until the asset in which it is created comes into existence.[212] It is emphasized that this delayed creation of the security right does not necessarily affect its priority.[213]

The ESR should meet the needs of businesses for a general security right. Combined with a debtor-based registration system,[214] it is perfectly possible to make the ESR a general security right. What is more, the *acquis* already provides for the possibility of creating rights *in rem* in 'collections of indefinite assets as a whole which change from time to time'.[215] The ESR should follow the *acquis* in this respect. Parties would still remain free to specify the objects in relation to which the ESR is created, if they so wish. It must be noted, though, that the development towards general securities is a step away from one of the leading principles of property law, namely the principle of specificity.[216] A choice whether or not to make the ESR a

where he describes that the registration system under the Cape Town Convention would originally have been debtor-based, and why it was later changed to an asset-based system.

207 *Cf* Hunter 1976, p. 324: '[I]t is felt that this form of security [the floating charge] and its mode of administration may have much to contribute to the more flexible and efficient financing of business throughout the Community.' Bouckaert pleads for a commercial general security right encompassing all movable assets, such as the company's inventory. He proposes to use the English floating charge as an example. Bouckaert 2006, p. 192.

208 Act of 25 October 1919 with regard to the pledge on a commercial fund, Belgian Official Gazette 5 November 1919; Van Erp & Akkermans 2012 Chapter 5 at III.A.4.b. *Belgian law* and excerpt 5.35 (BE).

209 See recently the Hoge Raad in *Dix* v *ING Bank NV*, 03 February 2012, LJN: BT6947 at 4.6.1.-4.6.4. See also: <http://www.debrauw.com/News/LegalAlerts/Pages/DutchSupremeCourt acceptsfloatingcharge.aspx#page=1>.

210 See e.g. Goode 1998, p. 459.

211 Sigman 2004, p. 57.

212 Comments under B to Art. IX.-2:102, p. 5412.

213 *Ibidem*.

214 See *infra* section 5.2.2.5. *Registration*.

215 See Chapter 4, Part I section 1.3. *Regulation 1346/2000/EC on insolvency proceedings*.

216 Van Erp 2009b; Kieninger 2004a, p. 669.

general security right is a reflection of an underlying choice whether and to what extent to uphold the principle of specificity in EU property law.[217]

### 5.2.2.4. *Accessory or Non-Accessory Security Right*

Should the ESR be an accessory or a non-accessory security right? The question of accessority already came up when the introduction of a Euromortgage was considered under the Commission's 2005 Green Paper on Mortgage Credit in the EU.[218] The Euromortgage would have been a non-accessory security right modelled after German and Swiss law.[219] Being non-accessory means that the security right can be transferred separately from the claim it secures, which is not possible if the two are accessory to each other. The Euromortgage was however discussed prior to the current mortgage credit crisis, which did not start until about three years after the Green Paper was published. During the credit crisis it became clear that non-accessory security rights could pose serious problems.[220] Under German law - after which the Euromortgage was modelled - accessority between a security right and a secured claim is reintroduced in the *Sicherungsvertrag*, the contract governing the loan relationship between the borrower and the lender. It appeared during the credit crisis that the borrower cannot always rely on the loan agreement with the holder of the mortgage as against the new holder of the mortgage.[221] This led to some dramatic instances where the new holder of the mortgage decided to execute the mortgage, even though the borrower had fulfilled his obligations under the loan agreement vis-à-vis the original holder of the mortgage.[222] Such a situation would constitute a violation of EU consumer protection principles.[223] I would therefore recommend that an ESR would either be an accessory security right or that the contractual constructions meant to create *Ersatzakzessorietät* (i.e. a reintroduction of accessority) are critically re-evaluated so that the borrower is adequately protected if the ESR were to become a non-accessory security right.

217 The fact that the Cape Town Convention provides for an asset-based registry in which only specified objects can be registered reflects an adherence to the specificity principle; Van Erp 2004, p. 98.

218 See *supra*, section 5.2.1. *Past proposals and existing cross-border security rights*. See also *The Costs and Benefits of Integration of EU Mortgage Markets*, Report for European Commission, DG Internal Market and Services, by London Economics, August 2005, p. 69; to be found at: <http://ec.europa.eu/internal_market/finservices-retail/docs/home-loans/2005-report-integration-mortgage-markets_en.pdf>.

219 Van Erp 2008b, p. 8. See also Wehrens 2004, p. 771.

220 *Cf* Van Erp 2009a, p. 268-269.

221 Van Erp & Akkermans 2013 at 3. *The impact of the financial crisis*.

222 For practical examples see: <http://www.verkaufte-kredite.de>, a website set up by the German law firm Hänssler & Häcker-Hollmann providing information for people whose credit agreements have been transferred to companies mostly located outside Germany.

223 Van Erp & Akkermans 2013 at 3. *The impact of the financial crisis*.

#### 5.2.2.5. *Registration*

It would be advisable to make registration in a public, European registry a constitutive element for the creation of an ESR. Hidden security rights might function fairly well within a limited national credit market but it is questionable whether that would still be the case in an internal market consisting of 27 Member States 'where personal reliance must be replaced by reliance on institutions'.[224] Kreuzer, who proposed the creation of a European Security Right already in 1990,[225] pleaded for registration of the ESR as a condition for its establishment.[226] The Cape Town Convention goes in the opposite direction: registration is not necessary for the creation of an international interest under the Convention, it merely serves to notify third parties of its existence, to establish a ranking and to preserve its effectiveness in insolvency proceedings.[227] Making registration a constitutive element for the creation of an ESR would ensure that it always acquires a ranking.[228] This would make it easier to establish its priority over other property rights created in relation to the same object,[229] and would preserve its effectiveness in insolvency.[230]

Given that the scope of the ESR would not be limited to particular kinds of objects - as is the case with the international interest under the Cape Town Convention - registration of security rights on movable assets could be burdensome if the register were asset-based. However, a debtor-based register would be feasible.[231] It would moreover match the choice for a general ESR which could be created in relation to groups of assets or future assets.[232] An asset-based registration system requires the registration of every separate transaction for every identifiable object, whereas a debtor-based registration system can accommodate the registration of groups of transactions for groups of assets which do not necessarily have to be identified.[233]

### 5.3. *European Use Right*

As much inspiration as there is for the creation of a European Security Right, in the form of previous proposals for and existing international, cross-border security

224 Kieninger 2004a, p. 670. See also Van Erp 2004, p. 109.
225 Kreuzer 1990, p. 635 *et seq.*
226 Kreuzer 1990, p. 640.
227 Goode 2008, p. 37, 49, 175.
228 *Cf* Kieninger 2004a, p. 671; Kreuzer 1990, p. 640.
229 Van Erp 2004, p. 97.
230 *Cf* Art. 30(1) of the Cape Town Convention: 'In insolvency proceedings against the debtor an international interest is effective if prior to the commencement of the insolvency proceedings that interest was registered in conformity with this Convention.'
231 Kieninger 2006, p. 168.
232 In comparison: debtor-based registries are used in England with respect to the floating charge, which is a general security right; Kieninger 2004a, p. 670.
233 *Cf* Goode 2008, p. 51.

rights, there is little inspiration for the creation of a European Use Right (EUR). To my knowledge, no proposal has yet been made for the creation of a cross-border limited property right to use. However, as was shown in Chapter 2, situations in which free movement is hindered by the differences between national systems of property law do not necessarily only concern security rights but may, and do, also concern rights to use, especially in cases of succession.[234] Under Dutch law, for instance, a usufructuary has the power to use up or consume the object in relation to which he holds a right of usufruct, in Dutch referred to as *verteringsbevoegdheid*.[235] Such a usufruct with *verteringsbevoegdheid* is however not generally known in other EU Member States. Therefore, if the object on which such a usufruct rests is transported to a country that is not familiar with this *verteringsbevoegdheid*, the powers of the usufructuary are likely to change under the *lex rei sitae* of the receiving country. The problematic mutual recognition of use rights, such as the usufruct (with our without *verteringsbevoegdheid*), but also such as the common law trust,[236] would be a reason for the adoption of a European Use Right that supercedes the national discussion on the recognition of foreign use rights.

In light of the foregoing, I would propose the creation of an EUR as well as an ESR. Below follows an analysis of each of the factors that would have to be taken into account in the development of an EUR.

### 5.3.1. Content of the Right

The content of a use right can vary from limited to extensive. The extent of the powers of the holder of the use right determines the extent of the powers the holder of the primary right - which is burdened by the use right - has left. The powers contained in the use right may be so extensive that the primary right on which it rests/from which it is carved out is completely hollowed out.[237] This is sometimes referred to as 'bare ownership'.[238] The content of a use right may vary.[239] It may contain a right to use another's object; this could, for instance, be a right of way. It may contain a right to take something from another's object; this could, for instance, be the right to take minerals from another's land or to hunt on another's land. It could also contain a right to benefit from another's object, i.e. to receive payments or services. Finally, it could simply impose an obligation on the holder of the primary right over the object to refrain from using their object in a certain way. The corollary to the rights enjoyed by the holder of the use right is that the grantor of the use right must accept that the grantee does something with the grantor's object.[240] The

234 Chapter 2 at 6.2. *Obstacles to the free movement of persons.*
235 Art. 207 of Book 3 of the Dutch civil code. See also Akkermans 2008, p. 275-276.
236 See e.g. Gaillard & Trautman 1987.
237 See e.g. Akkermans 2008, p. 421.
238 Van Erp & Akkermans 2012, Chapter 3 at I.C.1. *Usufruct*; Akkermans 2008, p. 414.
239 *Cf* French 2000-2001, p. 227.
240 *Cf* Van Erp & Akkermans 2012, p. 244 *et seq.*, Notes with excerpt 3.32 (NL).

content of the use right may further entail an obligation for the rightholder to pay a periodical compensation to the grantor.[241]

Another element of use rights is the question whether they can only entail a negative obligation for the grantor of the right or whether they can also entail a positive obligation for the grantor. In the first instance, the grantor of the right can only be obliged to accept that the grantee uses his object, or to refrain from using his object in a certain way. In the second instance, the grantor of the right is obliged to do something with the object for the benefit of the grantee of the use right. Use rights containing positive duties for the grantor are generally not allowed because they are seen as an unacceptable restriction of the right of ownership and because successors in title of the grantor would also be bound to these duties even though they had no say in their creation.[242] The EUR should only be able to contain a negative obligation for the grantor, in order to prevent parties from making use of the EUR to circumvent national rules against use rights containing positive obligations for the grantor.

### 5.3.2. Time-Limit

A right to use can be established for a limited or unlimited duration of time. Comparative research of national use rights indicates that the time-limit of the use right is often related to the content of the use right: a use right which is more extensive in content tends to be able to be established for a shorter period of time, whereas a use right which is more limited in content tends to be able to be established for a longer period of time.[243] A use right can, for instance, be established for the duration of the life of the rightholder or for a fixed period of time.[244] A fixed period of time might be relatively short (years or decades) or it might be so long that there barely remains a difference between the use right and the primary right from which it is derived.[245] Rights to use for an unlimited period of time exist at the national level;[246] it could be decided that a European Use Right can also be created for an unlimited period.

241 Sagaert 2006, p. 45.

242 Van Erp & Akkermans 2012, Chapter 3 at III.E. *A dislike of positive burdens*; Akkermans 2008, p. 438. A few countries do accept property rights containing a positive obligation for the grantor of the right: see Akkermans 2006, p. 181-182.

243 Akkermans 2008, p. 423; Sagaert 2006, p. 52.

244 Sagaert 2006, p. 39.

245 Akkermans 2008, p. 421; Sagaert 2006, p. 36.

246 Akkermans 2008, p. 423; Sagaert 2006, p. 47.

### 5.3.3. For what Type of Objects?

Given that the *acquis* already accepts that rights *in rem* can be created in relation to immovables, movables and intangibles, it would make sense that a European Use Right could be created in relation to each of these three categories of objects.

### 5.3.4. General or Specific Use Right

A use right can confer on its holder a general right to use another's object or a specific right to use another's object.[247] As stated before, the broader the powers conferred by a use right on the rightholder, the shorter the duration of time tends to be for which such a right can be created. An EUR should be able to be created both as a general and as a specific use right, establishing different time-limits for its existence depending on its content.

## 6. The Place of Private International Law in the Optional Instrument

The proposal presented in this chapter for the development of a European system of property law has covered what would be the most essential elements of such a system. However, some of the more detailed aspects of property law have not been dealt with in this proposal, and if the EU would decide at some point in the future to create legislation in the field of property law it would probably not deal with all possible aspects of property law. Such aspects are, for instance, acquisitive prescription or the relationship between European property rights and national priority rights.[248] It would therefore be necessary to include in an instrument on EU property law a conflict of laws rule that determines which law applies to those matters that have not been covered by the instrument itself. It is not uncommon for supranational legislation to include a conflict of laws provision, as can, for instance, be seen in the Cape Town Convention which states that '[r]eferences to the applicable law are to the domestic rules of the law applicable by virtue of the rules of private international law of the forum State'.[249]

It might be an obvious choice, for an instrument on EU property law, to include a reference to the *lex rei sitae* for all matters not covered by the instrument itself. It followed from the research done for Chapter 4 of this study that the *acquis* adheres to the *lex rei sitae* rule. It may be justifiable to maintain the *lex rei sitae* rule as regards immovable property but, where movable property is concerned, the *lex rei sitae* rule can and does cause hindrances to the internal market, and would therefore not be an appropriate conflicts rule to be included in an instrument on EU property

247 Sagaert 2006, p. 31 and 46.

248 Priority rights being rights that grant a kind of 'superpriority' to its rightholder - e.g. tax authorities - over other security rights.

249 Art. 5(3).

law which has as its purpose to overcome obstacles to the internal market. It was therefore discussed in Chapter 5 whether this rule should be replaced by a different conflicts rule, such as the *lex registrationis* or the *lex destinationis*. Until further study into these alternatives has been conducted, it cannot be said with certainty which conflicts rule would be best to be incorporated in an instrument on EU property law. Perhaps a solution such as can be found in the Regulation on international successions recently adopted by the Council and Parliament[250] could also be adopted in an optional instrument on EU property law. This Regulation provides parties with a limited choice of law to apply to their succession. According to Articles 21 and 22 of the Regulation, the law applicable to the succession as a whole is the law of the State in which the deceased had his habitual residence at the time of death. Alternatively, a person may choose as the applicable law to his succession as a whole the law of the State of his nationality.

The private international law issues could be circumvented if EU property law were implemented in the same way as the proposed Common European Sales Law, making it part of national law. However, until more is known about whether the proposed Common European Sales Law will become law and how it will operate, I would not propose to implement EU property law in this manner.

## Concluding Remarks to Part II

The purpose of this final chapter has been to outline the status quo of EU property law and to propose a framework for the future development of this field of law. My proposal in this chapter does not provide a complete system of property law that could be adopted by the EU. What it has done is identify the key elements and main policy issues that would have to be taken into account if the EU were to decide to enact legislation in the field of property law. In my opinion, the obstacles to the internal market that were identified earlier in this study, caused by the differences between the national property law systems and their closed and mandatory nature, would be best reduced or removed through the enactment of an optional instrument in the form of an EU Regulation containing European-autonomous rules on property law. The main advantages of an optional instrument are that it does not replace the national systems of property law, but exists next to them, and that – through parties' choice – we can get an indication to what extent there was actually a need for property law that functions in a cross-border situation, something which is difficult to measure empirically.

As outlined in this chapter, the optional instrument would first of all have to contain a set of operating rules, meaning rules governing the creation, transfer,

250 Reg. 650/2012/EU on jurisdiction, applicable law, recognition and enforcement of decisions and acceptance and enforcement of authentic instruments in matters of succession and on the creation of a European Certificate of Succession, [2012] *OJ* L 201/107. More about this Regulation in Chapter 4.

registration, destruction and third party effects of property rights. Secondly, the optional instrument should introduce European-autonomous property rights, namely a European Primary Right (which would be the most extensive property right available under European law), a European Security Right, and a European Use Right. These European property rights would function within the operating system set up for this purpose. Lastly, the optional instrument should contain a list of definitions of terms such as (im)movable, (in)tangible and possession, to ensure the consistent use of these key terms throughout the optional instrument and preferably in other secondary measures of EU law as well.

European property rights should be able to be created in relation to all types of objects, whether immovable, movable or tangible. As the results of the research conducted for Chapter 4 of this study showed, the *acquis* already accepts that all these types of objects can be the object of rights *in rem*. Registration should be a constitutive element for the creation and transfer of European property rights so as to avoid any confusion about their existence and to provide them with a ranking and guarantee their effect in insolvency. A European Registry should be set up for this purpose. Registration should be debtor-based, not asset-based, meaning European property rights should be registered against the debtor in case of a European Security Right and against the grantor in case of a European Use Right. A debtor-based registry makes it possible to register European property rights in relation to groups of assets and future assets, as well as individually specified assets. This is of particular importance for the European Security Right, which should be able to be created as a general security right and not merely as a specific security right, thereby following the trend of increasing popularity of general security rights. Only a debtor-based registration system can accommodate the registration of groups of transactions for groups of assets, which do not necessarily have to be identified. The European Security Right should be able to be created as a non-possessory right. Possessory security rights are ineffective in international business transactions because they deprive the debtor of the possibility to use the encumbered asset to generate funds to repay the secured loan. A non-possessory European Security Right would therefore be more appropriate for the internal market. The European Security Right should moreover be an accessory security right. Experiences from the ongoing financial crisis teach us that non-accessory security rights can cause severe problems for debtors. Thus, unless a sufficient substitute can be developed for the protection otherwise granted to a debtor by the accessory nature of a security right, it would be inadvisable to develop a non-accessory European Security Right.

The creation of a European Primary Right would have to occur by converting a national primary right into an EPR. This conversion would extinguish the national primary right, thereby avoiding the situation that two primary rights exist simultaneously in relation to the same object. As a consequence of the *nemo dat* rule, however, conversion could not lead to a loss of other, limited, property rights already burdening the original primary right. Once this conversion has been registered, the EPR can be transferred to another party. Finally, with regard to the European Use Right, clear time-limits should be indicated for the life of such a right.

The more extensive the content of a European Use Right, the more restricted the period of time should be for which it can be established.

This proposal may appear quite far-reaching at first. It may feel counter-intuitive to propose such an integrated approach by the EU in a field of law to which it has previously not paid much attention or at least not in a coherent and consistent way. But I believe that, for property law, this would be the way forward. Previous experiences, such as the 1973 Draft Directive and the proposal for a Euromortgage, show that projects which intend to leave too many aspects to national law will have limited or no success, perhaps not entirely for that reason but certainly in part for that reason. The property laws of the Member States are simply more divergent than other areas of law and their closed and mandatory nature is intended - particularly when it comes to land - to protect national interests. Therefore, if a European measure in the field of property law leaves too many aspects to be decided by national law, the effect will be that the national law, primarily due to the *lex rei sitae,* will draw these aspects entirely into its own closed system, thereby damaging the intended facilitating effects for cross-border trade of the European measure. The success of Article 9 UCC and the Cape Town Convention seems for a large part to result from their truly international - in the sense of cross-border - character: they provide for a self-standing international interest that is created in accordance with rules set up specifically for these international interests and they have their own registration system. Very little is left to be determined by national law. And yet, the existence of these international interests does not seem to have distorted national law. When it comes to Article 9 UCC, it might be said that it has competed with the national security rights of the states and won that competition but that is simply the outcome of a competition between legal systems. By introducing a European system of property law through an optional instrument as an alternative to national property law, national property law would not be distorted or replaced but it would be faced with a competitor, particularly in cross-border settings. Only practical experience can tell us what the outcome of such competition would be.

## ANNEX TO CHAPTER 4: TERMINOLOGY

| | |
|---|---|
| **Owner/ownership** | Artt. 75, 123(2), 345 TFEU<br><br>Reg. 678/2011/EU<br>Reg. 492/2011/EU<br>Reg. 474/2011/EU<br>Reg. 451/2011/EU<br>Reg. 442/2011/EU<br>Reg. 270/2011/EU<br>Reg. 258/2011/EU<br>Reg. 204/2011/EU<br>Reg. 1151/2010/EU<br>Reg. 1097/2010/EU<br>Reg. 920/2010/EU<br>Reg. 904/2010/EU<br>Reg. 856/2010/EU<br>Reg. 632/2010/EU<br>Reg. 356/2010/EU<br>Reg. 113/2010/EU<br>Reg. 1221/2009/EC<br>Reg. 1164/2009/EC<br>Reg. 1142/2009/EC<br>Reg. 1136/2009/EC<br>Reg. 846/2009/EC<br>Reg. 494/2009/EC<br>Reg. 392/2009/EC<br>Reg. 254/2009/EC<br>Reg. 80/2009/EC<br>Reg. 25/2009/EC<br>Reg. 1274/2008/EC<br>Reg. 1126/2008/EC<br>Reg. 1008/2008/EC<br>Reg. 800/2008/EC<br>Reg. 689/2008/EC<br>Reg. 683/2008/EC<br>Reg. 521/2008/EC |

| | |
|---|---|
| *(continued…)* | Reg. 504/2008/EC<br>Reg. 452/2008/EC<br>Reg. 177/2008/EC<br>Reg. 100/2008/EC<br>Reg. 1524/2007/EC<br>Reg. 1370/2007/EC<br>Reg. 617/2007/EC<br>Reg. 498/2007/EC<br>Reg. 1995/2006/EC<br>Reg. 1974/2006/EC<br>Reg. 1906/2006/EC<br>Reg. 1905/2006/EC<br>Reg. 1896/2006/EC<br>Reg. 1638/2006/EC<br>Reg. 1628/2006/EC<br>Reg. 1425/2006/EC<br>Reg. 1198/2006/EC<br>Reg. 1027/2006/EC<br>Reg. 865/2006/EC<br>Reg. 734/2006/EC<br>Reg. 62/2006/EC<br>Reg. 2110/2005/EC<br>Reg. 2096/2005/EC<br>Reg. 1915/2005/EC<br>Reg. 1073/2005/EC<br>Reg. 560/2005/EC<br>Reg. 184/2005/EC<br>Reg. 1/2005/EC<br>Reg. 1891/2004/EC<br>Reg. 1763/2004/EC<br>Reg. 1321/2004/EC<br>Reg. 802/2004/EC<br>Reg. 785/2004/EC<br>Reg. 782/2004/EC<br>Reg. 638/2004/EC<br>Reg. 550/2004/EC<br>Reg. 314/2004/EC<br>Reg. 139/2004/EC<br>Reg. 138/2004/EC<br>Reg. 2004/2003/EC<br>Reg. 1702/2003/EC<br>Reg. 1210/2003/EC<br>Reg. 304/2003/EC<br>Reg. 2321/2002/EC<br>Reg. 1400/2002/EC<br>Reg. 881/2002/EC<br>Reg. 876/2002/EC<br>Reg. 2580/2001/EC<br>Reg. 2130/2001/EC<br>Reg. 2909/2000/EC<br>Reg. 2887/2000/EC<br>Reg. 2488/2000/EC |

| | |
|---|---|
| *(continued…)* | Reg. 1917/2000/EC<br>Reg. 1685/2000/EC<br>Reg. 1673/2000/EC<br>Reg. 1346/2000/EC<br>Reg. 2533/1998/EC<br>Reg. 1687/98/EC<br>Reg. 2271/96/EC<br>Reg. 2223/96/EC<br>Reg. 2214/96/EC<br>Reg. 385/96/EC<br>Reg. 2897/95/EC<br>Reg. 3603/93/EC<br>Reg. 696/93/EEC<br>Reg. 2919/85/EEC<br>Reg. 2380/74/EEC<br><br>Dir. 2010/76/EU<br>Dir. 2010/31/EU<br>Dir. 2010/24/EU<br>Dir. 2010/13/EU<br>Dir. 2009/140/EC<br>Dir. 2009/136/EC<br>Dir. 2009/119/EC<br>Dir. 2009/111/EC<br>Dir. 2009/81/EC<br>Dir. 2009/73/EC<br>Dir. 2009/72/EC<br>Dir. 2009/65/EC<br>Dir. 2009/46/EC<br>Dir. 2009/44/EC<br>Dir. 2009/38/EC<br>Dir. 2009/18/EC<br>Dir. 2009/12/EC<br>Dir. 2008/71/EC<br>Dir. 2008/6/EC<br>Dir. 2007/65/EC<br>Dir. 2007/59/EC<br>Dir. 2007/2/EC<br>Dir. 2006/123/EC<br>Dir. 2006/114/EC<br>Dir. 2006/112/EC<br>Dir. 2006/70/EC<br>Dir. 2006/68/EC<br>Dir. 2006/48/EC<br>Dir. 2006/43/EC<br>Dir. 2005/68/EC<br>Dir. 2005/65/EC<br>Dir. 2005/60/EC<br>Dir. 2005/29/EC<br>Dir. 2005/28/EC<br>Dir. 2004/39/EC<br>Dir. 2004/17/EC |

| | |
|---|---|
| *(continued…)* | Dir. 2003/124/EC<br>Dir. 2003/98/EC<br>Dir. 2003/85/EC<br>Dir. 2003/63/EC<br>Dir. 2003/55/EC<br>Dir. 2003/54/EC<br>Dir. 2003/49/EC<br>Dir. 2002/96/EC<br>Dir. 2002/87/EC<br>Dir. 2002/83/EC<br>Dir. 2002/60/EC<br>Dir. 2002/48/EC<br>Dir. 2002/47/EC<br>Dir. 2002/21/EC<br>Dir. 2002/19/EC<br>Dir. 2001/108/EC<br>Dir. 2001/107/EC<br>Dir. 2001/97/EC<br>Dir. 2001/29/EC<br>Dir. 2000/52/EC<br>Dir. 1999/37/EC<br>Dir. 1999/5/EC<br>Dir. 98/26/EC<br>Dir. 95/26/EC<br>Dir. 94/22/EC<br>Dir. 93/37/EEC<br>Dir. 93/7/EEC<br>Dir. 92/35/EEC<br>Dir. 91/674/EEC<br>Dir. 90/167/EEC |
| **Proprietor** | Reg. 32/2010/EU<br>Reg. 24/2010/EU<br>Reg. 290/2009/EU<br>Reg. 250/2009/EC<br>Reg. 207/2009/EC<br>Reg. 25/2009/EC<br>Reg. 24/2009/EC<br>Reg. 1503/2006/EC<br>Reg. 1738/2005/EC<br>Reg. 1737/2005/EC<br>Reg. 138/2004/EC<br>Reg. 6/2002/EC<br>Reg. 1346/2000/EC<br>Reg. 1749/1999/EC<br>Reg. 1290/97/EC<br>Reg. 2223/96/EC<br>Reg. 2869/95/EC<br>Reg. 696/93/EEC<br>Reg. 1998/78/EEC<br>Reg. 7/63/EEC |

| | |
|---|---|
| *(continued…)* | Dir. 2008/95/EC<br>Dir. 2006/114/EC<br>Dir. 2006/111/EC<br>Dir. 2005/36/EC<br>Dir. 2004/39/EC<br>Dir. 2002/21/EC<br>Dir. 98/44/EC<br>Dir. 97/55/EC<br>Dir. 86/635/EEC<br>Dir. 74/556/EEC |
| **Possessor/possession** | Reg. 961/2010/EU<br>Reg. 1186/2009/EC<br>Reg. 1221/2008/EC<br>Reg. 669/2008/EC<br>Reg. 194/2008/EC<br>Reg. 423/2007/EC<br>Reg. 1013/2006/EC<br>Reg. 108/2006/EC<br>Reg. 1210/2003/EC<br>Reg. 881/2002/EC<br>Reg. 2488/2000/EC<br>Reg. 1346/2000/EC<br>Reg. 1081/2000/EC<br>Reg. 338/97/EC<br>Reg. 752/93/EEC<br><br>Dir. 2011/83/EU<br>Dir. 2009/132/EC<br>Dir. 2008/8/EC<br>Dir. 2007/64/EC<br>Dir. 2006/112/EC<br>Dir. 2006/21/EC<br>Dir. 2006/12/EC<br>Dir. 2005/60/EC<br>Dir. 2004/28/EC<br>Dir. 2001/24/EC<br>Dir. 2001/17/EC<br>Dir. 1999/31/EC<br>Dir. 93/7/EEC<br>Dir. 72/159/EEC |
| **In rem/in re** | Reg. 874/2009/EC<br>Reg. 207/2009/EC<br>Reg. 593/2008/EC<br>Reg. 6/2002/EC<br>Reg. 44/2001/EC<br>Reg. 1346/2000/EC<br><br>Dir. 2009/138/EC<br>Dir. 2006/112/EC<br>Dir. 2001/24/EC |
| **Real right/personal right** | Reg. 1722/2005/EC |

| | |
|---|---|
| **Proprietary** | Reg. 184/2005/EC<br>Reg. 2580/2001/EC<br>Reg. 385/96/EC<br><br>Dir. 2006/49/EC<br>Dir. 2002/47/EC<br>Dir. 2001/24/EC<br>Dir. 98/26/EC |
| **Numerus clausus** | *No results.* |
| **Lex rei sitae** | (Reg. 650/2012/EU on international successions; PE-CONS 14/12)<br><br>Dir. 2002/47/EC<br>Dir. 2001/24/EC |
| **Transfer** | Reg. 73/2009/EC<br>Reg. 555/2008/EC<br>Reg. 376/2008/EC<br>Reg. 614/2007/EC<br>Reg. 1974/2006/EC<br>Reg. 795/2004/EC<br>Reg. 1782/2003/EC<br>Reg. 1435/2003/EC<br>Reg. 1400/2002/EC<br>Reg. 1381/2002/EC<br>Reg. 2529/2001/EC<br>Reg. 1917/2000/EC<br>Reg. 1673/2000/EC<br>Reg. 385/96/EC<br><br>Dir. 2009/65/EC<br>Dir. 2006/112/EC<br>Dir. 2006/48/EC<br>Dir. 2005/68/EC<br>Dir. 2002/83/EC<br>Dir. 2001/34/EC<br>Dir. 2001/23/EC<br>Dir. 96/9/EC<br>Dir. 91/674/EEC<br>Dir. 86/635/EEC<br>Dir. 78/660/EEC |
| **Convey* WITH Land** | Artt. 192 and 50(2)(e) TFEU<br><br>Reg. 1126/2008/EC<br>Reg. 1910/2005/EC<br><br>Dir. 72/160/EC |
| **Assign* WITH Claim** | Reg. 825/2010/EU<br>Reg. 612/2009/EC<br>Reg. 495/2009/EC<br>Reg. 207/2009/EC |

| | |
|---|---|
| *(continued…)* | Reg. 593/2008/EC<br>Reg. 1042/2007/EC<br>Reg. 1908/2006/EC<br>Reg. 1906/2006/EC<br>Reg. 1435/2003/EC<br>Reg. 6/2002/EC<br>Reg. 1346/2000/EC<br>Reg. 2647/98/EC<br>Reg. 2100/94/EC<br>Reg. 17/62/EEC<br><br>Dir. 2009/144/EC<br>Dir. 2009/138/EC<br>Dir. 2008/48/EC<br>Dir. 2006/112/EC<br>Dir. 2001/24/EC<br>Dir. 98/29/EC<br>Dir. 86/635/EC |
| **Cession** | Dir. 2006/112/EC<br>Dir. 2006/69/EC |
| **Pledg*** | Reg. 254/2009/EC<br>Reg. 1126/2008/EC<br>Reg. 593/2008/EC<br>Reg. 108/2006/EC<br>Reg. 2454/93/EEC<br><br>Dir. 2009/138/EC<br>Dir. 2009/83/EC<br>Dir. 2009/44/EC<br>Dir. 2008/48/EC<br>Dir. 2006/49/EC<br>Dir. 2006/48/EC<br>Dir. 2006/46/EC<br>Dir. 2005/68/EC<br>Dir. 2004/109/EC<br>Dir. 2002/47/EC<br>Dir. 98/26/EC<br>Dir. 88/361/EEC<br>Dir. 86/635/EEC |
| **Mortgag*** | Reg. 667/2010/EU<br>Reg. 1201/2009/EC<br>Reg. 1071/2009/EC<br>Reg. 250/2009/EC<br>Reg. 4/2009/EC<br>Reg. 1126/2008/EC<br>Reg. 215/2007/EC<br>Reg. 881/2002/EC<br>Reg. 876/2002/EC<br>Reg. 1346/2000/EC<br>Reg. 2223/96/EC<br>Reg. 2454/93/EEC<br>Reg. 2220/85/EEC |

| | |
|---|---|
| *(continued…)* | Dir. 2009/138/EC<br>Dir. 2008/122/EC<br>Dir. 2008/48/EC<br>Dir. 2008/7/EC<br>Dir. 2006/48/EC<br>Dir. 2003/49/EC<br>Dir. 2003/48/EC<br>Dir. 2002/83/EC<br>Dir. 2002/65/EC<br>Dir. 2001/24/EC<br>Dir. 88/361/EEC |
| **Hypothec*** | *No results.* |
| **Lien** EXCEPT **Client** | Reg. 965/2011/EU<br>Reg. 442/2011/EU<br>Reg. 1346/2000/EU<br><br>Dir. 2010/76/EU<br>Dir. 2009/138/EC<br>Dir. 2008/122/EC<br>Dir. 2001/24/EC<br>Dir. 98/26/EC |
| **Charge/floating charge/fixed charge** | Dir. 95/18/EC |
| **Estate** | Art. 64(1) and (2) TFEU<br><br>Reg. 1346/2000/EC |
| **Tenure** | Reg. 995/2010/EU<br>Reg. 1201/2009/EC<br>Reg. 1200/2009/EC<br>Reg. 543/2009/EC<br>Reg. 1166/2008/EC<br>Reg. 868/2008/EC<br>Reg. 1444/2002/EC<br>Reg. 1837/2001/EC |
| **Freehold*** | Reg. 2909/2000/EC |
| **Fee simple** | *No results.* |
| **Lease*** | Reg. 243/2010/EU<br>Reg. 1120/2009/EC<br>Reg. 73/2009/EC<br>Reg. 1974/2006/EC<br>Reg. 1628/2006/EC<br>Reg. 1248/2006/EC<br>Reg. 318/2006/EC<br>Reg. 1910/2005/EC<br>Reg. 795/2004/EC<br>Reg. 1/2004/EC<br>Reg. 1606/2002/EC<br>Reg. 2550/2001/EC<br>Reg. 2342/1999/EC<br>Reg. 1256/1999/EC<br>Reg. 385/96/EC |

| | |
|---|---|
| *(continued…)* | Reg. 1768/95/EC<br>Reg. 1066/95/EC<br>Reg. 2407/92/EEC<br><br>Dir. 2009/140/EC<br>Dir. 2009/111/EC<br>Dir. 2008/122/EC<br>Dir. 2006/48/EC<br>Dir. 2002/96/EC<br>Dir. 98/20/EC<br>Dir. 93/38/EEC<br>Dir. 72/160/EEC<br>Dir. 67/531/EEC<br>Dir. 63/262/EEC |
| **Tenancy/tenancies** | Reg. 481/2010/EU<br>Reg. 1200/2009/EC<br>Reg. 868/2008/EC<br>Reg. 593/2008/EC<br>Reg. 1234/2007/EC<br>Reg. 861/2007/EC<br>Reg. 1722/2005/EC<br>Reg. 138/2004/EC<br>Reg. 1788/2003/EC<br>Reg. 1444/2002/EC<br>Reg. 1837/2001/EC<br>Reg. 44/2001/EC |
| **Title to WITH Interest in/Legal title** | Reg. 250/2009/EC<br>Reg. 1126/2008/EC<br>Reg. 1725/2003/EC<br>Reg. 1210/2003/EC<br>Reg. 310/2002/EC<br>Reg. 2580/2001/EC<br>Reg. 1826/1999/EC<br>Reg. 2223/96/EC<br><br>Dir. 2011/7/EU<br>Dir. 2008/122/EC<br>Dir. 2006/112/EC<br>Dir. 2006/49/EC<br>Dir. 2006/48/EC<br>Dir. 2002/47/EC<br>Dir. 2000/35/EC<br>Dir. 98/26/EC<br>Dir. 91/674/EEC<br>Dir. 86/635/EEC |
| **Retention of title/reservation of ownership** | Reg. 1346/2000/EC<br><br>Dir. 2009/138/EC<br>Dir. 2006/112/EC<br>Dir. 2006/69/EC<br>Dir. 2001/24/EC |

| | |
|---|---|
| *(continued...)* | Dir. 2001/17/EC<br>Dir. 2001/7/EU |
| **Servitude** | *No results.* |
| **Usufruct*** | Reg. 1200/2009/EC<br>Reg. 1248/2006/EC<br>Reg. 1444/2002/EC<br><br>Dir. 88/361/EEC |
| **Easement** | Dir. 88/361/EEC |
| **Restrictive covenant** | *No results.* |
| **Emphyteusis** | Dir. 72/160/EEC |
| **Superficies** | *No results.* |
| **Trust*** | Reg. 1259/2010/EU<br>Reg. 1200/2009/EC<br>Reg. 25/2009/EC<br>Reg. 1126/2008/EC<br>Reg. 1033/2008/EC<br>Reg. 593/2008/EC<br>Reg. 864/2007/EC<br>Reg. 680/2007/EC<br>Reg. 1027/2006/EC<br>Reg. 874/2004/EC<br>Reg. 2201/2003/EC<br>Reg. 44/2001/EC<br>Reg. 1444/2000/EC<br><br>Dir. 2011/16/EU<br>Dir. 2010/24/EU<br>Dir. 2009/138/EC<br>Dir. 2009/65/EC<br>Dir. 2007/16/EC<br>Dir. 2006/48/EC<br>Dir. 2005/60/EC<br>Dir. 2003/87/EC<br>Dir. 2003/41/EC<br>Dir. 2002/47/EC<br>Dir. 88/361/EC |
| **Beneficiary WITH Trust** | Reg. 25/2009/EC<br>Reg. 1027/2006/EC<br>Reg. 44/2001/EC<br><br>Dir. 2005/60/EC |
| **Movable*** | Art. 335 TFEU<br><br>Reg. 667/2010/EU<br>Reg. 439/2010/EU<br>Reg. 1211/2009/EC<br>Reg. 923/2009/EC<br>Reg. 723/2009/EC<br>Reg. 713/2009/EC |

| | |
|---|---|
| *(continued...)* | Reg. 471/2009/EC<br>Reg. 207/2009/EC<br>Reg. 1339/2008/EC<br>Reg. 521/2008/EC<br>Reg. 294/2008/EC<br>Reg. 215/2008/EC<br>Reg. 638/2004/EC<br>Reg. 138/2004/EC<br>Reg. 2004/2003/EC<br>Reg. 1798/2003/EC<br>Reg. 881/2002/EC<br>Reg. 44/2001/EC<br>Reg. 2909/2000/EC<br>Reg. 2454/93/EEC<br>Reg. 3330/91/EEC<br><br>Dir. 2009/138/EC<br>Dir. 2009/65/EC<br>Dir. 2008/122/EC<br>Dir. 2008/8/EC<br>Dir. 2006/112/EC<br>Dir. 2005/60/EC<br>Dir. 2002/83/EC<br>Dir. 2001/24/EC<br>Dir. 1999/44/EC<br>Dir. 1999/34/EC<br>Dir. 85/374/EEC |
| **Tangible* EXCEPT** | |
| **Tangible evidence/contribution/criteria** | Reg. 667/2010/EU<br>Reg. 356/2010/EU<br>Reg. 1284/2009/EC<br>Reg. 495/2009/EC<br>Reg. 250/2009/EC<br>Reg. 194/2009/EC<br>Reg. 1147/2008/EC<br>Reg. 800/2008/EC<br>Reg. 683/2008/EC<br>Reg. 219/2007/EC<br>Reg. 1942/2006/EC<br>Reg. 881/2002/EC<br>Reg. 1346/2000/EC<br>Reg. 218/92/EEC<br><br>Dir. 2009/138/EC<br>Dir. 2008/57/EC<br>Dir. 2008/8/EC<br>Dir. 2006/112/EC<br>Dir. 2005/60/EC<br>Dir. 2002/65/EC<br>Dir. 2001/24/EC<br>Dir. 1999/44/EC<br>Dir. 91/674/EEC |

| | |
|---|---|
| *(continued…)* | Dir. 91/308/EEC<br>Dir. 84/386/EEC<br>Dir. 78/660/EEC |
| **Corporeal*** | Dir. 2005/60/EC<br>Dir. 91/308/EEC |

## SAMENVATTING

Goederenrecht wordt traditioneel gezien als een zeer nationaal-georiënteerd rechtsgebied dat weinig tot geen invloed ondervindt van Europees recht. Over het algemeen wordt het begrip 'Europees goederenrecht' begrepen als nationaal goederenrecht van Europese landen in rechtsvergelijkend perspectief. Goederenrecht juristen gaan er vaak niet van uit dat er zoiets bestaat als EU goederenrecht, zijnde goederenrecht dat is gecreëerd door de Europese wetgever en dat voortvloeit uit Europese wetgeving en rechtspraak van het Hof van Justitie van de Europese Unie (HvJEU). Er hebben zich echter gedurende de laatste vijftien jaar ontwikkelingen voorgedaan die aantonen dat het Europese recht ook het nationale goederenrecht begint te raken en dat het wellicht tijd is voor de Europese wetgever om zich bewuster met goederenrecht bezig te gaan houden. Zo is er het snel groeiende corpus aan EU contractenrecht, dat zich in belangrijke mate, maar niet uitsluitend, richt op consumentencontracten. Een belangrijk voorbeeld is het Voorstel voor een Verordening van het Europees Parlement en de Raad betreffende een gemeenschappelijk Europees kooprecht.[1] Er wordt gepoogd om in zulke maatregelen van Europees privaatrecht een strikte scheiding aan te houden tussen contractenrecht en goederenrecht. Dit is echter een illusie.

Om te beginnen trekken de 27 Lidstaten niet allemaal op dezelfde manier de grens: wat voor de één contractenrecht is, is voor de ander goederenrecht. Een Europese richtlijn die als contractenrecht bedoeld is, kan desondanks onderdeel van nationaal goederenrecht worden op het moment dat hij door de Lidstaten wordt geïmplementeerd. Daarnaast is het Europese recht traditioneel gezien niet onderverdeeld in dezelfde categorieën als nationaal recht. Europees recht maakt in beginsel geen onderscheid tussen privaat- en publiekrecht, tussen administratief recht en strafrecht, etc. Europees recht kan alleen tot stand komen als er een rechtsbasis voor is in de Verdragen, en die rechtsbases richten zich op specifieke beleidsvelden, zoals mededingingsrecht, interne markt, en consumentenbescherming. Met

1 COM(2001) 635 definitief.

andere woorden: tenzij Europese regelgeving met zoveel woorden aangeeft dat het contractenrecht of goederenrecht (etc.) betreft, kan in principe elke richtlijn of verordening goederenrecht bevatten. Het is dus belangrijk om er voor te waken, dat in de groeiende ontwikkeling van het EU contractenrecht het goederenrecht niet achterblijft, en dat is op dit moment wel het geval.

Daarnaast wordt het steeds vaker duidelijk dat het nationale goederenrecht onderhevig is aan de invloed van de regels van de interne markt, meer in het bijzonder het vrij verkeer van goederen, diensten, personen en kapitaal. Goederenrecht is dwingend recht, en de nationale stelsels van goederenrecht kennen over het algemeen een *numerus clausus* - een beperkte lijst - van goederenrechtelijke rechten. Het is dus voor partijen niet mogelijk om van het goederenrecht af te wijken, of om andere rechten te creëren dan is toegestaan binnen de *numerus clausus*. Daarnaast maakt de internationaal privaatrechtelijke regel *lex rei sitae* het voor partijen onmogelijk om het recht van een ander land te kiezen als toepasselijk recht op hun goederenrechtelijke rechtsverhouding. Ingevolge de *lex rei sitae* wordt een dergelijke verhouding altijd beheerst door het recht van de plaats waar het goed gelegen is. Hierdoor kan het gebeuren, dat goederenrechtelijke rechten die rusten op een object dat zich over een landsgrens heen verplaatst, verloren gaan indien de *numerus clausus* van de nieuwe *situs* geen soortgelijk recht kent en het buitenlandse recht niet erkend wordt. In dit proefschrift worden een aantal uitspraken van het HvJEU geanalyseerd waaruit blijkt, dat dergelijke regelgeving in strijd kan zijn met de vier vrijheden van de interne markt en dus buiten toepassing verklaard dient te worden.

Het bovenstaande schetst de redenen waarom er meer onderzoek nodig is naar goederenrecht op EU-niveau. Het is vervolgens van belang om een overzicht te krijgen van het reeds bestaande EU-goederenrecht, alvorens een voorstel gedaan kan worden over de verdere ontwikkeling van dit rechtsgebied. Dit proefschrift bevat een dergelijk overzicht. Het aantal richtlijnen en verordeningen dat regels van goederenrecht bevat, of dat het nationaal goederenrecht raakt, is niet heel groot. Ongeveer een vijftiental maatregelen betreft onderwerpen met goederenrechtelijke aspecten zoals grensoverschrijdende insolventie, handel in emissierechten, en beperking van eigendom van grond dat tot natuurgebied is verklaard. Echter, een zoektocht naar maatregelen die goederenrechtelijke terminologie bevatten - zonder deze terminologie nader te verklaren - leverde een lijst van honderden, zo niet duizenden, richtlijnen en verordeningen op die termen bevatten zoals eigendom, bezit, overdracht, en erfpacht. Deze maatregelen betreffen zeer uiteenlopende onderwerpen, van landbouw tot terrorismebestrijding. Ze houden zich geen van alle echt concreet en bewust bezig met goederenrecht, en het gebruik van goederenrechtelijke terminologie is inconsequent. Er kan worden vastgesteld dat er weliswaar al EU goederenrecht bestaat, maar dat het nog zeer gefragmenteerd is en vaak een nevenproduct van een maatregel die hoofdzakelijk op een ander onderwerp is gericht. Het meest consequent is het EU goederenrecht nog als het gaat om het type objecten waarop een goederenrechtelijk recht kan rusten: zolang een object een economische waarde vertegenwoordigd kan er een goederenrechtelijk recht (inclusief eigendom) op rusten, ook wanneer het een niet-stoffelijk object betreft.

Gezien de onoverzichtelijke en ongestructureerde staat waarin het EU goederenrecht momenteel verkeert, presenteren de laatste twee hoofdstukken van dit proefschrift een raamwerk voor een meer consistente en coherente ontwikkeling van dit rechtsgebied. Daarbij is allereerst gekeken naar de vorm: kan het EU goederenrecht het best neergelegd worden in een richtlijn of een verordening, als dwingend recht of als optioneel instrument, of slechts als inter-institutioneel akkoord? Een optioneel instrument, neergelegd in een verordening, lijkt hier de beste keuze te zijn. Een optioneel instrument laat het nationale goederenrecht onaangeroerd en biedt enkel een Europees alternatief voor partijen, naast het bestaande nationale recht. Zo kan men ook zien in hoeverre er daadwerkelijk behoefte bestaat aan EU goederenrecht en of het optionele instrument voldoende beantwoordt aan de behoefte van partijen. Een optioneel instrument zou met name een belangrijke rol kunnen vervullen in grensoverschrijdende situaties, maar het zou ook beschikbaar moeten zijn voor partijen in zuiver interne situaties om te voorkomen dat bijvoorbeeld een bedrijf zich alsnog aan minimaal twee rechtsstelsels moet aanpassen: het Europese optionele stelsel en het eigen nationale recht. Het optionele instrument zou verder in een verordening moeten worden neergelegd en niet in een richtlijn, om ervoor te zorgen dat private partijen zich er rechtstreeks op kunnen beroepen en om te voorkomen dat er implementatieverschillen ontstaan tussen de Lidstaten.

Het laatste hoofdstuk van dit proefschrift richt zich op de vraag wat de inhoud van zo'n optioneel instrument zou moeten zijn. Als uitgangspunt is daarvoor een model genomen wat ontwikkeld is in het eerste hoofdstuk en wat op abstracte wijze weergeeft wat de kenmerken - of 'bouwblokken' - van het goederenrecht zijn. Kortweg toont dit model dat het goederenrecht bestaat uit een kern, de rechten, en een *operating system*, zijnde een stelsel van regels dat aangeeft hoe de rechten verworven en overgedragen kunnen worden, hoe zij tenietgaan, en wat hun derdenwerking is.[2] EU goederenrecht zou dit model moeten volgen. Indien er Europese goederenrechtelijke rechten zouden komen, die in de gehele EU gebruikt kunnen worden, zou veel van de erkenningsproblematiek waar partijen nu tegen aanlopen, opgelost worden. Deze Europese rechten zouden dan wel ook in een Europees *operating system* moeten kunnen functioneren, om ervoor te zorgen dat ze overal op dezelfde wijze gecreëerd en overgedragen kunnen worden, zonder dat partijen alsnog gedwongen zijn om hiervoor het nationale recht - waarmee ze wellicht niet bekend zijn - te gebruiken. Er zouden dus Europese regels van vestiging, overdracht, registratie etc. moeten komen.

Wat betreft de Europese goederenrechtelijke rechten: deze kunnen functioneel worden vormgegeven. Rechtsvergelijkend onderzoek toont aan dat goederenrechtelijke rechten ofwel tot gebruik, ofwel tot zekerheid strekken. Deze functies zijn verenigd in het recht van eigendom. Op Europees niveau zou het dus volstaan om

2 Eén van de onderscheidende kenmerken van goederenrechtelijke rechten is dat ze, in tegenstelling tot verbintenisrechtelijke rechten, derdenwerking hebben.

een eigendomsrecht, een gebruiksrecht en een zekerheidsrecht aan te bieden waar partijen gebruik van kunnen maken. Om te voorkomen dat men zich aan reeds eerder gevestigde, nationale beperkte rechten zou kunnen onttrekken door het vestigen van een Europees eigendomsrecht, zou het Europees eigendomsrecht alleen gevestigd moeten kunnen worden door omzetting van een reeds bestaand nationaal eigendomsrecht. Ingevolge de *nemo dat* regel, die bepaalt dat er niet meer rechten overgedragen kunnen worden dan de rechthebbende zelf bezit, zou de omzetting van het nationale eigendomsrecht naar het Europese eigendomsrecht met zich meebrengen dat het Europese eigendomsrecht met dezelfde beperkte rechten bezwaard zou zijn als het nationale eigendomsrecht waaruit het voortkomt.

Dit voorstel voor de verdere ontwikkeling van EU goederenrecht behandelt de meest essentiële aspecten, maar het kan geen allesomvattend systeem van goederenrecht bieden. Het is daarom nodig om in het optioneel instrument een regel van internationaal privaatrecht op te nemen die aangeeft welk recht van toepassing is op die gevallen die niet in het optioneel instrument geregeld zijn. Dit zou de *lex rei sitae* kunnen zijn, maar zoals eerder gezegd kan de *lex rei sitae* - al dan niet in samenhang met nationaal goederenrecht - tot belemmeringen in de interne markt leiden. Het is daarom de moeite waard om alternatieven voor de *lex rei sitae* te onderzoeken, zoals de *lex registrationis* of de *lex destinationis*,[3] om het recht aan te wijzen dat van toepassing is op zaken die niet door het optioneel instrument geregeld zijn. Deze alternatieven komen kort aan de orde in dit proefschrift en zullen onderwerp zijn van toekomstig onderzoek van de auteur.

3 Respectievelijk het recht van de plaats van registratie van een object en het recht van het land van bestemming van een object.

# BIBLIOGRAPHY

**Akkermans 2006**
Akkermans, B., 'The New Dutch Civil Code: the Borderline between Property and Contract', in: J.H.M. van Erp & B. Akkermans (eds.), *Towards a Unified System of Land Burdens?*, Antwerp/Oxford: Intersentia, 2006, p. 179-183.

**Akkermans 2008**
Akkermans, B., *The Principle of Numerus Clausus in European Property Law* (Ius Commune Europaeum; 75), Antwerp/Oxford/Portland: Intersentia, 2008.

**Akkermans 2010a**
Akkermans, B., *Common Frame of Reference, The EU Consumer Acquis and European Property Law*, M-EPLI working paper, Maastricht, 18 June 2010.

**Akkermans 2010b**
Akkermans, B., 'Hoorzitting van de Europese Commissie over collectieve verhaalsmogelijkheden (Collective Redress) in de Europese Unie, 29 mei 2009', *Tijdschrift voor de Procespraktijk*, 2010, p. 11-14.

**Akkermans 2011**
Akkermans, B., *The European Union Development of European Property Law*, M-EPLI Working Paper, 30; Maastricht, 2011.

**Akkermans 2012a**
Akkermans, B., 'Property Law and the Internal Market', in: J.H.M. van Erp, A.F. Salomons & B. Akkermans (eds.), *The Future of European Property Law*, Munich: Sellier European Law Publishers, 2012, p. 201-248.

**Akkermans 2012b**
Akkermans, B., 'The Role of the (D)CFR in the Making of European Property Law', in: V. Sagaert, E. Terryn & M. Storme (eds.), *The Draft Common Frame of Reference (DCFR): a National and Comparative Perspective,* (Ius Commune Europaeum, 99), Antwerp/Oxford/Portland: Intersentia, 2012, p. 265-288.

**Akkermans & Ramaekers 2010**
Akkermans, B. & Ramaekers, E., 'Article 345 TFEU (ex Article 295 EC), Its Meanings and Interpretations', *European Law Journal,* 2010 (16/3), p. 292-314.

**Akkermans & Ramaekers 2012**
Akkermans, B. & Ramaekers, E., 'Lex Rei Sitae in Perspective: National Developments of a Common Rule?', in: B. Akkermans & E. Ramaekers (eds.), Property Law Perspectives (Ius Commune Europaeum; 106), Antwerp/Oxford/Portland: Intersentia, 2012, p. 123-151.

**Akkermans & Ramaekers 2013**
Akkermans, B. & Ramaekers, E., 'Free Movement of Goods and Property Law', *European Law Journal,* 2013 (19/2), p. 237-266.

**Asser & Hartkamp 2011**
Asser, C. & Hartkamp, A., *Handleiding tot de beoefening van het Nederlands Burgerlijk Recht. 3: Vermogensrecht algemeen, I – Europees recht en Nederlands vermogensrecht* (2nd edition), Deventer: Kluwer, 2011.

**Avout 2006**
Avout, L. d', *Sur les solutions du conflit de lois en droit des biens,* Paris: Economica, 2006.

**Von Bar 2000**
Bar, C. von, *Sachenrecht in Europa: systematische Einführungen und Gesetzestexte,* 4 vols., Osnabrück: Universitätsverlag Rasch, 2000.

**Von Bar 2008**
Bar, C. von, 'A Common Frame of Reference for European Private Law – Academic Efforts and Political Realities', *Electronic Journal of Comparative Law,* 2008 (12/1), p. 1-10.

**Von Bar & Drobnig 2002**
Bar, C. von & Drobnig, U., *Study on Property Law and Non-contractual Liability Law as they relate to Contract Law,* Brussels: European Commission, 2002.

**Barnard 2001**
Barnard, C., 'Fitting the Remaining Pieces into the Goods and Persons Jigsaw?', *European Law Review,* 2001 (26), p. 35-59.

**Barnard 2010**
Barnard, C., *The Substantive Law of the EU - The Four Freedoms* (third edition) Oxford: Oxford University Press, 2010.

**Barnard 2012**
Barnard, C., 'What the Keck? Balancing the Needs of the Single Market with State Regulatory Autonomy in the EU (and the US)', *European Journal of Consumer Law*, 2012 (2), p. 201-216.

**Bartels 1995**
Bartels, S., 'Europees privaatrecht: over de bevoegdheidsverdeling tussen Unie en Lid-Staat met betrekking tot het eigendomsrecht', *Ars Aequi*, 1995 (44/4), p. 244-251.

**Basedow 1995**
Basedow, J., 'Der kollisionsrechtliche Gehalt der Produktfreiheiten im europäischen Binnenmarkt: favor offerentis', *Rabels Zeitschrift fuer Ausländisches und Internationales Privatrecht*, 1995 (59), p. 1-54.

**Basedow *et al.* 2011**
Basedow, J., *et al.*, *Policy Options for Progress Towards a European Contract Law - Comments on the issues raised in the Green Paper from the Commission of 1 July 2010, COM(2010) 348 final*, Max Planck Private Law Research Paper, 11, Hamburg: Max Planck Institute for Comparative and International Private Law, 2011.

**Basedow & Dutta 2010**
Basedow, J. & Dutta, A., 'Comments on the European Commission's Proposal for a Regulation of the European Parliament and of the Council on Jurisdiction, Applicable Law, Recognition and Enforcement of Decisions and Authentic Instruments in Matters of Succession and the Creation of a European Certificate of Succession', *Rabels Zeitschrift fuer Auslaendisches und Internationales Privatrecht*, 2010 (74/3), p. 522-720.

**Baur, Baur & Stürner 2009**
Baur, F., Baur, J.F. & Stürner, R., *Sachenrecht* (18. neubearb. Aufl.), München: Beck, 2009.

**Bitsch 2005**
Bitsch, M.-T., *Histoire de la construction européenne de 1945 à nos jours* (4th edition), Questions à l'histoire; Brussels: Complexe, 2005.

**Böhm 1962**
Böhm, P., 'Ownership of Nuclear Materials in Euratom', *American Journal of Comparative Law*, 1962 (11), p. 167-183.

**Bouckaert 2006**
Bouckaert, B., 'Divergences of the Law on Securities. A Law and Economics Approach', in: U. Drobnig, H.J. Snijders & E.-J. Zippro (eds.), *Divergences of Property Law, an Obstacle to the Internal Market?*, München: Sellier. European Law Publishers, 2006, p.175-194.

**Bright 2000**
Bright, S., 'Winning the Battle against Unfair Contract Terms', *Legal Studies*, 2000 (20/3), p. 331-352.

**Bright & Bright 1995**
Bright, S. & Bright, C., 'Unfair Terms in Land Contracts: Copy out or Cop out?', *Law Quarterly Review*, 1995 (111), p. 655-673.

**Bright & Bright 1998**
Bright, C. & Bright, S., 'Europe, The Nation State, and Land', in: S. Bright & J. Dewar (eds.), *Land Law: Themes and Perspectives*, Oxford: Oxford University Press, 1998, p. 356-376.

**Burdeau 1984**
Burdeau, G., *Die französischen Verstaatlichungen* (Abhandlungen aus dem gesamten Bürgerlichen Recht, Handelsrecht und Wirtschaftsrecht, 56); Heidelberg: Verlagsgesellschaft Recht u. Wirtschaft, 1984.

**Burghardt 1969**
Burghardt, G., *Die Eigentumsordnungen in den Mitgliedstaaten und der EWG-Vertrag – Zur Auslegung von Art. 222 EWGV* (Abhandlungen aus dem Seminar für Öffentliches Recht, 57), Universität Hamburg: Verlag Ludwig Appel & Sohn, 1969.

**Van Calster 1997**
Calster, G. van, 'The EU's Tower of Babel – The Interpretation by the European Court of Justice of Equally Authentic Texts Drafted in more than one Official Language', *Yearbook of European Law*, 1997 (17), p.363-393.

**Caramelo Gomes 2008**
Caramelo Gomes, J.L., 'Unification in the Field of Property Law from the Perspective of European Law', in: W. Faber & B. Lurger (eds.), *Rules for the transfer of Movables, a candidate for European Harmonisation or National Reform?*, Munich: Sellier European Law Publishers, 2008, p.239-248.

**Carruthers 2005**
Carruthers, J.M., *The Transfer of Property in the Conflict of Laws*, Oxford: Oxford University Press, 2005.

**Caruso 2004**
Caruso, D., 'Private Law and Public Stakes in European Integration: the Case of Property', *European Law Journal*, 2004 (10/6), p. 751-765.

**Claes 2006**
Claes, M., *The National Courts' Mandate in the European Constitution*, Oxford: Hart, 2006.

**Claessens 2008**
Claessens, S.J.F.J., *Free Movement of Lawyers in the European Union*, Nijmegen: Wolf Legal Publishers, 2008.

**Clarke & Kohler 2005**
Clarke, A. & Kohler, P., *Property Law – Commentary and Materials* (Law in Context), Cambridge: Cambridge University Press, 2005.

**Clarkson 2011**
Clarkson, C.M.V. & Hill, J., *The Conflict of Laws* (4th edition); Oxford: Oxford University Press, 2011.

**Colliard 1965**
Colliard, C.-A., 'L'entreprise publique et l'évolution du Marché commun', *Revue Trimestrielle de Droit Europeen*, 1965 (1), 1-10.

**Collins et al. 2006**
Collins, Sir L. *et al.* (eds.), Dicey, *Morris and Collins on The Conflict of Laws* (14th edition), London: Sweet & Maxwell, 2006.

**Constantinesco 2003**
Constantinesco, V., 'Brève note sur l'utilisation de la méthode comparative en droit européen', in: F.R. v.d. Mensbrugghe (ed.), *L'utilisation de la méthode comparative en droit européen* 25, Namur: Presses Universitaires de Namur, 2003, p. 169-183.

**Craig & De Búrca 2011**
Craig, P. & De Búrca, G., *EU Law: Text, Cases and Materials* (5th edition), Oxford: Oxford University Press, 2011.

**Curtin 1995**
Curtin, D., 'The Shaping of a European Constitution and the 1996 IGC', *Aussenwirtschaft*, 1995 (50), p. 237-251.

**Dannemann, Ferreri & Graziadei 2010**
Dannemann, G., Ferreri, S. & Graziadei, M., 'Language and Terminology', in: C. Twigg-Flesner (ed.), *The Cambridge Companion to European Union Private Law*, Cambridge: Cambridge University Press, 2010, p. 70-84.

**Devroe 1997**
Devroe, W., 'Privatizations and Community Law: Neutrality versus Policy', *Common Market Law Review*, 1997 (34), p. 267-306.

**Dickinson 2009**
Dickinson, A., *Response to the Green Paper on the Review of Council Regulation (EC) No 44/2001 on Jurisdiction and the Recognition and Enforcement of Judgments in Civil and Commercial Matters*, 30 June 2009, available at: <http://ec.euro pa.eu/justice/news/consulting_public/0002/contributions/civil_society_ngo_academics_others/mr_andrew_dickinson_en.pdf>.

**Dijck & Heuvel 2004**
Dijck, G. van & Heuvel, N.W.M. van de, 'Discussiëren over goederenrecht', *Tijdschrift voor Insolventierecht*, 2004 (4), p. 191-200.

**Dirix 2006**
Dirix, E., 'Effect of Security Rights vis-à-vis Third Persons', in: U. Drobnig, H.J. Snijders & E.-J. Zippro (eds.), *Divergences of Property Law, an Obstacle to the Internal Market?*, München: Sellier. European Law Publishers, 2006, p. 69-94.

**Doralt 2011**
Doralt, W., *The Optional European Contract Law and why Success or Failure may Depend on Scope Rather than Susbtance*, Max Planck Private Law Research Paper, 11/9, Hamburg: Max Planck Institute for Comparative and International Private Law, 2011.

**Drasch 1998**
Drasch, W., 'Die Rechtsgrundlagen des europäischen Einheitsrechts im Bereich des gewerblichen Eigentums (Artt.100a, 235, 36 und 222 EGV)', *Zeitschrift für Europäisches Privatrecht*, 1998 (6/1), p. 118-139.

**Drobnig 1997**
Drobnig, U., 'Scope and General Rules of a European Civil Code', *European Review of Privat Law*, 1997 (5), p. 489-496.

**Drobnig 2006**
Drobnig, U., 'Recognition and Adaptation of Foreign Security Rights', in: U. Drobnig, H.J. Snijders & E.-J. Zippro (eds.), *Divergences of Property Law, an Obstacle to the Internal Market*, München: Sellier, 2006, p. 105-116.

**Drobnig 2011**
Drobnig, U., 'European Conflict Rules for the Mutual Recognition of Security Rights in Goods', in: R. Westrik & J.A. van der Weide (eds.), *Party Autonomy in International Property Law*, München: Sellier. European Law Publishers, 2011, p. 165-188.

**Drobnig, Snijders & Zippro 2006**
Drobnig, U., Snijders, H.J. & Zippro, E.-J. (eds.), *Divergences of Property Law, an Obstacle to the Internal Market?*, München: Sellier. European Law Publishers, 2006.

**Eidenmüller *et al.* 2008**
Eidenmüller, H. *et al.*, 'The Common Frame of References for European Private Law - Policy Choices and Codification Problems', *Oxford J Legal Studies*, 28/4 (2008), p. 659-708.

**Van Erp 2001**
Erp, J.H.M. van, 'European Union Case Law as a Source of European Private Law: A Comparison with American Federal Common Law', *Electronic Journal of Comparative Law*, 2001 (5).

**Van Erp 2004**
Erp, J.H.M. van, 'The Cape Town Convention: a Model for a European System of Security Interests Registration?', *European Review of Private Law*, 2004 (12/1), p. 91-110.

**Van Erp 2006a**
Erp, J.H.M. van, 'Comparative Property Law', in: M. Reimann & R. Zimmermann (eds.), *The Oxford Handbook of Comparative Law*, Oxford: Oxford University Press, 2006, p. 1043-1071.

**Van Erp 2006b**
Erp, J.H.M. van, *European and National Property Law: Osmosis or Growing Antagonism?* (Sixth Walter van Gerven Lecture), Groningen: Europa Law Publishing, 2006.

**Van Erp 2006c**
Erp, J.H.M. van, 'Servitudes: The Borderline Between Contract and (Virtual) Property', in: J.H.M. van Erp & B. Akkermans (eds.), *Towards a Unified System of Land Burdens?* (Ius Commune Europaeum, 54), Antwerp/Oxford: Intersentia, 2006, p. 1-11.

**Van Erp 2008a**
Erp, J.H.M. van, 'L'Europe: Chacun pour soi?', *Electronic Journal of Comparative Law*, 2008 (12/2).

**Van Erp 2008b**
Erp, J.H.M. van, *Security Interests: A Secure Start for the Development of European Property Law*, Maastricht Faculty of Law Working Paper, No. 5, Maastricht, 2008.

**Van Erp 2009a**
Erp, J.H.M. van, 'DCFR and Property Law: The Need for Consistency and Coherence', in: R. Schulze (ed.), *Common Frame of Reference and Existing EC Contract Law* (2nd rev. Edition), Munich: Sellier. European Law Publishers, 2009, p. 249-262.

**Van Erp 2009b**
Erp, J.H.M. van, *From 'Classical' to Modern European Property Law?*, Maastricht Faculty of Law Working Paper, No. 4, Maastricht, 2009.

**Van Erp 2010**
Erp, J.H.M. van, *Matrimonial Property Regimes and Patrimonial Aspects of other Forms of Union: what Problems and Proposed Solutions?* (Proposal for EU Rome IV Regulation), Brussels: European Parliament, 2010.

**Van Erp 2011a**
Erp, J.H.M. van, 'Book X DCFR and the Introduction of the Trust in the Netherlands', Edinburgh Law Review, 2011 (15), p. 479-482.

**Van Erp 2011b**
Erp, J.H.M. van, *Teaching Law in Europe: From an Intrasystemic, via a Transsystemic to a Suprasystemic Approach*, Maastricht Faculty of Law Working Paper, No. 10, Maastricht, 2011.

**Van Erp 2011c**
Erp, J.H.M. van, 'European Property Law: a Methodology for the Future', in: R. Schulze & H. Schulte-Nölke (eds.), *European Private Law - Current Status and Perspectives*, Munich: Sellier. European Law Publishers, 2011, p. 227-249.

**Van Erp & Akkermans 2006**
Erp, J.H.M. van & Akkermans, B. (eds.), *Towards a Unified System of Land Burdens?*, Antwerp/Oxford: Intersentia, 2006.

**Van Erp & Akkermans 2010**
Erp, J.H.M. van & Akkermans, B., 'European Union Property Law', in: C. Twigg-Flesner (ed.), *The Cambridge Companion to European Union Private Law*, Cambridge: Cambridge University Press, 2010, p. 173-186.

**Van Erp & Akkermans 2012**
Erp, J.H.M. van & Akkermans, B. (eds.), *Cases, Materials and Text on Property Law*, Oxford: Hart Publishing, 2012.

**Van Erp, Akkermans & Ramaekers 2012**
Erp, J.H.M. van, Akkermans, B. & Ramaekers, E., 'Review of Von Bar, Christian and Clive, Eric (eds.), Principles, Definitions and Model Rules of European Private Law. Draft Common Frame of Reference (DCFR)', *Maastricht Journal of European and Comparative Law*, 2012 (19/1), p. 83-93.

**Van Erp & Akkermans 2013**
Erp, J.H.M. van & Akkermans, B., 'Public or Private Harmonisation of the EU Mortgage Market?', *Zeitschrift für Europäisches Privatrecht*, 2013 (1), p. 43-58.

**EBRD Model Law on Secured Transactions**
European Bank for Reconstruction and Development, *Model Law on Secured Transactions*, London, 1994.

**Faber & Lurger 2008**
Faber, W. & Lurger, B. (eds.), *National Reports on the Transfer of Movables in Europe*, Munich: Sellier. European law publishers, 2008.

**Fennelly 1996-1997**
Fennelly, N., 'Legal Interpretation at the European Court of Justice', *Fordham International Law Journal*, 1996-1997 (20), p. 656-679.

**Flessner 2010**
Flessner, A., 'Rechtswahl im internationalen Sachenrecht - neue Anstöße aus Europa', in: P. Apathy *et al.* (ed.), *Festschrift für Helmut Koziol zum 70. Geburtstag*, Wien: Jan Sramek Verlag, 2010, p. 125-146.

**Franzina 2011**
Franzina, P., 'The Proposed New Rule of Special Jurisdiction Regarding Rights in rem in Moveable Property: a Good Option for a Reformed Brussels I Regulation?', *Diritto del commercio internazionale*, 2011 (3), p. 789-808.

**French 2000-2001**
French, S.F., 'Highlights of the new Restatement (Third) of Property: Servitudes', Real Property, *Probate and Trust Journal*, 2000-2001 (35), p. 225-242.

**French 2006**
French, S.F., 'The American Restatement of Servitudes Law: Reforming Doctrine by Shifting From Ex Ante to Ex Post Controls on the Risks Posed by Servitudes', in: J.H.M. van Erp & B. Akkermans (eds.), *Towards a Unified System of Land Burdens?* (Ius Commune Europaeum, 59), Antwerp/Oxford: Intersentia, 2006, p. 109-116.

**Füller 2006**
Füller, J.T., *Eigenständiges Sachenrecht?* (Jus Privatum. Beitrage zum Privatrecht, 104), Tübingen: Mohr Siebeck, 2006.

**Gaillard & Trautman 1987**
Gaillard, E. & Trautman, D.T., 'Trusts in Non-Trust Countries: Conflict of Laws and the Hague Convention on Trusts', *American Journal of Comparative Law*, 1987 (35), p. 307-340.

**Gambaro 1997**
Gambaro, A., 'Perspectives on the Codification of the Law of Property: an Overview.', *European Review of Private Law*, 1997 (5), p. 497-504.

**Garb & Wood 2010**
Garb, L. & Wood, J. (eds.), *International Succession* (3rd edition), Oxford: Oxford University Press, 2010.

**Gardner 2011**
Gardner, S., *An Introduction to the Law of Trusts* (3rd edition), Oxford: Oxford University Press, 2011.

**Gaudemet-Tallon 2002**
Gaudemet-Tallon, H., *Compétence et exécution des jugements en Europe: Règlement no 44/2001, Conventions de Bruxelles et de Lugano* (3rd edition), Paris: LGDJ, 2002.

**Gerbet 1956**
Gerbet, P., 'La genèse du plan Schuman. Des origines à la déclaration du 9 mai 1950', *Revue française de science politique*, 1956 (6/3), p. 525-553.

**Van Gerven 1998**
Gerven, W. van, 'The ECJ Case-Law as a Means of Unification of Private Law?', in: M. Hesselink, A. Hartkamp, E. Hondius, C. Joustra, & E. du Perron (eds.), *Towards a European Civil Code* (2nd edition), Nijmegen: Ars Aequi Libri, 1998, p. 91-105.

**Van Gerven 2002**
Gerven, W. van, 'Codifying European Private Law? Yes, if...!', *European Law Review*, 2002 (27), p. 156-176.

**Van Gerven 2004**
Gerven, W. van, 'Harmonization of Private Law: Do we need it?', *Common Market Law Review*, 2004 (41/2), p. 505-532.

**Ginossar 1979**
Ginossar, S., 'Rights in rem – A new Approach', *Israel Law Review*, 1979 (14), p. 286-336.

**Goode 1998**
Goode, R., 'The Protection of Interests in Movables in Transnational Commercial Law', *Uniform Law Review n.s.*, 1998 (3-2/3), p. 453-465.

**Goode 2008**
Goode, R., *Convention on International Interests in Mobile Equipment and Protocol Thereto on Matters Specific to Aircraft Equipment - Official Commentary* (Revised edition), Rome: UNIDROIT, 2008.

**Grabitz 2005**
Grabitz, E., 'Art. 295 EGV [Eigentumsordnung]', *Das Recht der Europäischen Union - Kommentar* (III), München: Beck, 2005.

**Gretton 2007**
Gretton, G.L., 'Ownership and its Objects', *Rabels Zeitschrift für ausländisches und internationales Privatrecht*, 2007 (71/4), p. 802-851.

**Groeben 1997**
Groeben, H. Von der, *Kommentar zum EU-/EG-Vertrag* (5th revised edition 1) Baden-Baden: Nomos, 1997.

**De Groot 2008**
Groot, S. de, 'Fiduciary Transfer and Ownership', in: W. Faber (ed.), *Rules for the Transfer of Movables: a Candidate for European Harmonisation or National Reforms?*, München: Sellier. European Law Publishers, 2008, p. 161-174.

**De Groot & Bartels 1994**
Groot, G.-R. de & Bartels, S., 'Goederenrecht in de Europese Unie', *Ars Aequi*, 1994 (43/5), p. 57-66.

**De Groot & Salomons 2011**
Groot, S. de & Salomons, A.F., 'Zekerheidsoverdracht in het Nederlandse BW, de Franse Code civil en de Europese DCFR.', *Ars Aequi*, 2011, p. 383-390.

**Hage 2010**
Hage, J.C., 'Rechtstheoretische analyse van de partijautonomie in het overeenkomstenrecht. Twee dimensies van contractsvrijheid. Een bijdrage aan de algemene leer der overeenkomsten', in: I. Samoy (ed.), *Evolutie van de basisbeginselen van het contractenrecht* (Ius commune Europaeum, 90), Antwerpen: Intersentia, 2010, p. 241-262.

**Hartkamp 2007**
Hartkamp, A., *Ambtshalve aanvulling van rechtsgronden naar Europees recht en naar Nederlands recht*, Deventer: Kluwer, 2007.

**Hartkamp 2008**
Hartkamp, A.S., *Vermogensrecht algemeen - Europees recht en Nederlands vermogensrecht* (Asser-Serie, 3-I), Deventer: Kluwer, 2008.

**Hartkamp 2011**
Hartkamp, A. S., 'The influence of Primary European Law on Private Law', in: A.S. Hartkamp *et al.* (eds.), *Towards a European Civil Code* (4th revised and expanded edition), Alphen aan den Rijn/Nijmegen: Kluwer Law International BV/Ars Aequi Libri, 2011, p. 127-148.

**Heiderhoff 2007**
Heiderhoff, B., *Gemeinschaftsprivatrecht* (2nd edition), München: Sellier. European Law Publishers, 2007.

**Herfurth 1998**
Herfurth, U., *Immobilienerwerb in Europa*, Bonn: Economica-Verlag, 1998.

**Heß 1998**
Heß, B., 'Dienstbarkeit und Reallast im System dinglicher Nutzungs- und Verwertungsrechte', *Archiv für die civilistische Praxis*, 1998 (198), p. 489-516.

**Hesselink 2009**
Hesselink, M.W., 'A European Legal Method? On European Private Law and Scientific Method', *European Law Journal*, 2009 (15/1), p. 20-45.

**Hesselink, Rutgers & Booys 2007**
Hesselink, M.W., Rutgers, J.W. & Booys, T. de, *The Legal Basis for an Optional Instrument on European Contract Law*, CSECL, Working Paper Series, No. 2007/04 2007.

**Hinteregger & Borić 2009**
Hinteregger, M. & Borić, T. (eds.), *Sicherungsrechte an Immobilien in Europa (Grazer Beiträge zum Recht der Länder Südosteuropas und der Europäischen Integration*, Wien: Lit Verlag GmbH & Co. KG, 2009.

**Hohfeld 1916-1917**
Hohfeld, W.N., 'Fundamental Legal Conceptions as Applied in Judicial Reasoning', *Yale Law Journal*, 1916-1917 (26/8), p. 16-59.

**Honnebier 2006**
Honnebier, P., 'The Cape Town Convention and International Registry for Mortgages and other Secured Interests in Aircraft', *Notarius International*, 2006 (11/1-2), p. 21-27.

**Honoré 1961**
Honoré, A.M., 'Ownership', in: A.G. Guest (ed.), *Oxford Essays in Jurisprudence*, London: Oxford University Press, 1961, p. 107-147.

**Hunter 1976**
Hunter, M., 'The draft EEC Bankruptcy Convention - a Further Examination', *International and Comparative Law Quarterly*, 1976 (25), p. 310-328.

**Ioriatti Ferrari 2008**
Ioriatti Ferrari, E., *Interpretazione e Traduzione del Diritto*, Padova: CEDAM, 2008.

**Israël 2005**
Israël, J., *European Cross-Border Insolvency Regulation*, Antwerp: Intersentia, 2005.

**Israël & Saarloos 2007**
Israël, J. & Saarloos, K. J., 'Europees internationaal privaat- en procesrecht', in: A.S. Hartkamp, C.H. Sieburgh & L.A.D. Keus (eds.), *De invloed van het Europese recht op het Nederlandse privaatrecht* (Onderneming & Recht, 42-II), Deventer: Kluwer, 2007, p. 629-698.

**Johnston & Unberath 2010**
Johnston, A. & Unberath, H., 'European Private Law by Directives: Approach and Challenges', in: C. Twigg-Flesner (ed.), *The Cambridge Companion to European Union Private Law*, Cambridge: Cambridge University Press, 2010, p. 85-100.

**Kakouris 1994**
Kakouris, C.N., 'Use of the Comparative Method by the Court of Justice of the European Communities', *Pace International Law Review*, 1994 (6), p. 267-283.

**Karsten & Petri 2005**
Karsten, J. & Petri, G., 'Towards a Handbook on European Contract Law and Beyond: The Commission's 2004 Communication "European Contract Law and the Revision of the Acquis: The Way Forward"', *Journal of Consumer Policy*, 2005 (28), p. 31-51.

**Keirse & Veder 2010**
Keirse, A.L.M. & Veder, P.M., *Europeanisering van vermogensrecht* (Preadviezen uitgebracht voor de Vereniging voor Burgerlijk Recht), Deventer: Kluwer, 2010.

**Kenny 2006**
Kenny, M., 'Constructing a European Civil Code: Quis custodiet ipsos custodes?', *Columbia Journal of European Law*, 2006 (12), p. 775-808.

**Kieninger 1996**
Kieninger, E.-M., *Mobiliarsicherheiten im Europäischen Binnenmarkt: zum Einfluß der Warenverkehrsfreiheit auf das nationale und internationale Sachenrecht der Mitgliedstaaten*, Baden-Baden: Nomos Verlagsgesellschaft, 1996.

**Kieninger 2002**
Kieninger, E.-M., *Wettbewerb der Privatrechtsordnungen im Europäischen Binnenmarkt*, Tübingen: Mohr Siebeck, 2002.

**Kieninger 2004a**
Kieninger, E.-M., 'Evaluation: a Common Core? Convergences, Subsisting Differences and possible Ways for Harmonisation', in: E.-M. Kieninger (ed.), *Security Rights in Movable Property in European Private Law*, Cambridge: Cambridge University Press, 2004.

**Kieninger 2004b**
Kieninger, E.-M., *Security Rights in Movable Property in European Private Law*, Cambridge: Cambridge University Press, 2004.

**Kieninger 2006**
Kieninger, E.-M., 'European Regulation of Security Rights', in: U. Drobnig, H.J. Snijders & E.-J. Zippro (eds.), *Divergences of Property Law, an Obstacle to the Internal Market?*, München: Sellier. European Law Publishers, 2006, p. 165-174.

**Kieninger 2008a**
Kieninger, E.-M., 'Die Zukunft des deutschen und europäischen Mobiliarkreditsicherungsrechts', *Archiv für die civilistische Praxis*, 2008 (208), p. 182-226.

**Kieninger 2008b**
Kieninger, E.-M., 'Europäisches Mobiliarkreditsicherungsrecht', in: S. Emmenegger (ed.), *Kreditsicherheiten*, Bern: Helbing Lichtenhahn Verlag, 2008, p. 109-139.

**Kiiver & Kornet 2010**
Kiiver, P. & Kornet, N. (eds.), *The Maastricht Collection – Selected National, European and International Provisions from Public and Private Law* (2nd edition), Groningen: Europa Law Publishing, 2010.

**Klauer 1998**
Klauer, I., *Die Europäisierung des Privatrechts – Der EuGH als Zivilrichter*, Baden-Baden: Nomos Verlagsgesellschaft, 1998.

**Knot 2008**
Knot, J.G., *Internationale Boedelafwikkeling*, Deventer: Kluwer, 2008.

**Koch 1995**
Koch, H., 'Private International Law: A 'Soft' Alternative to the Harmonisation of Private Law?', *European Review of Private Law*, 1995 (3), p. 329-342.

**Kortmann 2005**
Kortmann, J.S., 'De overdracht van CO2-emissierechten nader beschouwd', *Nederlands Juristenblad,* 2005 (8), p. 392-396.

**Kreuzer 1990**
Kreuzer, K., 'Europäisches Mobiliarsicherungsrecht oder: Von den Grenzen des Internationalen Privatrechts', in: W.A. Stoffel & P. Volken (eds.), *Conflits et harmonisation - Kollision und Vereinheitlichung - Conflicts and Harmonization,* Fribourg: Éditions Universitaires Fribourg Suisse, 1990, p. 613-641.

**Kreuzer 1991**
Kreuzer, K., 'Gutachtliche Stellungnahme zum Referentenentwurf eines Gesetzes zur Ergänzung des Internationalen Privatrechts (Außervertragliche Schuldverhältnisse und Sachen) - Sachenrechtliche Bestimmungen', in: D. Henrich (ed.), *Vorschläge und Gutachten zur Reform des deutschen internationalen Sachen- und Immaterialgüterrechts,* Tübingen: J.C.B. Mohr (Paul Siebeck), 1991, p. 38-181.

**Kuipers 2009**
Kuipers, J.-J., 'Cartesio and Grunkin-Paul: Mutual Recognition as a Vested Rights Theory Based on Party Autonomy in Private Law', *European Journal of Legal Studies,* 2009 (2/2), p. 66-96.

**Kullerkupp 2008**
Kullerkupp, K., 'Private Autonomy in Property Law: Can the Parties 'Design' their Transfer?', in: W. Faber (ed.), *Rules for the Transfer of Movables: a Candidate for European Harmonisation or National Reforms?,* München: Sellier. European Law Publishers, 2008, p. 47-59.

**Lagarde 2009**
Lagarde, P., 'Cadre commun de réference et droit international privé', in: R. Schulze (ed.), *Common frame of reference and existing EC contract law* (2nd rev. edition), Munich: Sellier. European Law Publishers, 2009, p. 275-293.

**Landsmeer 2001**
Landsmeer, A., 'Movement of Capital and Other Freedoms', *Legal Issues of Economic Integration,* 2001 (28/1), p. 57-69.

**Lavranos 2008**
Lavranos, N., 'The Effect of UN Sanctions on Private Party Transactions', *European Law Reporter,* 2008, p. 137-143.

**Lawson & Rudden 2002**
Lawson, F.H. & Rudden, B., *The Law of Property* (3rd rev. edition), Oxford: Oxford University Press, 2002.

**Léger 2000**
Léger, P., 'Article 295 (ex-article 222)', in: *Commentaire article par article des traités UE et CE*, Paris: Dalloz, 2000, Article 295.

**Lehmann 2008**
Lehmann, M., 'Liberating the Individual from Battles between States: Justifying Party Autonomy in Conflict of Laws', *Vanderbilt Journal of Transnational Law*, 2008 (41), p. 381-434.

**Lenaerts 2003**
Lenaerts, K., 'Interlocking Legal Orders in the European Union and Comparative Law', *International and Comparative Law Quarterly*, 2003 (52), p. 873-906.

**Lenz 1999**
Lenz, C.-O., 'Art. 295 (ex-Art. 222) (Eigentumsordnung)', in: *EG-Vertrag: Kommentar* (2nd edition), Basel: Helbing & Lichtenhahn, 1999, Article 295.

**Libchaber 2004**
Libchaber, R., 'Les Biens', in: *Le Code civil 1804-2004: Livre du Bicentenaire*, Paris: Dalloz, 2004, p. 297-372.

**Low 2011**
Low, G., *European Contract Law between the Single Market and the Law Market – A Behavioural Perspective*, Nijmegen: Wolf Legal Publishers, 2011.

**Maitland 1936**
Chaytor, A.H., Whittaker, W.J. & Brunyate, J. (eds.), *Equity: a Course of Lectures – by F.W. Maitland* (2nd revised edition), Cambridge: Cambridge University Press, 1936.

**Mansel 2010**
Mansel, H.-P., 'The Impact of the European Union's Prohibition of Discrimination and the Right of Free Movement of Persons on the Private International Law Rules of Member States - With Comments on the Sayn-Wittgenstein Case before the European Court of Justice', in: K. Boele-Woelki *et al.* (eds.), *Convergence and Divergence in Private International Law – Liber Amicorum Kurt Siehr*, The Hague: Eleven International Publishing, 2010, p. 291-309.

**Marenco 1983**
Marenco, G., 'Public Sector and Community Law', *Common Market Law Review*, 1983 (20), p. 495-527.

**cFarlane, Hopkins & Nield 2009**
McFarlane, B., Hopkins, N. & Nield, S., *Land Law: Text, Cases and Materials*, Oxford: Oxford University Press, 2009.

**McFarlane & Stevens 2010**
McFarlane, B. & Stevens, R., 'The Nature of Equitable Property', *Journal of Equity*, 2010 (4/1), p. 495-527.

**McKendrick & Goode 2010**
McKendrick, E. & Goode, R. (eds.), *Goode on Commercial Law* (4th edition), London: Penguin, 2010.

**Mensbrugghe 2003**
Mensbrugghe, F.R. van der, *L'utilisation de la méthode comparative en droit européen*, Namur: Presses Universitaires de Namur, 2003.

**Merrill & Smith 2000-2001**
Merrill, T.W. & Smith, H.E., 'Optimal Standardization in the Law of Property: The Numerus Clausus Principle', *Yale Law Journal*, 2000-2001 (110/1), p. 1-70.

**Merrill & Smith 2001**
Merrill, T.W. & Smith, H.E., 'The Property/Contract Interface', *Columbia Law Review*, 2001, p. 773-852.

**Michaels 2006a**
Michaels, R., 'EU Law as Private International Law? Reconceptualising the Country-of-Origin Principle as Vested-Rights Theory', *Journal of Private International Law*, 2006 (2/2), p. 195-242.

**Michaels 2006b**
Michaels, R., 'The Functional Method of Comparative Law', in: M. Reimann & R. Zimmermann (eds.), *The Oxford Handbook of Comparative Law* (1st edition), Oxford: Oxford University Press, 2006, p. 339-382.

**Michaels & Jansen 2006**
Michaels, R. & Jansen, N., 'Private Law beyond the State? Europeanization, Globalization, Privatization', *American Journal of Comparative Law*, 2006 (54/4), p. 843-890.

**Micklitz 2009**
Micklitz, H.-W., 'The Visible Hand of European Regulatory Private Law - The Transformation of European Private Law from Autonomy to Functionalism in Competition and Regulation', *Yearbook of European Law*, 2009 (28/1),p. 3-60.

**Milo 2003**
Milo, J.M., 'Retention of Title in European Business Transactions', *Washburn Law Journal*, 2003 (43), p. 121-139.

**Müller-Graff 2004**
Müller-Graff, P.-C., 'EC Directives as a Means of Private Law Unification', in: A. Hartkamp *et al.* (eds.), *Towards a European Civil Code* (3rd fully revised and expanded edition), Nijmegen/The Hague: Ars Aequi Libri/Kluwer Law International, 2004.

**Neri & Sperl 1960**
Neri, S. & Sperl, H., 'Article 222; I.-Historique', in: *Traité instituant la Communauté Économique Européenne: travaux préparatoires, déclarations interprétatives des six gouvernements, documents parlementaires,* Luxembourg: Cour de Justice des Communautés Européennes, 1960, 410, Article 222.

**Ploeger 2000**
Ploeger, H.D., 'De gemobiliseerde onroerende zaak', *Nederlands Tijdschrift voor Burgerlijk Recht,* 2000 (17/1), p. 16-18.

**Ploeger 2002**
Ploeger, H.D., 'Onroerende stacaravans: hoe lang is duurzaam?', *Weekblad voor Privaatrecht, Notariaat en Registratie,* 2002 (6497), p. 519-522.

**Ploeger & Loenen 2004**
Ploeger, H.D. & Loenen, B. van, 'EULIS - At the Beginning of the Road to Harmonization of Land Registry in Europe', *European Review of Private Law,* 2004 (12/3), p. 379-387.

**Polak 2006**
Polak, M.V., 'Recognition, Enforcement and Transformation of Foreign Proprietary Rights - a handful of observations and suggestions', in: U. Drobnig, H.J. Snijders & E.-J. Zippro (eds.), *Divergences of Property Law, an Obstacle to the Internal Market?,* München: Sellier, 2006, 117-130.

**Pozzo 2003**
Pozzo, B., 'Harmonisation of European Contract Law and the Need of Creating a Common Terminology', *European Review of Private Law,* 2003 (6), p. 754-767.

**Pozzo 2008**
Pozzo, B., 'L'interpretazione della Corte del Lussemburgo del testo multilingue: una rassegna giurisprudenziale', in: E.I. Ferrari (ed.), *Interpretazione e Traduzione del Diritto,* Padova: Kluwer Italia, 2008, p. 73-113.

**Pozzo & Jacometti 2006**
Pozzo, B. & Jacometti, V. (eds.), *Multilingualism and the Harmonisation of European Law,* The Hague: Kluwer Law International, 2006.

**Van Praagh 2005**
Praagh, S. Van, 'Preface - Navigating the Transsystemic: A Course Syllabus', *McGill Law Journal*, 2005 (50/4), p. 701-706.

**Ramaekers 2012**
Ramaekers, E., 'Cross-border Successions - The New Commission Proposal: Contents and Way Forward. A Report on the 2010 Academy of European Law Conference', *Electronic Journal of Comparative Law*, 2012 (15).

**Rauscher 2009**
Rauscher, T., *Internationales Privatrecht - mit internationalem und europäischem Verfahrensrecht* (3rd edition), München: Verlag C.H. Beck, 2009.

**Reimann & Zimmermann 2006**
Reimann, M. & Zimmermann, R. (eds.), *The Oxford Handbook of Comparative Law*, Oxford: Oxford University Press, 2006.

**Review of the Brussels I Regulation (EC 44/2001) - Comments from the United Kingdom**
UK Ministry of Justice, *Review of the Brussels I Regulation (EC 44/2001) - Comments from the United Kingdom*, 2009.

**Rieber 1957**
Rieber, H., *Der Gemeinsame Markt - Wortlaut des Vertrages über die Europäische Wirtschaftsgemeinschaft vom 25. März 1957 mit den Erläuterungen der Bundesregierung und einer Einführung von Ministerialrat Dr. Rieber* (Schriftenreihe zum Handbuch für Europäische Wirtschaft, 1), Frankfurt am Mainz: Verlag August Lutzeyer Baden-Baden, 1957.

**Riegel 1979**
Riegel, R., 'Die Einwirkung des europäischen Gemeinschaftsrechts auf die Eigentumsordnung der Mitgliedstaaten - Zugleich ein Beitrag zur Auslegung von Art. 222 EWGV', *Recht der Internationalen Wirtschaft*, 1979 (11), p. 744-749.

**Riesenhuber 2006**
Riesenhuber, K., *Die Europäisierung des Privatrechts*, Berlin: De Gruyter Rechtswissenschaften Verlags-GmbH, 2006.

**Rodriguez Murillo 2007**
Rodriguez Murillo, N., 'The Revision of the Timeshare Directive', *International Travel Law Journal*, 2007, p. 81-89.

**Roth 1994**
Roth, W.-H., 'Die Freiheiten des EG-Vertrages und das nationale Privatrecht - Zur Entwicklung internationaler Sachnormen für europäische Sachverhalte', *Zeitschrift für Europäisches Privatrecht*, 1994, p. 5-33.

**Roth 2003**
Roth, W.-H., 'From Centros to Ueberseering: Free Movement of Companies, Private International Law, and Community Law', *International & Comparative Law Quarterly*, 2003 (52), p. 177-208.

**Roth 2009**
Roth, W.-H., 'Kompetenzen der EG zur vollharmonisierenden Angleichung des Privatrechts', in: B. Gsell & C. Herresthal (eds.), *Vollharmonisierung im Privatrecht*, Tübingen: Mohr Siebeck, 2009, p. 14-44.

**Rushworth & Scott 2010**
Rushworth, A. & Scott, A., 'Total Chaos?', *Lloyd's Maritime and Commercial Law Quarterly*, 2010, p. 536-543.

**Rutgers 1999**
Rutgers, J.W., *International Reservation of Title Clauses: a Study of Dutch, French and German Private International Law in the Light of European law*, The Hague: T.M.C. Asser Press, 1999.

**Rutgers 2005**
Rutgers, J.W., 'The Rule of Reason and Private Law or the Limits to Harmonization', in: A. Schrauwen (ed.), *Rule of Reason; Rethinking another Classic of EC Legal Doctrine* (The Hogendorp Papers), Groningen: Europa Law Publishers, 2005.

**Rutgers 2012**
Rutgers, J.W., 'Registered European Security Instrument in a Multilingual European Union', in: J.H.M. van Erp, A.F. Salomons & B. Akkermans (eds.), *The Future of European Property Law*, Munich: Sellier European Law Publishers, 2012, p. 153-163

**Saarloos 2010**
Saarloos, K. J., *European Private International Law on Legal Parentage? – Thoughts on a European Instrument Implementing the Principle of Mutual Recognition in Legal Parentage*, Maastricht: Océ Business Services, 2010.

**Sagaert 2005**
Sagaert, V., 'Het goederenrecht als open systeem van verbintenissen? Poging tot een nieuwe kwalificatie van de vermogensrechten', *Tijdschrift voor Privaatrecht*, 2005 (42/3), p. 983-1086.

**Sagaert 2006**
Sagaert, V., 'The Fragmented System of Land Burdens in French and Belgian law', in: J.H.M. van Erp & B. Akkermans (eds.), *Towards a Unified System of Land Burdens?* (Ius Commune Europaeum, 59), Antwerp/Oxford: Intersentia, 2006, p. 31-53.

**Sagaert 2007**
Sagaert, V., 'De verworvenheden van het Europese goederenrecht', in: A.S. Hartkamp, C.H. Sieburgh & L.A.D. Keus (eds.), *De invloed van het Europese recht op het Nederlandse privaatrecht* (Onderneming & Recht, 42-I), Deventer: Kluwer, 2007, p. 301-333.

**Sagaert 2011**
Sagaert, V., 'Harmonization of Security Rights on Immoveables: An Ongoing Story', in: A.S. Hartkamp *et al.* (eds.), *Towards a European Civil Code* (4th revised and expanded edition), Alphen aan den Rijn/Nijmegen: Kluwer Law International/Ars Aequi Libri, 2011, p. 1043-1064.

**Sara 2011**
Sara, C., *Boundaries and Easements* (5th edition), London: Sweet & Maxwell, 2011.

**Sauter 1998**
Sauter, W., 'The Economic Constitution of the European Union', *Columbia Journal of European Law*, 1998 (4), p. 27-68.

**Scharpf 2002**
Scharpf, F.W., *The European Social Model: Coping with the Challenges of Diversity*, MPIfG Working Paper, 02/8, July 2002.

**Scheltema 2011**
Scheltema, A.H., 'Art. 7:69 BW: stille cessie afgeschaft en verrekening verruimd?', *Maandblad voor Vermogensrecht*, 2011 (11), p. 283-291.

**Schlosser Report 1979**
Schlosser, P., *Report on the Convention on the Association of the Kingdom of Denmark, Ireland and the United Kingdom of Great Britain and Northern Ireland to the Convention on jurisdiction and the enforcement of judgments in civil and commercial matters and to the Protocol on its interpretation by the Court of Justice*, Luxembourg, 1979.

**Schmid, Hertel & Wicke 2005**
Schmid, C.U., Hertel, C. & Wicke, H., *Real Property Law and Procedure in the European Union*, Florence/Würzburg: EUI/DNotI, 2005.

**Schneider 1995**
Schneider, H.E.G.S., *Die Anerkennung von Diplomen in der Europäischen Gemeinschaft*, Maastricht: Rijksuniversiteit Limburg, 1995.

**Schulte-Nölke 2007**
Schulte-Nölke, H., 'EC Law on the Formation of Contract - from the Common Frame of Reference to the "Blue Button"', *European Review of Common Law*, 2007 (3), p. 332-349.

**Schulte-Nölke 2010**
Schulte-Nölke, H., 'The Way forward in European Consumer Contract Law: Optional Instrument instead of Further Deconstruction of National Private Laws', in: C. Twigg-Flesner (ed.), *The Cambridge Companion to European Union Private Law*, Cambridge: Cambridge University Press, 2010, p. 131-146.

**Schulte-Nölke, Twigg-Flessner & Ebers 2008**
Schulte-Nölke, H., Twigg-Flesner, C. & Ebers, M. (eds.), *EC Consumer Law Compendium*, Munich: Sellier. European law publishers, 2008.

**Schulze 2009**
Schulze, G., 'Ökonomik der Vollharmonisierung im Gemeinschaftsprivatrecht', in: B. Gsell & C. Herresthal (eds.), *Vollharmonisierung im Privatrecht*, Tübingen: Mohr Siebeck, 2009.

**Schwarze 2000**
Schwarze, J., 'Art. 295 (ex-Art. 222) [Eigentumsordnung]', in: *EU-Kommentar* (1st edition), Baden-Baden: Nomos, 2000.

**Sigman 2004**
Sigman, H.C., 'Security in Movables in the United States - Uniform Commercial Code Article 9: a Basis for Comparison', in: E.-M. Kieninger (ed.), *Security Rights in Movable Property in European Private Law*, Cambridge: Cambridge University Press, 2004, p. 54-80.

**Simón Moreno 2011**
Simón Moreno, H., 'Towards a European System of Property Law', *European Review of Private Law*, 2011 (5), p. 579-612.

**Smit & Herzog 1976-1996**
Smit, H. & Herzog, P.E., *The Law of the European Community: A Commentary on the EEC Treaty*, (5), New York: Bender, 1976-1996.

**Smits 1998**
Smits, J.M., 'A European Private Law as a Mixed Legal System', *Maastricht Journal of European and Comparative Law*, 1998 (5/4), p. 328-340.

**Smits 2002**
Smits, J.M., *The Making of European Private Law – Toward a Ius Commune Europaeum as a Mixed Legal System*, Antwerp/Oxford/New York: Intersentia, 2002.

**Smits 2006a**
Smits, J.M., 'European Private Law: A Plea for a Spontaneous Legal Order', in: *European Integration and Law* (Ius Commune Europaeum, 56), Antwerp/Oxford: Intersentia, 2006, p. 55-107.

**Smits 2006b**
Smits, J.M., 'Europese integratie in het vermogensrecht: een pleidooi voor keuzevrijheid', in: *Preadvies Nederlandse Juristen-Vereniging 2006* (Handelingen Nederlandse Juristen-Vereniging, 136), Deventer: Kluwer, 2006, p. 57-104.

**Smits 2008a**
Smits, J.M., *The Draft Common Frame of Reference, Methodological Nationalism and the Way Forward*, TICOM Working Paper, Tilburg: SSRN, 2008.

**Smits 2008b**
Smits, J.M., 'The Draft-Common Frame of Reference for a European Private Law: Fit for Purpose?', *Maastricht Journal of European and Comparative Law*, 2008, p. 145-148.

**Smits 2009a**
Smits, J.M., 'Democracy and (European) Private Law: A Functional Approach', *European Journal of Legal Studies*, 2009 (2/2), p. 26-40.

**Smits 2009b**
Smits, J.M., 'Europees Recht als Alternatief: de Charme van het 28ste Rechtsstelsel', *Tijdschrift voor Privaatrecht*, 2009 (46), p. 1731-135.

**Smits 2010**
Smits, J.M., 'Europeanisering van vermogensrecht: een bespreking van de preadviezen uitgebracht voor de Vereniging voor Burgerlijk Recht', *Nederlands Tijdschrift voor Burgerlijk Recht*, 2010 (27/10), p. 428-431.

**Smits 2011**
Smits, J.M., 'Over de ongekende legitimiteit van een optionele code', in: M.W. Hesselink *et al.* (eds.), *Het Groenboek Europees contractenrecht: naar een optioneel instrument?*, Den Haag: Boom Juridische uitgevers, 2011, p. 25-33.

**Snijders 2006**
Snijders, H.J., 'Access to Civil Securities and Free Competition in the EU, a Plea for One European Security Right in Movables', in: U. Drobnig, H.J. Snijders & E.-J. Zippro (eds.), *Divergences of Property Law, an Obstacle to the Internal Market?*, München: Sellier. European Law Publishers, 2006, p. 153-164.

**Sparkes 2007**
Sparkes, P., *European Land Law*, Oxford and Portland, Oregon: Hart Publishing, 2007.

**Spaventa 2009**
Spaventa, E., 'Leaving Keck behind? The Free Movement of Goods after the Rulings in Commission v Italy and Mickelsson and Roos', *European Law Review*, 2009 (34/6), p. 914-932.

**Steiner & Woods 2009**
Steiner, J. & Woods, L., *EU Law* (10th edition), Oxford: Oxford University Press, 2009.

**Stöcker 2012**
Stöcker, O., 'The Eurohypothec', in: J.H.M. van Erp, A.F. Salomons & B. Akkermans (eds.), *The Future of European Property Law*, Munich: Sellier. European Law Publishers, 2012, p. 65-77.

**Strese 2006**
Strese, J., *Die Kompetenzen der Europäischen Gemeinschaft zur Privatrechtsangleichung im Binnenmarkt*, Baden-Baden: Nomos Verlag, 2006.

**Strikwerda 2008**
Strikwerda, L., *Inleiding tot het Nederlandse Internationaal Privaatrecht* (9th edition), Deventer: Kluwer, 2008.

**Struycken 2007**
Struycken, T.H.D., *De Numerus Clausus in het Goederenrecht*, Deventer: Kluwer, 2007.

**Study Group on a European Civil Code 2006**
Study Group on a European Civil Code, *Principles of European Law*, Munich: Sellier, 2006.

**Stürner 1994**
Stürner, R., 'Dienstbarkeit heute', *Archiv für die civilistische Praxis*, 1994 (194), p. 265-294.

**Teuben 2005**
Teuben, R., *Verhandelbare emissierechten: juridische aspecten van emissiehandel voor CO2 in Nederland en de Europese Unie* (Europese monografieën), Deventer: Kluwer, 2005.

**Thunis 2003**
Thunis, X., 'L'empire de la comparaison', in: F.R.van der Mensbrugghe (ed.), *L'Utilisation de la Méthode Comparative en Droit Européen* (25), Namur: Presses Universitaires de Namur, 2003, p. 5-15.

**Tichý 2011**
Tichý, L., 'A New Role for Private International and Procedural Law in European Integration? A Critical Comment', in: R. Brownsword *et al.* (eds.), *The Foundations of European Private Law*, Oxford and Portland, Oregon: Hart, 2011, p. 393-412.

**Twigg-Flessner 2011**
Twigg-Flesner, C., 'The Acquis Principles: an Insider's Critical Reflections on the Drafting Process', *Zeitschrift für Gemeinschaftsprivatrecht*, 2011 (8/2), p. 54-63.

**UCC: Official Text and Comments 2008 Edition**
American Law Institute and National Conference of Commissioners on Uniform State Laws, *Uniform Commercial Code: Official Text and Comments*, St Paul, Minn: West Pub. Co, 2008 Edition.

**Usher 2002**
Usher, J.A., 'Enhanced Cooperation or Flexibility in the Post-Nice Era', in: A. Arnull & D. Wincott (eds.), *Accountability and legitimacy in the European Union*, Oxford: Oxford University Press, 2002, p. 97-112.

**Verhagen 2007a**
Verhagen, H.L.E., *Conflit mobile bij roerende zaken: assimilatie of transformatie?*, Deventer: Kluwer, 2007.

**Verhagen 2007b**
Verhagen, H.L.E., 'Kritische beschouwingen over het wetsontwerp voor een "Wet conflictenrecht goederenrecht"', *Weekblad voor Privaatrecht, Notariaat en Registratie*, 2007, nos. 6711 & 6712.

**Verhagen & Dongen 2010**
Verhagen, H.L.E. & Dongen, S. van, 'Cross-Border Assignments under Rome I', *Journal of Private International Law*, 2010 (6/1), p. 1-21.

**Verhoeven 1996**
Verhoeven, A., 'Privatisation and EC Law: Is the European Commission "Neutral" with Respect to Public Versus Private Ownership of Companies?', *International & Comparative Law Quarterly*, 1996 (45), p. 861-887.

**VerLoren van Themaat 1982**
VerLoren van Themaat, P., 'Het economisch grondslagenrecht van de Europese Gemeenschappen', in: W. van Gerven (ed.), *Liber amicorum Josse Mertens de Wilmars*, Antwerpen: Kluwer, 1982, p. 353-383.

**Vírgos & Schmit 1996**
Vírgos, M. & Schmit, E., *Report on the Convention of Insolvency Proceedings*, Brussels: Council of the European Union, 1996.

**Virole 1965**
Virole, J., 'Questions posées par l'interprétation du traité du 25 mars 1957 instituant la Communauté Economique Européenne à propos de la nationalisation de l'électricité en Italie', *Revue Trimestrielle de Droit Europeen*, 1965 (1), p. 369-398.

**Vismara 2006**
Vismara, F., 'The Role of the Court of Justice of the European Communities in the Interpretation of Multilingual Texts', in: B. Pozzo & V. Jacometti (eds.), *Multilingualism and the Harmonisation of European Law*, Alphen a/d Rijn: Kluwer Law International, 2006.

**Van Vliet 2000**
Vliet, L.P.W. van, *Transfer of movables in German, French, English and Dutch law*, Nijmegen: Ars Aequi Libri, 2000.

**Van Vliet 2005**
Vliet, L.P.W. van, 'De financiëlezekerheidsovereenkomst, een tussenbalans', *Nederlands Tijdschrift voor Burgerlijk Recht*, 2005 (5), p. 190-204.

**Vogenauer & Weatherill 2006**
Vogenauer, S. & Weatherill, S. (eds.), *The Harmonisation of European Contract Law – Implications for European Private Laws, Business and Legal Practice* (Studies of the Oxford Institute of European and Comparative Law, 1 (Oxford and Portland, Oregon: Hart Publishing, 2006.

**Wagner 2002**
Wagner, G., 'The Economics of Harmonization: the Case of Contract Law', *Common Market Law Review*, 2002 (39), p. 995-1023.

**Wallis 2006**
Wallis, D., 'Is it a Code?', *Zeitschrift für Europäisches Privatrecht*, 2006 (3), p. 513-514.

**Wallis & Allanson 2011**
Wallis, D. & Allanson, S. (eds.), *European Property Rights & Wrongs*, Markprint, Lahti: Diana Wallis, 2011.

**Van der Walt & Kleyn 1989**
Walt, A.J. van der & Kleyn, D.G., 'Duplex Dominium: The History and Significance of the Concept of Divided Ownership', in: D.P. Visser (ed.), *Essays on the History of Law*, Cape Town: Juta, 1989, p. 213-260.

**Watson 2000**
Watson, A., 'Legal Transplants and European Private Law', *Electric Journal of Comparative Law*, 2000 (4/4).

**Weatherill 2004a**
Weatherill, S., 'Why Harmonise?', in: T. Tridimas & P. Nebbia (eds.), *European Union Law for the Twenty-First Century: Rethinking the New Legal Order* (Volume 2: proceedings of the 2003 W.G. Hart Workshop); Oxford: Hart, 2004, p. 11-32.

**Weatherill 2004b**
Weatherill, S., 'Why Object to the Harmonization of Private Law by the EC?', *European Review of Private Law*, 2004 (5), p. 633-660.

**Weatherill 2006**
Weatherill, S., 'Diversity between National Laws in the Internal Market', in: U. Drobnig, H.J. Snijders & E.-J. Zippro (eds.), *Divergences of Property Law, an Obstacle to the Internal Market?*, München: Sellier, 2006, p. 131-152.

**Weatherill 2010a**
Weatherill, S., *Cases & Materials on EU Law* (9th edition), Oxford: Oxford University Press, 2010.

**Weatherill 2010b**
Weatherill, S., 'Competence and European Private Law', in: C. Twigg-Flesner (ed.), *The Cambridge Companion to European Union Private Law*, Cambridge: Cambridge University Press, 2010, p. 58-69.

**Weatherill 2011**
Weatherill, S., 'The Limits of Legislative Harmonization Ten Years after Tobacco Advertising: How the Court's Case Law has become a "Drafting Guide"', *German Law Journal*, 2011 (12/3), p. 827-864.

**Wehrens 2004**
Wehrens, H.G., 'Real Security regarding Immovable Objects – Reflections on a Euro-Mortgage', in: A. Hartkamp *et al.* (eds.), *Towards a European Civil Code* (3rd fully revised and expanded edition), Nijmegen/The Hague: Ars Aequi Libri/Kluwer Law International, 2004).

**Van der Weide 2006**
Weide, J.A. van der, *Mobiliteit van goederen in het IPR – tussen situsregel en partijautonomie*, Deventer: Kluwer, 2006.

**Weller 2011**
Weller, M.-P., 'Anknüpfungsprinzipien im Europäischen Kollisionsrecht: Abschied von der "klassischen" IPR-Dogmatik?', *IPRax*, 2011 (31/5), p. 429-437.

**Westrik & Van der Weide 2011**
Westrik, R. & Weide, J.A. van der (eds.), *Party Autonomy in International Property Law*, Munich: Sellier. European law publishers, 2011.

**Von Wilmowsky 1996**
Wilmowsky, P. von, *Europäisches Kreditsicherungsrecht: Sachenrecht und Insolvenzrecht unter dem EG-Vertrag*, Tübingen: Mohr/Siebeck, 1996.

**Von Wilmowsky 1998**
Wilmowsky, P. von, 'EG-Vertrag und kollisionsrechtliche Rechtswahlfreiheit', *Rabels Zeitschrift fuer Auslaendisches und Internationales Privatrecht*, 1998 (62/1), p. 1-37.

**Zevenbergen 2002**
Zevenbergen, J., *Systems of Land Registration: Aspects and Effects* (Publications on Geodesy 51), Delft: Nederlandse Commissie voor Geodesie/Netherlands Geodetic Commission, 2002.

**Zimmermann 2006**
Zimmermann, R., 'Comparative Law and the Europeanization of Private Law', in: M. Reimann & R. Zimmermann (eds.), *The Oxford Handbook of Comparative Law*, Oxford: Oxford University Press, 2006, p. 539-578.

## CURRICULUM VITAE

Eveline Ramaekers (1985) studied law at the European Law School, Maastricht University (LL.B., LL.M. *cum laude*). She subsequently held a post as PhD researcher in Maastricht, during which time she spent several months as a visiting researcher and lecturer in Münster, Stellenbosch, and at the China-EU School of Law in Beijing. She has published on European developments in property law and is at present researching the relationship between EU law and private international law, particularly in relation to property law. She co-founded the Young Property Lawyers Forum, a network for young property law researchers, which has organized four international conferences and published its collected essays in two volumes of *Property Law Perspectives*. Since the completion of her doctoral thesis, Eveline has held a post as Fellow and Tutor in Law at Wadham College, Oxford, where apart from doing research she teaches EU law and English land and trust law.

**IUS COMMUNE EUROPAEUM**

A peer-reviewed book series in which the common foundations of the legal systems of the Member States of the European Union are the central focus.

The *Ius Commune Europaeum* series includes horizontal comparative legal studies as well as studies on the effect of treaties within the national legal systems. All the classic fields of law are covered. The books are published in various European languages under the auspices of METRO, the Institute for Transnational Legal Research at the Maastricht University.



Recently published:

Volume 102: *The Changing Role of the European Council in the Institutional Framework of the European Union*, F. EGGERMONT
Volume 103: *Linked Contracts*, I. SAMOY and M.B.M. LOOS (eds.)
Volume 104: *Constitutions Compared* (3rd ed.), A.W. HERINGA and PH. KIIVER
Volume 105: *Alternative Ways to Ius Commune*, A.L.M. KEIRSE and M.B.M. LOOS (eds.)
Volume 106: *Property Law Perspectives*, B. AKKERMANS and E. RAMAEKERS (eds.)
Volume 107: *Constitutional Conversations*, C. VAN DE HEYNING and M. DE VISSER (eds.)
Volume 108: *Enforcing Health and Safety Regulation*, L. TILINDYTĖ
Volume 109: *Administrative Law of the European Union, its Member States and the United States. A Comparative Analysis*, R. SEERDEN (ed.)
Volume 110: *Market Integration through 'Network Governance': The Role of European Agencies and Networks of Regulators*, M. ZINZANI
Volume 111: *Truth and Efficiency in Civil Litigation. Fundamental Aspects of Fact-finding and Evidence-taking in a Comparative Context*, C.H. VAN RHEE and A. UZELAC (eds.)
Volume 112: *Law and Security in Europe: Reconsidering the Security Constitution*, M. FICHERA and J. KREMER (eds.)
Volume 113: *Inside Policy Custody: An Empirical Account of Suspect's Rights in Four Jurisdictions*, T. SPRONKEN, E. CAPE and J. HODGSON (eds.)
Volume 114: *Motive Matters! An Exploration of the Notion 'Deliberate Breach of Contract' and its Consequences for the Application of Remedies*, M. VAN KOGELENBERG
Volume 115: *Legal Education*, A.W. HERINGA
Volume 116: *Standing Up for your Right(s) in Europe. A Comparative Study on Legal Standing (Locus Standi) before the EU and Member States' Courts*, M. ELIANTONIO, C. BACKES, C.H. VAN RHEE, T. SPRONKEN and A. BERLEE

www.ingramcontent.com/pod-product-compliance
Ingram Content Group UK Ltd.
Pitfield, Milton Keynes, MK11 3LW, UK
UKHW051926100926
8556IPUK00022B/1390

9 781780 681719